N

s Bitschy
162

B Miller

J. Yoder
152

Coal Bank

J. Knerp
63

J. C. Miller
80

Fine Cherry & Pear Orch.
80

Coal Bank

M. J. Miller
126

Lime Stone & Coal

Schweitzer

Peter Shutt
51

John Shutt
86

J. J. Kaser
21

Conrod Dorfer
171 1/4

113 67/100

Peter

J. J. Pion

15

J. Kyr

Fine Orchard

56

M. Yoder

John Speicher

staham

40

J. J. Miller

Coal

John Shutt
30

Jacob Olin
160

s Hershberger
195

Kaufman
49

M. Deiss

M. B. 13   Schumaker

J. C. Miller
76

Mich Yoder

I. D. Miller
99

29

60

J. & M. Troyer

Moses Olinger
80

V. H.

Coal Bank

C. D. Slabach
140

133

Helmuth
60

G. Stahuch
64

40

Coal

19

C. Hershberger

S H

60

90

J. & M. Troyer

66

Seth Troyer
158

Lime S. & Coal

Coal Bank

C. Miller
60

FARMERS TOWN

Lime Stone

John B. Miller

C. D. Starbaugh
126

C. D. Starbaugh

J. Bower
100

M. Bower
30

M. Domer
30

Michael Domer
156

Domer
156

M. C. Fint
53

Christian Miller
40

F. Helmuth
80

40

Lime Stone & Coal

116

Lime Stone & Coal

J. Kerns

Jacob Stuber

Christian Miller
160

Lime Stone & Iron Ore
162 1/2

C. D. Starbaugh
40

Lime Stone & Coal

Peter Bitschy
140

Jacob D. Sta
160

Charles Fair

H. Shutt
48

J. D. Troyer

4 Bitschy
32

D. S. T. 10

P. B. 14

J. Kerns

Thos. Syler
140

Sugar Creek Valley Farm

E. Fair Fisher

C. H. Shutt

David S. Troyer

Sugar Creek

20

P Bitschy

Elah Fair
160

J. F. fous
158

Alfa Bitschy
140

Peter Mi
131

s Shaffer
160

N. Row
80

Pleasant Valley Home
177

14 40/100

Andrew Raber
147

S H
No 4

Henry M. Dom
160

Shaffer
160

John C. Speicher

Wm Christman

Nathaniel Fair
95

John S. Barger

Lime Stone & Coal

Seth Domer

H D Christman
40

N. Fair
60

holmes

Tobias Barger

Lime Stone Coal & Iron Ore

Dunkard Ch.

Black Band Iron Ore 10 foot Vein

C. D. Gorbe
80

School House

C. Fisher

C. Fisher

Historical Album

of

Charm, Ohio

by Vernon J. Miller

— 1995 —

Vernon J. Miller
4755 County Rd. 19
Millersburg, OH 44654

ISBN 0-9642548-3-2

 Printed on acid-free paper.

Front Cover: A sketch of Charm, ca 1912, by artist and historian Leroy Beachy, using factual information supplied by the author.

CARLISLE
PRINTING
◆ Walnut Creek ◆

2727 TOWNSHIP RD. 421 • SUGARCREEK, OHIO 44681
— PRINTING and PUBLISHING —

Historical Album of
Charm, Ohio

1995

Vernon J. Miller

Preface

Seemingly, during recent decades, there has been an avid and increasing interest in history. Preserving past illustrations tends to be a fascinating and rewarding endeavor. The *Historical Album of Charm, Ohio* promotes the view of preserving and presenting to the public the life of a small country town in central Ohio. Lest we forget its story, its people, or its activity, a collection of reminisces can hopefully be shared with today's and future generations.

Locally, the album embraces business history, school history, local happenings, and biographical sketches, and uses quotes along with illustrations to enhance its story. Excerpts connected with prominent industries like cheesemaking and sawmilling share details to their historical background. Insights into the life of Troyer's Hollow on the Doughty Creek, or of tramps, once commonplace across the country, give reality to their former existence. In a broader sense, the history focuses briefly on early land claims, Indian treaties, placement within the Northwest Territory, county formation, and early settlement that encircled the unique Holmes County village. To the tourists who are discovering Charm along their rural scenic route it contains background to its places, its people, and its community.

Thus the volume now enables you to view more of the historical life of Charm than has ever been previously available, in factual and documented work.

V

178/ A northeast view of Charm soon after the store was destroyed by fire, November 24, 1894. Places are identified from left to right: Storeowner, Isaac J. Miller house (later known as "the boarding house") — People standing on remaining store foundation — Jeweler's shop and doctor's office — Barn that was later moved and presently on the John O. Miller residence — House of Lewis Geib (Mose L. Yoder home); the small building partly seen on the right of the house is, supposedly, the shoe repair shop — Planing mill and buggy shop — House where today's bank is located — Roof of first wagon shop can be seen — Today's Jonas J. Yoder house — Cider press building in foreground — Dr. Guittard house presently owned by Joe Erb — Emanuel Oswald farm in background — Blacksmith shop built by George Price in 1894 — Only the roof of the town's first blacksmith shop is seen above the one built by Price — Cheese factory and home of Fred Nickles.

189/

Charm in 1992

VI

✒ *Foreword* ⎯⎯⎯⎯⎯⎯⎯⎯⎯⎯⎯⎯⎯⎯⎯⎯⎯

The *Historical Album of Charm, Ohio* is a historical composition of a small village in southeastern Holmes County. Springing up at a rural country crossroad in a farming area of early German (Clark) Township, the town has been situated within a populous Amish community since infancy. From the initial business of a blacksmith shop, ca 1840, along an aged Indian trail, a town developed to become known as Stevenson. After the establishment of a post office in 1885 its name was changed to Charm. Throughout most of the town's years of existence it has also been known by its nickname of "Putschtown," meaning "a small clump."

Business activities have always been prominent in the small village, and have been more extensive in proportion to the population. Much of the business in the hamlet was of local trade until the 1970s and 80s. At this time great steps of change took place, primarily that of a progressive building material center, along with the advancement of tourism in Holmes County. Charm has in no way escaped this increasing flow of visitors and businesses have responded accordingly as indicated herein.

As an introduction to the dominant business section of the volume, a brief outline is given of earlier events which eventually formed our governing bodies as they are known today. This will help form a general idea of the early land claims held by various countries until the establishing of Ohio and its counties and townships that pertain to the area of interest. Following businesses, are accounts of school records, local happenings, biographical sketches, and tramps, along with a brief history of the renowned Troyer's Hollow.

The basic information contained in the album is primarily confined to a four square mile area. This area consists of Sections 4, 5, 6, and 7 of Township 8, Range 5, and their respective corners join in the village (see Maps of Interest – page 27). The perimeter of these four sections has been used as a principal boundary.

Being unique, Charm has always been of service to the community and visitors, who marvel at its homey atmosphere, its picturesque countryside, and its Amish lifestyle, reminiscent of American life a century ago. For these reasons, people of different walks of life have found the small country town a "charm." ✒

Table of Contents

Date following the entry is when the business was established.

(continued on page 10)

9

♊

❧ Acknowledgments ————————————

The author can never adequately repay the contributions made to this work by numerous individuals who not only devoted time and effort to the project, but also generously contributed ideas, materials, and factual details. Without their help, this work would have been impossible.

Although it would be impracticable to name everyone who contributed, I would, nevertheless, like to mention the support and help given by the following:

Atlee Keim of Mt. Hope still recalls minute details and happenings of his boyhood in Charm, even though he is now 87 years of age. Tobias M. Yoder, at 93, is the oldest living person in Charm; but his strong memory allowed him to provide much historical background. Dey Troyer, 86, a former Charm resident, willingly shared historical details and his photographic collection.

Henry L. Erb read and copied newsletters from *The Budget*, which shed light on everyday life and business in early Charm. Brooks Harris, who has shown significant interest in Charm history, generously shared his findings.

Thanks go to Daniel Hershberger for his help on the manuscript.

The Wayne Hostetler family shared memorabilia. Vera Nussbaum provided information on the Nickles history, Janet Korns contributed historical background on Sanford Leander Korn, and the Herb Miller family, along with Evelyn Culp, supplied details on Isaac J. Miller.

I also thank the following offices for their cooperation and for granting me research privileges: The Holmes County Public Library, the Holmes County Recorders Office, the Holmes County Office of Education, and the East Holmes Local School District Administrative Office.

I extend gratitude to my immediate family, including my parents, my brother, Ivan Miller, and my wife, Sara Ann Miller, all of whom gave me help, support, and information.

The contributions and friendships of all those named are deeply treasured, as well as the help and support of others too numerous to name.

Also, numerous friends who contributed items of interest passed away during the seven years I worked on this project; but they remain deep in my memory. They include: Mose D. Troyer, Emanuel J. Yoder, John P. Troyer, Lorene Kaser, Paul Hummel, John B. Kurtz, John L. Yoder, Adrian Sheetz, John B. Yoder, John L. Mueller, Levi L. Yoder, Sarah Weaver, Ammon H. Miller, Sarah Hershberger, Mattie Yoder, Jacob A. Miller, Levi D. Schlabach, Atlee D. Schlabach, Melvin A. Raber, Anna Keim, Jonas T. Miller, Jacob Amos Miller, Lula Beachy (Schlabach), Edward R. Miller, Rollin McClelland, Henry A. Hershberger, Mervin Shetler, Noah A. Keim, and Ura J. Miller.

The writings of late local historians Clarence Troyer, Warner Farver, and Harry C. Logsdon have been very helpful, and their research and work has been of great value to me. ❧

❧

❧ Introduction

This introduction will help the reader to understand the following chapters of the volume more clearly, and to discover a broader usefulness of this history of Charm. Though numerous prior articles have been written concerning Charm[1], the *Historical Album* is the first attempt to bring a researched and documented composition of the village to the public.

Because the volume aims to preserve past illustrations for the future, I deemed it necessary to use a form of documentation that can be readily referred to. With the use of county records, newspaper articles, published materials, and various sources, more historical background can thus be revealed, which brings insight, detail, and life to our town of interest.

The compilation relies notably on primary sources of information. Cited source codes to documentation are shown along the margin and are given by letters and/or numbers followed by a /. These will relate to the credits and sources at the latter part of the volume, or as further explained. Biographical identification follows the same procedure and, where applicable, some form of identity is given.

Detail of documentation: Example:
- Numbers followed by a / relate to
  Credits and Sources   19/
- Page numbers relating to Credits and Sources   22/ p.15
- Dates relating to Credits and Sources   50/ 7-16-1895
- Deeds (Holmes County)
  (volume-page-date)   V35-82-1872
- Harvey Hostetler, *Descendants of Jacob Hoch-stetler*, Council Bluffs, Iowa: n.p., 1912.   DJH 3541
- Harvey Hostetler, *Descendants of Barbara Hochstetler and Christian Stutzman*, Scottdale, Pa.: Mennonite Publishing House, 1935.   DBH 4520
- Harold E. Cross, *Ohio Amish Genealogy*, Baltimore, Maryland: n.p., 1964.   OAG 6552

Leroy Beachy, *Cemetery Directory of the Amish Community in Eastern Holmes and Adjoining Counties in Ohio* [2nd Ed.], N.p.: n.p., 1975.   CD-L-33

Hugh F. Gingerich, et al, *Amish and Amish Mennonite Genealogies*, Gordonville, Pa.: Pequea Publishers, 1986.   YR 26111

It is my hope that the history can aid other persons researching within the same line of interest and such documentation can be helpful.

Two indexes give ready reference to individuals referred to throughout the history. One pertains only to school enrollments and teachers, while the other contains the remaining names in the volume.

Credits to pictures are recognized and are listed in the numerical Credits and Sources section.

Though it has been my intention to remain as accurate as possible within the limits of the sources available to me, it is nevertheless safe to say the album will not be found without human error.

Quite often during the time of compiling the information contained herein, I was amazed at what turned up within the short span of years. This led to a seeming ever-expanding project whereby I was often reminded of a poem recited at the Charm School:

> Labor with what zeal we will,
> Something still remains undone;
> Something uncompleted still,
> Awaits the rising of the sun.
> By the bedside, on the stair,
> At the threshold, near the gate;
> By the cares of yesterday,
> Each today is heavier made.

Giving all honor to Him who has given us the privileges to be born and to live on the lands that He at one time created and which we may know as home.

The earth is the Lord's, and the fulness thereof; the world, and they that dwell therein. Psalm 24:1.

Vernon J. Miller ❧

---

1 Clarence Troyer, *History of Villages – People – Places in Eastern Holmes County*, Berlin, Ohio: Berlin Printing, 1975.

178 /   A north view of Charm, ca 1914. Stevenson – Stevensville became Charm in 1885 and a greater part of its existence has also been known as "Putschtown." Places of business from left to right: Charm Flour Mills — Keim Brothers Lumber Co. — Store — Meat Market (windows trimmed in white) — Wagon Shop — Cider Press — Two Black-smith Shops. The Jeweler, Joni J. Yoder house on the left — Center foreground, Andy I. Miller log cabin — Far right, two-story schoolhouse.

Names Pertaining to Charm

Connecting the various names of the town to Charm is an interesting and, to some extent, a puzzling subject of deliberation. Various versions have originated and have been passed along from generation to generation. Such names as Stevenson, Stevensville, Charm, and Putschtown have all related to the small country village in eastern Holmes County.

While in its infancy the tiny village became known as Stevenson. The most widely accepted account of how the name originated has been attributed to a neighboring farmer, Stephen Yoder. *19/ p.34* For a number of years Yoder and his son lived on the present Albert N. Schrock farm, which is immediately north of the town. Thus, when an identification was needed for the locality, "Steven-son" fit rather appropriately. According to historians interviewing early Charm residents, the Yoders had occupied this farm during the period of the Civil War, ca 1860.

Another account states that a son of Stephen *CD- p.125* Yoder operated a wagon and blacksmith shop around which a small village eventually formed. The oft-used phrase "down by Stephen's son" caught on, and the village became known as Stevenson.

During these early days of Stevenson in the nineteenth century, another title for the town was being used. Here, also, various accounts have survived, as has the nickname itself. Perhaps the most distinguishing story tells how a visitor to the area was traveling across the countryside. When overlooking the tiny village from one of the surrounding hills, he is said to have remarked, *"Es is usht ein glehne putscha."* Its equivalent in English would be, "It is only a small clump (or bunch)." Thus "Putsch" or "Putschtown" was passed along to eventually be a commonly used term. Being used repeatedly, it has clung to the town until the present day.

To mention a second theory—a long time Charm area resident during the first half of the twentieth *280/ ?-?- 1945* century, Seth Erb, related how one New Year's Day two boisterous boys placed some gunpowder between two anvils. When lit, the resulting explosion was jokingly called a "putsch."

Yet another story indicated a person smoking a *19/ p.34* pipe, and when the smoke was blown out, it went "putsch."

Ironically, no documentation has been able to verify any of these circulating sketches. Nevertheless, in analyzing the word "putsch," it would seem the most likely theory would be connected to the visitor's observation of the "small clump of houses." *"Putscha"* is still readily used in the Pennsylvania Dutch language, which is widely spoken throughout the community, having been brought into the area by pioneers in the early 1800s. Thus, with identifying the "putsch" account with the native language and interpretation, its weight seems favorable, whereas the remaining reports are merely phonic expressions and do not relate directly to the town as suggested here.

Perhaps we can also get a more distinct view regarding the name of Stevenson, or rather the events occurring that related to that name. In chronological order, we find that Stephen Yoder (YR26111) was deeded the lands of the Southeast quarter of Sec. 5 Twp. 8 Range 5 in 1830, from John *V2-73- 1830* Yoder. John had been the original grant holder from the government, acquiring the land in 1815, and was a grandfather to Stephen on his mother's side. As noted on the deed, the grantor was residing in Sugarcreek Township, Tuscarawas County, while Stephen was named as being from Somerset County, Pennsylvania. This land extended from the present Charm School and included most of Charm, the Albert N. Schrock farm to northwest, and part of the Henry Schlabach farm on the west.

225/
1840

On the 1840 census, one of the Yoder family is listed as being engaged in a trade which we can suppose to be that of a blacksmith. With the oldest child only six years old, the father would have been operating it himself. It appears to have been the only business there at that time.

249/   Looking east, the former Stephen Yoder farm on the left on whose land most of Charm was built – 1992.

189/   Cornerstone of the Stephen Yoder barn, S Y 1848.

189/   S. Yoder 1856 — House cornerstone

16/

❀

16

The Yoders apparently first lived in a log cabin which stood along the north bank of the small stream, south of the present buildings. Later, at the turn of the century, the cabin was dismantled

and some of the lumber was used to build a hog shed that still remains on the farm today. According to the cornerstones, the large barn was built in 1848 and the farmhouse in 1856, respectively. In addition to this farm, Stephen also owned 120 acres immediately west and southwest of Charm (today the Henry A. Schlabach and Jonas N. Yoder farms).

V12-67-
1844

309/

By 1847 Stephen Yoder had sold 1³/₄ acres to Daniel Lawer. Though no deed was recorded in Holmes County, Daniel nevertheless began paying taxes that year for the acreage, situated in the southeast corner of the southeast quarter of Section 5. Also, a building value of $288.00 is shown on the tax record, which, presumably, was that of, or included, the blacksmith shop. On the 1850 census Daniel Lawer is identified as being a blacksmith along with George Snellenberger, whereas Stephen Yoder is listed only as a farmer.

225/
1850

V 17-
322-
1851

The blacksmith shop acreage consisted of the land from the present schoolhouse north to CR 70, which is described in an 1851 deed transfer from Daniel and Susan Lawer to Levi S. Miller ($850.00). This first blacksmith shop had been built where Old Blacksmith Shop Gifts is located today.

The above facts would indicate that Yoder became more greatly involved with farming by selling his place of business in 1847 then building the large bank barn on the farm in 1848.

231/
281/
DBH
2287
DJH
2246

Stephen Yoder died during the winter of early 1858 and was buried (CD-0-2) on the farm bordering the town that was named after him. A sale to dispose of his earthly belongings was held October 21, 1858. Within the next two years the widow remarried to a neighbor, Andrew Troyer (TYC1) who died in 1867. It is apparent the widow thereafter moved to her children living in Indiana, where she died in 1876.

V28-18-
1865

Interestingly, we find Yoder's son, Daniel, engaged in farming the home farm at the time of the 1860 census. By '65 he had sold the farm and also located at Indiana.

According to these articles, it would be logical to reason that the town was named Stevenson because of Stephen Yoder's association with the town. The added "son" could well suggest the son Daniel's presence as a farmer, or merely imply that it was a town name.

This would point to a time frame from Yoder's first land purchase of 1830 to Daniel's transfer of '65, which would include the Civil War period, as noted earlier.

The 1861 Holmes County map does not make mention of Stevenson. However, this would not appear uncommon, since Stevenson included only a small place of business besides a schoolhouse. Moreover, the town was never laid out in lots;

therefore Stevenson was never officialized.

Appearing in *Caldwell's Atlas of Holmes Co. Ohio* (1875), Stevenson is now readily identified as a town and is even shown with a layout of the village.

A decade later enough interest was created that the town decided to try establishing a post office. With this accomplished in 1885, the village was renamed Charm.

Once again, various accounts exist of how the name Charm came into existence. Commonly accepted is the story that from a list of names submitted by the postal department to the post office patrons, Charm was chosen. Why? No one can be sure. However, attached to this is an opinion that one of the patrons at Stevenson was Joni J. Yoder, who was a jeweler. During that period, the late 1800s, it was customary to attach a large ornament, called a watch charm, to a watch chain. Since the name Charm appeared on the government's list and Yoder's business was also connected to that name, it was the one chosen. *343/*

A second account states, no other town with the same name within a state could apply for a post office. Therefore Stevenson was not acceptable, and Charm was submitted and approved by the Postmaster General.

Another theory has surfaced lately from an aged gentleman who spent his boyhood years at Charm at the turn of the century. From his account, there were two towns in Ohio using the name Stevenson. When a name change was sought, businessmen of the village went to Columbus to pursue the matter. Not having agreed to a new name, the person in charge inquired how the village was located and situated. The men described the town as having a store and meat market, shoe shop, cider press, cheese house, blacksmith shop, and a road and a stream going through the town, along with hills and farms in the area. Visualizing the little town, the official replied, "This must be a charming place, so I'd call it Charm." *57/*

However, research would make the watch charm account more plausible, as Joni J. Yoder was supposedly engaged in the jeweler's business at that time. Joni had begun in the watch and clock trade while yet single. Later, in 1887, he purchased the lot "it being the jewelry shop and the ground on which it stands" from John W. Hershberger, located where the Homestead Restaurant is today. Yoder was involved in the business until he sold out because of ill health in 1911. Incidentally, J. J. Yoder also served as the town's postmaster from 1888 to 1890. *V51-447-1887*

School and postal records also reveal the fact that the village had been using the name Stevensville prior to Charm. An 1879 school record *100/2-5-1911 136/ 311/*

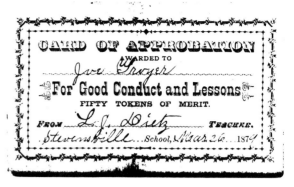

311/

The earliest known record showing the name of Stevensville – 1879 school approval.

of approval gives evidence of this, as well as the postal record for the application of a new post office. (See "Post Office" for copy.) In 1885, when the required form was filled out, the new name was initially proposed to be Stevensville. Of interest is the location paper application which states: "Select a short name for the proposed office, which, when written will not resemble the name of any other post office in the United States." Here the first name inserted, "Stevensville," is blotted out and the selection changed to "Charm."

There is evidence of a Stephensville post office in existence in Stark County in 1830, whereas today the name is not found as a town in Ohio (see "Post Office"). *136/*

In reviewing the mentioned form, it would appear evident that the name Charm was chosen by the local people because of the instruction "select a name." Also, the handwritten Charm on the document corresponds with the handwriting of H. L. Giaugue, the postmaster of Berlin.

Exactly how or why Charm was chosen still remains unproven. In sum, despite the numerous suggestions and explanations, it remains unclear how the name Charm was chosen.

On December 10, 1885 the postal document was stamped by the First Assistant Postmaster General, A. E. Stevenson, at Washington, D.C., making Charm an official town in the United States. *138/ 9-30-1886*

A short notice appeared in the *Holmes County Republican* concerning the newly named town, stating: "The new post office at Stevensville in German Township is called Charm." This, also, would indicate that Stevensville, as a name, was somewhat in usage at the time.

Today, in the United States, no other post office is identified by the name Charm. However, five Stevenson – Stephensons exist, and five Stevensvilles show up. *291/*

Presently (1995), the small village of Charm has a population of 107 residents. ❧ ❧

❧ Maps of Interest ——————

CANADA

Lake
Superior

Lake
Michigan

Lake
Huron

NORTHWEST

Lake
Erie

Lake
Ontario

MISSISSIPPI
RIVER

PENNSYLVANIA

TERRITORY

VIRGINIA

OHIO
RIVER

KENTUCKY
TERRITORY

NORTHWEST TERRITORY
1787

247/
p.3

The U.S. Military District with other principal land subdivisions in relation to present county boundaries.

254/
p.341

The extensive Washington County as it was originally laid out in 1788 in the Ohio Wilderness of the Northwest Territory.

1803

247/
p.17

Ohio counties when statehood was established in 1803.

1806

254/
p.368

Washington County being further reduced with the formation of Muskingum County in 1804.

❧

254/ Coshocton County formed from Muskin-
p.404 gum County in 1811.

1820

254/ Holmes County organized in 1825 from
p.412 parts of Coshocton, Tuscarawas, and Wayne
Counties.

1828

Pioneer Yost Miller (ML221) map – ca 1835. The Charm area would be Sections 4 - 5 - 6 - 7 in the left center.

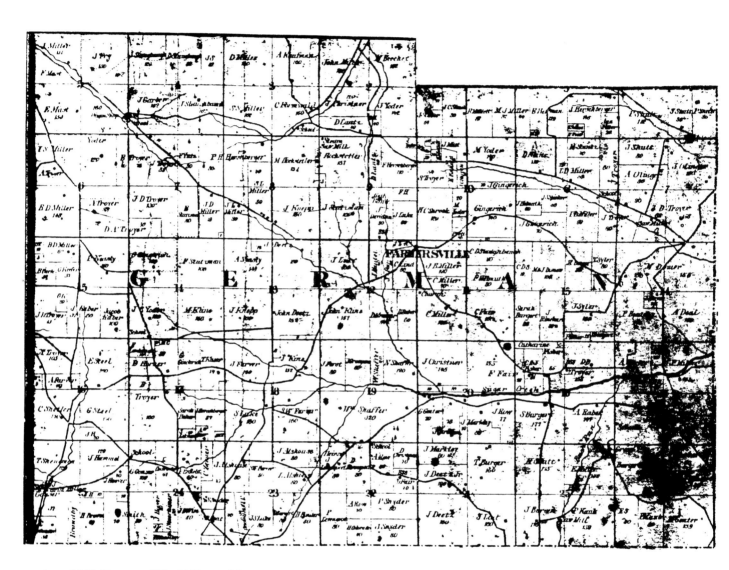

313/   1861 German (Clark) Township

GERMAN

Scale 3 Inches to the Mile

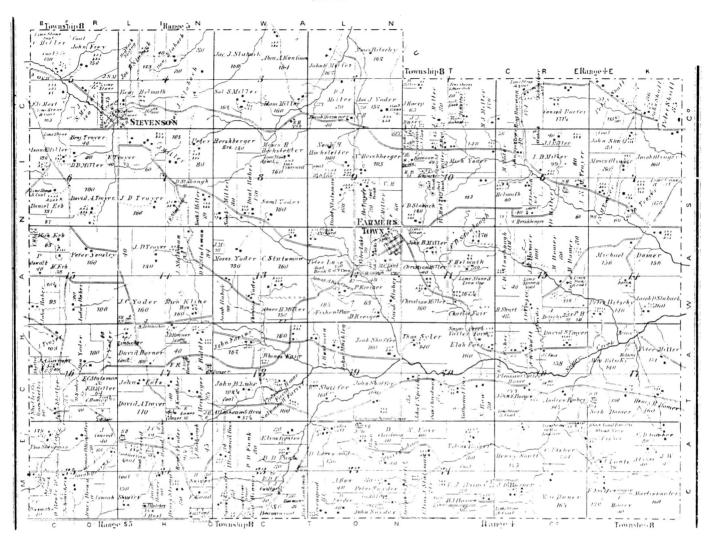

German (Clark) Township – 1875

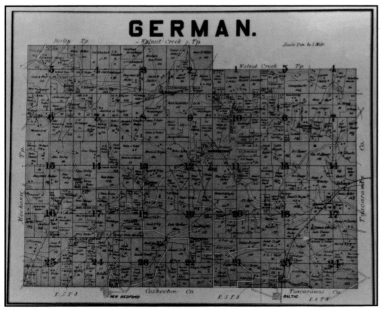

201/   Stevenson (Charm) – 1875
p.87

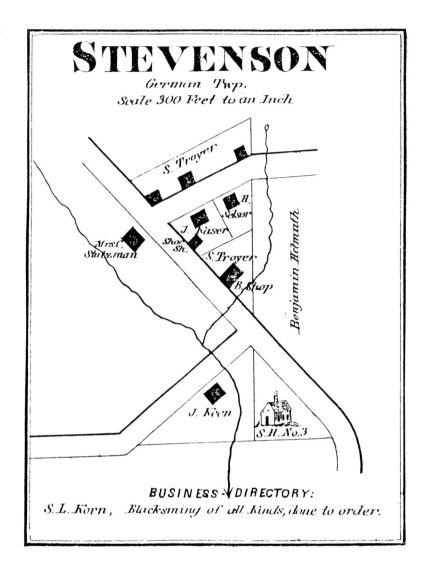

314/   Charm – ca 1895

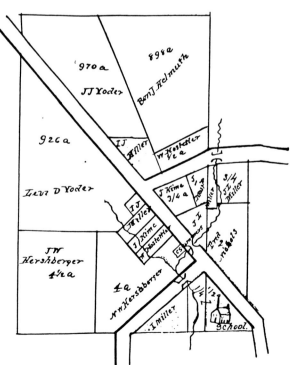

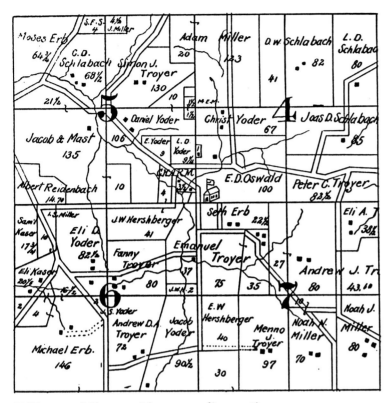

1907 map of Charm with surrounding sections.

223/
p.28

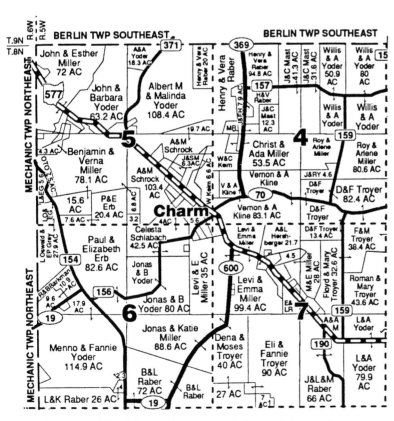

1992 plat map. (This history focuses mainly on this area.)

230/
p.22

Maps of Interest

364/
377/ Topographic map of Charm and surrounding sections; 4 - 5 - 6 - 7.

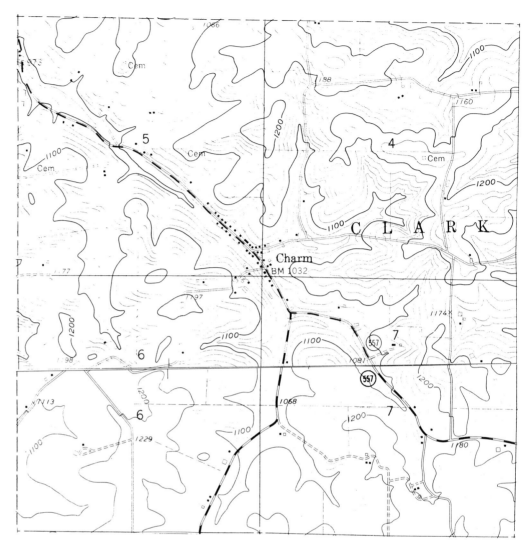

171/ Charm, looking east - ca 1915. The martin box in the middle of the intersection was made by Joel Beiler.

Charm – ca 1915. On right: wagon shop, cider press, blacksmith shop, schoolhouse.   *171/*

Coming into town from the northwest (SR 557) – ca 1912. The newly built flour mill on the right.   *178/*

8/   Charm street corner – ca 1915

333/   Butcher shop and store from the east

Right: schoolhouse — cheese factory — the town's first blacksmith shop — second blacksmith shop, built across the street — "Isaac Andy" log cabin, foreground – ca 1914.   *178 /*

Charm – 1974   *218 /*

Bird's eye view – Charm – 1985

295/

Charm situated in a val-   249/
ley – from the east – 1992

❧

249/   From the south – 1992

❦   *249/*   Street scene – 1991

Area History

The Early Paleo and Delaware Indians

The lone Indian paused briefly before stepping into the clearing[1]. Before him lay a narrow valley which he had often passed through. The dry seasons had cleared up the swampy lowlands and his coming home would be hastened with the direct course he could be taking toward the setting sun. Along a ridge he had just passed[2] were the almost-vanished remains of stone campfire dugouts which, he had often been reminded, his earlier ancestors had used.

Again, his thoughts were drawn to the concern that rested heavily in his heart. A number of seasons ago at a great battle between the Indians and whites[3], his tribe had wished to remain at peace[4]. However, the great loss of his kind had also forced them to join in the signing of a treaty[5] which fell heavily on his heart. The very land he had been using to survive on was now no longer his to nourish his family, his tribe, or himself. Two seasons later[6], as more preparations were made to move westward to lands allotted to them, he had come across a party of men striking off division lines and placing stone markers as cornerstones. The advancing whites from the rising sun were becoming more real.

Knowing the day was getting late, he again started homeward. Nearing the lowlands of the valley, he crossed a narrow path[7] that had been readily worn from the many years of Indian travel. But now his trained eyes spied a different set of prints in the dusty path. Two—no, three[8]—hard-soled moccasins had left their prints plainly. Crossing the next ridge slowly, he keenly felt the push and encroachment of the whites on his being. Before him lay a beautifully wooded valley[9] that would lead him to his home. Only yesterday, at the beginning of his journey, he had taken refuge from a sudden thunderstorm in a cave[10] within the narrow gorge to his right.

About to wade the now shallow creek, he again felt the tinge of anger. Yes, today, while explaining through gestures of his whereabouts at the trading post[11], he was told the stream of his homeland had been named Doughty[12]. Even the waters could not escape being invaded by the language of the whites.

Getting closer to home, his wandering thoughts were suddenly interrupted. Up until now this had only been a dream. Only he knew how much he cherished the highly polished steel, the bone handle, and the keen edge of the knife hanging at his side. By whom else could this wish for a knife have been made possible but by the white men? To trade for a knife is what the trek had been for. The carefully tanned hides he had been saving were readily exchanged at the trading post, with each one valued as "a buck[13]."

---

1 An allegory. Evidence of Indians remaining in Holmes County after their larger numbers had moved out may be found in: 19/ p.156; 22/ p.19; 26/ p.17; 214/ p.24.

2 94/ 129/   On the ridge east of Charm, on the present David J. Troyer, Roy L. Miller, and Eli M. Shetler farms, were found campfire sites when miners were excavating for coal in the 1970s. The sites had been dug out, then stones laid in the bottom or up its sides. Charcoaled wood or ashes were still present. Other locations found in the area were on the Mose L. Troyer and Abe M. Troyer farms, $^{1}/_{2}$ and 1 mile south of Charm, respectively.

3 The Battle of Fallen Timber in 1794 between General Anthony Wayne's forces and the Indians in northwestern Ohio.

4 214/ p.17   As a whole, the Delaware Indians were peaceful toward the whites because of the kindness shown to them by William Penn.

5 Greenville Treaty of 1795.

6 The United States Military District surveyed 1797.

7 26/ p.14   An Indian trail passing through Charm.

8 CD p.113   In 1808, three Amishmen, Jacob Miller and sons Henry and Jacob, came to the area and built a log cabin a mile east of Sugarcreek.

9 The Doughty Valley of the Beck's Mills area.

10 The cave along the Doughty Creek in Troyer's Hollow.

11 224/ V.2 p.694   New Philadelphia was laid out in 1804 on the east bank of the Tuscarawas River.

12 214/ p.31. Supposedly named after Col. Doughty who was head of the Zanesville Land Office, and a local Indian, Chief Doughty.

13 220/ p.15, 705. "A buck" was a deerskin and could be traded with a one-dollar value at trading posts.

Quickening his pace, he could now see the Indian village[14]—or could it still be called a village? It was dotted with abandoned huts, save the few he had been using for himself. Not long before, the tribe had moved west because the peace agreement had turned the home grounds over to a different people.

Tonight, again, he was alone, close to the stream now known as the Military[15]. Accordingly, the outlying lands were being assigned to white warriors who had fought for the great nation's independence.

Curled up in the warmth of his hut, the already useful knife lay at his head. He knew that one day he would also be joining his kin on new grounds. However, they would need to tell their children how greatly they had cherished the fullness of life along the Doughty and Military, and encourage them to someday return to visit the valley of their forebears[16].

——————— * ———————

94/   Fluted Paleo Point arrowhead found 1 mile east of Charm.

94/   The earliest inhabitants recognized as having occupied the hunting grounds are known today as the Paleos. Their presence is recorded by the flint hunting point they left behind as they wandered through the vicinity. One of the few "fluted Paleo points" found in Holmes County was discovered a mile east of Charm on the David J. Troyer farm. Of superb quality, the 3-inch flint head is grooved on both sides to accept its wooden shaft.

At this time no small town had yet existed. The future site of habitation was yet a land of the Indians that the white men were to claim. Its valley was one of the many valleys that lay in the vast stretches of wilderness. Its hills and ridges were still heavily covered with oaks, maples, walnut, hickory, and chestnut—virgin timber that had not yet heard the sound of the axe. Its valley lay like a low swampland as the bubbling springs gurgled from the hillside and meandered their courses to that "beautiful river."

214/   The Delaware Indians had originally come from
p.25-26   the lands west of the Mississippi River and were,
221/   at that time, known as Lenni Lenapes. Moving east
p.32,35   over a long period of time and up the Ohio River Valley, they eventually came into the Delaware River Basin. This area consisted of parts of New York, New Jersey, Pennsylvania, and Delaware, from which they received their name.

It was the Delawares who welcomed William Penn; generations later, they still respected him and remained his peaceful fellowmen.

Being confronted and pushed westward again by the Iroquois of New York, they gradually located in the Muskingum River Valley of Ohio, which was assigned to them by these northeast Indians. The Delawares were the fourth most important Indian tribe of Ohio, after the Miami, Shawnee, and Wyandot. They were of the Algonquin Indian family, and eventually ended up on reservations in Oklahoma.

The closest Indian village to the area of interest was located four miles southwest of Charm, close to the Military Creek and the intersection of CR 58 in Mechanic Township (see footnote p.36 #14).

There is no exact date when the last group of Indians abandoned the village, but, supposedly,
26/   they left before the 1812 Greenville Treaty dead-
p.17   line. Even later, the area was frequently visited by
214/   Indian hunting parties or individuals who stayed
p.34   around the locality. Of the better known Indians were Tom Lions, who had a hut in the valley between Berlin and Bunker Hill, and Chief Doughty, whom the pioneers remembered as a peaceable Indian going from home to home asking for food.

*

---

14 214/ p.20–26. A Delaware Indian village had been located 2¹/₂ miles west of Beck's Mills in Mechanic Township. Situated on lands today owned by Roy O. Keim and Lester Hochstetler of Sections 1, 10, and 11. The semi-circle encampment had been wisely chosen in a small valley with two abundant springs (Twin Springs) nearby.

15 22/ p.6. About 20 of the 34 100-acre lots in Mechanic Township which were surveyed for Revolutionary War veterans are drained by this stream, and it was, accordingly, named "Military Creek."

16 312/ 97/ p.245. In 1958 a group of Indians had stopped at the Noah J. B. Miller farm, east of Clark in the Doughty Valley, and told him how their ancestors had originated from this area.

❧ Early Claims, Rights, Treaties, Statehood, Counties, and Townships

Spain

The first country from abroad to lay claim to the ascribed lands was Spain. Soon after Columbus found lands in the west, the Spanish and Portuguese became rivals in seafaring ventures to further discover and explore in the newfound land. As opposition arose between them on rights to claim, the Pope at Rome, who had strong influence on international affairs, issued a "papal decree," or law, which created in 1494 a "Line of Demarcation" along the 45th meridian. This line was slightly altered soon afterward and passed north and south through the Cape Verde Islands off the west coast of Africa. It entitled Portugal to the rights of exploration of lands east of said line, with Spain having the rights to the west, which included North America.

221/ p.37-38 222/ p.22-28

From 1539 to 1542 Hernando De Soto, a Spanish explorer, spent three years in the southern part of the country, ranging through Florida and into the Mississippi River Valley. He had searched in vain for gold that he hoped to find; yet, in doing so, he laid claim to all of the lands drained by the Mississippi River and its tributaries. Thus our land was originally claimed by Spain, first by the Pope's decree and lastly by De Soto's rights to exploration.

In the meantime, France and England were also readying their own exploration voyages of the new western lands and would not heed the former Demarcation line, inquiring by what right they could claim to own all the earth.

At the turn of the sixteenth century England was still regarded as a poor country. Developing their shipbuilding brought them to superior sea power, which enabled them to defeat the Spanish Armada in 1588. This defeat shattered Spain's hope of preventing England from establishing colonies along the east coast of North America.

The Indians, claiming possession to the American lands, were, at first, awed with the appearance of the white men. However, they soon realized that the whites were not only harvesting Indian game, but taking up their hunting lands as well. In due time this encroachment would cause many skirmishes between the two nations.

France

At the early onset of the establishment of America, explorers were finding their way into the western wilderness. Robert Cavalier, Sieur de LaSalle, a Frenchman, is considered the first white to actually come into the Ohio lands, and thereby claiming the vast area for France, ca 1670.

213/ p.3 221/ p.40-42

La Salle was born in France in 1635. In 1667 he came to Canada as a Jesuit missionary, but spent most of his life thereafter as an explorer for his country, with association with the French governor of Canada. Learning from New York's Seneca Indians of a shorter route from Lake Erie to the Ohio River, he began the envisioned exploration that year. Crossing Lake Erie, La Salle entered the Cuyahoga River traveling southward, then crossed the Portage to a smaller stream. Records would suggest that on his way to the Muskingum Forks, he probably traveled through lands now being Wayne, Holmes, and Coshocton Counties. Proceeding down the Muskingum River, he did eventually reach the Ohio River, and he claimed all of present-day Ohio in the name of France.

11/ 1-10- 1968

In 1683, after another trip into the Mississippi River Basin, he laid claim to the entire Mississippi Valley.

214/ p.5

The English, after claiming the Atlantic coast, were also maintaining that they had the right to all of the lands from the Atlantic to the Pacific. With England already granting tracts of land to individuals and colonies and the French claiming

❧

rights to discovery, including agreements with the Indians, there was bound to be conflict, which led to the French and Indian War. The French and Indian War of 1755–1763 was, in reality, fought between France and England for possession of disputed American lands, with their Indian allies of either side.

222/
p.27

(Note: England and Scotland were united in 1707 and since then known as "Great Britain." Thereafter, the English have also been called the British.)

England

213/
p.3

The Treaty of Paris ceded all of the French claims to the victorious English on February 10, 1763.

America

221/
p.54

The Ohio lands were now included in the possessions of England until the Revolutionary War. The American colonists' demand for independence from the mother country led to the Revolution (1775–1783).

Finally, the last remaining British hopes to land claims were shattered when George Rogers Clark and his men marched into the "Great West" to capture their fort stronghold at Vincennes in Illinois country on February 24, 1779. The Clark expedition is regarded as one of the most daring maneuvers of all military history. Setting out on a 250-mile march in the midst of winter with close to 170 Virginia volunteers, he crossed the snow- and ice-covered plains of the swamp lands of northern Ohio and Indiana. At times the soldiers were wading in the icy waters. The terrible journey was completed in 3 weeks and the fort taken completely by surprise. The British Governor Henry Hamilton, not anticipating any action until the following spring, surrendered to Clark; morever, he had miscalculated the attacking force, thinking it was 3 times its actual size—so clever were the military maneuvers of the well-drilled Virginians.

Well-known scouts Simon Kenton and Daniel b ne had been a part of the said expedition through the Indian territory.

Northwest Territory (see map p.19)

221/
p.43,
57-58

As the Americans now took control of the disputed lands, Great Britain turned over all of their rights, including the Northwest Territories, at the Treaty of Paris of 1783. The treaty of '83 included provisions to Spain which relinquished her rights to lands east of the Mississippi, but retained their claims west of the "father of waters."

⠦

Even though England had allotted to the Indians claims to western New York and the Lake Ontario-Lake Erie-Ohio Valley at their meeting of alliance at Albany, New York in 1701, the 1783 Paris treaty made no mention of the Indians; the English ceded all of the lands east of the Mississippi to the American colonists only. This, in due time, would cause more problems, with the Indians being deprived of their home grounds and the colonists constantly pushing westward to lands allotted to them from England.

214/
p.29

An interesting note should be included here concerning our local Delaware Indians. Early in 1777, at the onset of the Revolutionary War, the Shawnees, Wyandots, and Mingoes had joined with the British, whose base was at Detroit, to fight against the colonists. According to their tribal custom, to bid a tribe to join for war, "the hatchet" was sent to the Delawares. On March 9, 1777, the Delawares met in council at the forks of the Muskingum at Coshocton to discuss the matter. After a lengthy conference which included Chief White Eyes, Killbuck, and other friendly chiefs, the decision to remain peaceful was affirmed. Three times during that summer "the hatchet" was offered to them, but it was turned down each time. Their outstanding adherence to peace is regarded by historians as a highly important victory for the colonists during the years of the Revolution. Had their numbers joined against the colonists, the war might easily have ended in favor of the British.

214/
p.6-11

After the Revolutionary War, Congress created an office of commissioners to negotiate Indian treaties. The first of these treaties connected to Ohio was made on October 22, 1784 at Fort Stanwix, New York by the Iroquois, who ceded to the U.S. all their claimed lands. Though the Iroquois had allotted Ohio lands to other tribes, they still claimed this as their earlier conquered rights. The Iroquois chiefs present were Cornplanter and Red Jacket, who negotiated with commissioners Arthur Lee, Richard Butler, and Oliver Wolcott. The terms of the treaty included the delivery of prisoners taken during the war. The agreed-upon goods for payment was made to the Indians as soon as the treaty was signed, and the prisoners were returned.

After the Iroquois lands were secured by the U.S. Commissioners, their next step was to procure treaties with the lesser western tribes. The next treaty, at Fort McIntosh, a few miles below Fort Pitt (Pittsburgh, Pennsylvania) on the Ohio River, was completed January 21, 1785. The U.S. representatives were George Rogers Clark, Richard Butler, and Arthur Lee. The Indian tribes in attendance were the Delaware, Chippewa, Ottawa, and Wyandot.

The following are the terms of the Fort McIntosh Treaty:

"Article I: Three chiefs, one from among the Wyandot and two from the Delaware nations shall be d[e]livered up to the Commissioners of the U.S. to be by them retained till all the prisoners white and black taken by said nations or any of them, shall be restored."

"Article II: The said Indian nations do acknowledge themselves and all their tribes to be under the protection of the U.S. and of no other sovereign whatever [sic]."

"Article III: The boundary line between the U.S. and the Wyandot and Delaware nations shall begin at the mouth of the river Cuyahoga and run thence up said river to the portage [Akron] between it and the Tuscarawas branch of the Muskingum, thence down said branch to the forks at the crossing place above Fort Laurens [Bolivar]; thence westerly to the portage of the Big Miami which runs into the Ohio and where the fort stood taken by the French in 1752 [Fort Laramie]; thence along said portage to the Great Miami or Ome river and down the south west side of same to its mouth [Toledo], thence along the south shore of Lake Erie to the mouth of the Cuyahoga where it began."

"Article IV: The United States allot[s] all the lands contained within the said lines, to the Wyandots and Delaware nations to live and to hunt on and to such of the Ottawa nation as now live thereon; saving and reserving for the establishment of trading posts, six miles square at the mouth of the Miami or Ome river and the same at the portage on the branch of the Big Miami, which runs into the Ohio and the same on the lake at Sandusky where the fort formerly stood and also two miles square on each side of the lower rapids of the Sandusky river which posts and lands annexed to them shall be for the use and under the government of the United States."

"Article V: If any citizen of the United States or other person not being an Indian shall attempt to settle on any of the lands allotted to the Wyandot and Delaware nations, in this treaty, except on lands reserved to the U.S. in the preceding articles, such persons shall forfeit the protection of the U.S. and the Indians may punish him as they please."

"Article VI: The Indians who sign this treaty as well as in behalf of all their tribes as of themselves, do acknowledge the lands east, south[,] and west of the lines described in the third article, so far as the said Indians formerly claimed the same, to belong to the U.S. and none of their tribes shall presume to settle upon the same or any part of it."

"Article VII: [Pertains to land in Michigan.]"

"Article VIII: [Pertains to the distribution of goods among the Indians – goods given to them

68 / p.4-7

in payment for land ceded to the whites.]"

"Article IX: If any Indian or Indians commit robbery or murder on any citizen of the U.S. the tribe to which the offenders may belong shall be bound to deliver them up at the nearest post to [be] punished according to the ordinances of the United States."

"Article X: The commissioners of the U.S. in pursuance of the humane and liberal vows of Congress, will as soon as this treaty is signed, cause the goods agreed upon to be distributed among the various tribes."

"Supplemental Article: It is agreed that the Delaware Chiefs, Oelelemend or lieutenant Colonel Henry alias Killbuck; Hengue Pushees, or Big Cat Wicocalind or White Eyes, who took up the hatchet for the U.S. they and their families shall be received into the Delaware Nation, in the same situation and rank as before the war and enjoy their due portion of the lands given to the Wyandot and Delaware Nations in this treaty, as fully as if they had not taken part with the Americans or as any other person or persons in said nation."

The treaty was signed by the three U.S. commissioners: Clark, Butler, and Lee; along with eleven chiefs and braves of the Indian tribes: Daunghquat, Hopocan, Abraham Kuhn, Walendughtun, Talapoxie, Wingemund, Packelant, Cinge-wanno, Waonoos, Konalewass, Shawngum, and Quecookia.

This Indian treaty gave the United States title to the Ohio lands except the northern quarter. After the Fort McIntosh agreement, efforts were made to secure a treaty with the Miami and Shawnee tribes who still had white prisoners taken during the Revolutionary War.

A year later on January 31, 1786, commissioners Clark, Parsons, and Butler met and agreed to a payment of goods in exchange for white prisoners and lands of the Shawnee tribe, at Fort Finney, near the mouth of the Miami River. The treaty terms were close to those of the former treaty, except that the boundaries extended farther west.

As agreements were made with the main tribes during the years after the Revolution, and the western push by the whites to settle on the newly acquired lands was beginning, other tribes not bound to the treaties still claimed title rights to Ohio lands. In turn, this caused more unrest and uprisings against the frontier pioneers who were now settling on lands claimed by the U.S. government. The powerful Shawnee nation was one tribe not bound by earlier treaties, and they strongly defended their claim to the lands concerned.

The Continental Congress, by now exasperated by the numerous unrelenting Indian nations, determined to establish a civil government in the

213 / p.1

214 / p.11

223 / p.11

213 / p.10

214 / p.10-11

Northwest Territory, which included lands of Ohio, Indiana, Illinois, Michigan, Wisconsin, and Minnesota. To fulfill this attempt, the Northwest Ordinance was enacted July 13, 1787, which gave the new territory the procedures to obtain state-hoods and its groundwork to government. This historic ordinance was the first legislation by Congress which concerned real property, and has formed the guidelines by which most subsequent states entered the Union. The document contains provisions for religious freedom, trial by jury, encouragement of schools and education, prohibition of slavery, and the encouragement of good faith toward the Indians. It also established the primary boundaries of the later-formed states in the Northwest Territory.

213/
p.43-46

APPENDIX
ORDINANCE OF JULY 13, 1787
An ordinance for the government of the territory of the United States northwest of the river Ohio.

Be it ordained by the United States in congress assembled, That the said territory, for the purposes of temporary government, be one district; subject, however, to be divided into two districts, as future circumstances may, in the opinion of congress, make it expedient.

Be it ordained by the authority aforesaid, That the estates both of resident and nonresident proprietors in the said territory, dying intestate, shall descend to, and be distributed among their children, and the descendants of a deceased child, in equal parts; the descendants of a deceased child or grand child to take the share of their deceased parent in equal parts among them: and where there shall be no children or descendants, then in equal parts to the next of kin, in equal degree; and among collaterals, the children of a deceased brother or sister of the intestate shall have, in equal parts among them, their deceased parents' share; and there shall, in no case, be a distinction between kindred of the whole and half blood; saving in all cases to the widow of the intestate, her third part of the real estate for life, and one third part of the personal estate; and this law relative to descents and dower, shall remain in full force until altered by the legislature of the district. And until the governor and judges shall adopt laws as hereinafter mentioned, estate in the said territory may be devised or bequeathed by wills in writing, signed and sealed by him or her, in whom the estate may be, (being of full age,) and attested by three witnesses; and real estates may be conveyed by lease and release, or bargain and sale, signed, sealed, and delivered, by the person, being of full age, in whom the estate may be, and attested by two witnesses, provided such wills be duly proved, and such conveyances be acknowledged, or the execution thereof duly proved, and be recorded within one year after proper magistrates, courts, and registers, shall be appointed for that purpose; and personal property may be transferred by delivery; saving, however, to the French and Canadian inhabitants, and other settlers of the Kaskaskies, Saint Vincents, and the neighboring villages, who have heretofore professed themselves citizens of Virginia, their laws and customs now in force among them, relative to the descent and conveyance of property.

Be it ordained by the authority aforesaid, That there shall be appointed, from time to time, by congress, a governor, whose commission shall continue in force for the term of three years, unless sooner revoked by congress: he shall reside in the district, and have a freehold estate therein, in one thousand acres of land, while in the exercise of this office.

There shall be appointed, from time to time, by congress, a secretary, whose commission shall continue in force for four years, unless sooner revoked; he shall reside in the district, and have a freehold estate therein, in five hundred acres of land, while in the exercise of his office; it shall be his duty to keep and preserve the acts and laws passed by the legislature, and the public records of the district, and the proceedings of the governor in his executive department; and transmit authentic copies of such acts and proceedings, every six months, to the secretary of congress: There shall also be appointed a court, to consist of three judges, any two of whom to form a court, who shall have a common law jurisdiction, and reside in the district, and have each therein a freehold estate, in five hundred acres of land, while in the exercise of their offices; and their commissions shall continue in force during good behavior.

The governor and judges, or a majority of them, shall adopt and publish in the district, such laws of the original states, criminal and civil, as may be necessary, and best suited to the circumstances of the district, and report them to congress from time to time; which laws shall be in force in the district until the organization of the general assembly therein, unless disapproved of by congress; but afterwards the legislature shall have authority to alter them as they shall think fit.

The governor for the time being, shall be commander in chief of the militia, appoint and commission all officers in the same, below the rank of general officers; all general officers shall be appointed and commissioned by congress.

Previous to the organization of the general assembly, the governor shall appoint such magistrates and other civil officers, in each county or township, as he shall find necessary for the preservation of the peace and good order in the same. After the general assembly shall be organized, the powers and duties of magistrates and other civil officers shall be regulated and defined by the said assembly; but all magistrates and other civil officers, not herein otherwise directed, shall, during the continuance of this temporary government, be appointed by the governor.

For the prevention of crimes and injuries, the laws to be adopted or made shall have force in all parts of the district, and for the execution of process, criminal and civil, the governor shall make proper divisions thereof; and he shall proceed from time to time, as circumstances may require, to lay out the parts of the district in which the Indian title shall have been extinguished, into counties and townships, subject, however, to such alterations as may thereafter be made by the legislature.

So soon as there shall be five thousand free male inhabitants, of full age, in the district, upon giving proof thereof to the governor, they shall receive authority, with time and place, to elect representatives from their counties or townships, to represent them in the general assembly; provided that, for every five hundred free male inhabitants, there shall be one representative, and so on, progressively, with the number of free male inhabitants, shall the right of representation increase, until the number of representatives shall amount to twenty-five; after which the number and proportion of representatives shall be regulated by the legislature; provided, that no person be eligible or qualified to act as a representative, unless he shall have been a citizen of one of the United States three years, and be a resident in the district, or unless he shall have resided in the district three years; and in either case, shall likewise hold in his own right, in fee simple, two hundred acres of land within the same; provided also, that a freehold in fifty acres of land in the district, having been a citizen of one of the states, and being resident in the district, or the like freehold and two years residence in the district, shall be necessary to qualify a man as an elector of a representative.

The representatives thus elected, shall serve for the term of two years; and in case of the death of a representative, or removal from office, the governor shall issue a writ to the county or township, for which he was a member, to elect another in his stead, to serve for the residue of the term.

The general assembly, or legislature, shall consist of the governor, legislative council, and a house of representatives . The legislative council shall consist of five members, to continue in office five years, unless sooner removed by congress; any three of whom to be a quorum: and the members of the council shall be nominated and appointed in the following manner, to wit: As soon as representatives shall be elected, the governor shall appoint a time and place for them to meet together, and when met, they shall nominate ten persons, residents in the district, and each possessed of a freehold in five hundred acres of land, and return their names to congress; five of whom congress shall appoint and commission to serve as aforesaid: and whenever a vacancy shall happen in the council, by death or removal from office, the house of representatives shall nominate two persons, qualified as aforesaid, for each vacancy, and return their names to congress; one of whom congress shall appoint and commission for the residue of the term: And every five years, four months at least before the expiration of the time of service of the members of council, the said house shall nominate ten persons, qualified as aforesaid, and return their names to congress; five of whom congress shall appoint and commission to serve as members of the council five years, unless sooner removed. And the governor, legislative council, and house of representatives, shall have authority to make laws, in all cases, for the good government of the district, not repugnant to the principles and articles in this ordinance established and declared. And all bills, having passed by a majority in the house, and by a majority in the council, shall be referred to the governor for his assent; but no bill or legislative act whatever, shall be of any force without his assent. The governor shall have power to convene, prorogue, and dissolve the general assembly, when in his opinion is shall be expedient.

The governor, judges, legislative council, secretary, and such other officers as congress shall appoint in the district, shall take an oath or affirmation of fidelity, and of office; the governor before the president of congress, and all other officers before the governor. As soon as a legislature shall be formed in the district, the council and house assembled, in one room, shall have authority, by joint ballot, to elect a delegate to congress, who shall have a seat in congress, with a right of debating, but not of voting during this temporary government.

And for extending the fundamental principles of civil and religious liberty, which form the basis whereon these republics, their laws, and constitutions, are erected; to fix and establish those principles as the basis of all laws, constitutions, and governments which forever hereafter shall be formed in the said territory; to provide, also, for the establishment of states, and permanent government therein, and for their admission to share in the federal councils on an equal footing with the original states, at as early periods as may be consistent with the general interest:

It is hereby ordained and declared, by the authority, aforesaid, That the following articles shall be considered as articles of compact, between the original states and the people and states in the said territory, and forever remain unalterable, unless by common consent, to wit:

ART. 1. No person, demeaning himself in a peaceable and orderly manner, shall ever be molested on account of his mode of worship or religious sentiments, in the said territory.

ART. 2. The inhabitants of the said territory shall always be entitled to the benefit of the writ of habeas corpus, and of the trial by jury; of a proportionate representation of the people in the legislature, and of judicial proceedings according to the course of the common law. All persons shall be bailable, unless for capital offences, where the proof shall be evident, or the presumption great. All finds shall be moderate; and no cruel or unusual punishments shall be inflicted. No man shall be deprived of his liberty or property, but by the judgment of his peers, or the law of the land, and should the public exigencies make it necessary, for the common preservation, to take any person's property, or to demand his particular services, full compensation shall be made for the same. And, in the just preservation of rights and property, it is understood and declared, that no law ought ever to be made, or have force in the said territory, that shall, in any manner whatever, interfere with, or affect, private contracts or engagements, bona fide, and without fraud, previously formed.

ART. 3. Religion, morality, and knowledge, being necessary to good government and the happiness of mankind, schools and the means of education shall forever be encouraged. The utmost good faith shall always be observed towards the Indians; their lands and property shall never be taken from them without their consent; and in their property, rights, and liberty, they never shall be invaded or disturbed, unless in just and lawful wars authorized by congress; but laws founded in justice and humanity shall, from time to time, be made, for preventing wrongs being done to them, and for preserving peace and friendship with them.

ART. 4. The said territory, and the states which may be formed therein, shall forever remain a part of this confederacy of the United States of America, subject to the articles of confederation, and to such alterations therein as shall be constitutionally made; and to all the acts and ordinances of the United States in congress assembled, conformable thereto. The inhabitants and settlers in the said territory shall be subject to pay a part of the federal debts, contracted or to be contracted, and a proportional part of the expenses of government, to be apportioned on them by congress, according to the same common rule and measure by which apportionments thereof shall be made on the other states; and the taxes for paying their proportion, shall be laid and levied by the authority and direction of the legislatures of the district or districts, or new states, as in the original states, within the time agreed upon by the United States in congress assembled. The legislatures of those districts, or new states, shall never interfere with the primary disposal of the soil by the United States in congress assembled, nor with any regulations congress may find necessary, for securing the title in such soil, to the bona fide purchasers. No tax shall be imposed on lands the property of the United States; and in no case shall nonresident proprietors be taxed higher than residents. The navigable waters leading into the Mississippi and St. Lawrence, and the carrying places between the same, shall be common highways, and forever free, as well to inhabitants of the said territory, as to the citizens of the United States, and those of any other states that may be admitted into the confederacy, without any tax, impost, or duty therefor.

ART. 5. There shall be formed in the said territory, not less than three, nor more than five states; and the boundaries of the states, as soon as Virginia shall alter her act of cession, and consent to the same, shall become fixed and established as follows, to wit: the western state in the said territory, shall be bounded by the Mississippi, the Ohio, and Wabash rivers; a direct line drawn from the Wabash and Post Vincents, due north, to the territorial line between the United States and Canada; and by the said territorial line to the lake of the Woods and Mississippi. The middle states shall be bounded by the said direct line, the Wabash, from Post Vincents to the Ohio, by the Ohio, by a direct line drawn due north from the mouth of the Great Miami to the said territorial line, and by the said territorial line. The eastern state shall be bounded by the last mentioned direct line, the Ohio, Pennsylvania, and the said territorial line: provided however, and it is further understood and declared, that the boundaries of these three states shall be subject so far to be altered, that, if congress shall hereafter find it expedient, they shall have authority to form one or two states in that part of the said territory which lies north of an east and west line drawn through the southerly bend or extreme of lake Michigan. And whenever any of the said states shall have sixty thousand free inhabitants therein, such state shall be admitted, by its delegates, into the congress of the United States, on an equal footing with the original states, in all respects whatever; and shall be at liberty to form a permanent constitution and state government: provided the constitution and government, so to be formed, shall be republican, and in conformity to the principles contained in these articles; and, so far as it can be consistent with the general interest of the confederacy, such admission shall be allowed at an earlier period, and when there may be a less number of free inhabitants in the state than sixty thousand.

ART. 6. There shall neither be slavery nor involuntary servitude in the said territory, otherwise than in the punishment of crimes, where of the party shall have been duly convicted; provided always, that any person escaping into the same, from whom labor or service is lawfully claimed in any one of the original states, such fugitive may be lawfully reclaimed, and conveyed to the person claiming his or her service as aforesaid.

Be it ordained by the authority aforesaid, That the resolutions of the 23rd of April, 1784, relative to the subject of this ordinance, be, and the same are hereby repealed and declared null and void.

Done by the United States, in congress assembled, the 13th day of July, in the year of our Lord 1787, and of their sovereignty and independence the twelfth.

Laws of United States, Volume 1, Page 475.

Washington County (see map p. 20)

Arthur St. Clair was appointed governor of the new establishment in the Northwest Territory, and arrived at Marietta July 9, 1788. On July 26 he gave proclamation for the formation of Washington County as follows: "Beginning on the bank of the Ohio [R]iver, where the western boundary line of Pennsylvania crosses it [East Liverpool], and running with that line to Lake Erie; thence along the southern shore of said lake to the mouth of the Cuyahoga [R]iver [Cleveland]; thence up said river to the portage [Akron] between it and the Tuscarawas branch of the Muskingum; thence down that branch to the forks, at the crossing place above Fort Laurens [Bolivar]; thence with a line to be drawn westerly to the portage on that branch of the Big Miami on which the fort stood that was taken by the French in 1752, until it meets the road from the lower Shawnese town to Sandusky [Marion]; thence south to the Scioto river, and thence with that river to the mouth [Portsmouth], and thence up the Ohio [R]iver to the place of beginning."

214 / p.6-11

223 p.11

224 / *VJJ-* p777

68 / p.6

The above described line running west of Fort Laurens was similar to the treaty boundaries and later what was to become known as the Greenville Treaty Line, which extends through northern Holmes County.

Incidentally, Charm is located south of this line, and its territory lies within the Northwest's first county of Washington. The treaty line, passing immediately south of Mt. Hope, is a mere eight miles north of Charm.

The attempt to establish a government again stirred more Indian troubles, and Governor St. Clair took further action to establish peace along the frontier. On January 9, 1789, he called the chiefs of various tribes to Fort Harmar, where he obtained separate treaties and confirmed those made at Fort Stanwix, Fort McIntosh, and Fort Finney. Here, again, the Indians were paid with goods ($6,000) for agreeing and signing the treaty.

With still no permanent peace in sight, Congress felt that force was the only means left to secure peace. Expeditions into the wilderness were led by General Harmer in 1790 and Governor St. Clair in 1791, but both were dealt defeat. It was in August of 1794 that General Anthony Wayne, at the Battle of Fallen Timbers, shattered the Indian Confederacy; they never recovered from the blow, and Indian strength of the Northwest was extinguished.

After this U.S. victory, the government sought another treaty at Fort Greenville (Greenville, Ohio) on August 3, 1795. A large number of Indian tribes, along with General Anthony Wayne and his party, assembled to further relinquish their claim to lands south and east of the boundary line in the Northwest Territory permanently. The articles involved were more minutely expressed than the former pacts. The boundary was described as follows: "beginning at the mouth of the Cuyahoga [R]iver; thence up said river to the portage; thence across said portage and down the Tuscarawas branch of the Muskingum to the crossing place above Fort Laurens; thence in a westerly direction to that branch of the Great Miami at or near which stood Loramie's store; thence northwest to Fort Recovery; thence in a southerly direction to the mouth of the Kentucky River."

The third article reserves the Indian chiefs' right to accompany the surveyors whenever the U.S. shall decide to survey and mark the boundaries. The fourth article states the value of goods to be paid to the tribes. An amount of $20,000.00 was to be paid immediately, and thereafter, every year, the U.S. would deliver, at some point on the Ohio River, goods valued at $9,500.00. The fifth article agrees that should the Indians sell any of their land, it must be sold only to the U.S. and, until that, the U.S. shall protect all tribes in their full enjoyment of their lands against white people. Further articles provided that intruders on Indian lands be punished; that Indians be permitted to hunt on ceded lands with no injury to person or property of white settlers; that trade between tribes and U.S. citizens be established; and that all former treaties be cancelled.

It is of interest to note some of the boundary points that were widely known to both the Indians and white men. Rivers, of course, were a known and definite reference point. The Portage Path, between the Cuyahoga and Tuscarawas, was a narrow strip of land between the said rivers that could be crossed quickly if one were going in the direction of either course. The portage was an east-west path, and it was the only place between Lake Erie and the Ohio River that no river had to be forded for access to lands farther west. This, in fact, would have been a well-known reference point for the early inhabitants. The importance of Fort Laurens (Bolivar) was also of keen interest. The Tuscarawas river was shallow enough a short distance above the fort so that it could be forded. It was therefore also a familiar western point used by the Indians and the advancing whites. Loramie's store, close to the Indiana border, became another good reference, as stores and trading posts were scarce and far apart in the unsettled wilderness. Located deeply in Indian territory, it was an ideal bearing point to them and the frontiersmen. With these locations in the vast, unsettled wilderness known by both the Indians and white people, they could be readily used and understood

for the boundary points when agreeing on a treaty.

As the Battle of Fallen Timber was the turning point in the establishment of peace and the settlement of the Northwest, some further notes of the expedition will be included.

Although the British had lost control to American lands during the Revolutionary War, some were still stimulating the Indians to harass the frontiersmen and the treaty's terms. The Indians, at the same time, felt they were being "driven out and ill-treated" by the advancing white men.

The victory at the Battle of Fallen Timber is considered important in both American and Ohio history. Although the actual confrontation occurred approximately 115 miles northwest of our town of interest, our lands were nevertheless included in the resulting treaty of peace of Fort Greenville.

General Anthony Wayne was joined by an army of 1600 Kentuckians as he began his march into northwestern Ohio on July 28, 1794 from headquarters at Fort Greenville. Wayne's aim was to

68/
p.6-9

308/

224/
VJJ
p.137-
139

224/
VJJ
p.139

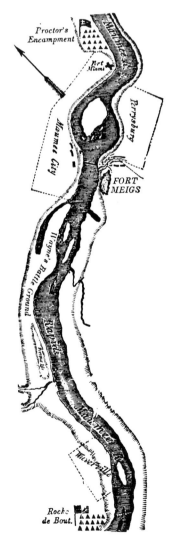

General Anthony Wayne's route at the Battle of Fallen Timber in northwestern Ohio.

bid for peace, as recommended by the government, or otherwise shatter the Indian stronghold that was being aided by the British.

After the well-trained army left Fort Greenville, they continued north toward the Maumee river. The Indians, by this time, were well aware of Wayne's movements and had received British assistance from Detroit.

By August 13 a scout, Christopher Miller, was sent to the Indians as a special messenger to offer terms of friendship, as advised by Washington. Wayne, becoming impatient by the delayed message, moved forward and met Miller returning with the reply stating that, could the army wait ten days, the Indians would decide for peace or war. By August 18 the army arrived at a place immediately south of Waterville, where they built a site to contain some of their heavy baggage.

The Indians, anticipating an attack any time, were making their final preparations. In doing so, they would not eat in the morning on the day of the expected siege, for noted reasons. Returning that night to the village, which was located at Presque Isle Hill two miles south of Maumee City, the prepared evening meal was eaten by the warriors. Day number two was a repeat of the first. Only one meal was received, and still the white men had not appeared. By now the Indians were showing signs of weakness, and the following morning did partake of the food.

Meanwhile Wayne, not having received a peace message, was ready to march head-on into Indian-occupied territory. His camp was a mere two miles south of the stronghold.

Around 8:00 on the morning of August 20, 1794, the army began to head north again. Following the Maumee River, they came to a wooded land of broken and downed trees which were apparently felled by a tornado or high winds. It was here among the fallen timber that the Indians lay hidden and met their oncoming foe with gunfire. Thus, this battle would henceforth be remembered as the "Battle of Fallen Timber." After the first volley of fire from the Indians, Wayne gave immediate command to charge forward. The immediate action of the troops was executed with swiftness and precision that resulted from months of extensive previous training.

The early morning encounter caught the Indians off guard, even though they were anticipating their coming. Since this was the third day they had lain in wait, some Indians were still in camp that morning when the first shots were heard. Rushing toward the scene of action, they were met with retreating comrades. The Indian fighters were rushing in both directions during Wayne's advancing movement, which created great confusion. Thus, the Indians' very first stand was crushed, and they were thoroughly defeated. They retreated to the vicinity of the British's Fort Meigs, which was their supplying ally.

Wayne, knowing the fort was heavy with artillery and trying to avoid yet another conflict with the British, did not attack the fortification. Staying in the area a week, the army returned to their headquarters while laying waste to the Indian villages and corn fields for miles on each side of the Maumee. The army hoped that the fear of hunger

"The Signing of the Treaty of Greenville" – Painting by Howard Chandler Christy.

resulting from this destruction would compel the Indians to terms of peace.

221/
p.66-67 Had Wayne's proposal been met, the plundering of the natives' lands and lives could have been spared. At the earlier offer of peace, Chief Little Turtle of the Miamis had advised his nations to accept the bid. Foreseeing the strength of Wayne and certain defeat, he said to his fellowmen, "We have beaten the enemy twice under different commanders; we cannot expect the same good fortune again. The Americans now have a chief who never sleeps. The night and day are alike to him. There is something, whispers in my mind, it would be well to listen to his offers of peace."

But the other chiefs would not agree with Little Turtle's proposal and were dealt the crushing defeat.

221/
p.33 Little Turtle and the Miamis had helped defeat General Harmer near Fort Wayne, Indiana in 1790 and then, in 1791, the courageous and skillful chief had led the Miamis and Shawnees against St. Clair, to his defeat.

The peace treaty drawn up by General Wayne would remain well-known and important. The general prepared the terms with the same care as he had readied his army before the battle. In June of 1795 there assembled with him at Fort Greenville over 1,000 chiefs and warriors from close to twenty tribes. The dramatic scene lasted nearly two months. Countless speeches later, under the agreement of both camps to adhere to peace, the historic Treaty of Greenville was signed. Chiefs of each tribe were present and included: Little Turtle, Blue Jacket, Tarhe, and Buckongahelas. Of the Americans to sign were General Anthony Wayne, William Henry Harrison, and other white leaders. On December 22, 1795, with the advice and agreement of Congress, it was signed by the commander-in-chief of the expedition, President George Washington.

The young and advancing America was now more confident with a settled peace treaty, and the gateway to the northwest was opened.

223/
p.11 The following year provisions were made to survey the boundary lines set forth in the treaty. Israel Ludlow was appointed Deputy Surveyor of the United States, and the courses were under his personal direction. His chain carriers were William C. Shenk and Israel Shreve. In 1797, a random line was surveyed from Loramie's store east to Fort Laurens to determine the true magnetic bearing of the line. On Sunday, July 9, 1797, Ludlow began the initial survey near present Bolivar, Ohio. His notes read: ". . . according to the treaty of Greenville by General Wayne of August 5, 1795, at the crossing place of Tuscarawas branch of the Muskingum [R]iver above Fort

Laurens at a bottom oak ten inches in diameter, standing on the west bank of said fork, which tree is notched with three notches on the north and west sides with this inscription: 'surveyed according to Treaty by Gen. Wayne, a line to Loramie's store, 78 degrees 50 minutes W.'" On August 29 he came to the designated point close to the Indiana state line. The continuing line to Fort Recovery and Kentucky was completed in August of 1799.

The assurance of a lasting peace treaty now generated yet even more interest in settlement of the Territory of the Northwest.

214/
p.6-7 In 1805, ten years after the Greenville agreement, another treaty was signed at Fort Industry. Under the terms of this treaty, the Indians gave up their claim north of the "Treaty line" and west of the Cuyahoga River to the west end of Lake Erie. In 1817 and 1818 other treaties relinquished the remaining Indian lands of Ohio to the government.

220/
p.490 In 1796, prior to these treaties, the Northwest's governor, Arthur St. Clair, had established Wayne County, naming it in honor of General Wayne. The vast area consisted of lands north and west of the Greenville Treaty Line, northeastern Indiana, and Michigan Territory. Although the area was of Indian lands at this time, its establishment may not really have been intended to its settlement, but rather a tribute to its namesake, General Anthony Wayne.

United States Military District
(see map p.20)

Congress was apparently anxious to settle the Northwest, and soon various surveys were conducted on Ohio lands, granting and later selling claims to pioneer settlers. In 1796, two decades after the Revolution and one year after the Greenville Treaty, Congress established an act to survey and set aside lands to be credited to Revolutionary War veterans. This survey is known as the U.S. Military District and our lands of interest lie within the area.

213/
p.11,
23-24

224/
09
p.935 The layout was begun in March, 1797, and contains 2,560,000 acres. The district is bounded on the north by the Greenville Treaty Line, which was also the northern edge of Washington County at the time. On the eastern border lie the Seven Ranges that were the first public lands to be surveyed in the United States. To the south are Congress Lands and Refugee Tract, and the Scioto River on the west. The U.S. Military District is presently found in counties of Tuscarawas, Holmes, Coshocton, Knox, Morrow, Marion, Delaware, Franklin, Licking, Muskingum, Guernsey, and Noble.

The tract was divided into surveying townships

Copy of an original U.S. Military Land Grant, signed December 9, 1829 by President Andrew Jackson. The lands are located in Monroe Township at the SR 39-TR 257 intersection, and the remaining 100 acres is 6 miles northwest of Welcome in Knox Township.

five miles square containing 16,000 acres then subdivided into quarter-townships of 4,000 acres. Soldiers were to receive the land according to their rank, which was: Major General 1,100 acres, Brigadier General 850, Colonel 500, Lieutenant Colonel 450, Major 400, Captain 300, Lieutenant 200, Ensign 150, and noncommissioned officer or soldier 100.

Since no one person had a warrant to 4,000 acres, the grants were pooled. Only about one half of the two million-plus acres was claimed. The 262 quarter-townships claimed were determined by drawing. Apparently, not a great amount of land was actually settled by these veterans. Some were well-satisfied to stay in populated areas of the east and took no liking to life in the unsettled wilderness. Others receiving warrants sold them, so that, finally, about one half of the claimed acres (569,542) were owned by only 22 persons. Later surveys in 1800 and 1802 divided some of the fractional townships into 100- and 50-acre lots. Within the area of present-day Holmes County, 480 of these 100-acre lots were given to the said soldiers.

A later law of 1830 gave the warrant holders the opportunity to exchange the warrant for land script good for $1.25 an acre, and issued in 80-acre amounts anywhere on public lands.

With the lack of interest shown by the war sol-

diers, an Act of March 3, 1803 provided that all remaining lands be surveyed into 640-acre sections 1 mile square and to be sold as any other public land. The earlier 5-mile square township surveys were numbered east to west in ranges with Range 1 beginning at the west line of the Seven Ranges (see map p. 20). Townships, in turn, were numbered northward from the southern boundary. As the 1-mile sections were surveyed, they were also numbered individually within the 5-mile square block starting at the northeast corner and going westward (5 - 4 - 3 - 2 - 1). At the fifth section, number 6 was the next one south and (6 - 7 - 8 - 9 - 10) were numbered eastward, and so on, to 25. Thus Charm would be located in the U.S. Military District, within the Eighth Township north of its southern boundary, and in the Fifth Range west of the Seven Ranges, situated on the adjoining corners of Sections 4 - 5 - 6 - 7 of the latter survey.

The surveys of Township 8 – Range 5 were conducted between May 27 and June 3, 1798 by deputy surveyor Absalom Martin. The work was under the general management of the Surveyor General, Rufus Putman. The later division of the township into 1-mile square sections containing 640-acre areas was surveyed by Ebenezer Buckingham and was laid out between November 5 and November 11, 1803.

287/

☙

The original plats and field notes of these United States Government surveys are in the custody of the Ohio Historical Society at Columbus, Ohio.

As the sections were surveyed, sandstones were placed at the corners, which served as markers. The approximate 6x6-inch, topped stones have a cross etched on the surface, which serves as their identification. These were placed with the cross pointing in true directions respectively. The stones are still readily found throughout the area. It was from them that the early pioneers first laid claim to their lands.

213/
p.18,56

As the demand for land increased, land offices were established in 1800 at Steubenville, Cincinnati, Chillicothe, and Marietta. From 1804 to 1840 the Land Office was in operation at Zanesville. It was at this office that all of our original patents were issued from the designated area of Sections 4 - 5 - 6 - 7.

Different payment arrangements were used during the early years of land purchasing. Once the final settlement was made, a certificate was issued at the land office which was sent to Washington, D.C. so a U.S. Patent could be issued. Return of the deeds was often delayed because of checking accounts and records, plus the fact that the president needed to sign each one. Up until March 3, 1833 a presidential signature was required on each U.S. Patent Deed.

292/

The earliest deeds issued were generally made up using a deerskin to record the land layout and agreement. Also of interest is the fact that the early deed was an indenture-type document in appearance. This means that at the time of issuing, a top part was randomly cut off, with that part kept at the courthouse as a receipt. If suspicion later arose concerning the identity of a deed, it could be taken to the records office to see if it matched the cut lines of its counterpart. On closer examination, the skin's leather grains could be checked to see if they corresponded. This procedure served as a hedge against lands being stolen by means of falsification of deeds.

12/

Copy of an original U.S. Patent Deed, signed December 19, 1814 by President James Madison. The land was located in the southwest quarter of Section 21, Township 9, Range 5, today being a mile south of Walnut Creek. The grantee, Elizabeth Miller (ML 227) was the first white woman to own land in Holmes County, and also the first girl to marry in the county. She immigrated from Somerset County, Pennsylvania, then married Moses Beachy, also of Somerset, who had acquired the adjoining quarter section to the south.

Ohio (see map p.21)

With more and more Easterners making the Ohio lands their home, there was an ever-increasing population that was getting closer to the 1787 Ordinance provision—that once a territory had 60,000 free inhabitants, it could obtain statehood.

Census records for Ohio indicate this gigantic increase during those early years: 1790, 3,000 inhabitants; 1800–45,365; 1810 – 230,760. In 1802 Congress passed a law enabling the people of the eastern part of the Northwest Territory to form a state. On January 11, 1803 an election was held and Edward Tiffin was elected as Ohio's first governor, along with the members of the assembly. Governor Tiffin took the oath of office March 1, 1803, and Ohio was admitted into the Union as the seventeenth state.

224/
VII
p.54
221/
p.85-86

Muskingum County (see map p.21)

A large north-central portion of the former vast Washington County was organized March 1, 1804 to become Muskingum County. Its northern border extended to the Greenville Treaty Line, which would later become an area of Holmes County.

224/
VIII
p.324

Tuscarawas and Coshocton Counties
(see map p. 22)

The formation of Tuscarawas County on February 15, 1808 reduced the size of Muskingum County, for the new county included the northeastern portion of Muskingum. The county was further diminished through the organization of Coshocton County on April 1, 1811, as Coshocton included the northwestern part of Muskingum. (The two newer counties were bordered on the north by the well-known treaty line.)

224/
VI
p.466-
VIII
p.679

By the second decade of the nineteenth century, the large area of the former Washington County, named after President George Washington, had substantially decreased in size. As areas increased in population and came within the provisions of the 1787 Ordinance, smaller counties were formed with individual legislative bodies. By this time the newly organized counties that consisted of land taken from Washington County were: Fairfield, Muskingum, Coshocton, and Tuscarawas Counties.

Coshocton County, within which lie our lands of interest, was so named after the Delaware Indian village "Goshachgunk." The village was located within the limits of present-day Coshocton on the forks of the Walhonding and Tuscarawas Rivers.

Holmes County (see map p. 22)

Holmes County was formed January 20, 1824

and organized a year later on January 4, 1825. The territory contained within the county was taken from the southern part of Wayne County; 87,440 acres lay north of the Greenville Treaty Line. A 2-mile wide strip consisting of 16,200 acres was taken from Tuscarawas County's western border, extending from the south boundary of Township 8 to the treaty line on the north. The remaining portion, 162,200 acres, was made up of lands from Coshocton County.

224/
VII
p.934

The boundaries of Holmes County were designated by the state legislature as follows (the statements in parentheses were added later by George F. Newton to enable the reader to better visualize the layout):

68/
p.33-35

"Section I: Be it enacted, etc., That such parts of the counties of Coshocton, Tuscarawas and Wayne as lies within the boundaries herein set forth, be, and the same is hereby erected into a separate county by the name of Holmes: Beginning on the old Indian boundary line where the east boundary line of Wayne [C]ounty intersects the same: thence north with the line of Wayne County to the northeast corner of Section 25, of Township 15 in Range 11, (that being the northeast corner of present Paint [T]ownship), thence west with the sectional lines to the west boundary of Wayne County, (that being the northwest corner of our present Washington [T]ownship); thence south to the aforesaid old Indian boundary line (being the south west corner of fractional Section 30, of [T]p. 19, [R]ange 15 and western corner of present Knox [T]ownship) thence (eastwardly) with said Indian boundary line to the northeast corner of Knox Co.; thence south with the east line of Knox Co. to the line between the 7th and 8th [T]ps. (at the southwest corner of [S]ection 25, [T]p. 8, [R]ange 9, that being the present southwest corner of our present Richland Township); thence east with the line between the 7th and 8th tier of townships to the southeast corner of [S]ection 24, of [T]p. 8 in [R]ange 4, (that being the present southeast corner of German [T]p.); thence north to the aforesaid old Indian boundary line; thence east with said Indian boundary line to place of beginning.

Section 2: That the said county of Holmes, be and remain attached to the counties from which it was taken, until the legislature shall think proper to organize the same.

Section 3: That there shall be commissioners appointed to fix the seat of Justice in said county of Holmes agreeably to the act, entitled an "act establishing seats of justice," who shall report to the court of common pleas, to be holden in the county of Coshocton, which court shall take such order on said report as is directed by the aforesaid act; and the commissioners shall be paid for their

❧

services under this act out of any money in the treasury of Coshocton county; which sum shall be remunerated by the said county of Holmes so soon as the same shall be organized.

Section 4: That the county of Holmes shall be and the same is hereby attached to the eleventh congressional district for the election of representatives to Congress; provided however that the several parts of the territory taken from the counties of Wayne, Coshocton and Tuscarawas, shall remain attached to the original counties for other purposes until the said county of Holmes shall be organized."

To locate a seat of justice for Holmes County, the legislature appointed David Huston of Green County, Daniel Converse of Muskingum County, and John Wallace of Champaign County to fulfill that duty.

26/
p.14
With the county seat at stake, Millersburg, Lima, and Berlin entered the competition. Millersburg was chosen as the county seat in 1825.

Lima was laid out by Moses Knowles when the county seat issue came up. The town was platted in the southeast corner of Section 13 at the US 62-TR 351 intersection (Holmes Lumber and Building Supply area), halfway between Berlin and Millersburg. After two years, the idea to build Lima was abandoned and the town never developed.

145/
3-13-
1990
Holmes County was named after Major Andrew Hunter Holmes, 1790–1814. Major Holmes grew up in Virginia and the family was acquainted with Thomas Jefferson. During the War of 1812 the young, 24-year-old officer was engaged at Mackinac Island. On August 4, 1814 he was killed during an unsuccessful attack on the island. A brother, David, was appointed by President Jefferson as the first governor of Mississippi; therefore that state also has a Holmes Co.

German Township (see map p. 24, 25)

At the time of Coshocton County's organization in 1811, its area was laid off in townships. German Township, which later became known as Clark, was formed at this early time before Holmes County had come into existence.

Soon after German Township was renamed

Clark, a newspaper article concerning the township was written by W. S. Hanna in 1918, from which the following has been taken:

50/
6-27-
1918
"... It was one of the three townships formed in northern Coshocton County when it was organized in 1811. It covered the entire east end of what is now Holmes County, except the two mile strip taken from Tuscarawas county, and extended from the Indian Boundary Line southward across what is now Holmes County into Coshocton County. All of Range five and the east half of Range six, now being parts of Salt Creek, Paint, Walnut Creek, German, Mechanic and all of Berlin township was included within its boundaries. In 1819 Mechanic [T]ownship was formed partly from German, Tuscarawas and Hardy and in 1820 the whole north end of German [T]ownship was struck off to form Berlin [T]ownship, which extended from the Indian Boundary Line south to the north line of what is now Clark [T]ownship. When Holmes County was formed [in 1824] that part of German [T]ownship contained within its boundaries was Range 5, Township 8, having an area of twenty-five square miles ..."

70/
At the time of the county's organization, the two-mile wide strip connected to Holmes County from Tuscarawas was added to the previously formed German Township on June 8, 1825 by the county commissioners. On December 7 of that year the commissioners ordered the townships within the county to be organized and named. As already noted, our township's territory was German and, at the time of this act, it was not altered in size.

It has been assumed that the name German had derived from the German descent of the numerous early pioneer settlers.

Clark Township

26/ p.2
50/
6-27-
1918
On June 3, 1918 the county commissioners, on petition of a majority of electors and notice as provided by law, renamed German Township to Clark Township. The conception for a new name derived from the resentment felt toward the Germans during World War I.

This was the first and only successful change of a township's name since the county was organized in 1825. ❧

Early Settlement

The first pioneer known to locate within the Holmes County boundaries was Peter Jolly. Peter appeared in Killbuck Township as a squatter around 1798 and later moved to Richland County. By 1809 more attention was focused on the Killbuck and Tuscarawas Valleys of the Muskingum River Basin. The Killbuck River Valley was still a part of Washington County and the Tuscarawas Valley a part of the newly formed Tuscarawas County. The Killbuck area was later to become a part of Coshocton, then, eventually, Holmes County.

61/
p.653

It was to have been one mile east of the Killbuck River that Jonathan Grant and his son built a cabin along Salt Creek in Prairie Township in July of 1809. The Grants had come on foot from Beaver County, Pennsylvania carrying their meager provisions.

224/
VJ
p.936

Later that summer Jonathan Butler and his father-in-law James Morgan arrived at the Big Spring west of Holmesville. Their timely arrival greatly aided Grant, who had fallen quite sick. With their care he regained good health.

100/
2-15-
1984

The same year, 1809, 21-year-old Jonas Stutzman came to Ohio with the Jacob Millers, whose wife was an aunt to him. Miller had chosen land northeast of Sugar Creek in Tuscarawas County the previous year. As Jonas carefully picked his building site, he was also mindful of a new and expanding Amish settlement of the future. By fall he had built a cabin on the quarter section south of present Walnut Creek, at a good spring location. With a stream close by he could, eventually, also build a sawmill. The time spent scouting the area was well worth the effort. His decision to locate in the fertile Valley was a wise one. Although unknown to him at the time, it would someday become the largest Amish community in history.

DJH
9147

The first wagon to arrive in the Walnut Creek Valley came May 6, 1810, bringing the belongings of the Joseph Masts, Christian Yoders, John Troyers, and Jonas Millers. The families all settled within 1½ miles of the Stutzman cabin.

The Grants had returned to Pennsylvania as cold weather set in during the winter of 1809–1810. However, by the spring of 1810 they returned, and others were also arriving and choosing sites in their neighborhood. In April of 1810 Edwin Martin, then John L. Dawson, David Knox, and Robert Knox settled along Martin's Creek, a mile south of the Grant cabin. In the same year and in the following, Peter Casey settled along the Killbuck River close to Millersburg, along with Abraham Shrimplin farther south. The Carpenters and Morrisons were settling in the Doughty Valley as Peter Shimer, Jacob Korn, Thomas Edgar, and others laid their respective claims near Berlin in 1810–1811. The earliest known deed (1812) of Berlin Township was held by Jacob Troyer, who occupied the west half of Section 6 immediately north of Berlin.

224/
VJ
p.936

The first white children known to be born within the boundaries of later-formed Holmes County were: Hannah Butler, born February 4, 1810 to Jonathan Butlers at the Big Spring northwest of Holmesville; Yost, son of pioneers Christian and Anna (Hershberger) Yoder (YR2612) of the Walnut Creek Valley, was born November 8, 1810; and Moses, born January 12, 1811 to Jonas and Catherine (Hershberger) Miller (ML244), also of the Walnut Creek settlement. The young couple's first child was the second Amish child born in Holmes County, and would eventually serve as a highly respected and influential bishop of the growing Amish community. He was known as "Glay (Little) Mose."

26/
p.1

Given the relatively late settlement of the Holmes County lands, the question arises—why? Primarily, the area was settled late because it was not located on or within chief waterways like the

Ohio River and its tributaries to the south, or along the Lake Erie and the bigger rivers flowing northward into it. Holmes County was sandwiched between the main waters of the Ohio country, and its overland passes were not yet improved to readily bring in the earlier settlers.

Furthermore, since the survey of military lands closed land grants to the public, people were prevented from scouting and building on land not available to them.

Nevertheless, only six short years after the land sales were opened to the public throughout the Military District, the pioneers found their way into the unclaimed wilderness. They found beneath the buffalo grass valleys a fertile, tillable soil ready for the farmer's plow. Springs were bubbling from the hillside, giving an abundant water supply. Adequate streams would sufficiently supply power of the water-wheeled sawmill and gristmill so vitally important to a new community. The early pioneers had learned that soils could vary from one ridge to the next—but with the big oak, maple, chestnut, and walnut trees, they knew that beneath the brush would be the fertile soil highly adaptable to crop lands. They wisely understood that a good layer of topsoil would also produce big trees. ❧

100 /
2-5-
1984

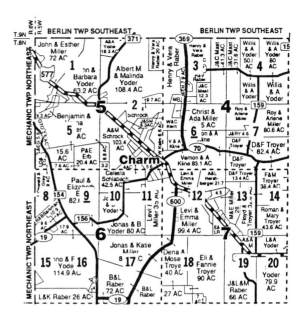

Land Grant entries in relation to present-day ownerships (name, date filed, residency).

1. Jacob Stutzman, June 6, 1815, Coshocton Co., O.
2. John Yoder, June 6, 1815, Coshocton Co., O.
3. Henry Yoder, December 30, 1815
4. Henry Yoder, February 28, 1820, Somerset Co., Pa.
5. Daniel Miller, June 13, 1815, Coshocton Co., O.
6. Joseph Troyer, June 6, 1815, Coshocton Co., O.
7. Henry Yoder, May 9, 1816, Coshocton Co., O.
8. Jonas Miller, November 20, 1830
9. Jonas Miller, March 14, 1828
10. Valentine Mikler [Mishler?], June 5, 1826
11. George Thomas, October 16, 1828
12. Moses Bitchey, June 6, 1815, Coshocton Co., O.
13. John Fornwald [Farmwald], June 4, 1828
14. Christian Henderick, March 29, 1828
15. David Troyer, October 22, 1830
16. David Troyer, September 9, 1830
17. Peter Miller, Jr., April 23, 1816, Coshocton Co., O.
18. Christian Aicsh, July 27, 1831
19. Peter Ostwald, October 8, 1829
20. Daniel Miller, September 23, 1826

✌ The Amish ─────────────────────

Charm, aside from its geographical location in the southeastern corner of Holmes County, is also situated within the largest Amish population in existence today. The populous community extends from Holmes County to surrounding counties of Wayne, Stark, Tuscarawas, and Coshocton. Recent estimates would indicate this population to number over 20,000 persons.

The Amish, a religious group, were influential in the early settlement of Holmes County. As a whole, they were farmers, but some also worked in the trades of blacksmithing, sawmilling, and gristmilling during the pioneer period of the county. Early settlement (1809–10), along with a close-knit adherence to church and family ties, have been basic reasons for the growth in population of the group during the past two centuries.

Religiously, they are a remnant of the persecuted Christian church of the Reformation Period in the sixteenth century. Known as an Anabaptist body of believers, their views on adult baptism, nonresistance, and non-swearing of oaths could not be tolerated by state-church authorities. This resulted in great measures of persecution, as the Anabaptists could not conscientiously obey the government rulings.

The Reformation began in the early 1500s under the recognized leadership of Martin Luther *300/* (1483–1546) in Germany, and Ulrich Zwingli *p.10-85* (1484–1531) in Switzerland. As the cause gained momentum, others, in turn, took steps toward greater reforms. In 1525 George Blaurock, Felix Manz, Conrad Grebel, and Wilhelm Reublin introduced adult baptism upon confession of faith, in adherence to their firm views on religious beliefs.

The new wave of Anabaptism was met with heavy persecution from unmerciful authorities. By use of confinement, sword, and fire, thousands were killed for their deeply held religious views.

Zurich, Switzerland, the center of the controversial movement, witnessed the first death—that of Felix Manz. With hands tied at his knees, he was tossed into the Limmat River in 1527.

Driven to hiding and exile, the blood of the martyrs only spread the spirit more intensely. To the north, in Holland, Anabaptism was taking new roots. Menno Simons (1496–1561) was converted to the cause in 1536 and became an influential leader. His followers became known as *Menists* or Mennonites.

Another group of Swiss Anabaptists had taken exile in the Alsace region of France. By 1660 this *301/* congregation adopted the Holland Mennonites' 18 *p.214* articles of the confession of faith originally accepted in 1632 at Dortrecht, Holland. Among this community arose another leader, Jacob Amman, whose schism with liberally inclined Swiss Brethren in 1693 is recognized today as the founding year of the Amish church.

For the Amish, the settling of America brought new possibilities for the future. Religiously, America offered religious freedom. Agriculturally, the opportunities to continue with their long-held practice of farming looked promising. As early as 1737 an Amish church was established in Berks *AA/NG* County, Pennsylvania. From this initial settlement, *p.XIX* several routes of migration were followed; one was to Somerset County in southwestern Pennsylvania by 1773. Out of this parent colony came the nucleus of the Amish group settling in Ohio during the first quarter of the nineteenth century.

One of the first Amish pioneers to seek a new home in the Tuscarawas Valley was Bishop Jacob *CD-* "Yockel" Miller (ML23). Seeking a claim and build- *p.113* ing a cabin a mile east of present Sugarcreek in 1808, Miller and his son Jacob returned to Somerset County. Another son, Henry, supposedly wintered in the Ohio wilderness. Coming back the following year, they were joined by nephew Jonas Stutz-

✌

man, who built the first cabin in the Walnut Creek Valley of Holmes County. The next year, 1810, the Jacob Millers and Stutzman were joined by the Jonas Millers, Christian Yoders, John Troyers, and Jacob Masts. There were now enough members, and the first Amish church service for the new community was held that year.

The long-accepted practice among the Amish has been to hold church services in the homes for the surrounding community or districts. Thus, when the congregation eventually overflows the meeting places, the church district is divided and ministers are ordained accordingly.

287 /

At Charm, the outlying lands were primarily occupied from 1815 to 1830, and mainly by Amish people. Their church district, at this early settling, would have extended to Sugarcreek. This was under the leadership of bishop and pioneer Jacob Miller.

211 /
307 /
318 /
p. 2-3

As the church of the new settlement grew, pioneer Moses Beachy (BC 17) of Walnut Creek was ordained the first bishop in Holmes County. After dividing the district in 1840, "Gross" Mose Miller (ML 249) became bishop of the Walnut Creek area. Moses Beachy died in September of that year, and Levi Miller (ML626) of Farmerstown was chosen soon thereafter to fill the senior's vacancy.

After the Miller congregation was divided again, David A. Troyer (TYc12) was ordained as leader in 1849, while Shem Miller (ML 2295) became the first bishop of a Doughty district immediately west of Charm in 1850. Bishop Troyer was succeeded by Joni J. Troyer (OAG 2099) in 1898, then Gideon Troyer (OAG 3042) in 1924. With Gideon's district being divided in the mid '30s, Abe D. Troyer, for-

merly of Stark County, became bishop in 1939 for the congregation south of Charm that extended to the New Bedford area. Serving as bishops after Troyer were David L. Raber – 1948, Valentine A. Hershberger – 1962, John J. C. Yoder – 1972, and Henry A. Nisley – 1984, whose district is presently Flat Ridge Northwest, southwest of Charm. From a Valentine Hershberger branch, Dan G. Yoder became bishop in 1969. When his district was divided, Delbert J. Erb was ordained and has been bishop of Flat Ridge East, south of Charm, since 1988, and Roy J. C. Yoder of Flat Ridge since 1989.

Bishop Gideon Troyer was succeeded by Melvin A. Raber in 1957, then John B. Yoder in 1988, who is bishop of the present Charm North district. From a division of Raber's district, Andy M. Hershberger was ordained to Charm South in 1984.

To the east of Charm, and of the Charm East District, the district derives from the earlier Levi Miller church. Noah P. Beachy was ordained bishop in 1895, followed by Dan J. A. Miller, ordained in 1931, Dan N. Stutzman, in 1951, and Aden R. Miller, in 1973.

From a branch of Noah P. Beachy, the following bishops were: Enos Mast, 1923; Dan P. Barkman, 1926; Benjamin Yoder, Eli M. Miller, 1946; Eli E. Hershberger, 1951, and Floyd E. Troyer, 1974 of Farmerstown West, located southeast of Charm.

7 / 1-5-
1994
319 /
1994
p. 28-33

From this early settlement of Amish pioneer families in Tuscarawas, Holmes, Coshocton, and Wayne Counties, there has grown the largest Amish community in existence today. Presently church districts number approximately 150, with each averaging around 30 families per district. ও

❧ Roads ————————————————

The first road or trail passing through Charm was originally an Indian path that connected to buffalo trails. This area of Ohio was often used by the vast herds of buffalo on their migration routes from the western Great Lakes area southward to the Ohio River and beyond. Of the three main buffalo trails in Ohio, the Great Trail meandered its way through Holmes County.

26 /
p.14
214 /
p.66
215 /
p.17

Originating at Detroit, Michigan, the route passed Toledo on a southeastern course to Tiffin, Bucyrus, and Mansfield. From there it closely followed US 62 to Millersburg, continuing across the back country route of Ohio's first state road, the well known Port Washington Road, through Saltillo, Beck's Mills, Baltic, Port Washington, Cambridge, and Marietta.

At Millersburg a path branched from the Great Trail eastward past Berlin and Walnut Creek, and into the Tuscarawas Valley. From this branch an intermediate Indian trail led southward and again connected with the Great Trail. This middle route left the branch trail two miles east of Berlin at Kline Lumber Company on TR 369 and headed due south. Passing through Charm, it met the main trail between Beck's Mills and New Bedford.

These trails, trodden by thousands of buffalo during past centuries, served well for the Indians to travel on, and were found very useful to early pioneer settlers. The paths instinctively chosen by the American bison were the groundwork for early roads and, as evident in their usage today, they have remained similar in geographic location.

The building of roads has been an important factor in the layout and establishment of a community. One of their chief purposes was to connect places of business and/or towns, thereby providing better access to services being offered. Also, along these early roads, other towns eventually grew to serve the needs of an area. Thus these early establishments became the basis of our road map of today.

One such illustration may be found at Charm and SR 557. Incidentally, part of SR 557 was the second of the first four roads petitioned for and presented to the commissioners of Holmes County to be designated and later laid out as a county road. The road was to begin at Jacob Fisher's blacksmith shop at the northwest corner of Section 16. Jacob had moved his family there in 1818. This is where SR 557 begins at the present Andy A. Raber farm, two miles southeast of Farmerstown.

68 /
p.44

The following is copied from the Commissioners Journal #1, 1825: "A petition was presented praying for a road to be established, beginning at Jacob Fisher's blacksmith shop on the N.W. [Quarter] of Section Sixteen Range [F]our[,] Township Eight, thence to Andrew Sipes thence to Jonathan Miller's mill on Doughty fork of Killbuck. A view and survey being granted on same road by the commissioners. John Deitz, Samuel Berger and William Farver be and they are hereby appointed to view and cause the same to be surveyed and make return thereof to the commissioners at their next meeting. Samuel Robertson appointed to survey the same. Jacob Deitz and Jacob Fisher gave bond in the final sum of one hundred dollars for the payment of the costs on order issued to the views accordingly."

70 /

This interesting document makes known and describes this early route well. From the Fisher blacksmith shop, to Andrew Sipes farm in the S.W. Qtr. of Sec. 9 at the present Melvin A. Raber farm, the course was laid out in a northwest direction. Continuing in the same direction to the mill along the Doughty Creek, the road led to the N.E. Qtr. of Sec. 1 at the extreme northeast corner of Mechanic Township at the head of the Doughty Glens. Jonathan Miller had acquired this quarter section from Peter Nowels on January 29, 1825. (Nowels, supposedly, had built this mill around 1820.)

108 /
p.133
V5-377-
1825
309 /
1837

Tax records indicate this first mill to have been

❧

a grist mill; then, by 1837, a sawmill had also been added. It was common during the early settlement period to operate both mills at one place before larger mills were placed along the streams. The site where this early mill was located is owned today by Mrs. Jonas D. J. Miller. This was on the north side of TR 123 and on the west bank of the Doughty, immediately before the stream enters the narrow gorge. Evidence of this mill was still present in the early 1900s when Daniel Miller, better known as "John Dannie," and the Joseph Keim family operated a water-powered sawmill here. Remains of the embankment of the dam are still visible. (See Charm Flour Mills and Sawmilling histories.)

201/
p.41
223/
p.28

The present SR 557 closely follows this early route. Two villages were later built along the road, namely Stevenson (Charm) and Farmerstown. At Farmerstown the route was altered between 1861 and 1875. The earlier layout had continued northwest through the town to the dividing line of section 9 and 12, then headed due west two miles to the point where the said section line intersects SR 557, between the present Perry and Sam Miller farm and the Jonas D. Yoder farm. (See 1861 German Township map, p. 24.) This road was also changed at Charm at the turn of the century. The present route going south from town to the first farm buildings on the Levi A. Miller farm is shown on the 1875 Atlas as being a lane. Instead, the road

112/

had ascended the hill opposite the schoolhouse, passed the cemetery, then, winding east of the buildings, it angled to the Charm–Farmerstown route between the Miller farm buildings and the Andy Hershberger acreage.

By 1907 this portion of the road had been changed to its present route. It is understandable that in the early nineteenth century it would have been more practical to climb the hill at the Abe Mast property, than to build the grade of the present road from the schoolhouse to the Miller barn. Also, part of it would have been undrained bottom land. By the time the change did take place, the farm buildings had been placed and the road needed to circle around the barn. This created the bad curve at the south edge of town.

Another road closely related to business was a

201/
p.41

direct route from Charm to the Doughty Glens or Troyer's Hollow. The Hollow and Beck's Mills lie one and two miles, respectively, to the west, and had an abundant source of water to run the sawmills, gristmills, and woolen mills. Because of the importance of these businesses, a road had led directly from early Stevenson to the Glens, heading from town, up the schoolhouse hill (TR 156), then angled right. It passed just below the Henry Schlabach farm buildings, then headed due west

▪
54

along the 5 – 6 section line before descending into the Doughty hollow. No doubt this readily served

57/

its purpose, as the glens themselves had a wool, grist, and sawmill, along with a shoe shop and a retinning business. Also, its residents had a short route to Charm for a blacksmith, jeweler, cheese factory, store, etc.

At the turn of the twentieth century, when flooding caused the trades to close down or be moved from the hollow, this road was abandoned. The only remaining portion of the roadbed used after closing is the first 1,000 feet at the village and the lane going into the glens. Some evidence of the former route is still visible today.

201/
p.41
223/
p.28

During its early use as a road, the route had continued across the Doughty Creek and divided. The road angling south joined today's TR 124 on the Dean Yoder farm, while the northwest route connected to the same road on the Wayne Miller farm. Two more roads also connected the Hollow's activities to the surrounding community. Both exited downstream along the Doughty Creek. The one on the right side routed out of the ravine along its west bank, then arrived at the small village of Beck's Mills. On the east side, the roadbed followed the stream's bank, then intersected with today's CR 19 at the Henry D. Yoder acreage, a short distance east of Beck's Mills. Along this road, along the Doughty, another road had angled southeast to the Port Washington Road. Traveling

274/

in that direction from the hollow, it came to the present Marty Kuhns property, crossed CR 19, then passed the Menno A. Yoder farm buildings. From there it crossed farm fields and, winding past the old Erb farm at Levi V. Raber's buildings, it came to the Abe A. Yoder farm, which was only a short distance before intersecting with the Port Washington Road.

This early highway, the Port Washington Road, was Ohio's first state road, adopted by state legis-

100/
4-27-
1988

lature on February 6, 1832. It connected the towns of Millersburg and Port Washington. The important roadway, along with the building of the Ohio Canal from Portsmouth at the Ohio River via Port Washington to Cleveland on Lake Erie, opened grain and livestock trade to outside markets. The wagon freight and livestock transported to Port Washington were then loaded on boats and taken through the canal to their destination.

During the days of horseback travel, mail was transported on this road by a post rider, with one postal stopping point at Beck's Mills. In the late 1850s a route established between Millersburg

22/
p.31

and New Philadelphia, though, earlier, this road had also been used as a postal route. The express rider would leave Millersburg, starting out on the Port Washington Road, for the post offices at Saltillo, Beck's Mills, and New Bedford, along with other towns on the route to New Philadelphia. The following day the mail bags were then carried on the return trip, and postal deliveries made westward.

Another east–west road is known to have existed south of Charm. Branching off to the right of present CR 600, the road crossed the Charm creek ¹/₄ mile south of town, then extended along the right side of a small trickle stream. It passed on the north side of the Jonas N. Yoder farm buildings and south of the Sam D. Erbs, to where the only remaining stretch that is still used today connects with today's CR 19.

At one time a lane had connected this Yoder farm with the earlier mentioned Charm–Doughty road to the north. Later, part of the lane was used for a roadway when the present road (TR 156) was put in and the two former ones were eliminated. Considering that these farm buildings were built prior to the said later-built road, it is only logical that the road now winds narrowly past the buildings. The *Standard Atlas of Holmes County, Ohio –*

223/

249/

Cut sandstone culvert from an earlier road along CR 600, a mile south of Charm (road built in 1881).

249/

The inside of an arched cut sandstone culvert along CR 70, 1¹/₂ miles east of Charm. Of the original portion, the bottom, sides, and top are made of sandstone which had been mined on the present Jonas L. Yoder farm.

1907 gives reference to these roads, and portions of the roadbeds can still be seen today.

The *1907 Atlas* indicates CR 600 taking another course at that time. One mile south of Charm, at the Mose L. Troyer farm buildings, the road had extended across the fields to the present lane between the Henry M. Miller and Abe M. Troyer farm in section 14. This old stretch of unimproved road from Charm was known as "the lane." Also, at the Mose L. Troyers, a roadway had branched east of the buildings, passed the Eli A. Troyer buildings and exited on the Marvin Raber farm.

76/
288/

The stretch of road, formerly known as "the cut," between the Ben D. Rabers and Mose V. Hershbergers on CR 600, was built in 1931. Prior to this a road had angled southwest at the Raber buildings and connected with a ridge roadway, which then, in turn, swung southeast to the Hershbergers. A lane and a cut sandstone culvert are still reminders of this former path.

181/

Also along CR 600 at the Jonas M. Miller farm, formerly known as the "Davy Jake farm," a road branched west, passed the cemetery, and teed into present CR 19 close to the Erb cemetery on the former Valentine Erb farm.

Along Clark Township's northern border, another roadbed is still partially visible today. It had angled northwest at the present Mose A. Raber farm in Section 3 until intersecting Section 4. Heading north, it crossed the extreme southwest corner of Walnut Creek Township and exited into Berlin Township on the Andy Y. Miller farm to TR 124. The lane leading to the Miller farm is still part of the former roadway.

95/

The last car to go this stretch of road was a Roadster driven by Dr. Swarts of Charm. As he was coming up the hill, the old car got hot and caught fire. The bewildered veterinarian jumped from the car and scooped handfuls of dirt from the road onto the burning engine to extinguish the flames.

94/

During 1971, when mining for coal a mile east of Charm, the CR 600–TR 159 intersection was altered. The township road, on the David Troyer farm, had exited a short distance farther east on the small knoll. As the land was reclaimed and gullies were filled in at that time, the present route was made possible.

The narrow, winding dirt roads of the pioneer past served their purpose well at the time. As noted, some followed Indian or animal trails, while others originated according to the settlement and needs of the community. These early roads consisted merely of a narrow-tracked path for horse drawn vehicles, avoiding gullies and the wet, swampy bottom lands. Shallow creek beds were often forded until bridges could be built. Over the years, road changes and improvements were made, with wider and better bridges being built.

75/   Local farmers along the roads were hired to help with the road work, using a team and slip scraper. With one driver per team, one man loading, and one dumping at the fill site, tons of dirt were moved as banks were cut down and gullies filled up. Numerous teams would be working on one project as they gradually formed the groundwork of many of our local roadways of today.

    The slip scraper consisted of a small scoop-type implement with two handles on the back side and an outside frame that was hooked to a team. The scoop and frame would pivot on the sides; that would allow the filler to raise the handles and dig into the soil until filled. Pushing down on the handles, the raised tip would ride to the fill site, where the load was dumped as the scoop was turned upside down. As the handles were raised and the cutting edge dug into the soil, a sturdy, heavy-set person was needed at the handles to keep control. It is said that Levi J. Raber of the Charm area was a good hand at filling the scraper.

71/   Local farmers also helped out with spreading gravel on the roads. This, too, was done with teams and shovels. By removing the wagon box from the running gears and laying planks as a floor, the rig was converted to haul gravel. At the pit the gravel was loaded by hand. Side boards were placed along the side and a fair amount of gravel could be hauled on a load. Upon arrival at the work site, the side boards were removed and some part of the load spilled from the wagon. Next, the planks of the floor were set on edge one by one, and the remaining gravel would dump below the rig on the roadway.

73/
100/
2-2-
1916   Locally, a gravel pit was opened on the Sharp farm (then owned by Jacob Miller), along SR 557, one mile south of US 62, presently the Alvin A. Hershberger farm. Gravel was sold at the pit for 25¢ per yard. As early as 1916, signatures were collected by Noah W. Hershberger to gravel the road from Charm to US 62.

71/
183/   In 1924, SR 557 was improved and graveled for the first time, from US 62 to the south edge of Charm. Thereafter, this roadway was at one time known as the "gravel pike."

72/   During that same year a portion of this road in Charm was cemented. With the store and butcher shop alongside a dirt road, the intersection badly needed a hard surface. Dirt, dust, and mud were

19/
p.40 a problem. Earlier, Mose J. Keim had applied a thick layer of sawdust on the road from his mill in town, which served its purpose well at the time. After agreeing to the idea of cementing the road surface at the midst of the village, Griggs and Anderson of Millersburg were contracted to do the work during the summer of 1924. The cement

hitching rail along the east side of the road was constructed at the same time. The cement was mixed at the site using a large portable mixer. Gravel and mortar were shoveled into a hopper, which was hoisted with cables and dumped into the mixer. Helping with construction were foreman Amon Mullet and Jonas T. Miller. The concrete now buried under layers of asphalt was not removed when the blacktop was applied years later. The old landmark hitching rail, though not used during the last decade, was removed December 19, 1990, when the former watch repair shop was remodeled for a bed and breakfast.

74/   Four years after the first section of 557 was improved, in 1928, the project continued from Charm toward Farmerstown.

    The Griggs and Anderson firm, with one or two slip scraper teams, was aided by farmers and teams along the road as they cut down banks and filled in low places. The banks were sloped by hand with picks and mattocks. Among the mecha-

113/
140/ nized equipment used at the time was a grader pulled by a tractor, a steam-powered shovel, and an "iron mule," which was a tractor with a bucket dump mounted on the rear axle. A driver's seat was positioned above the one front wheel.

75/   The following year, 1929, CR 70 east of Charm was widened and improved. The road ascending the hill one-half mile from town was cut down and the fill made at Henry B. Yoders.

69/
181/   Referring to the previously mentioned "cut": when a road change was sought, a proposal was brought to the community to find out their interest in the new road. This change was for CR 600, a mile south of Charm. As it turned out, the number of signatures on the petition was evenly divided.

    One day Valentine Hershberger stopped by and asked neighbor Benjamin Kurtz how he felt about the road change. Benj said he was still rather undecided, but had placed a "no" on the petition. However, he asked Hershberger, "What would I do with the corner lot between the road and the supposed new one?"

    Valentine answered, "It would make an ideal place for a pig pen," to which Kurtz agreed. As Benjamin now placed a "yes" vote, the proposal carried for the new road change.

    The Griggs and Anderson firm of Millersburg also did this excavating and road building. John

90/
113/
181/ Tash was foreman of the operation. A gasoline engine–powered shovel was used to cut the embankments for the new section of highway. John Oswald, who owned a truck at this time, helped with fill dirt hauling. During this undertaking, Orie Oswald purchased a truck and engaged in the road building. A neighbor boy, Mose D. Troyer,

worked 8-hour days on the project and was paid 20¢ per hour.

At the time, this was a major undertaking—moving the great amount of fill dirt from the Hershberger farm to the Kurtz farm, or present Ben Raber farm. This portion of new roadway is located where present CR 19 begins at CR 600, close to the former Hershberger Gun Shop.

With the increasing amount of traffic, roads were being further improved and, eventually, were blacktopped. SR 557 was first blacktopped in the late 1940s. A Huber tractor-type roller was used to finish off the new pavement. CR 70 east of Charm was originally blacktopped in the late 1950s.

Clark Township purchased their first motor-driven road grader in 1954, which greatly aided

76/

road maintenance and improvements.

During the summer of 1992, guard rail sections were placed along SR 557 as a safety measure, because of the increasing amount of traffic.

A year later, in 1993, the cement bridge a half mile northwest of Charm on SR 557 was replaced. The new bridge was built a slight distance northwest of the former one to eliminate some of the curve along the winding stretch of road. During construction, traffic was routed past the site on a one-way basis, using traffic lights to aid the busy flow. By late summer the Menuez Brothers' construction of the widened and improved bridge was completed.

Earlier in 1983 a SR 557 cement bridge a mile northwest of town had also been replaced with a wider structure. 🦢

ᴂ Locality and Agriculture —

Locality

Geographically, Charm is located in the northwest corner of Clark Township in Holmes County, Ohio. As previously noted, the village is situated in the corners of Sections 4 - 5 - 6 - 7 in Township 8, Range 5. The exact corners of the sections center at the Charm School playground. Most of the town is located in the northeast corner of Section 5.

Latitude and longitude, respectively, are 40°30' north of the equator and 81°47' west of the Meridian of Greenwich, which passes through London, England.

As an example of sun time for the immediate area, time zones are equally spaced around the world at 15° apart, and each represents one hour. Further defined, one degree would be equal to four minutes. The local time zone, Eastern Standard, is taken from the seventy-fifth to the ninetieth meridian, which are located basically from Philadelphia, Pennsylvania to St. Louis, Missouri. With Charm situated at $6^3/_4$° west of the seventy-fifth degree longitude and each degree representing four minutes, 27 minutes need to be compensated. Thus, when the sun is due south at Philadelphia at 12:00 noon, it will be directly south of Charm at 12:27 P.M. (1:27 D.S.T.). Slight allowances must be made throughout the year for time equation.

The Charm elevation is 1,032 feet above sea level. In 1959 a survey marker was placed at the southwest corner of the bridge on SR 557 at the Ole Mill Furniture store. The hills surrounding the village ascend gradually a few hundred feet above the town's valley. To the east they attain a height of 1,240 feet, and the highest lie to the south and southwest, at 1,300 feet. Its water is drained into the Doughty Creek $1^1/_4$ mile northwest of Charm, and will drop approximately 72 feet to that point.

249/

Agriculture

Agriculture is farming and, as of the late 1990s, some produce growing has been introduced to the area. The contour, or strip, farming method is practiced because of the hilly lay of the land. This practice serves well to prevent soil erosion and to facilitate the rotation of crops.

Hay, corn, oats, and barley are the chief crops raised, and are mostly consumed on the farm itself by the horses, cattle, sheep, and hogs.

A change from wheat to barley growing was seen during the last decade, although some wheat is still being grown. Barley is better adaptable to the cold winter climate and low wheat prices also relate to this change.

Before the cane pressing equipment was sold in the 1970s at the east edge of Charm, some cane was grown in the area.

Earlier, in the 1800s, flax was also raised. The

Survey elevation marker at Charm – 1,032 feet above sea level.

plant's fibrous stalks were broken and cleaned, then spun into a linen thread for use during early pioneer life. The flax seed could be crushed and pressed to produce linseed oil.

Soils are variable, from sandy and light to heavy loam, and well adaptable to farming and pasture land. Analysis and proper applications of fertilizer and lime have contributed to good crop yields. Because of regular manure spreading, the soil has become better organically balanced than soils on which only chemicals are applied. This practice will allow better water absorption. In case of dry weather, such soils will also retain a moisture content longer. Not only is the manure application more economical than the high-priced chemicals, but, in addition, it improves soil structure and increases aeration.

Dairying has been the chief farming practice of the area during the past years. More recently there has been a trend to change from milk production because of unsatisfactory milk prices. During the past decade many farms have added poultry growing to their farm operation. ❧

69/
50/
5-4-
1989

❧ Natural Resources ────────────

Water

Springs are greatly depended on as a water supply today, and were even more so during the early settling of the locality. During pioneer days water had been a main concern when locating a dwelling or farm building. As plumbing supplies were not available at the time, the buildings were situated close to a good supply of spring-fed water. At the spring outcropping, the water course would usually be followed back into the hillside a short distance and a cut sandstone catch basin erected, or clay tile would be laid, with which abundant water supplies have been brought to use. Most of these provide an excellent, cool, fresh drinking water. On the farm, these have served well for cooling foods and milk. They would usually spring from an outcropping of sandstone or limestone, and are dependent on rainfall, which regulates the rise and fall of the flow.

As other water supplies were needed where no spring-fed flow was available, shallow wells were introduced. These were usually from 15 to 30 feet deep and were dug by hand. Some are still in use today. The digging was begun with pick and shovel, and as the hole got deeper, a scaffold was set up to hoist out the remaining dirt with rope and bucket. When the desired depth was reached below the water level, most wells were laid up with fieldstones to keep the sides from caving in. The width of the finished well ranged from 3 to 5 feet. These wells could be extremely dangerous if not covered properly.

A safer well with less labor involved was also built by stacking clay tile up through the center of the newly dug hole, then refilling the outside perimeter with dirt. With a hand pump mounted on the top, this type of well was an affordable and ample water supply. The last two wells known to have been dug in the area are on the Floyd E.

Troyer farm and on the John O. Miller acreage. With two already on the Troyer farm, former owner Simon P. Troyer dug one in the cellar of the house. Coming to completion, they were disappointed when the well produce a red, sulfur water and was never used. Apparently, an outcropping of coal was nearby. The other is located in the Miller pasture field and was dug by Lee Miller and Mose L. Yoder. Other wells in the immediate Charm area are, or were, located on lands owned by: Harry Kauffman, Amanda Miller, Keim sisters, Keim Lumber Co., Ben M. Miller, Mose L. Troyer, John O. Miller, Robert Barkman, Marty Kuhns, Joe Erb (Delbert Troyer), Vernon Kline, Andy M. Hershberger, Jonas N. Yoder, Abe A. Mast, Charm Cheese Factory, Noah Raber, and three on the Levi A. Miller farm. *293/* *171/*

The earlier John O. Miller well and one at the Noah A. Raber home were dug in 1899 by Noah Farver. *100/* *11-30-1899*

Today most of the dwellings also rely on a deeper, drilled well as a water supply aside from the spring water that is frequently found. Most of these wells range from 90 to 300 feet. The primary water sources come from sandstones known as "Big Injun" or "White Massillon," with each producing a good quality, soft water. *77/* *285/* *303/* *p.78*

Various types of pump setups are driven by gasoline engine, compressed air, electricity, or a windmill. Though most of the drilling was done with bit and cable, the more recent rotary rigs have greatly reduced the labor involved. Well casing was generally set in the top $1/2$ or $3/4$ of the depth using a 5-inch steel or plastic tubing. Recently, more casing is being set down on the water-veined sandstone, thereby preventing the problems of a caved-in well.

Among the drillers for the area have been: the Erbs, Peter and nephew John; Vic Kaser; Harold Mullet and Sons; Andy N. Miller of Charm Drilling; Frontz Drilling Inc.; Burgan Drilling; and Moravy Drilling.

81/   During the early 1900s the Erbs were using a steam-powered drilling rig.

Water drainage from the 2-square-mile area of interest is largely dependent on the Charm Creek.

The creek, flowing northwest, empties into the upper Doughty Creek $1^1/_4$ miles beyond the village, then the Doughty, in turn, flows southwest to the Killbuck Creek 4 miles below Clark. East of Warsaw the Killbuck merges with the Walhonding River that joins the Tuscarawas at Coshocton to form the Muskingum. The waters from the western portions of Sections 5 and 6 either drain directly or by the way of a small stream into the Doughty.

Drainage along the eastern edge of Sections 4 and 7 takes an interesting route as its waters flow from the dividing ridge in opposite directions to begin their course to the bigger rivers. The ridge $^3/_4$ mile east of Charm makes this divide. Five different headwater streams of the Walnut Creek originate along this border. Eventually they join, to meander through Mud Valley and flow into the South Fork Sugar Creek at Dundee. The extreme southeast corner of Section 7 lies in the Sugar Creek Watershed Area and also drains into the South Fork Sugar Creek. This creek, flowing through the towns of Sugar Creek, Barrs Mill, and Dundee, empties into the Beach City Dam. Beyond the lake and joining with the Sugar Creek, it circles to Dover and the Tuscarawas River. The Tuscarawas then meets the Walhonding to form the Muskingum River at the Three Rivers Bridge at Coshocton. It is here that the waters from the dividing ridge east of Charm join again, having descended the slopes in a completely opposite direction. Flowing south, the Muskingum passes the famous Y-bridge at Zanesville and empties into the Ohio River at Marietta.

Trees

Forests, trees, or logs have been important resources to the settlement and establishment of the Charm community. The surrounding hills and valleys had been a vast forest of mixed timber. With years of accumulation of leaves and decaying matter, the forest floor became a rich, fertile soil. After the early settlers had felled the trees and the brush was cleared off, the humus-filled earth was ready for the farmer's plow.

Clearing land was by no means easy work in the early 1800s. Using axes and crosscut saws, forests were slowly cut down and cleared.

The timber could be used in constructing buildings and furniture, for firewood, or in numerous other ways. Many trees were first deadened by cut-

22/
p.29

ting through the inner bark layer. Later they were felled and many split into rails for building fences. Miles of this criss-cross fence were strung across the countryside. Hardly any of this type of fence remains today. The last seen in the area was replaced in the 1970s along CR 19, south of Charm, on the Hershberger farm along the southern border of Section 6.

All kinds of hardwoods could be found in the forested area, which included oak, maple, cherry, walnut, elm, ash, poplar, beech, hickory, and chestnut. This large variety gave the woodworker choice for his needs and uses while also providing food for humans and wildlife.

302/
p.262   The chestnut trees, which were at one time a prime source of wood, have almost completely vanished from the United States. This handsome, deciduous tree was valuable as an enormous producer, not only of quality lumber but also of edible nuts as well. The fatal, parasitic fungus (*Endothia parasitica*) epidemic affected all species of American chestnuts.

In 1904, in New York City, the disease was first noticed on the deadened trees. It is believed to have been brought into this country from Japan. Measures were taken to control it at the start, but it was practically impossible to keep the problem within a limited area. The spores of fungus are spread by wind, rain, insects, birds, animals, and the transfer of diseased plants, timber, or lumber

78/   from which the bark is not removed. By 1948 all chestnuts were considered dead. The potential of these stately trees, reaching heights of 100 feet, to produce innumerable volumes of high quality lumber while bearing enormous amounts of nuts as a food, will never be replaced. This great loss is regarded as the single, most devastating natural disaster in North American history. Today an occasional decaying trunk or a young tree struggling to survive are reminders of the once-prominent, mighty chestnuts.

Its lumber has become a highly sought-after product, as there still seems to be limited amounts
79/   available. Today's high price will reflect this. In 1912 and 1933 Keim Lumber at Charm was selling small amounts of this lumber at 2¢ and 3¢ a foot, whereas in 1994, they retailed select pieces of chestnut at $7.00 per board foot. Most of the lumber found today is wormy because of insects riddling the trees after they had deadened, but before they were sawed. To the admirer of today, these tiny pinholes are a remembrance of their fateful past.

78/   Of similar fate were the diseased elm trees.
302/   Though a large percentage of the trees were killed
p.409   off, the effect was not nearly as critical as was the case with the chestnut, because its lumber is of

lesser quality and it is not a food-producing tree. It is believed that the fungus or a disease-carrying beetle were imported into this country from Europe. The infection was originally noticed in Holland in 1919 and was accordingly known as the Dutch Elm disease. In the U.S., four diseased trees were found in Ohio in 1930. By 1940 the virus had spread through the mid-eastern states. The immediate area was mainly affected during the 1960s. However, not all of the elms died, and the few surviving ones seen across the countryside remain yet a gracefully branched tree. The first few years after dying, they attracted a lot of attention by producing the sough-after morel mushroom in the spring. Today the elm tree is growing again, and large quantities of healthy young growth may be found.

Hard maples, or sugar maples, are of valuable importance to a community. In late winter these sap-producing trees supply great amounts of water that is boiled down to a thickened syrup. Maple syrup is a valued addition to any kitchen and is often produced as an additional source of income. 294/

The few Catulpa trees remaining along CR 600 south of Charm are remnants of a Catulpa grove planted by Jacob S. Yoder at the turn of the century. The trees had been planted in the field east of the farm buildings, but have since been removed, save the few along the roadway.

Coal

An abundance of coal has been mined in our four-Section area at various periods of time. The coal mined was mostly taken from Sections 4 and 6, with a good quality #6 found throughout. Underground mining of the early 1900s was quite a contrast to the strip mining in the 1960s. Determination, hard work, and courage are what kept the underground mines in production: the determination to keep on digging, the hard work of picking and shoveling tons of dirt and coal, and the courage to crawl underground on hands and knees in total darkness, except for the flicker of the carbide lamp.

Though no actual remains of an area mine are standing today, there is still evidence of their former existence in some locations. No mine is known to have been in Sections 4 or 5. In Section 6 a mine was located along the western border and shared with Mechanic Township. The entry was immediately west of the Martin Kuhns buildings a mile west of Charm along CR 19.

Along the southern border of the southwest quarter on the Levi V. Raber farm was the Erb mine. On the same farm, in Section 15, a sister mine was produced on the opposite side of the hill. Extending northward, the two were finally joined 81/
121/

together, with their entrances approximately 750 feet apart. Uniting both mines was meant to create better ventilation. Later an airshaft was dug between the mines and set up with clay tile to further help ventilation.

As the Erbs' miners had been thorough with their work, it was said they had taken out most of the coal from that hill. This was later proven with strip mining by Holmes Limestone; therefore no further attempt was made to uncover that area when the second cut opened up to empty coal rooms. For an extended period of time this underground mine was operated by Tom Sheneman.

Two more mines were opened a short time in the southwest quarter, but with the coal layer sloping the wrong way, water drainage became a problem and both had to be abandoned. One was located on the Valentine Erb farm between the Menno Yoder farm buildings and the cemetery. The other belonged to Jacob S. Yoder, and its entrance was along the west side of the Vernon J. Miller house along CR 19. This was the last mine opened by Yoder. 90/

Across the hill in the southeast quarter were the other Yoder mines, and two on the Benjamin Kurtz farm. It is not known exactly how many were opened by these two men but, from available sources, it would appear seven could be correct, Yoder five and Kurtz two. Some coal bank waste may still be seen at the heads of the two trickle streams on the former Kurtz and Yoder farms.

The Kurtz mines were first opened in 1918 or 1919. The initial mine stretched south toward CR 19. Later the second one opened, using the same shanty, and extended toward the Yoders to the north. The west draw up the slope divided the two mines where the coal from both thinned down. 80/
90/

The coal was from 38" to 44" thick, which was ideal for this type of back breaking and crawl mining. With the coal slanting toward the opening, these stayed dry and hard-surfaced, and were considered the best in the area to work in.

John B. Kurtz recalled helping his father build the track scaffolding on the outside as a young boy.

At this particular mine no ramp was needed, as the bank below the entrance had enough slope to give adequate room for the coal pile.

Most of the miners working here live along the Doughty area and included: Amos Ledrich, Ammon Kaser, Floyd Kaser, Peter J. Troyer, Adam Oswald, Ab Kaser, Otto Scherer, Earl Kaser, Carl Kaser, Lester Scherer, Robert Clark, and John B. Kurtz.

In the early mornings they would come walking from their homes, south and west of the mine. Ab Kaser, who had had a sawmill accident earlier and lost one of his legs, came hobbling across the fields on crutches. He and his son Earl worked the mine together. Earl would push his father into the mine on an empty car, then Ab would load the coal and Earl would take it out. At quitting time Ab would crawl on top of a partly filled car and be pushed out again, along with the coal.

The Kurtz mines were run by Ammon Kaser.

Coal was used locally or hauled to area towns as a fuel source. After Floyd Kaser got his first truck, he would supply the Baltic Brickyard with coal from this mine. Labor during the 1930s was $1.20 per ton, and a day's wages would average to $5.00 or $6.00.

It was customary for mines to be safety inspected periodically. After one such inspection, which determined that the Kurtz mine was safe, a portion caved in the following day. No casualties resulted, but the broken-down roof had to be hauled out and other reinforcements made.

For the immediate area, this mine was one of the last to shut down.

Section 7 had two mines. The first was in the southeast quarter on the Henry N. Miller farm, presently owned by Marvin J. Raber. This well known mine was operating south of the buildings, entering the north slope of the hill. Apparently this was the first of the mines within our area of interest, as this is the only "coal bank" shown on the 1875 Atlas (*Caldwell's Atlas of Holmes Co. Ohio*).

The other was east of the buildings on the Melvin J. Miller farm in the northeast quarter of the section. This mine also had drainage problems, so its existence was brief.

Picks, shovels, hammers, wedges, knee pads, and carbide lamps all played a significant part in the role of the coal miner. Equipped with these and fighting the dust in the coolness of the mine, the miners brought tons of coal to the use of mankind.

75/ In opening a mine, the layer depth of the proposed coal bed was determined by outcroppings with test drilling and surveying. As the entrance (often called the entry) was cut into the hillside, posts and planks were set as a retaining wall and roof in the mine. Throughout the channel, boards were laid lengthwise and rails placed on these. Shorter slats were then nailed between the rails for a footing when pushing the coal cart. Earlier, wooden rails had been used, but were usually replaced later with steel, which would allow the carts to roll more easily. Laid 3 to $3^1/_2$ feet apart, they carried the 5- to 7-foot mine cars loaded with coal, dirt, rocks, and supplies.

The inside height of the mine varied from 2 to $3^1/_2$ feet, depending on the coal thickness. Crawling on hands and knees was a must in the cramped depth of a coal vein. The miner, in a crouching

position, or while lying on his side, would pick out the bottom of the coal layer. The top part was then easily broken down by driving a long, slim wedge along the grain of the coal, or by blasting. When explosives were used, they were usually set up and blasted as the last labor of the day. By the next morning the dust had settled and the coal was ready to be brought out.

80/ Locally, two brands of blasting powder were used: Kings, handled by Benjamin Kurtz, and Austin, sold by John B. Yoder of Berlin.

The loose coal was then loaded onto the cars and pushed outside to be dumped. Whenever suitable when transporting coal to the outside, a few cars would be latched together.

Depending on the slope of the terrain, some tipples were level with the entry, while others needed a ramp to get the height needed for the coal piles below. On the higher tipple, the loaded mine cars were winched up with cables. On the tipple, they were emptied onto a screen to separate the various sized coal lumps.

As an area, or room, was emptied, portions were left to support the roof and another opening or adjoining room was mined out. Wooden support posts were placed in the empty room to keep the mine as safe as possible. As needed, more tracks were laid out. Leading from one opening into the next, the mine would eventually become a network of rooms and passages.

The carbide lamp worn on the forehead gave the miner sufficient light for working in the depth of total darkness. It was simply designed, yet readily served its purpose until it was replaced by the battery-operated light. It consisted of two chambers, a valve, a shiner, and the flint striker. Carbide was placed in the bottom chamber and water in the top. By opening the valve, the water dripped onto the carbide, which produced a gas. This was ignited by the striker mounted on the edge of the shiner. Used properly, the brass lamp would burn for hours on one filling.

90/ A shanty was built close to the entry for supply storage, doing repair work, and taking rest breaks. One of the repairing jobs was resharpening the coal picks. To resharpen, the dull end of the pick was brought to a red-hot glow in a forge or through the hole in the side of a pot bellied stove, then pounded with a hammer to the desired shape and point.

While the pick was being heated for reshaping, the temper of the steel would be lost. To retrieve this again, various methods were used. One of these was reheating to a cherry-red, then quenching in oil. Another method was heating to the desired color, then momentarily dipping the tip in water. This instantly cooled the tip. With the

316/

heavier part still hot, the heat crept out into the sharpened point again. Then, by laying a thin wooden shaving on the tip, the returning heat would light the wood, which indicated the correct temperature, and the pick was plunged in cold water again until cool. Incorrect tempering would cause the pick to break off or bend more easily.

Strip mining for coal has been seen in all four sections. With the amount of coal still remaining beneath the hills and ridges, in spite of the earlier underground mining, the Amish farmers were reluctant to give up their productive farm lands. Harvesting the coal and leaving the farm as a neglected strip mine was not to their liking.

The breakthrough to local, open pit mining and reclamation came to reality in 1967. The forethought of two area businessmen, Joe Erb and Emanuel Mullet, eventually provided the landowner with an acceptable method of mining.

11/12-29-1979 129/

The first coal strip mined by Charm resident and excavator Joe Erb was on the Cletus Fender farm four miles south of Charm, using a D-6 Caterpillar. The site was an abandoned underground mine, with coal still remaining up to five feet thick. The unusual bed of coal lay with the slant of the hillside and was down only approximately twelve feet.

Emanuel Mullet, owner of Hardy Coal operations of Sugar Creek, shared his idea with Erb and Raymond Raber, a dwarf living in Charm, during the 1960s. A further break materialized as Erb and Mullet planned and worked out a system of mining and reclaiming that was satisfactory to the farming community and the state's requirements.

Raber, a close friend to Mullet, in turn found an Amishman, John B. Kurtz, who was willing to test the men's theories. The Kurtz farm was located 1/2 mile southwest of Charm in the northeast quarter of Section 6. This initial venture began in 1967, at which time their first new D-8 bulldozer was purchased. The following year, mining was begun on the Gideon B. Yoder farm southwest of New Bedford, followed by the John L. Raber farm two miles south of Charm.

The firm that grew from this enterprise was originally known as Joe Erb Excavating. It changed at this time to Charm Mining. Eventually it merged with Holmes Limestone, which is owned by Emanuel Mullet and known as Charm Mining Division of Holmes Limestone, Inc. They are the only company that has done strip mining in the immediate area. Under Erb's helpful supervision, their dream was brought to fulfillment.

After their initial venture in mining and reclamation, interest has grown to the extent that most of the local coal has been removed. Hills and ridges were completely renovated. The top and subsoils were removed with pan scrapers. Remaining layers of sandstone, limestone, and shale were pushed aside with bulldozers or hauled out with front-end loaders, down to the coal bed. The removal of hard rock formations was greatly hastened by drilling and blasting. Once the pit was opened and the coal exposed, it was hauled out. Careful attention was stressed once the coal layer was reached. Mullet's philosophy of financial management required not removing any coal with the shale layer. His view was, "If we can harvest coal at a ten percent profit and if the top ten percent is ruined, we are automatically cutting from that profit." Thickness in coal beds averaged from two to three feet.

Truck traffic on local roads was greatly increased as pit after pit was emptied. Once a pit was exhausted, the rock layering of the next cut was transferred to the former one.

The final step was reclaiming to bring the land back again to tillable use. After the shale and rocks were leveled off, the subsoils and topsoils were spread back on top. Often this resulted in more tillable acreage, because steep slopes, gullies, and boulders were eliminated. Some timber was removed to mine coal, thus also adding to the farming land.

After proper cultivation, these fields have been producing high crop yields again, though some places have a problem with proper soil drainage.

11/12-29-1979

In a newspaper article, Emanuel Mullet is quoted, telling a farmer's wife who questioned his mining operations: "I've used this illustration many times," he said. "I start out by saying that a bed wouldn't look right with the mattress on top or the spread on the bottom. I tell them that I take the spread off and put it over here on a pile, then the comforter and place it over here on another pile. Then I shake up the mattress, take out the coal, level it back and replace the comforter and spread. They have no difficulty in following me."

Reclamation has left a lasting impression on the community. Its original beginning at Charm has encouraged the state so that presently no coal mining is carried out without a total reclamation.

Other farms mined in Section 6 were lands of Phineas M. Yoder, Dan J. Raber, and Levi V. Raber. Section 4 had coal removed from the David J. Troyer, Jonas R. Yoder, Eli J. Mast, Crist U. Miller, and Henry M. Raber farms. Only the northeast corner of Section 5 had been strip mined, on a portion of the Henry M. Raber farm. In Section 7, the Mose L. Troyer, Eli A. Troyer, Melvin J. Miller, and Floyd E. Troyer farms have had coal removed.

Considering the tremendous amount of man hours involved in strip mining, the tons of coal that were mined is unimaginable. With a 3-foot cube of coal weighing approximately one ton, thousands of tons have been harvested.

Gas and Oil

274/
329/

Numerous oil and gas producing wells have been drilled in the Charm area. Of the more recent wells, the first to be drilled were on the Levi N. Yoder farm 1^1/$_2$ miles southeast of Charm ca 1970 by Pennzoil, and a mile southwest on the Menno A. Yoder farm in 1978 by Jade Oil Co. Since then, most local farms have been tapped for oil and gas reserves.

100/
3-8-
1906
124/

Prior to these later wells, in the early 1900s, some shallow Berea gas wells had existed in the area. In early 1906 a William McHendry of the Pittsburgh (Pennsylvania) Oil and Gas Company began leasing area farms. His lease agreements were drawn up for five years in consideration of one dollar. Should the well produce oil, a ^{1}/$_8$ part would be paid to the lessor. Gas, when marketed, would be paid at the rate of $200.00 per year, with the landowner receiving free use of gas for domestic purposes. A total of 2,763 acres were leased from lands mostly in German (Clark) Township. Two years later another 1,174 acres were obtained in lease agreements.

V71-
489-
1906

In August of 1906 McHendry bought 1.71 acres in Charm, this acreage being the land of the present Roman Keim house and that of the former "Getz boarding house" across the road from the store.

100/
9-13-
1906
86/
303/
p.266

The exploration was known as the Charm Oil Company or the Charm Oil Fields.

The Pittsburgh-based company began drilling in August, 1906 on the Andrew J. Troyer farm of Section 7 – northeast quarter, a mile southeast of Charm. This is the Melvin J. Miller and Roman J. Troyer farms today.

The first venture of 1,000 feet produced no oil, and a second well was begun the first part of September on the same farm. It is known that a producing well was located here, a short distance east of the Lester Scherer dwelling. The oil tanks were set to the northwest of the well along SR 557. By November a gas producing well was completed in Section 4 on the Peter C. Troyer farm (present David J. Troyer farm), and in December a third attempt was made at the Andrew J. Troyers. In June of 1907 the drilling machinery was hauled to Millersburg, from where it was shipped back east to Pittsburgh. Three oil producing wells had been brought to production during the past year. By September a "deep well" rig was received at Baltic by railroad, with McHendry also planning to reopen and drill one of his well still deeper. On September 5, 1907, Levi D. Yoder, a local farmer, hauled the engine from Baltic. On October 19 he brought in drilling rope from the same town for the Charm Oil Company.

100/
11-15-
1906
100/
12-13-
1906
100/
6-13-
1907
50/
9-12-
1907
304/
83/

🍂

During this time and until 1920, a heavy rope was used instead of wire cable for drilling. Even then, a rope was spliced to the fore end of the cable which was intended to give more flexibility than an all steel run. Not until 1946 was cable used by itself on the rig drum.

85/

At the time the rig was brought into the area, a bachelor, Joe Sneer, was working at the livery stable at Baltic, and brought the well investors to observe the operations. Supposedly, the first site for the new rig was on the present Marvin J. Raber farm in the southeast quarter of Section 7. It was reported by Sneer, local teams brought the equipment to the location, including the heavy rig itself. As they attempted to make the last steep grade north of the farm buildings, teams were hooked to every place where there was room to be hitched; since mud had made footing slippery for the horses.

100/
12-12-
1907
85/

Another well was placed on the Raber farm (which was owned by Noah N. Miller at the time) in December of 1907. Two wells are remembered as being active there, one on the east and another on the west side of TR 160.

124/

Apparently drilling ceased a few years until 1910. In October of 1908 William McHendry assigned all of his lease holdings in Holmes, Tuscarawas, and Coshocton counties to Morris Aronson, also of Pittsburg, for $200.00. Seemingly this was for untapped lands.

100/
11-18-
1910
303/
p.266
181/
76/

During 1910 four wells were reportedly drilled, including one producing on the Menno J. Troyer farm in the southwest quarter of Section 7. Another three had also been located in this quarter—the Eli A. Troyer–Mose L. Troyer farms today. One was located immediately behind the Mose Troyer barn and another close to the Eli Troyer–Abe M. Troyer line fence. Some of these wells had been placed around the 1920s, including three on the Noah J. Miller farm in the southeast quarter of Section 7, owned today by Levi N. Yoder.

188/

Charm itself had a well in production, about 100 feet south of the Charm Flour Mill. It was drilled around 1910 to a depth of 2,800 feet. Immediately west of Charm in the extreme southwest corner of the southeast quarter of Section 5 (Henry A. Schlabach farm), another dry hole was reached during this early period of gas well exploration.

Newspapers reported a depth of 2,800 feet using the deep well rig.

303/
p.266

During 1917 a Clinton sandstone test was placed on the Dan Mast farm, 1^1/$_2$ miles northwest of Charm in Berlin Township. The Clinton horizon was reached at 3,775 feet and no production was secured from the well.

8/

As the community now had a tapped and available natural gas supply, pipelines were laid out, which brought gas lighting to the schoolhouse and store at Charm. In 1916 Noah W. Hershberger came close to a leaking gas line with a lantern, and almost set the blacksmith shop on fire. From Charm the line extended northwest a distance of ten miles to Millersburg, where the Millersburg Glass Factory needed a reserve gas supply. Their main source was furnished by the Killbuck Gas Company, which had shallow wells in Killbuck, Clark, and Millersburg areas. The president of the factory, J. W. Fenton, had a total of eighteen drilled for reserve purposes, of which he personally drilled two.

The short-lived factory would become widely known during its brief existence for manufacturing the Carnival glass of Millersburg. The first piece of glass was made May 20, 1909 in the newly erected 100 x 300 foot building. During the next eighteen months the company so excelled in the glass industry that even today the quality and color of the product have not been matched. However, lawsuits for unpaid accounts were soon filed against the company. On September 20, 1911 the District Court of the United States held a public sale, selling the building and contents to Samuel B. Fair, who renamed the factory Radium Glass Company. During 1912 the Radium Glass Company had also shut its doors, and the manufacturing of the Carnival glass would permanently cease.

In 1913 the plant was sold to Jefferson Glass Company and, reportedly, the molds were sold as scrap iron. Jefferson produced a line of electric and gas lighting fixtures, but by 1916 was forced to shut its doors because of a shortage of natural gas.

Apparently the reserve wells also did not have a long holdout, which is not uncommon with the shallow 1,000-foot wells.

After the gas was no longer used at Millersburg, the line was recollected. Local farmers with teams and wagon gears were hired to haul the pipe to Millersburg.

The abandoning of the early gas wells brought drilling to a standstill for a long period of time. Though farms were leased to petroleum companies, gas exploration was unheard of in the area.

As previously mentioned, the two Yoder wells were the first to be brought to production in the 1970s. From then on, company competition has been intensified for lease contracts. Jadoil Inc., Lake Region Oil Inc., Bakerwell Inc., Derby Oil Company, Jerry Moore Inc., and Wallick Petroleum Company have been responsible for bringing most of the local wells into existence today.

Usually they would contract with a drilling company, mainly G and H Drilling and Sherman Drilling. These were stem type drilling rigs.

During the race for gas and oil wells in the 1980s,

the 4,000-foot Clinton rock formation was sought. At times, the Berea would also produce some natural gas at 1,000 to 1,200 feet.

Once a well was drilled, its potential was usually not known until after a log record and fracture were completed.

In 1986 the town of Charm also got a gas well. With the cooperation of Lake Region Oil Co. and the Charm residents, the idea came in to reality.

An earlier attempt with Columbia Gas Company to supply the village with gas had not been successful.

After the whole Charm community agreed to a lease contract with Lake Region, enough adjoining acreage was leased to place a well, which required a minimum of forty acres.

John Waltman, a lawyer of Millersburg, did the necessary legal paperwork. At this time a board of directors was also formed to take care of the project known as Charm Development. The nonprofit organization, formed in 1985, consists of seven members: John O. Miller, Leroy J. Raber, Abe A. Mast, John A. Miller, Noah A. Raber, Melvin H. Raber, and treasurer, Ivan J. Miller. This committee also serves as the intermediate council between the producer, Lake Region Oil Company, and the consumer.

After surveying the area, only a small circle remained suitable to place a well. Regulations limit a well to be at least 500 feet from any outlying

Drilling the gas well at Charm, January, 1986.

boundaries. The chosen site was on the John O. Miller property, 50 feet east of the barn.

In the latter part of December, 1985, the cable drum rig was moved to the location. On January 2, 1986, drilling had begun and on the 28th was completed at a depth of 4,082 feet. During the next months steel pipes were placed throughout town and trenched in by Miller Roustabout Service Inc. That spring, after hookups were completed, natural gas was available to the Charm people. Later, in 1988, a tap was supplied to a private line that was extended to residents north of town.

In 1989 the neighborhood community a mile southeast of town, along SR 557, obtained a gas supply from Lake Region Oil Co. The line was placed and serviced by Raber Machine Shop. A similar line was installed in 1987 in the western part of Section 6. This line has since (in 1994) been transferred to Northern Industrial Energy Development, Inc. of New Concord, Ohio.

Drilling of the Clinton gas and oil wells throughout the area greatly diminished by the late 1980s. In its place began the bid to produce a deeper Roserun well, attaining depth from 6,000 to 7,000 feet. The earliest of these wells were drilled in 1988, with some producing pressures of 2,000+ pounds. Because a few of the violent, highly pressured wells got out of hand, special task forces were brought in to drown them out. One, at the Roman D. Yoders, 2^1/$_2$ miles south of Charm, broke a connection that allowed the explosive natural gas to be breathed into the air cleaner of the engines, which immediately ran wild, set the gas flow on fire and extensively damaged the rig. The roar, smoke, and glow of the fire late into the night were seen and heard miles away.

65/

To aid potential site locations, geophysical surveys were conducted. This study of the earth's layering formation was done by seismograph readings. Once a designated line was agreed upon by gas well lease holders, a layout was surveyed across the countryside, usually stretching a mile or more. Teams of workers on foot surveyed, placed flags, drilled small diameter, 4-foot deep holes, charged the holes, placed wires, and attached geophones. The holes were loaded with a 4-ounce explosive that was discharged, creating sound waves to the layering rock formations which, in turn, were received by the geophones and seismograph. The readings would indicate the rise and fall of the underground formation. High points supposedly held possible gas or petroleum reserves. As these were found, other series of wires were criss-crossed at the spot to further explore and recheck the previous findings. At the high cost of drilling the mile depth well, this added knowledge proved helpful for locating a likely site. Most

☙
68

of the surveys were done by Paragon Geophysical Inc. of Mt. Gilead, with branch headquarters at Millersburg, and Precision Geophysical, located south of Millersburg along SR 83.

232/

The first try for a Roserun well in our designated area was made by Sherman Drilling for Joe Cross on the David J. Troyer farm, ^{3}/$_4$ mile east of Charm. Drilling began July 5, 1990, and with a short layover, it was completed on July 18. No gas was found and it was termed a "dry hole."

66/

The next Roserun attempt was on the Menno A. Yoder farm on the southwest quarter of Section 6. The pad was leveled Wednesday, August 1, 1990, immediately northwest of the buildings. By Saturday the rig moved in. From 8:00 A.M. until noon trucks were bringing loads of equipment, which included the rig platform with engines, two-piece derrick, two diesel powered screw air compressors, water pumps, electrical power plant, five boat-type containers with drilling stems and equipment, and five water supply tanks. The rotary, cable drum, Gardner Denver rig was owned by Sherman Drilling of Mineral City. Rig crews working frantically had the 116-foot derrick erected by noon. At 2:00 P.M., only six hours after the first trucks had arrived with equipment, the setup was completed and they began drilling.

On Sunday at 11:00 A.M. they stopped and retrieved the stems, then placed casing to cement a top seal. Universal cement trucks had arrived by 2:00 P.M., but delays of a water truck arrival and malfunctioning pumps put the cementing off until 5:00. This cementing was a state requirement to check for leakage. After it had set for eight hours, five or six hundred pounds of air pressure was applied. Leaking connections beneath the rig platform caused another delay, so drilling did not begin until 12:00 noon on Monday, August 6. Operations the following week went smoothly, with only minor interruptions.

Accuracy of a straight hole was highly stressed, and periodical checks were conducted at various times, with the readings of an instrument suspended by cable into the depth of the hole. Five thousand feet were attained Friday evening with less than one degree off center. It was rumored that Sherman Drilling guaranteed a hole within three degrees of accuracy. Though three degrees seems slight, at the depth of the Roserun, a degree equals approximately one hundred feet.

Early Sunday at 1:30 P.M., the Trenton sandstone was reached, which indicated another twenty hours of drilling to completion. There was still good alignment. Stems were being lowered more slowly, at six inches per minute.

A fuel oil burning fire pot had been lit at 1:00 P.M. at the water outlet at the pit. This would instantly ignite any gases reaching the surface and thereby avoid an explosion.

Speed was increased again Sunday evening to approximately one foot per minute. As the desired depth of 6,317 feet was closely reached, drilling was halted at 9:45. This allowed frac trucks, which arrived ten minutes later, to set up. Connections of the three Universal owned trucks were made at the well head and drilling resumed at 10:30. At this time only a few drilling stems remained on the platform. This was enough to reach the anticipated depth. Frequent cutting samples were collected and analyzed by a geologist who was present at the time. After another stem and a half, the first signs of eruption were noticed, as the salt water rushed from the outlet tubing and hit the opposite side of the pit with increasing intensity.

The suspense was like that caused by an eruption of a western geyser, unusually anxious and uncertain.

The gradual lowering of the drilling was stopped. All eyes were on the sludge pit as the water kept gushing forth. The stockholders and well personnel had awaited this moment with sheer nerve wracking anticipation. Salt water was hissing against the bank for about one minute when the first gas ignited. The eruption was met with a shout from the tense onlookers. The shooting flames extended 25 feet across the pit and upwards to 15 feet as they illuminated the smoke-filled night sky with a red, flickering glow.

The frac trucks, waiting nearby, soon began forcing water into the well to override its force of gas pressure. As the flames were subsiding, rig personnel began disassembling equipment no longer needed. Throughout the night stems were retrieved and the following afternoon the casing was set. During the rest of the week the equipment was moved out. Later a service rig was brought in to place the tubing and bring the well to production.

A third Roserun for the area was drilled on the Larry Gray acreage along the east side of the Doughty Glens of Troyer's Hollow. The Section 6 located site was started on March 12, 1992, on a Thursday evening. The Lake Region leased well was drilled by G and H Drilling of Mt. Hope, Ohio with their automatized rig. On the sixth day of drilling, the 6,000-foot depth was reached, so that by March 18 at 2:00 A.M., a small pocket of gas ignited at 6,320 feet. However, the source was soon exhausted and drilling was continued to a greater depth.

Later the well was fractured in hopes of developing a producing well. After no sufficient showing of mineral resources, the well was sealed off up to the Clinton sandstone depth and is being produced from there.

On November 15, 1993 a fourth Roserun well was begun, with its leases extending within the area of interest. The Lake Region Oil Co. owned well, located on the Sheneman, or Ruth Miller, farm, was termed a "community lease," with several property acreages also being leased in order to accumulate the required surrounding area for the chosen well site. It was located between Charm and Beck's Mills off of CR 19. The drilling was done by G and H Drilling.

A week later, on Monday, March 22, gas erupted at 6,358 feet. With the recently improved rig, they were able to extinguish the gas fire themselves by pumping a water solution into the well. After the required amount was pumped to contain the pressure, drilling "with mud" was continued for several hundred feet in hopes of accumulating all of the gas reserves within the Roserun formation. By the last week of December the well was brought into production.

In 1994 the Eli J. Mast farm, in Section 4, was drilled. However, no production was secured. In December of the same year, a well was placed in Section 6, on the Jonas M. Miller farm.

Sandstone

Sandstone foundations for buildings and their use in constructing bridges were the principal uses of sandstone resources found in the area. Their early use from the pioneer period until the advancement to cement blocks and poured walls in the first quarter of the present century have left lasting impressions of their durability. Many walls constructed well over 100 years ago and still in good repair today are evidence that this type of work was substantial.

In the area are found foundations of two different types of stone walls. The one consists of a smaller and irregular stone size, while the other is of the larger, cut and dressed stone set in neat rows.

248/

Drilling for the Roserun formation on the Larry Gray acreage, March, 1992.

317 /
Aug.,
1969

Here again, with the larger stone setup, two different types of work exist. The most magnificent is stones shaped to cubes, with the six sides dressed and laid lengthwise along the course. The other type is a double-faced wall with the inside or hidden face rough, whereas the showing or outside surface was dressed off. However, some stones were placed the full width of the wall to bind it solidly together. Walls varied in thickness and are usually found from 16 to 24 inches wide.

The amount of work needed to build these foundations seems incomprehensible today. With no heavy equipment to rely on, the endeavor depended greatly on hard manual labor along with skill and knowledge gained through years of experience. With hardly any stone mason work being done anymore, the techniques and know-how have largely become a lost art. Accounts related by the "old timers" will help form an idea of how sandstone masonry was done.

To begin with, a sandstone site was usually chosen as close to the building location as possible.

317 /
Aug.,
1969

Work was begun by drilling a hole so a sizable chunk (4 to 6 feet) could be blasted off. Drilling a 2-inch hole was done by tamping an 8-foot rod with a hardened tip, while slowly turning it. The loose sand was cleaned out of the hole with a hickory pole that had many small notches at the end to pull the sand to the top. Next a "creaser" rod was driven down the hole to score two lines on opposite sides of the hole to make the rock split in the direction of the crease. After blasting powder and a fuse were placed in the hole and closed firmly with clay, the stone was split apart. One charge could blast a 12-foot rock, so larger stones were drilled and set accordingly. Two men could drill a hole in two hours with the drill rod.

Next, the chunk was split along the grain direction into smaller pieces. Splitting was done by first picking shallow slots about 3 inches long and placed 2 to 4 inches apart, then driving blunt wedges into them. A wedge touching the bottom would simply bounce out when hit with a sledge, so care was taken that only the tapered sides had contact. Equally important was the way to drive the wedges: usually one tap per wedge working along the full length of the split to maintain an even pressure and ensure a clean break.

Once the correct size was roughly split out, the dimensions were scratched on the top, which would be the bottom once the stone was turned over. Because of the grain of the sandstone, this surface was reasonable flat and would be finished off with a small, pointed pick. The excess on the sides and ends was knocked off with glancing blows from a "mash hammer." Correct use of this tool would allow the surface to be hit as close as

A collection of stone cutting tools includes: pipe rollers on left, 8-foot drill bar, stone wedges, pick heads, level, bars, drafting chisel (center), stone turning hook, picks, and sledge. In the background are: chisels, grannel, mash hammer, and wedges.

an inch to the dimension marks.

Next, a blunt steel, or "rock facing chisel," and a wooden mallet were used. "Spaulds" were flaked off the edges until the sides and ends were vertical with the marked-off surface. This produced a "rock faced finish," but was good enough for exposed sides. Both ends, however, needed to be dressed smoother for the stones to fit closely against each other on the wall. Here a "grannel" was used—a tool about the size of a large axe. About a dozen small, sharp picks are clamped in a row, forming the head, and when used will neatly dress down the surface.

Usually the stones were then taken to the foundation site. With the use of a derrick at the quarry, they could be loaded onto wagons and taken to the foundation, where another hand cranked derrick hoisted them onto the wall. By picking small holes into both sides, the heavy stone could be grasped with hooks when any lifting was done. Pipe rollers were used to roll the stones in place whenever the derrick would not reach out.

Once the stone was set in place on the wall, the crew dressed down the top, creating a flat bed for the next layer later. Here the sides were now also dressed if required. With the small pick and "grannel" the wall could be neatly dressed off, with the "grannel" leaving the attractive, dimpled surface readily seen on cut sandstone.

For a final touch, some stones had a border cut around the exposed side. The surface was expertly marked off by tapping a "drafting chisel" all around the border. This narrow chisel had a serrated edge and its use greatly enhanced the stone mason's work of art.

Walls were built to lean back slightly from the base. A crew of four men could be expected to dress 40 to 50 running feet of stone per day. Circulating reports would say that during early barn building, the stone basement was built one summer and the wooden structure placed the following year. However, during the early 1900s, a typical barn foundation was expected to take 3 to 4 weeks to construct. Stone mason crews were often involved in a seasonal pattern of the work. During spring, work was done on barn walls, houses in the summer, and bridge abutments by fall.

Although cut stone work was replaced by cement blocks and poured walls, much work was still being done later with stone in order to reconstruct or repair an existing foundation.

Quarry sites of the immediate area have mostly disappeared. Remaining evidence on the Levi A. Miller and Jonas N. Yoder farms immediately south of Charm would indicate stone activity there. Between Charm and Beck's Mills along CR 19 on the Amos C. Yoder farm was to have been a quarry. The Troyer's Hollow of the Doughty also produced quantities of stone with the ready supply of boulders found there.

Limestone

With the use and application of lime, the correct ph levels can be maintained in the soil. Its use contributes to better crop yields. As of today, limestone is finely ground by commercial plants, then brought to the farm to be distributed as needed. Up to the mid-1900s a burnt limestone was used. This is still referred to as the highest quality of lime, more readily available for soil absorption. *Caldwell's Atlas of Holmes Co. Ohio* – 1875 indicates limestone locations in Sections 5 and 6.   *75/*

Various types of setups were made to burn limestone. The following is the method used by Dan J.

A limestone pile being set up for burning.

303/
p.206

249/

A remaining area lime pile set up and burnt by Tom Sheneman along CR 19.

Schlabach, who lived northeast of Charm.

During summer whenever time allowed, work was undertaken to build lime piles. Sites were usually selected on a hill to avoid the bothersome smoke. First to be laid were four air channels made of three 8- or 10-inch, 16-foot long planks. These were arranged to form a cross, which would cover a 32-foot area. In the center a wooden chimney was erected as an aid to a draft for the fire.

Next, firewood, old posts, or old rail fence (which was plentiful at the time) was placed in between and to the height of the plank ducts, then covered with straw. Coal was then brought from local underground mines with team and wagon and a layer put on the straw.

The limestone outcroppings, which the Schlabachs found on their own and adjoining farm, were further uncovered by using a team and slip scraper. Once the rock was exposed, it was drilled with a bar drill and sledge, then blasted into manageable pieces. Brought to the pile foundation, the stone was placed on top of the coal. The first pieces were leaned against the wooden chimney, then the next laid against each other to the outside edge of the pile. Usually another couple of layers of coal and limestone were added to make a sizeable heap. Dirt was then shoveled around the outside height to maintain the heat once it was burning.

When the stack was finally completed, kindlings were put into the air chambers and ignited. Once they were burning, they would burn and smolder for days.

The last step, slacking, was simply applying water to the burnt limestone. Once the stones got wet, they pulverized into a usable lime. Usually after the fire had burned out, the stones were hauled to smaller piles throughout the fields. After rain had slacked the burnt stone, the lime was spread out by hand. A pile set up with 1,000 bushels of stone would produce about 2,000 bushels of

303/
p.185,
206

❧

slacked lime.

With all the hard manual labor involved, the results were seen in the fertility of the crop lands.

Limestone in its original state consists mainly of calcium carbonate. Once it is burned it becomes a calcium oxide.

A geological look at the limestone found in Clark Township would reveal it to be that known as Putnam Hill. It is found solely in Ohio, basically throughout the interior of the state. In Holmes County it is the most important limestone to that extent, and the most useful stratigraphic marker.

It is a dense, hard, dove gray to bluish gray colored stone that is sometimes impregnated with fossils. Around Charm the Putman hill lies 1,065 to 1,100 feet above sea level and is somewhat unusual, not lying as a flat bed as noticed elsewhere throughout its formation. Generally this limestone is found to be two feet in depth. Springs are often produced at outcroppings along the hilly terrain throughout the area. The Putman Hill limestone produced a quality burnt limestone and has since been mined to be ground into agricultural lime, road beds, and cement. ❧

Business History

The following business section has primarily been arranged in accordance with the dates the businesses were established. The table of contents at the beginning of the album also list these years in chronological order.

Holmes County Farmer
February 20, 1896

We do not claim that Charm is the largest town in Holmes County nor that it is destined to ever be the metropolis of Ohio, but we do claim that in proportion to its size, our little village can not be surpassed in business enterprise and activity by towns of larger and older growth.

115/

The German fraktur *(below left)* describing Charm business places was done by Joas D. Schlabach, who resided a mile east of town. Its English equivalent would read:

Charm is the
Best Business Place in the County
Mast and Gerber – Dealer in
Shoes and Boots – Dry Goods – Hardware – Sugar
Coffee, etc.   Harvey Oswald, Clerk
B. E. Kaser – Butcher
Meat – Bologna – Ice Cream – Pop, etc.
Keim Brothers – Dealer in Lumber
Sawmilling – Planing Machinery, etc.
Joel Beiler builds traps
to catch sparrow birds, etc.
D. J. Mast – Grinding Mill
Flour grinding – chicken powder, etc.
J. J. Yoder – Dealer in watches – clocks
glasses – gates. I also grind bones
in the new grinding mill.

J. D. Schlabach   Baltic, Ohio

The broadside may be dated with reasonable accuracy using the above information. The new grist mill mentioned was first opened for business in December of 1912, and Schlabach died in April of 1914, thus indicating a date of ca 1913.

Oil Mill

Oil extracting mills had an essential place in early pioneer life. By producing much-needed oils used in a wide range of applications, their existence was a valued asset until they became available commercially.

Linseed oil is pressed from the seeds of the flax plant and is the most common of drying oils. Linseed oil was widely used in hardwood floor finishing and as a paint additive. Peanut oil is extracted from peanuts and used in cooking and soap making.

Daniel C. Miller (ML 616) was born at Somerset County, Pennsylvania in 1793. On June 13, 1815

287 / he applied for a land grant from the U.S. government at the Zanesville Land Office. The 153-acre tract was located between the later built town of Charm and the Doughty Creek.

Daniel was a son of Christian (Schmidt) Miller, who was a blacksmith. Likely learning the skills of mechanics from his father, Daniel built an oil extracting mill a short distance northwest of the later built town site. No exact date is known when
309 / the mill was built. However, he was taxed for an oil mill in 1837. The mill likely functioned with a flat, horizontal stone as a bed, while a heavy top, vertical wheelstone traveling in a small circle would crush the seeds, thereby pressing the oil from them.

Located close to a creek, the mill was supposedly operated with water power.

The exact location of the Daniel Miller oil mill has remained somewhat in question because of various accounts. DJH 1939 note states: "Daniel Miller, the third son of Schmidt Miller, resided between Charm, Ohio and Doughty Creek where he had an oil mill." From this statement some have felt the mill was located on Doughty Creek. Three different locations have been reported to have been along the Charm Creek, a tributary to the Doughty. The farthest downstream would have been along
308 / the stone bank a short distance upstream from
266 / Charm Tractor. Next was in the bottom land on the John B. Yoder farm close to the present cider press building. Here some old foundation stones still remain where a building had stood at one time. A third location was a couple of hundred feet upstream from the SR 557 bridge on the Ben M. Miller farm. This would seem as the most likely site of the mill.

By noting that Daniel was taxed for the mill in German (Clark) Township, the proposed site on the Doughty would be ruled out, as this stream does not flow through Clark Township. The next two would be in German Township, but on his brother Jonathan's land. The last one would be precisely along the edge of the Daniel Miller farm.
71 / Among the Miller descendants of today the state-
167 / ment can be heard, "My uncles used to say the oil mill stood a short distance above the bridge. Its site was in a recessed spot along the creek which was in later years filled in. The stone foundation existing downstream from the bridge was that of an early cider press."

The mentioned "uncles" would have been grandsons of Daniel, thus the account would appear to be authentic. Also passed along from these
288 / uncles is the story that when the early farmer
167 / wanted to drain his swampy bottom land, he
🙖 plowed a furrow along this section of the creek that gradually deepened, forming the creek bed

and draining the adjoining land.

On the 1839 tax list the mill is valued at $50.00, similar to that of a small sawmill or a tannery.
208 / Referring to an old ledger (1859–1890) of the locality, "flax seed oil" was being sold in 1860 at 87¢ for "about a quart." Most of the oil extracted here was probably linseed oil. Since the flax plant stalk was also usable at that early time, it made raising the plant more advantageous. The ledger also makes reference to "breaking flax" (1862). By breaking the stalk, the fibrous strands were thus revealed. These were cleaned with a sharp-toothed hetchel, then later spun into a linen thread.

With the extensive process involved in raising flax until the strands could be ready for the spinning wheels, its usage was discontinued as commercial dry goods became available. Of course, the small hand-cranked cotton gin perfected by Eli Whitney in 1793 was a great step in America's textile industry.

No exact years can be established when the oil mill was in use on the Daniel Miller farm, though from the 1837 taxing until Daniel's death in 1861 may be a close guess. Because of Miller's involvement with the mill, he became known as *"Ölich Daniel"* (Oily Daniel). Today this title is the only reminder of the early place of business; the headstone at Daniel's grave (CD-0-4) bears that inscription. "Ölich Daniel" was buried on his farm which today is owned by a fifth generation descendant, Ben M. Miller.

Blacksmith Shop

The early community blacksmith shops were of great importance to their people. Though today primarily known as horseshoeing businesses, these early smiths produced and provided iron work of many descriptions. Reputable blacksmiths were known by their skill and quality of workmanship.

At Charm, and also earlier Stevenson, we find a long and colorful history of blacksmith shops and their relation to the village. From all appearances the town had four different blacksmith buildings at three locations. Connecting these to the correct ownerships and apprentices in their respective times has been one of the most confusing of all the town's business histories to compile. The fact that early deeds do not always state the full description of a small lot, that copying errors do occur, and that some transfers were never recorded, greatly complicates the work.

Deed records, along with censuses, map layouts, histories, and newspaper articles have been used to form a sketch of the dim past of some of the early blacksmiths who had located at Charm, sharing their skill and expertise.

Interestingly, the blacksmith shop may also be linked with the early or original naming of the village. Though there is no exact documentation of this, secondary evidence would point that way, along with the oral tradition which suggests that an Amish farmer, Stephen Yoder, had connection with the first blacksmith shop. Yoder had lived immediately northwest of town and his farmlands extended to the "early country crossroad" that eventually was named Stevenson, in relation to his name. (See *Names Pertaining to Charm.*)

As may be further noted, the early blacksmith shops have been designated as "east" and "west," relating to their location on the east or west side of the road (SR 557).

132/

Two blacksmith shops at Charm. The low-gabled building in the center is believed to have been the first blacksmith shop (east) and place of business in the town. The west shop, located across the street, is seen to the left.

Stephen Yoder was deeded the farm, which included most of the later built town's land in 1830. At the time of the 1840 census, one of the family was engaged in a trade that we suppose to be that of a blacksmith, according to a traditional story. As the oldest son was only six years old at the time, the elder Yoder himself would have been operating the shop, which appears to have been the first and only business there at that time.

By 1847 Yoder had sold 1³/₄ acres of land to a Daniel Lawer, who was paying taxes that year which included a building value of $288.00. Lawer, 28, is listed on the 1850 census as a blacksmith, along with an apprentice, George Snellenberger, 23 and single. From Lawer's land transfer four years later, the real estate can be described as being lands from the present schoolhouse to the former blacksmith shop, Jonas J. Yoder home, and bank building lot. This first blacksmith shop had stood on the east side of SR 557, where today's Old Blacksmith Shop Gifts is located, at the south side of town.

In 1851 Daniel Lawer sold the acreage to Levi S. Miller (ML 6235) for $850.00. Levi was a grandson

$\mathcal{V}$2-
73-
1830

309/

$\mathcal{V}$17-
322-
1851

of "Broad Run John," an early pioneer, and a brother to Isaac S. Miller, who acquired the wagon shop the same year. For a number of years later the Miller blacksmith owned both the wagon maker's shop and the blacksmith shop (east), which were, in turn, sold to Joseph Jones when the Millers moved to Elkhart County, Indiana.

Joseph Jones, 1834–1862, bought the blacksmithing interest in 1857 when he was 23 years of age. At the time of the 1860 census David Troyer, a teenager, and Jacob Farmwald, 23, are listed along with Jones as being engaged in the blacksmith trade. Jacob bought the undivided half interest of the Jones real estate in 1860. In March of 1862, Jacob bought the remaining undivided half interest from Jones, four months prior to his death.

Jacob Farmwald (FW 71) was born April 14, 1837 at Alsace, France. He had come to America when he was ten, in 1847, with his apparently widowed mother, Magdalena, and his aunt Elizabeth. In 1860 the mother was staying with Jacob and his wife Lydia (Miller) at Stevenson. The Farmwalds owned 3¹/₈ acres of land in town which extended from the present land of the school playground to the harness shop.

In 1867 Jacob bought the northwest quarter of Section 25, now owned by Stevie A. Raber, located 3 ¹/₂ miles south of the village. After his wife Lydia died in 1870, he remarried to Catherine Raber the following year, then later moved to Geauga County, where he died in 1902.

The Farmwald real estate at Stevenson was sold in 1868, 1869, and 1875. The 1868 transaction consisted of the 1¹/₂-acre tract from the school to CR 70 being sold to Solomon J. Farver, who was a shoemaker by trade. At the time of the transfer the blacksmith shop (east) was "excepted" and Jacob kept ownership until 1875, although he had moved out town earlier. The 1¹/₂-acre tract sold in 1869 included land presently to the north of CR 70. This was sold to Charles Nice, who is listed on the 1870 census as the blacksmith. Charles, 26, a German immigrant, apparently lived in one of the former houses across the street from today's restaurant, and presumably leased the shop from Farmwald. His wife Caroline was born in Ohio.

As noted, Jacob Farmwald sold the blacksmith shop (east) in 1875 to John H. Lawer and Christian Kempf.

Referring to *Caldwell's Atlas of Holmes Co. Ohio* – 1875, we find the first map layout of the town, which also indicates the blacksmith shop as being located on the east side of the street. According to the *Atlas*, a Samuel S. Troyer was connected with blacksmithing, as was S. L. Korn. The atlas business directory refers to Korn, of German township, as doing "blacksmithing of all kinds; also carriages

$\mathcal{AA}$
$\mathcal{MG}$
p.311

$\mathcal{V}$25-
271-
1857
$\mathcal{V}$25-
210-
1860
$\mathcal{V}$25-
211-
1862

$\mathcal{AA}$
$\mathcal{MG}$
$\mathcal{V}$29-
269-
1866
$\mathcal{V}$30-
541-
1867
$\mathcal{CD}$
p.133
$\mathcal{AA}$
$\mathcal{MG}$

$\mathcal{V}$32-
317-
1868
225/
1870

$\mathcal{V}$32-
458-
1869

$\mathcal{V}$35-
259-
1875

201/
p.29

❧

and wagons ironed with all work promptly done to order and warranted." As noted here, blacksmithing during the 1800s included a much broader range of iron work than what is done today.

At Millersburg, Korn is also listed among other town smiths. Apparently he was working in both towns. Since he never owned land in Stevenson, his blacksmithing engagement in the two towns may well have been the practice of a young and energetic blacksmith.

26/
p.17
153/

Sanford Leander Korn was born ca 1853 and was raised in Berlin, Ohio. His father, John, was a son of Jacob Korn, who had come to early Holmes County and settled at Berlin. He was one of the first known blacksmiths in the county. On January 16, 1873, Sanford married Sarah Marie Christopher of Killbuck and, in 1876, they bought a lot and moved to her hometown. From there the family moved to Defiance County in the early 1880s. Here Korn worked on the Miami and Erie Canals, along with shoeing mules. On August 12, 1882, Korn was riding home on a passenger train from Defiance and had intended to get off at a B. & O. junction. Instead, he jumped from the moving train when it passed his residence. Striking an embankment, he rolled back under the train, which crushed his head and arms, causing instant death.

26/
p.20

In 1876, the year that the Korns moved to Killbuck, a J. Korns was blacksmith at Charm. Most likely this was Sanford's father, John.

225/
1880

Two smiths appear in town in 1880, namely the previously mentioned John H. Lawer and Christian J. Miller. On the census John is listed with his wife Fredericka and six children.

305/
1162

Christian J. Miller (ML 61375) was raised a mile northwest of Stevenson. From Holmes County the Millers moved to Geauga County, where Christian died in 1912, having been a farmer and blacksmith throughout his life. Christian was a great-grandson of Christian "Schmidt" Miller, a widely known blacksmith and Amish bishop of Somerset County, Pennsylvania.

𝒱46-
336-
1882
𝒱41-
522-
1885
50/2-
20-1896
𝒱51-
555-
1887

The Lawer and Kempf transfer of 1875 also included the wagonmaker's shop where it is assumed Kempf was engaged. By 1882 the partnership sold their interest to Phillip Kerch for $1,050.00, which included the one acre north of CR 70. Later Phillip and Mahalah Kerch sold their real estate to George Price in 1885 for $1,500.00. George and his wife Lucy were residents of the town when the post office was established in 1885 and the village became known as Charm. The father, along with son William, conducted a flourishing blacksmithing trade for the next eleven years. George sold the wagon shop, from the acquired tract, in 1887 to former smith Christian J. Miller.

⁔

100/4-
12-1894
19/
p.36
𝒱54-
362-
1894

In 1894, when Price was laid up with erysipelas, Christian Hummel helped out in the blacksmith shop (west) during his sickness. Hummel was an apprentice to George Price for two years, receiving for his labor $85.00 plus room and board.

According to deed records, George Price built the second blacksmith shop in town. In 1894 Price bought 3.73 acres from jeweler Joni J. Yoder for $192.00, which included land on the west side of SR 557 presently owned by Albert A. Keim. On this lot a blacksmith shop was built during the years of Price's blacksmithing (1885–1896) in town. The new shop was located directly across the street from the other shop, supposedly on leased ground from J. J. Yoder until the 1894 transfer. Price had located in the new shop prior to 1890 when the old shop structure (east) was sold.

171/

Blacksmith shop (west) built by George Price ca 1890.

50/
2-20-
1896

With regret the community saw the George and Lucy Price family take leave in April of 1896. Out-of-state land agents had been in the vicinity and, as Price had taken serious interest in the agent's offering, they would be leaving Charm for a farm at Mecosa County, Michigan. The family left with the well wishes of the locality, who regarded the Price general blacksmithing business as "a shop noted for good and honest work."

𝒱55-
55-1890
𝒱59-
76-1896

George had owned numerous parcels of real estate in the village, including the two blacksmith shops. He sold the .03-acre lot on the east side of the street, "known as the ground on which the old blacksmith used to stand," to Jacob L. Miller in 1890. At the time of their departure, the other shop, .1 acre, was transferred to Christian Sommers. The trade was taken on by Eli Sommers who, supposedly, was a son of the Christian buying the real estate. Mention is made in a Millersburg newspaper, stating: "Eli Sommers of Walnut Creek has purchased the shop and goodwill of George Price and will continue the blacksmithing business at the old stand. Mr. Sommers comes well recommended and no doubt will receive the good wishes of all and the patronage of a wide territory."

50 /
2-20-
1896

The same year, William H. Hochstetler of Sugar Creek was employed at the Charm business. By 1899 Hochstetler was apparently the main blacksmith. He was so busy that he mentioned erecting a new shop after harvest, but apparently this never materialized.

100 /
10-26-
1896
100 /
6-29-
1899

Along with Hochstetler, a John Lanzer is listed as blacksmith on the 1900 census. Lanzer seemingly came to town the previous year.

50 /
4-13-
1899

William Henry Hochstetler (DBH 5027) was born July 27, 1874 at Sugar Creek, Ohio and married Anna Miller of Charm in 1898. They bought the triangle tract in town in 1903 that, today, is the Charm Building, and Jonas J. Yoder land, where they apparently lived in one of the two houses on the lot.

V68-
100-
1903

The couple had three children, with the youngest, Ruth, born April 11, 1904. By June, two months after her birth, the mother passed away. After her death, Ruth was adopted by William and Ida Fisher (DJH 1211). William was a schoolteacher at Charm and his wife a sister to the deceased Anna Hostetler. Both were daughters of the former Charm storekeeper and late Isaac J. Miller. The remaining children were also adopted by their aunts, with the oldest, Neva, going to the home of Frank and Nettie Lehman of Nappanee, Indiana, and Bernice to Rollie and Fannie Miller (late) of Uniontown, Ohio.

27 /

William H. Hochstetler later remarried to Mamie Hoffman and resided at Mio, Michigan.

The mentioned John Lanzer was still a practicing smith at Charm in 1910. No exact date is known when he left the village. The Lanzer family had been living at the "cheesemaker" Nickles home after they moved out of town, and had sold this property to Fred Groosen in 1901. There is supporting evidence that Lanzer had also been involved with business in the west shop.

225 /
1910
50 /
4-25-
1901
V64-
531-
1901

Since 1896 Christian Sommers had owned the shop building on the west side of the street. In 1907

178 /

One of these two men is smith John Lanzer. Charm blacksmith shop (west) ca 1905.

V74-
413-
1907
206/
p.104

he sold it and "all the tools therein" to Christian Hummel for $350.00. As previously stated, Christ had been at Charm earlier, employed by black-smith Jones. He became an artist in iron work and horseshoeing, which remained his occupation throughout most of his lifetime.

56/

Charm blacksmith, Christ Hummel, son Dean, and wife Amanda.

V80-
204-
1911
V80-
168-
1911

The tall, muscular, and heavily built blacksmith, whose great-grandmother was a full-blooded Cherokee, tipped the scales at 240 pounds. By 1911 he sold the old blacksmith shop and the present Abe A. Mast property to Henry N. Miller.

From Charm the Hummels moved a mile south to a small acre farm, presently owned by LaRue Oswald, at the head of the Doughty Glens. While living here Christ also worked the blacksmith trade.

9/
262/

Before moving, their oldest daughter, Verna Irene, was affected with appendicitis. Surgery was performed at the home on the customary "kitchen table." She died later because of pneumonia caused by too much ether during her surgery.

67/

Meanwhile, at Charm, Henry N. Miller (OAG 3569) had been employed by Christ Hummel be-fore taking on the blacksmithing himself. Becom-ing a well known smith in the area, Miller was readily known as "Black Hen," which related to his blacksmithing occupation. When he purchased the business, Henry was still single.

The Miller blacksmith met with a near-fatal ac-cident at his shop on September 17, 1912. Noah J.

100/
9-25-
1912

Raber (OAG 2390) came to the shop, an oft-used congregating and visiting spot, with one of the first repeating shotguns to be seen in the area. Arriv-ing in town, Raber removed the shell from the chamber, but left the ones in the magazine. Jacob J. Hershberger, in examining and handling the fire-arm, repeated and accidentally discharged the gun. The blast entered the blacksmith shop, hit the forge and its stone base, then glanced off and hit Henry, spraying lead shot in his face, chest, and legs, and breaking some of his teeth. Turning, he walked to the doorway, where he collapsed.

100/
11-20-
1912

He recovered from the accident with medical treatment. Later, x-rays showed seventy pellets had penetrated his body. They remained there throughout his lifetime. By the middle of Novem-ber Henry was back at work again.

67/
140/
100/
5-12-
1915
100/
11-17-
1915

Henry married Bena Nisley in 1914, lived at Charm, and was the blacksmith in town until 1920. During this time the old shop building (west) was removed and Henry built a new shop in its place in 1915. A notice appearing in *The Budget* of May 12 stated: "no blacksmithing will be done in Charm until our new blacksmith shop is completed which will be only a short time." By November Henry was buying some new machinery for the business, which turned out to be a repair shop.

V89-
202-
1919

In 1919 the Millers bought interest in the home farm from his father and moved there the follow-ing year. Today Marvin J. Raber owns the acreage 1 1/2 miles southeast of Charm. Later, in 1929, Henry also built a blacksmith shop at the farm. A son, Ammon, would later recall that the cut sand-stones they used for the foundation were obtained at the unused culvert at the turn on SR 557, 1/2 mile east of town. The road originally had made a sharper turn where the small pond is located on the east side of the present route, and its sandstone culvert was no longer being used.

67/

V89-
329-
1920

At Charm, Henry N. Miller sold the repair shop to three town businessmen, William A. Mast, Albert J. Keim, and Daniel J. Mast, in 1920.

In the 1970s the lot's owner, Albert A. Keim, moved the building back from the road a short distance; it was now used primarily for storage. In May, 1993 the aging structure was razed.

As noted on the opposite or east side of the street, John Lanzer was smith in 1910.

156/
100/2-
23-1916
100/6-
7-1916
100/7-
26-1916
V85-
128-1916

Sometime prior to 1916 Samuel H. Miller (DJH 5100) was blacksmith at the east shop, and by March he was erecting a new building. In June of that year the shop was finished and ready for busi-ness. Miller's activity in the new structure was short-lived and, by the latter part of July, he sold the smithing inventory to Wilbert Fraelich. The real estate was transferred to a brother, John H. Miller. Later in life Samuel was also a blacksmith at Goshen, Indiana.

Wilbert Henry Fraelich (1887–1978), whose father Adam was a blacksmith, began the trade himself at New Bedford ca 1910, soon after marriage. After helping his father at the flour mill at Beck's Mills, he took up blacksmithing at Charm again in 1916.

97 / p.44 157 / 100/7- 26-1916

Moving to Sugar Creek in 1918, he continued the trade there. Wilbert reached 90 years of age, and he and his wife, Celesta Pearl (Fett) are buried at the Oak Hill Cemetery.

Irvin Kaser continued with the blacksmithing after the Fraelichs left town, and also moved onto the rented property they had vacated in 1918. The former blacksmith of Sugar Creek then bought the Charm property and blacksmith shop (east) in early 1919 from John H. Miller. They resided here until 1920, when the tract was sold to Christian A. Hummel.

114 / V89- 217- 1919 V89- 400- 1920

Irvin died unexpectedly in his sleep, April 12, 1956. His wife of 43 years, Hulda (Brand-Kaser) Miller, is today a resident at Walnut Hills Nursing Home. At 102 years old, she still had an outstanding memory. She could readily recall living at Charm, as well as her earlier childhood days. Hulda referred to her life as a "happy life with many blessings," while of her secret to a long life

325 /

Blacksmith Irvin Kaser and wife Hulda

she remarked with a giggle, "I just keep breathing." Presently she responds very little to visiting. Hulda was born August 24, 1890.

Christ Hummel, the former Charm blacksmith, returned to the village as smith in 1920, although he had been on the opposite (west) side of the street during his earlier engagement. His oldest son, Ray, moved onto the property and helped his father in the blacksmith shop. At the time, the Hummels lived a short distance southeast of town at the present Andy M. Hershberger farm. Hummel was a man of business and would live on a property a few years, making some improvements and painting, then reselling at a profit and moving on to the next one. Later, at Charm, they lived at the Jonas J. Yoder home of today, where son Ray had lived.

9 / 19 / p.36

In 1924 they moved to the corner lot which stood where the present Keim Lumber driveway is located. While living there they built a garage with an upstairs room for "Isaac Andy" (Miller) to stay in when he was no longer able to care for himself. Andy was a half brother to Mrs. Amanda Hummel and had been a longtime Charm resident. Christ sold the blacksmith shop (east) and present real estate to Mose P. Troyer in 1925. In 1927 the Hummel family and "Isaac Andy" left Charm, selling the corner lot to Mose L. Yoder. They moved to Berlin; Christ later operated a butcher shop there.

V93- 581- 1925 V96- 445- 1926

Mose P. Troyer (OAG 0934) was raised a mile east of Charm, where he was born to Peter C. and Catherine (Schlabach) Troyer in 1894. Living in town, Mose continued the well known blacksmithing business located at the south side of the village.

155 / 156 /

During Troyer's involvement with the business, a cousin, John S. Miller, was employed at the shop. This was during the years when he was a widower—1925 to 1928. John was known as "Sim John" or "Ness John," which referred to his earlier residence of Ness County, Kansas. He was a talented and prolific worker of iron and, while at Charm, he also constructed water wheels designed for pumping water. The wheels were rigged to cables that extended to the pump. One of these wheels was erected on the Jonas N. Yoder farm southwest of town.

154 /

During his lifetime, he is credited with making a single cylinder, double action, double piston engine – which he used to run his shop, two wool carding machines, corn shellers, hammer mills, and hydraulic cider presses. He also worked on and repaired steam engines. John had lived in Missouri, Kansas, Indiana, and Ohio, then returned to Indiana, where he remarried in 1928.

Mose P. Troyer, or "Pit Mose," was blacksmith for 22 years. He sold the home and shop to Jonas J. Yoder in the fall of 1946, then moved to Wayne

155/
𝒱118-
419-
1946
156/

County in 1947. Troyer's son Aden and former smith "Hen" Miller helped out at the shop during the beginning of the new ownership.

Jonas Yoder brought the longstanding black-smithing business to the present age. By now the weatherbeaten old shop was in need of replacement. After an auction held at the premises, the building was razed and a new block structure was placed at the same site in 1969. Interestingly, Jonas, better known as "Schmit Jonas," was one of the last local blacksmiths to do any amount of repairing or iron work along with serving the horse-shoeing needs of the community. With today's Amish population which brings an extensive amount of horses into the area, the present day smiths are mainly kept busy serving horseshoeing needs. Jonas J. Yoder (OAG 2767) was active with horseshoeing until 1973. The hard labor involved with the art forced the older gentleman to quit at 59 years of age. The years of working in a bent over position have allowed the retired blacksmith to retain the exercise of keeping his knees straight while bending over to touch the ground with the palm of his hands. His advice: "Just lay your belly on your legs, bend over and touch the ground." Incidentally, Jonas and his wife, Sarah (Wengerd), were both born on Ground Hog Day, 1917. She passed away February 9, 1995, seven days after her seventy-eighth birthday.

Yoder continued with general repair work until March 31, 1989, and soon thereafter had another sale. The block building was completely refurnished that year, and by September it opened as the "Old Blacksmith Shop Gifts," owned by the Yoders' son, Jacob.

110/

Now, with no horseshoeing service in town, a village resident, Leroy J. Raber, who grew up on a Standardbred horse farm, took interest in the business. Beginning in 1975, he worked in the "Schmit Jonas" shop from February until May, then moved

249/

In 1969 Jonas J. Yoder replaced the aging blacksmith shop (east) with a new building, presently used as a gift shop.

126/

The Jonas J. Yoder blacksmith shop before it was razed in 1969.

into the newly built block building on his property at the northwest side of town. The business, known as "Raber's Shoeing Service," was the only active blacksmith shop in town. During 1994 a new shop was placed on their property, 1¹/₂ miles west of Charm. During the fall of 1994 the family moved to their new home.

With the Raber business moving out of town, the notable blacksmithing came to an end for the hamlet which has seen this business through almost the entirety of its existence as a village.

Numerous blacksmith shops have also been operated in the area surrounding Charm. As noted, blacksmith Christ Hummel operated a shop along TR 154 at the head of the road leading to the Doughty Glens from 1911 to 1920. Previously mentioned Henry N. Miller was an active smith while living on the farm, 1¹/₂ miles southeast of town, from 1929 until again moving to Charm in 1947.

67/
𝒱118-
566-
1947
140/
𝒱118-
213-1946
𝒱126-
599-1952
𝒱130-
182-1954
289/

The previous year, Henry had sold to his brother Ammon .4 acre, on which he built a blacksmith shop, located at the intersection of TR 190 and SR 557 a mile southeast of Charm.

In 1952 this acreage was sold to Perry S. Miller, who, in turn, sold it to Albert S. Miller in 1954. Albert was blacksmith for an extended period of time until sickness caused him to quit prior to his death in 1980. His well established business was known as Miller's Blacksmith Shop.

Since the early 1990s Melvin J. Miller did some amount of horseshoeing at the Sunny Slope Farm, a mile southeast of Charm along SR 557.

Wagon and Buggy Shop

When early settlers began arriving in Holmes County during the first quarter of the nineteenth century, they left behind them trails which eventually became roads that were beaten by horses and buggy and wagon wheels. Throughout the next century, horse travel was the chief means of transportation within the community. Thus wagon, carriage, and wheel shops were of vital importance during the period, and readily appeared in early towns.

From all known documentation, the wagon shop in our town of interest appeared ca 1848 and was preceded only by the blacksmith shop as a place of business. In September of 1848 Stephen J. Yoder, a farmer living northwest of the small country crossroad, and whose lands extended to the same, sold ½ acre to Manasseh Lawver for $40.00. *V15-569-1848* This acreage today includes the harness shop, the Keim Lumber driveway, and the Watchman's Cottage. The wagon shop later built on this lot was located immediately across the street from the Jonas J. Yoder house of today. A town layout in *Caldwell's Atlas of Holmes Co. Ohio – 1875* shows this placement of a building, as well as the 1894 Charm picture, where only the roof protrudes from behind the above mentioned Yoder house. Later deed transfers would identify transactions as "the wagon maker's shop and the ground upon which it stands."

Manasseh Lawver, age 24, is listed on the 1850 census along with his wife Mary, 28, as being a wagon maker. Also, at this time Elijah Row, 19 and single, was included in the Lawver household and employed as a wagon maker.

By 1851 the lot was sold to Isaac S. Miller for $450.00. This increase in settlement indicates the presence of a building now being on the tract. *V17-146-1851 309/1852* Miller, in turn, sold the business to his brother Levi in March, 1853, for the same price. The brothers were sons of Simon Miller (ML 623) and had grown up 1½ miles east of town on the present Eli M. Shetler farm. *V19-27-1853*

At age 21 Isaac married Rachel Troyer, and during the same year he took on with the wagon shop. Miller upholstered buggy tops, made sleighs, and did iron work related to the business. In addition, he was also a cobbler. After selling the trade to his brother Levi Miller in 1853, the Isaac Millers moved a mile west of town on the present Paul S. Erb farm. *206/ p.10,90* *V19-238-1853*

Levi owned the ½-acre tract four years, then sold it in 1857 to blacksmith Joseph Jones. Sometime during the next two years, the Miller family moved to Elkhart County, Indiana. *V25-271-1857 /ML 6235*

During this time, as indicated on the 1860 census, John Banen, a native of Switzerland, was en-

Wagon maker Andrew Forsch and wife Mary

123/

gaged in the wagon maker's trade. He did not own any real estate.

As indicated, Jones acquired the wagon shop in 1857. Upon his death in 1862, the shop was transferred to Valentine and Christian Limbacher. They then sold the wagon shop to Jacob Farmwald in 1866. Jacob was 29 at the time and had earlier been the town's blacksmith. *V25-272-1862 V29-269-1866 225/ 1860*

Within the next two years, Eli Mast became owner of the now separately sold .03-acre "wagon maker shop," which he resold to Andrew Forsch in 1868. Andrew was another immigrant who found his way to the small village of Stevenson. He was single and 22 years old when he arrived at Shanes-ville in 1867 from Bestersheid, Germany. Soon thereafter he met and married Marion (Mary) Zahner, also a German immigrant, whom he supposedly did not know until he had come to live in America. *V32-516-1868 97/p.43 123/*

Along with the wagon shop purchase of 1868, he bought an ¹¹/₁₆-acre tract, which is now the western part of the school playground. The following year, the Forsches bought the house across

V32-
515-1869 the street from the shop and $^3/_{16}$-acre ground for $115.00. On the 1870 census Andrew is listed as a wagon maker by trade.

V36-
195-1873
V44-
281-1880
V44-
70-1880 Andrew and Mary sold the wagon shop and home to Henry F. Selzer of Tuscarawas County in 1873, then purchased a home in the Doughty Glens, a mile west of town, which they resold in 1880. In 1879, the Forsches had located at Berlin, where he was also engaged as a wagon maker. After remaining there the rest of their life, both were buried in the town's cemetery.

V38-
104-1875
225/
1880
V46-
265-1882
V46-
336-1882
V41-
522-1885 As indicated on *Caldwell's Atlas of Holmes Co. Ohio* – 1875, Samuel S. Troyer was owner of the lot north and east of the town's intersection, which also shows a placement of a building where the wagon shop was located. The same year, Troyer sold the 1$^1/_2$-acre tract to John H. Lawer and Christian Kempf for $1,300.00. It is assumed Christian was engaged as a wagon maker, as John was known to have been a blacksmith. From this partner ownership, half an acre along the west side was sold in May, 1882, where the first store would later be built. Four months later the remaining acre, including the wagon and blacksmith shop (east), were transferred to Phillip Kerch. Phillip and his wife, Mahalah, in turn sold the acreage and buildings of business to George and Lucy Price in 1885.

V51-
555-
1887 Price, who was a blacksmith, sold the .03-acre "wagon maker shop and the ground on which it stands" to Christian J. Miller in 1887. Miller was a former town smith.

V53-
503-1889
V55-
55-1890
100/6-
8-1891 Two years later, in 1889, Christian sold the tract to Jacob L. Miller for $140.00. The following year Jacob bought the "old blacksmith shop" (east) from George Price. He apparently saw a need for expansion, as in the spring of 1891 he built a new wagon shop and planing mill. The former wagon maker's building was later used as a livery stable.

The new business was located between the newly built blacksmith shop (west) and the jeweler's shop. This would be immediately south of today's restaurant, and was the building that later housed the Isaac Bontrager harness shop, or what was known as the Harry Kauffman house.

100/7-
23-1891
50/2-
20-1896
100/1-
21-1897 By July, 1891 Miller had already sold a well recommended, new, Charm-made buggy. Within the next few years, Jacob moved to Illinois so that in 1896 Andy I. Miller was the wagon maker and wood worker. In January, 1897 Jacob L. Miller returned from the western state and was again engaged with his former business: ". . . engaged in planing mill and lumber business, he will soon have it arranged to do all kinds of wood work."

John J. Keim was operating the wagon shop in the early 1900s. Available information would indicate he was the wagon maker from 1906 until 1911. John married in 1905 to Saloma Miller, and

V73-
162-
1906
8/
279/ within the following year he moved to Charm. They purchased the lot on the northeast street corner in town in 1906 from the former blacksmith William H. Hostetler, who had moved to Michigan.

At Charm, Keim sold the Columbus Post, factory-made buggies. These arrived in shipping crates, then were fully assembled at the wagon shop.

It is interesting to note that during the period of horse-drawn vehicle travel, Cincinnati, Ohio was the center of carriage making in America.

In 1911 John Keim became involved with his brother Mose in sawmilling and with building their new planing mill. Engaged with this milling work at Charm, he quit the wagoneer trade.

CD-
0-4-18 John's wife died December 24, 1907, eight days after the birth of their firstborn child, Atlee. At 87 years of age, the son was recently still involved in the lumber company his father founded at Mt. Hope in 1923. Atlee J. Keim was born in the house formerly located on the corner across from the restaurant, and spent most of his boyhood years in the Charm area. His memory has served him well throughout the years and today he remains a favorite at relating accounts and happenings of life in early Charm.

The widower John Keim remarried in 1908 to Mary Ann Yoder.

V89-
288-
1920 The wagon shop was later owned by John's brother Albert, who sold it to Isaac J. Bontrager in 1920. At this time it was remodeled and used as living quarters and a harness shop, thus ending the period of a wagoneer trade at Charm.

140/ Later, from 1921 to 1947, when the blacksmith Henry N. Miller was living on the farm a mile southeast of town, he bought, repaired, and sold buggies. During this period many non-Amish people were buying cars, so Henry bought their unneeded vehicles. Numerous buggies had the fold-down tops which were taken off, with some being mounted on corn cultivators, much to the delight of the farmer working the fields on a warm summer day.

196/ Interestingly, among the Amish population, the buggy with the enclosed top, as it is made today, was not used until the 1930s. Earlier only open or topless buggies had been used.

140/
100/
1-?-1938
194/
CD-K-
15-33 To the north of Charm, Menno D. Miller had a buggy shop from the 1930s into the 1950s. As a dealer in new, factory-built buggies, he sold Standard Vehicle, and also built new, made-to-order buggies.

Menno was originally from Geauga County, but moved to Holmes County to the present Henry M. Raber farm when he married Mrs. Yost (Anna) Miller in 1932. In 1935 he built a buggy shop, which he operated until her death in 1951. After she passed away, Menno again moved back to Geauga County.

From his *The Budget* news column, Miller was known as the "Charming Charmer of Charm."

More recently, the Andy E. Raber family operated a buggy shop, from 1980 to 1989.

195/

Andy had been employed at the Charm Cheese Factory for a number of years. For health reasons, he sought a different livelihood, and built a new shop on his home property at the south edge of the village. The "Charm Buggy Shop" repaired and built new buggies, along with doing wheelwork.

In 1985, Ben, of the above named Raber family, had moved onto a property a mile southeast of Charm and put up a shop building. By 1987 the "SR 557 Carriage Shop" was engaged in restoring and painting carriages and sleighs.

During 1992 the Rabers took up farming and the business was discontinued.

Presently, only one buggy shop is located and in business in the immediate area. This one, owned by Albert N. Schrock, is situated immediately north of Charm. Since 1987, Albert has retired from farming and was thus able to pursue his interest of buggy making. Earlier in life he had been employed by a buggy maker, so he was not a newcomer to the trade. Schrock does any work required in buggy making, from wheelwork to repairing and building new ones.

The business of "Hillside Carriage and Buggy" was moved a mile northwest of Charm from Beck's Mills in 1988. Owner James Yoder started in buggy work at the former location and afterward proceeded to build the new shop along TR 154. Yoder did buggy and carriage repair work, along with making new vehicles. In 1993 the shop was converted into a craft store, although some buggy work was yet being done until early 1994.

Harness Shop

From available sources, Isaac S. Miller (ML 6238) would appear to be the first harness shop proprietor in town. Early records use different names for the leather workers, including: "harness maker," "cobbler," and "shoemaker." In this early period, "cobbler" or "shoemaker" identified their livelihood well, as they brought to the community their skill of shoemaking. This consisted of flattening out leather for soles, then cutting, nailing, and sewing the all-leather uppers to the hardened sole.

In 1851, at age 21, Isaac became a shoemaker by trade. The same year, he bought the wagon shop at Stevenson, where he apparently had the two businesses in one building during his short, three-

206/
p.90
ʊ17-
146-1851

223/
p.115

Harness and wagon maker Isaac S. Miller

year stay there. At the time, a younger brother, Jacob (DJH 6374), was known to have been a shoemaker, and quite likely was helping his brother as a cobbler.

225/
1850

Continuing with deed and census records, we find that Solomon S. Farver bought the Jacob Farmwald (blacksmith) interest in 1868, then is listed on the 1870 census as a shoemaker, at which time he was 35. His wife, Drusilla, and three children are also shown. The 1870 listing indicates a Jacob Kaser as being an apprentice to Farver, and by 1873 the real estate was transferred from Farver to Kaser.

ʊ32-
317-1868
ʊ36-
422-
1873

Jacob Kaser is named in *Caldwell's Atlas of Holmes Co. Ohio – 1875*, Stevenson map (see p. 26), as owning the shoe shop. Interestingly, at this time the early town layout indicates the location of the shop to have been on the east side of the road (along present SR 557, between the bank and the former blacksmith shop). This was probably only a small building, as two decades later no indication of its presence there is shown on a town picture.

225/
1880
ʊ48-

By 1880 Jonathan Kaser was a shoemaker in town. Jonathan had owned the Atlee Schlabach property at this time period. Lewis Geib also appears on this census and by 1896 is noted as being ". . . our saddler, who has achieved a just reputation for careful and accurate workmanship." The same year an apprentice, Will Hoover of New Bedford, was working in the harness shop, as was a brother, John Geib.

248-
1884
50/2-
20-1896
50/1-
9-1896
50/12-
13-1894
ʊ60-

During this period the Post Office was temporarily housed in the harness shop when the store was burned in 1894.

368-
1895
ʊ60-

In 1895 Lewis was deeded the property and house on the northeast corner lot in town. The following year the acreage was sold to Gideon B. Helmuth.

470-
1896

As noted, the shoe shop placement on the 1875 town map is not seen by 1894 (town picture). However, the 1894 picture reveals a small building with

8/ a chimney to the east of his house, possibly the shoe shop that had been moved, and likely had been Geib's interest in purchasing the property.

Around the turn of the century, Isaac J. Bontrager appears as the saddler at Charm. He is the first harness shop proprietor in town that our older residents recall, and has provided us with an extended period of business. Bontrager was a resident in the village during three separate periods before moving back to his home state of Indiana.

219/ Isaac (BN 222a) was born at LaGrange County, Indiana, September 26, 1856, and married Elizabeth Hattery in 1879. She died in 1896, leaving Isaac with three children. The oldest child, Lydia, married at fifteen years of age. In 1901 the widowed father married Savilla Kauffman, his son-in-law's half sister, who was 24 years his junior.

𝒱68- In 1903 the Bontragers bought the present Joe
26-1903 Erb property at the east edge of Charm for $825.00.
100/3- On February 28 of the following year, the family
3-1904 arrived by train at Millersburg with their belong-
57/ ings to make their future home at Charm. It is
100/2- known that part of the house was used as a
3-1938 saddler's shop at the time.

Isaac had been stricken with infantile paralysis when was a year old, so he was a cripple, using crutches throughout his life. Despite the handicap he was an active, well-respected businessman.
100/7- Because of his physical condition, he narrowly
28-1904 escaped injury the first summer they lived in Ohio. He had been at Millersburg and was attempting to hand the postal clerk on the train a letter as the train began to move from the station. Walking alongside the train, he stumbled over mail sacks piled on the ground and fell into a two-foot-wide space between the platform and the moving cars. Realizing the situation he was in, he remained there without moving until the entire train had passed, and miraculously, he was not injured.
100/7- In 1909 the Bontragers were living in the Goose
8-1909 Bottom, a mile west of Walnut Creek. After hav-
225/ ing a public sale there in 1911, they moved back to
1910 Charm in February.

A year later, the harness maker moved to a 29-
100/1- acre farm close to Winesburg, two miles south of
10-1912 the town, along the east side of the Seven Lick Hill.
93/ While living there, Isaac's wife, Sevilla, died dur-
250/ ing the onset of the flu epidemic in 1918. She died on October 20, and three days later a 9-month-old
100/9- daughter also passed away.
8-1919 The father, again a widower, once more made
𝒱89- the move back to Charm in 1919, buying the build-
288- ing in the center of town which had been a wagon
1920 shop and was now refurnished as a harness shop and dwelling. The south part of the building
❧ served as a repair shop. The opposite side, the
84 upstairs and downstairs, were living quarters for

Isaac and the five girls.

During those early years, Bontrager would fix
43/ a shoe for five or ten cents. He also served as den-
75/ tist when teeth needed to be pulled. For children, the kindly businessman had the tooth extracted before the child knew what had happened. As the young patient, suffering from toothache, was beaming over a piece of candy, the older gentleman lost no time in bringing out the troublesome tooth.

161/ Isaac is also remembered as having an unusual spot Arabian as a buggy horse.

Bontrager sold the building and equipment to Eli P. Troyer ca 1930, and moved back to Shipshewana, Indiana. Isaac died there in 1938 at 82 years of age, the father of fifteen children.

160/ The Eli P. Troyer family also used the building as a dwelling and shop, operating the business
𝒱103- until 1936, at which time the lot was transferred
499- to the Getz Brothers and the equipment sold to
1936 John J. Raber. At this time the harness shop build-
51/ ing was thoroughly cleaned out and further remodeled as a dwelling. The Paul R. Millers, who were living in the "Mose L. house" and working for the Getz Brothers, then moved into the former place of business.

John J. Raber, born in 1909, was a son of John B. and Susan Raber, and located at the Emanuel J.
56/ Miller home, adjacent to the flour mill, at the time
52/ Troyer closed shop. Purchasing Eli's equipment, he built a new harness shop at the northwest end of town, which is part of the present Miller's Dry Goods building.
𝒱106- In 1937 the property was sold to Levi J. Raber,
376- and Johns moved to Plain City, Ohio. His brother
1937 Crist had helped in the shop a year before it was sold, then rented the building from Rabers and continued with the business. He was single and boarded at Levis at the time. Crist repaired shoes and harness along with making new harnesses. He was at Charm approximately two years, then moved his equipment to Berlin and relocated in the former Christ Hummel butcher shop. Raber is presently in his late seventies and living in Plain City, Ohio.
53/ After Raber moved out in 1939, Howard Mast
43/ of Walnut Creek put the shop back into business again with other equipment. Within a short time he moved to Ferdericktown and was engaged in harness making until his death in an automobile accident. While at Charm, Howard was making new harnesses with extra heavy traces for twenty dollars.

At the time Howard moved, his father, Ura, resumed the harness business in Charm until 1941. Ura Mast was living at Walnut Creek and came to work with his Model A Ford coupe. When Mast

The Charm Harness Shop at Miller's Dry Goods ca 1945.

sold the trade, he worked on road construction a number of years, then opened another shoe repair and harness business in Walnut Creek, which turned out to be the forerunner of nationally known Mast Leather of Walnut Creek, Ohio.

John H. Miller (son of Henry N.) had been working for Mast and would have liked to keep the shop going. He approached Malva H. Shetler, who was "batching" in town at the time, and asked him to buy the business, offering to run it for him. Malva bought the inventory in the spring of 1941. John operated the business well, so that by fall he bought the contents from Shetler. In 1942 John sold it to his brother Henry. Along with harness and shoe parts, Henry also sold fishing supplies and block ice. He was the last owner for that shop location, and had public sale for the inventory when he discontinued business in 1948.

In 1949 Christian B. Miller, who lived on the Joe Erb–Delbert Troyer property in town, built a harness shop on skids adjacent to his house. Since not all of Henry H. Miller's equipment had been sold, Crist bought it later and moved it to its new location. Crist was sixty years old at the time he started in harness and shoe work. The nearby business kept the semi-retired gentleman busy, serving the community's needs. The shop was set up on a steep bank on the land where the present harness shop is, and this original building is still used there today. The large Charm Harness Shop sign on the outside gave indication of the business, while the ash-covered driveway led to and from the Miller-owned shop.

After the death of Crist in 1967, the shop and land were sold to Joe D. Erb. Soon after this, the owner moved the skid building and did extensive excavating, taking off the high bank for better accessibility. After getting the shop back to the site, Mrs. Erb and Henry E. Mast did business in 1968.

Charm was without a saddler a number of years until Abner V. Hershberger, living two miles south

of town, opened the shop two days a week. He was employed at Belden Brick at the time, but did repair work for the communities, a much needed service. Abner was at Charm from March of 1974 to February of 1975.

Levi D. Troyer was the town's next harness maker. The retired farmer living at the east edge of Charm, and a son-in-law to Crist Miller, re-opened the shop. Levi did well as a saddler and the farmer–minister's shop is remembered as having a pleasant atmosphere and as being a favorite place to visit and share news.

With Levi's sudden death in July of 1982, the harness shop was closed a short time, until resident Roy A. Miller bought the inventory and resumed business. Roy was not a stranger to this type of work, as he had grown up in his father's harness shop in New Bedford.

Within a few years he had built a reputable shoe

Charm Harness Shop and Erb's Sports and Archery – 1991

business selling Redwing shoes, so that a small addition was put to the back side for more ample room. After the Post Office moved into the Charm Center building in July of 1988, a new two-story building was put up on the south side, adjoining the former shop. The new addition was completed in October and was first used during the Charm Days on the 7th and 8th. Since this time, more varieties of shoes and boots have been added to the ever growing inventory.

In early 1989, Charm Harness was set up as a feed supply branch of Maysville Elevator. Selling a "Kent" brand name feed, Roy was enthused, when first approached by their representative, on the quality of the products. Since he was a former feed mill worker, Miller knew what to look for. Since no feed mill is operating in town anymore, the community welcomed the feed and animal health care products which now were available in the village again. A delivery service is scheduled for every Thursday, bringing feeds to supply the area's needs.

The present shop has seen the most substantial

149/

331/

218/
76/

249/

150/

58/
19/
p.36

223/
p.128

John Burkey and family, who built the first store, ca 1882.

331/

growth of any harness shop in the town's history. Aside from being family-operated, Roy employs Mose M. Miller, a local retired farmer, to help with the work.

Store

As the crossroad of Stevenson brought people through the small country town, or as they stopped at the established places of business, it would seem evident that a merchandising retailer would be welcome along the often used route. Already by the 1870s, the blacksmith, wagon, and shoe shops were bringing their services to the community.

100/5-
16-1990

Other small towns circling the village with general stores prior to the one at Stevenson would have been: Berlin (store established 1850s); Farmerstown (store established 1855); Beck's Mills (store established 1872); Walnut Creek; along with Millersburg to the northwest, a distance of ten miles. Millersburg was the center of buying and selling for the area. As noted on *Caldwell's Atlas of Holmes Co. Ohio – 1875*, no store had yet located in Stevenson at this time.

𝒱46-
265-
1882

The first indication of a store shows up in the deed records. In May, 1882, the west ½ acre of the 1½-acre tract owned by blacksmith and wagon maker John H. Lawer and Christian Kempf was sold to John Burkey (DJH 3025) for $95.00. This lot was located across the street from today's store and restaurant and included the lands of the for-

27/
374/

❧
Storekeeper and Civil War veteran Isaac J. Miller and children (left to right): Fannie, Ida, Nettie, Anna, Franklin, Isaac, Charlie, Edward, Cora, and their dog, Major.

189/

first three years of selling them, they sold over 200 of the spring tooth harrows.

Within its first decade the store had seen great prosperity until tragedy struck in 1894. One late Saturday evening, November 24, Moses J. Keim, a 13-year-old lad, was walking home from Charm after visiting a sick friend. The kerosene lantern he was carrying dimly lit his mile-long walk northwest of town when he was suddenly stopped by strangers who wanted to know if gasoline could be purchased close by. The frightened boy told them there was none available at that time around there and continued on his way home. The stranger's disguised inquiry would soon be known as false, and the intended purpose revealed. With the sleeping town unaware of their presence, the strangers gained entrance to the blacksmith and wagon shop. At the latter they entered through a window and took a bit, two chisels, and a brace, then broke into the store building. Once inside, the burglars concentrated largely on opening the safe. With powder and squibs the door was blown off. Neighbors living close by heard the explosion around midnight, but didn't get up to investigate. The money drawer with approximately $75.00 in cash was taken, along with mittens, shirts, cuffs, collars, and pocket knives. Stamps were taken from the post office, which was housed in the same building at the time. To cover up their work, the store was set on fire before they left the building. The men, making their escape, headed northwest from town. At the edge of the village along the J. J. Yoder–Levi D. Yoder (present Eli E. Miller–John A. Miller) line fence corner, the money drawer and a chisel were discarded.

110/

*50/11-
29-1894*

*100/12-
6-1894*

Back in town the disastrous fire was discovered at 1:00 A.M. Sunday morning. Despite the efforts of a bucket brigade to extinguish the flames, the store and contents were completely destroyed. The blown-up safe which contained books, notes, in-

*50/7-
11-1974*

mer watch repair shop, hitching rail area, and Keim Lumber driveway.

The following year Burkey sold an undivided ¹/₂ interest of ¹/₁₀ acre, "being the store house and the ground on which it stands," to his brother-in-law Emanuel D. Oswald. From this information it is assumed that the first store of Stevenson was built by John Burkey in 1882. John was the father of widely known Dr. Benjamin Oscar Burkey of Baltic. In 1884 he sold the remaining ⁴/₁₀ acre to Peter H. Remington for $850.00, which apparently included the house later known as "the Keim house." Mr. Remington was associated with the merchandising business, as during the same year he is known to have been selling dry goods.

*V48-
58-1883*

*V48-
240-
1884
208/
p.92*

Peter was instrumental in establishing a post office in town. A year after assuming storekeeping duties, an office proposal was accepted by the U.S. Postal Department and he was appointed the first postmaster in town on September 4, 1886. At the time of this establishment the town was renamed Charm. There is no indication of the type or size of this first store building. The only evidence of the structure is a Charm picture of 1896 (see p. VI) which shows people standing on the remaining foundation after a fire had completely destroyed the store and contents.

In 1888 the Remingtons moved to Plevna (Howard Co.), Indiana. (His wife, Susie (Buzzard) died there in 1906.) At Charm the storekeeping was continued by Isaac J. Miller and Noah W. Hershberger. Peter made a return trip in 1891 and sold the .4-acre property to Isaac for $500.00. The Miller family then moved to Charm in November. The partnership, known as Hershberger and Miller, not only sold dry goods and groceries, but were dealers in machinery as well. They were distributors in a large territory for the Hench and Drumgold harrows, a highly reputable items. During their

*253/
100/11-
5-1891*

*100/12-
8-1892*

*100/2-
8-1892*

189/

A wooden box featuring a Noah W. Hershberger and Isaac J. Miller store advertisement.

surance policies, and other valuable papers perished in the fire as well. Once the fire had subsided, the safe was inspected; only then was it discovered that it had been tampered with and busted. Charm had been hit by robbers. The peaceful little village's only store was reduced to ashes. Its stock of goods was valued at $5,000.000 and the building at $1,000.000. The insurance coverage carried for the business amounted to $3,500.00.

Isaac Miller was postmaster. Everything from that office was gone in the disaster. Soon after the fire it was arranged that the postal service be set up in the harness shop. No clues as to the suspects or their whereabouts were known except that the Keim lad had met some suspicious-looking characters only hours before the fire. A liberal reward for the arrest of the thieves was published.

On Thanksgiving Day, November 29, the chisel and money drawer, which still contained over $400.00 in notes and a small amount of change, were found by Frank Miller and Noah J. Yoder.

50/12-6-1894 The following week arrangements were already made to rebuild a new store at the site of the old one. Isaac J. Miller would take on the merchandising himself and his nephew–partner Noah W. Hershberger would take leave from the business.

50/12-13-1894 *50/3-7-1895* Meanwhile, around Coshocton, a town 22 miles to the south, suspicion arose as a number of tramps were selling postage stamps below par, along with clothing items and cutlery. The incident was brought to the attention of Marshal Sayer who, upon further investigation, found a gang of tramps sitting listlessly around a huge bonfire, then placed five of them in custody of the town jail. After a search which revealed knives, gloves, stamps, and other articles, and a preliminary trial on December 7, sufficient evidence was obtained to hold the five prisoners. The discovery of another article—postage-due stamps—could also not be justified by the tramps, because these stamps were used only by postmasters, who attached them to mail that had been sent with insufficient postage, and never got into the hands of individuals.

100/12-6-1894 On Monday, December 10, Postal Inspectors appeared and questioned the men, then had them arraigned in Federal Court on charges of robbing a post office. Storeowner Isaac J. Miller also went to Coshocton, and identified confiscated items as the same products he was selling at Charm. Sending a card back to town, he stated he felt sure the guilty party was apprehended.

50/12-13-1894 The accused gave their names as Edward Carr, Michael Grant, James Williams, Elmer Good, and Joseph Quinn, although there was suspicion that all of these names might have been false.

❧
88 After being kept in jail at Coshocton until February, the tramp–robbers were taken to Cleveland

50/2-28-1895 for a trial, which began February 26. Store owners Isaac and Noah of Charm were present at the trial as witnesses, along with Marshal Sayer, J. E. Owens, Thomas McDermott, Jr., Harry Horn, Evan Harris, and George Galentine of Coshocton.

50/3-7-1895 An account of the unusual trial was published in the March 7, 1895 *Holmes County Farmer*.

"Charm Robbers Sentence— Two Receive a Prize of Three Years—They Talked Well, [b]ut the Evidence [w]as Against Them"

"The most peculiar case in the history of the federal court came to an end Friday. Jos[eph] Quinn, the tramp, made his last appeal to the jury, and the verdict was guilty in the case of Quinn and Mike Grant and not guilty in the cases of Elmer Good, James Williams and Edward Carr.

". . . In court they conducted their own defence and did it with ability. Quinn was at times eloquent, although he was a professional hobo and admitted it. The prisoners had nothing in common except that they were all tramps. They just happened to drift together.

"When the jury returned its verdict, Good, Williams and Carr grabbed their hats and fled. District Attorney Cook wanted to speak to Good, but the young man refused to wait a minute. He said that he proposed to get out of Cleveland quick, and keep traveling until he struck a land where the name of this town was not even known.

"Quinn and Grant were called before Judge Ricks and the judge said, 'In conducting your case you have shown that you are men of intelligence. You have used good language, have shown ability and your addresses have been more clear and concise than many arguments made by professional lawyers. It is plain that you are educated men and should have been in better business than tramping and robbing and burning post offices.' The court gave each man a sentence of three years in the penitentiary at hard labor."

100/3-4-1895 A quote in *The Budget* mentions Quinn as the "leading spirit in the novel trial, but as far as his own fate was concerned, his cleverness was in vain."

50/2-28-1895 Back at Charm preparations were made to erect a new store. The plan to build on the same site was changed and the new structure was to be built on the opposite side of the street as soon as the weather permitted. (This is where today's newly *𝒱54-571-1895* built store is located.) Fifteen hundredths-acre of land was acquired from Levi D. Yoder as a building site.

50/3-16-1895 *50/5-23-1895* By mid-March of 1895 work had actively begun. The Flinner brothers were rapidly working on the stone foundation walls, which were completed in May. It was reported . . . "that our enterprising merchant, Isaac Miller, will have at his disposal a

The new Isaac Miller store soon after it was built in 1895. The Miller children are (left to right): William, Anna, Edward, Cora, and Ida, along with their dog, Major.

model store-room in every respect. Mr. Miller is a hustler and will make things hum."

Meanwhile, a "Dissolution Notice" had ap- *100/3-* peared in local papers: "We kindly ask all persons *21-1895* indebted to us by note or book account to call and settle for same not later than March 28, 1895 as we are heavy losers on account of being burned out and having dissolved partnership, we are therefore in need of cash to make prompt settlement. Thanking you for your past patronage, we remain Yours Respectfully, Hershberger and Miller, Charm, Ohio."

The new store was completed in August and the *100/8-* merchandising business would continue at the *19-1895* small but busy location. The following year in *The Holmes County Farmer*, the town's store is noted as *50/2-* the . . . "chief and foremost of local industries for *20-1896* Mr. Miller will sell you anything from a pin to a threshing machine. His strict attention to business has brought him a large share of success and constantly increasing trade attests to the satisfaction and confidence of his customers."

He also had a good market for eggs. During May *100/5-* of 1897 Isaac sold 2,000 dozen eggs in one week. *20-1897*

To the community the store proprietor was *42/* known as "Store Isaac." Unfortunately, in Decem- *100/12-* ber of 1899, he was on the sick list, so he hired *21-1899* William Hostetler to help as clerk in the store.

(Isaac had never regained good health since hav- *100/4-* ing typhoid fever during the Civil War.) However, *8-1900* on January 28, 1900 the respected citizen and merchant died from paralysis at 57 years of age, leaving a wife, the former Mary Lint, four sons, and five daughters. He was buried at the Dunkard Cemetery near Baltic (Shutt–Burger Cemetery).

Isaac J. Miller (ML 7718) was a veteran of the Civil War. On December 9, 1861, at 19 years of age, Isaac had volunteered in Company C of the 67th *8/* Ohio Volunteer Infantry. This regiment was orga- *111/* nized in the State of Ohio, at Large, from October, *38/* 1861 to January, 1862, to serve three years. On Sep- *117/* tember 1, 1865 the 62nd Regiment Ohio Infantry was consolidated with it. According to orders from the War Department, both regiments were mustered out December 7, 1865, after the war had ended in April of that year.

A partial list of battles in which this regiment took an active part is as follows:
Blooming Gap, W. Va. – February 14, 1862
Winchester, Va. – March 23, 1862
Strasburg, Va. – March 27, 1862
Front Royal, Va. – May 30, 1862
Port Republic – June 9, 1862
Harrison's Landing, Va. – July 4, 1862
Malvern Hill, Va. – August 5, 1862
Franklin, Va. – October 5, 1862

🍂

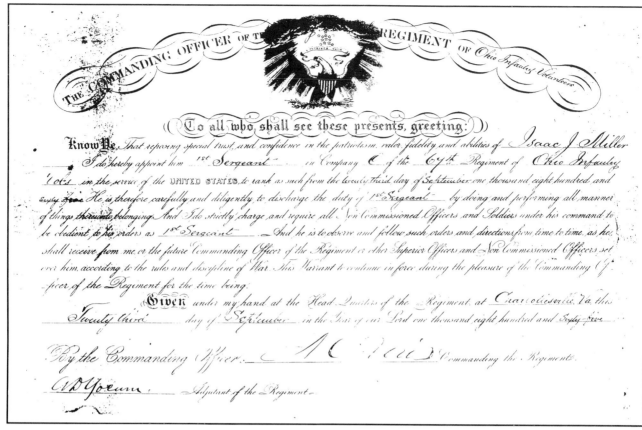

Isaac J. Miller's record of promotion to 1st Sergeant.

Isaac J. Miller's Civil War record. Commanding officers – Dates of promotion – Battles engaged in – Mustered out.

Blackwater, Va. – December 11, 12, 1862
Fort Wagner, S.C. (siege of) – July 10 to September 6, 1863
Fort Wagner, S.C. (second assault) – July 18, 1863
Fort Wagner and Grogg (capture of) – September 7, 1863
Chester Station, Va. – May 9–10, 1864
Bermuda Hundred, Va. – May 16–30, 1864
Wier Bottom Church, Va. – May 20, 1864
Howtell House – June 16, 1864
Petersburg, Va. (siege of) – June 15, 1864 to April 2, 1865
Wier Bottom Church, Va. – June 17–18, 1864
Deep Bottom Run, Va. – August 14–18, 1864
Newmarket – October 7, 1864
Darby Town Road, Va. – October 17–28, 1864
Petersburg, Va. (fall of) – April 2, 1865
Appomattox, Va. – April 8–9, 1865
Surrender of Lee's Army – April 9, 1865

Isaac entered the service at Camp Chase, in Columbus, Ohio. He was appointed Sergeant from Corporal on January 17, 1865, and a 1st Sergeant on September 23, 1865. At the fall of Petersburg, Virginia he was wounded and on December 7, 1865 mustered out with the Company at City Point, Virginia as a veteran. Two brothers, Tobias and Stephen, had enlisted ten days after Isaac and were both killed July 18, 1863 during the assault of Fort Wagner, South Carolina.

A gathering at the store porch at Charm, ca 1898. Storekeeper Isaac J. Miller and daughter are standing at the doorway.

After Isaac Miller left the military service, he came back to live in Holmes County for a year, then lived in Michigan for three years and Indiana another year before coming back to Ohio. Before coming to Charm he had been a farmer and had worked in a woolen mill.

After her husband's death, Mrs. Miller sold the store interest to Henry A. Hostetler of Berlin in early 1900 and moved to Nappanee, Indiana, where a daughter Cora resided. Moving along with grandmother Mary were: daughters, Nettie (Mrs. Frank Lehman); Fanny (Mrs. Rollie Miller); and granddaughters, Neva and Bernice Hochstetler, whose mother had died at Charm (Mrs. William Hochstetler). Later Neva was raised by the Lehmans and Bernice by Rollie Millers. Initially Cora, a former teacher at Charm, had gone to Indiana to pursue her career in music, and there married Clayton Stahly.

During 1910 Hostetler transferred the store lot to Jacob J. Hershberger (DBH 12906). Hershberger was an area native (son of Joni), raised two miles

109/

𝒱65-
414-
1900

100/5-
3-1900
27/
109/

𝒱77-
400-
1910

northeast of Charm. In 1914 he started an automobile business in Oregon and in 1963 was killed in a car accident in the western state.

William A. Mast (DJH 3885) and William Perry Miller (DJH 4476) had taken charge of the storekeeping in 1907, at which time both men moved to Charm. Mast was also appointed post-

82/
236/

223/
p.31
100/4-
4-1907

82/
236/

Storeowner Jacob J. and Melinda Hershberger in their 1911 Oldsmobile.

℘

136 /
114 /
115 /
241 /

master the following year. He was a grandson of Dr. Abraham Mast of Walnut Creek and a brother-in-law to Miller. Both were married to daughters of Albert Jaberg. The two men engaged in the business did not own the building and lot at this time. Around 1910, Mast was in partnership with Percy Gerber, who had taught school for two years at Charm. During this period Gerber was still single and was boarding at Joni J. Yoders. Within a few years Percy moved to Baltic and helped his father, Seth, in the early years of the establishment of the Gerber and Sons feed milling. At the time of his marriage in 1911, Harvey E. Oswald had been clerking at the Charm store.

100 / 11-
29-1911
𝒱80-
233-1911
𝒱80-
478-1912
8 /

Deeds indicate J. J. Hershberger sold the store to Gideon B. Helmuth in 1911, who sold it the following year to Jerry E. Schlabach.

W. A. Mast was fulfilling his storekeeping role well. As they were living on the corner lot where today's bank is located and close to the store, he could have business hours from early morning to late evening. As the first milk wagons arrived at the cheese factory in town, the store was opened. Opening his store early to satisfy their needs, he thereby was recognized as a well respected storekeeper.

16 /

Grocery supplies for the store were purchased at a Millersburg wholesaler, Smith and Shutt, located across the road from the depot. Mose L. Yoder and his sons would often take W. A. Mast's team and wagon to bring in the needed supplies. Taking the team—Rex, a white horse, and a black mare that was blind, a trip was made to Millersburg each Tuesday and Friday. With the wagon they would take a load of chickens and eggs that were then shipped by rail to markets in Cleveland. After the groceries were loaded at the wholesaler, the return ten-mile trip was made to Charm. Usually a large wooden box, containing the bread supply, was set at the back end of the wagon.

73 /
8 /

100 / 9-
14-1918

During Mast's proprietorship, natural gas lights were used in the store, supplied by local wells. In September of 1918 a Delco light plant was purchased for lighting purposes.

147 /

The Masts' only son, Harold, helped with store duties. As a young boy he left Charm for the west coast. Spending a short time there, he later lived for a year in Alaska, where he worked as a forest ranger. Returning east again, Harold attended school in Indiana before coming back to Charm and aiding his father in the store. Owning one of the first trucks in the area, he now trucked the gro-

178 /

🌰 The Charm store during the first quarter of the 1900s, probably under W. A., Mast's ownership. Chicken crates and egg cases are stacked on the porch. The butcher shop on the left housed a meat market and living quarters.

ceries to their store from Millersburg.

Two girls, Grace and Helen, completed the family.

On November 1, 1921, a Mast and Troyer of Millersburg took possession of the store and a month later it was sold to Arletus B. Miller. *100/10-20-1921* *100/12-1-1921*

The W. A. Masts sold the property in town in 1925 to Abner Schlabach and moved to Sugarcreek to operate a grocery store there. *V92-184-1925*

Meanwhile, in 1916, William Perry Miller, better known as Perry Miller, bought the Farmerstown store, then resold it in 1922 and located at Charm again, in 1923. He bought the Dr. Swarts property across the street from the store, and they, too, were close to their place of business. The same year he took on postmaster duties, and it is assumed the store transferred to him in this year, also. Around 1925 financial problems arose, and that year the store transferred to Abner Schlabach. During his youth, Perry Miller attended Wooster University and American Normal College to obtain a teacher's degree. While at Charm he began teaching at the local school ca 1926 and continued until his death. *100/5-16-1990* *116/* *98/* *50/4-?-1925* *DJH 4476*

In 1929 the Millers bought the present Atlee Schlabach property on the south side of town and built the new house. Selling again in 1935, they moved to the Tena Graefe acreage two miles west of Charm, which he had acquired in 1931 from local resident Albert J. Keim. Perry died at 59 years of age on March 4, 1937, of pneumonia. Because *V100-77-1929* *98/* *V102-427-1935* *V101-56/*

Lew Kaser, furniture maker, and storekeeper Waldo Getz.

Storekeeper Dennis Getz

of the road conditions, the long lane leading to the home was impassable for a vehicle, so the body was brought out to the road by neighbor Menno W. Troyer with a team and spring wagon. The funeral was held at the German Reformed Church at Walnut Creek and the large concourse of people overflowing the church was seated in the nearby schoolhouse, where a P.A. system was set up to transmit the sermon. From the obituary of the highly respected teacher, we quote: "As a husband and father he was kind, loving, and considerate. As a teacher he had a rare ability of inspiring his pupils and winning their confidence. He was of pleasant and jovial disposition." *60-1931* *44/* *274/* *118/*

Abner Schlabach, who had acquired the store from Perry, was the jeweler at Charm. In 1933 he sold the store lot to the Getz Brothers, Dennis, Waldo, and Reno. The brothers apparently had charge of the store some years before, as they appeared in Charm already in 1928, at which time Perry Miller had taken leave. They had acquired the house across the street, later known as "the boarding house." *V101-572-1933* *98/* *V100-31-1928*

Dennis was previously involved in merchandising, as he had owned the store at New Bedford since 1926. After a ten-year business there, he purchased the remaining interest of the store and house at Charm from his two brothers in 1936. *100/5-16-1990*

The Getz name has brought a touch of distinction to the history of Charm. Their adherence to business and their community support are still

Getz Brothers Store – 1934; Doris Miller

vividly recalled by today's older residents.

They—Dennis, Waldo, and Reno—were the sons of Ernest and Louise Getz. Dennis was married to Joyce Nadine Mullet, who died in 1963, then later he remarried to Lillian Todd. Reno's wife was Edna Engle, and Waldo had married Cora Frock. Cora was appointed postmaster in 1929, soon after locating in Charm. Waldos brought with them a nephew, Eddie Ott, who was under their guardianship. (See Biographical Sketches.) Eddie's touch of mischievousness has left a lasting impression on his former acquaintances.

The Getz ownership of the "boarding house" was unique with their merchandising business. During the 1930s, Susan M. Yoder, an Amish girl, was living in the house along with store employee Mary Yoder (Mrs. Paul Hummel) and did the cooking for the store's owners. On the days when a salesman called at the store during the noon hour, he would also be invited across the street for lunches made by Susan.

Another well known figure associated with the Getz boys was Carl Barthelmeh. During the time Dennis had the store at New Bedford, Carl was already employed there, taking care of the egg route. At Charm, the egg business was continued, with Barthelmeh's involvement. Driving a green, enclosed International truck, he would pick up eggs along the numerous routes within a large radius. He brought them to the store, where they were graded and candled, then placed in cartons for transport. The egg market at the store served

121/

9/

120/
121/

🍂

Storeowner Orie Oswald and son LaRue.

the community well. With the constant need for groceries, egg producers from the area could barter their eggs for grocery supplies. From Charm the sorted and graded eggs were again transported by "Buck" Barthelmeh and the dark green International to Pittsburgh, Pennsylvania, where they were distributed to restaurants.

75 /
268 /

Though at Charm he was known as a bachelor, "Buck" did marry Mary E. Howell during the latter years of his life. Carl was born February 3, 1909 and died February 27, 1964. He is buried at the Baltic Cemetery.

100 / 3-
5-1964

A poultry market also operated at the store during the Getz Brothers ownership. Along the west side of the building an addition had been built, within which the basement served as a holding room for poultry. Pens of hens and roosters lined the small room. Selling chickens raised on the farms or small acreages was yet another way of making a living. Jewish chicken buyers from Canton provided a ready market for the area's poultry.

171 /
56 /

These markets at the Charm store were of great importance during the Depression era. Exchanging eggs, poultry, and butter for the store necessities helped many families who were hit by the hard times of the mid-'30s.

The Getz ownership still saw the flour, sugar, and salt line of groceries coming in barrel or bulk containers. Bread was brought to the store in large wooden boxes. Outside on the front porch sat the gas pump with the glass measuring globe. (See Getz store picture, p. 94.) As the lever on the side was operated, gas was pumped up into the glass bulb, which was marked off in gallon and lesser amounts. After the needed amount was attained, a valve was opened and the globe drained with a short length of hose into the vehicle or container.

56 /

After the extended period of time that the Getz name was attached to storekeeping at Charm, the business was sold to Orie T. Oswald in 1942. Marie, daughter of Melvin B. Miller, had been employed by Getz as clerk, and continued working for Oswald at the time. The egg trade at the store was also continued by Dennis Getz and "Buck" for a number of years after the transfer. The Post Office continued to be housed in the building, and Orie eventually became postmaster in 1951. The store sold "Dannemiller" brand groceries, of Canton, until they went out of business, at which time the "Surefine" products were first introduced in Charm.

By 1952 the Charm General Store was greatly expanded by an addition onto the back side, thus increasing to almost twice the original size. About this time a change was made in storekeeping. Earlier, from behind the long counter, the clerk would

gather the needed items for the customer who came into the store. A ladder on casters was pushed along to reach the upper shelves of highly stacked groceries. The change brought along self-serve to customers, which greatly quickened sales and service during busy hours. With the expanded inventory and a larger volume of groceries being sold, the former practice became obsolete.

Aside from groceries, the store's inventory included footwear, hardware, glassware, dry goods, and health care products.

The Oswalds, Orie and Emma Oswald, who lived at Charm during most of their storekeeping years, were aided by their two children, LaRue and Eleanor. Their other hired help at the village store included Ruth Miller, Doris Miller, Lydia J. Raber, Lizzie S. Beachy, Fannie A. Troyer, Erma M. Miller, Mary E. Hershberger, Barbara A. Raber, Ada S. Erb, and Betty J. Kurtz.

During Orie's ownership he remodeled the room used by the Getz Brothers as a poultry holding pen to a freezer housing, renting out freezers to the Amish community. Orie operated the business almost thirty years, then upon retirement he sold the store to Forrest and Ivan Miller, in 1970.

𝒱175-
131-
1970

The Millers had been acquainted with storekeeping for a long time. Forrest was owner at the

322 /
9-1-
1958

Store after remodeling – 1958. Left to right: LaRue Oswald, Orie Oswald, Norman Snyder – salesman.

295 /

Charm General Store – 1970

122/

Storeowners Forrest and Margaret Miller

Miller's IGA immediately to the south, and his son Ivan was also involved with the business. Both stores were operated by them a short time, until the IGA building was remodeled as a restaurant. Ivan sold his half interest of the store to his father in 1974.

𝒱188-
406-
1974

Forrest had been a lifelong resident of the area. Born in Charm, a son of Arletus and Priscilla Miller, he married Margaret Ely; they resided most of their life a mile northwest of town along SR 557. In addition to being occupied at the store, he did general hauling and taxi service with a pickup. Earlier he had also assumed ownership of the Charm bologna business.

The Millers' eight years of proprietorship with the business was met by disaster on July 20, 1978. In the afternoon of the hot summer day, with temperatures in the nineties, a fire completely destroyed the 83-year-old store building. Since it was on a Thursday, when the store closed at noon, the daily trash was being burned behind the store in the forenoon. With grasses tinder dry, the fire had crept to a wooden coal shanty, which went up in flames and ignited the cornice on the back side of

50/7-
26-1978

295/

July 20, 1978 – the Charm Store destroyed by fire.

the store. Some smoke had been seen by town residents, but not enough to cause alarm, until it had gained headway and was out of control. The Berlin Fire Department was first notified at 2:30 P.M., and eventually seven area departments responded to the call. Fire crews felt confident that the blaze could have been contained if more water had been available when they first arrived. One supply tanker sent out broke down with transmission problems. During the course of the fire fighting, five crewmen were transported to the hospital at Millersburg, four suffering from smoke inhalation and the fifth from injuries sustained when he fell off a ladder.

Because of the large number of boxes, cartons, and flammable materials in a grocery store, it makes this type of fire hard to extinguish; flames quickly raced throughout the building. The restaurant, less than twenty feet away, was constantly kept sprayed and thereby was luckily saved from damage. After the fire, the loss was estimated at

218/

295/

The store fire from the south end of town.

145/
5-5-
1992

approximately $90,000.00. On Saturday, July 22, the town residents helped the owners salvage whatever usable items could be found—mostly dishes, tools, and boots from the basement. By this time, the stench of ruptured food was getting bad, so two weeks later the remains were burned, with the Baltic and Berlin Fire Departments guarding the blaze. The first week after the disaster, a bake sale was held in town to aid the Miller family in their loss. On August 26 the salvaged goods were sold at auction in the Keim Lumber planing mill.

The loss of the store was greatly felt by the local people. Since Miller had reached the age of retirement, he was not interested in rebuilding. At this time, local residents Edward and Lorene Raber took an interest in the sorrowful looking tract, and by fall the land was transferred to the new owners.

𝒱203-
443-
1978

Work was actively begun in October, after being delayed by insurance regulations. The new cement block building was set back farther from the road for needed front parking space. Ivan Weaver Construction was the contractor for the two-story structure. By January 10 the drywall was already being finished, and on February 12, 1979, the new Charm General Store opened. The completion was less than seven months after the former store was destroyed.

During this time, another building was added below the store, to house the freezers again. The service, known as Charm Freezer Service, houses around 85 freezers at Charm and is an expanding and highly regarded asset in the community, by now also having other locations. At the time of the fire, the freezers were undamaged and were moved into the restaurant basement until the new facility, with all new appliances, was set up.

The store's new owners were residents of Charm and presently reside a mile southeast of the village along SR 557. Edward was born at Charm and has been a familiar figure in business during the last several decades. His wife, Lorene, is a native of Nappanee, Indiana.

The newly built store opened February 12, 1979.

The small country grocery store nestled in the center of a tiny countryside village has been highly successful in satisfying the needs and wants of the community, as well as distant shoppers. The densely populated Amish area greatly benefits from their business.

The store continued to sell the "Surefine" brand foods, which had been a reputable products since Oswald introduced it in the 1950s. However, by 1989 problems had begun to arise because of the merger of the supplier, Associated Groceries, with Allied Groceries. As financial difficulties arose, the company ended up in bankruptcy court. As more and more stock was being back-ordered for the Charm store, a switch was made in October, 1989 to "Fame" brand groceries. They are distributed by Super Foods of Bellefontaine, Ohio.

The general store's added lines of sandwiches and pizza readily serves to the people stopping in for a quick meal. A specialty of the store is its hand-

249/

125/

Miller's IGA Market – 1969 (center)

dipped ice cream, which appeals to both local and out-of-town shoppers. Various cheese cuts are sold, which include the local Guggisberg-made Baby Swiss and the state champion quality Swiss cheese of Steiner's Cheese Company from Baltic.

The second grocery store at Charm was in the present Homestead Restaurant building. Part of the building had been a meat market and, with frequent customers, a small amount of groceries were stocked even as early as the 1920s. In 1950 Arletus Miller sold the butcher shop to Paul Hummel and brother-in-law Ray Mast, Jr.

The new ownership converted the former meat department and living quarters into a grocery store and eating bar. IGA brand foods were stocked at this time. The mini-restaurant consisted of a single counter and bar stools, along with a grill, french fryer, and soda fountain. The Masts, who were in charge of the business, lived in the upstairs quarters. Ray, Jr. was occupied with carpenter work, while his wife Gladys attended storekeeping. She recalls fondly the good times they experienced from the "family" ties with the people of the Charm community. Because they received and delivered many wedding orders, they were often also invited to the weddings of their Amish friends. They remember the late hours of keeping store with the idea that the young people needed a place to gather instead of being out and getting into trouble; they were often open until 11:00 P.M.

Though the well established business was prosperous, it remained in the partnership only three years. The Hummels had other commitments at their hometown of Berlin, and Ray, Jr. and Gladys, along with their two children, Rodney (5) and Cathy (4), moved to Florida. The building and inventory was sold to Forrest and Margaret Miller in 1953. They continued with the small, heavily stocked store and eating place until the building was completely remodeled as a restaurant in 1970. By this time the Millers were also owners of the

295/

169/
19/p.37
9/
96/
122/

🍂

General Store in town, along with making the well known Charm Bologna, which was discontinued shortly afterward. The former store had been known as Miller's Grocery and Market, Charm IGA Market, IGA Food Store, and Miller's IGA Market.

Jeweler

Clock and watch repair shops have long been associated with towns, villages, and communities, to which Charm can also interestingly relate to. Even the name of Charm itself has a unique connection to the jeweler's trade.

V48-542-1883

In 1883, while the small town was yet known as Stevensville, John W. Hershberger (HB 44d1) bought 1/20 acre from his father William and brother Noah for $10.00. This lot was located where the present restaurant is now. A small, gable-roofed building placed there was, undoubtedly, originally built as a jeweler's shop. The structure and its placement in the village can be seen on the old photos of the town, across the road from the first store, which burned in 1894 (see p. VI).

42/

It was long assumed that Joni J. Yoder was the town's first jeweler, but indications point otherwise, as John W. Hershberger (1851–1913) is known to have been selling clocks in the locality. One of his timepieces is still in Charm and owned today by Amanda A. Miller. The hanging wall clock had been given to her grandfather, Emanuel Troyer, in a land settlement for a misplaced line fence, during the time he operated the repair shop (See *Reflection Collection*).

19/
p.34

By 1885, when Stevensville applied for and was granted its first Post Office and was renamed Charm, Joni J. Yoder is recognized as a jeweler at that time. One account passed along as to the naming of Charm has it that at the time it was a common practice to wear quite long watch chains, to which an ornament called a "watch charm" was attached. With Joni supposedly jeweler at this time and with the name's apparent connection to his business, he is regarded as having been instrumental in the choice of the name of Charm.

V51-447-1887

Hershberger sold the 1/20-acre lot, "it being the jewelry shop and the ground on which it stands," to Joni in 1887 for $400.00. He was 24 years old and still single when he bought the lot, which was the first known tract of real estate he owned in the village. Joni J. Yoder (YR 261a8) was born in 1863 to Jacob C. and Lydia (Miller) Yoder. Throughout the community he was known by his German name of "Yune."

136/
137/

On May 15, 1888, the year after buying the real estate, he was appointed the second postmaster of the young village, and served for two years. During this time he married Elizabeth Schlabach.

With Joni unable to do heavy farm work because of poor health, he had taken up the jeweler's trade as an occupation.

100/
12-17-1891

According to a local newspaper ad appearing in 1891, it is apparent that the business was located at the Post Office, or rather, the postal service was housed in the clock and watch repair shop. Isaac J. Miller, the store owner, served as postmaster. However, by 1894 the Post Office was located in the store building when both were destroyed in the disastrous fire that year.

100/3-2-1893
100/3-9-1893

On Saturday, March 4, 1893, an auction was held to dispose of a large lot of clocks, watches, and jewelry. After the auction Yoder started up again with the repair work. A newspaper of the period stated, "We hope he will have better success." The next year he was transferring six tracts of land to various owners in the village.

Joni Yoder was the first to build a house (ca 1890) in the northwest part of Charm, locating and building a three-story structure on the present John Oren Miller property. While the Yoders lived there

50/8-16-1900

284/

The clock and watch repair shop built in 1916.

the clock and watch shop was housed in the bedroom, while their bed stood in a corner of the living room. A skillful and reputable jeweler, "Yune" furnished the community with anything in the jewelry line. Along with his main business, he sold farm gates and Superior grain drills, and made and distributed Rose Queen Salve. The small, round, red tins which sold for ten cents were well recommended for the eyes, lips, nose, nipples, chapped hands, burns, bruises, and earache, ". . . in fact for all sores."

The Yoder business came to an end in 1911 due to his failing eyesight. An ad appearing in *The Budget* on February 5, 1911 stated: "For sale: I have for sale my entire outfit of [w]atches, [c]locks, [o]ptical goods . . . and also a complete outfit of material. This is a good location for this business. I am compelled to quit on account of my eyes and will give possession April 1st. J. J. Yoder – Charm, O." Yoder sold the property to Arletus Miller in 1916 and moved to the corner lot (Mose L. house) for a short time before moving out of town.

At the time, Mrs. Yoder's nephew, Abner J. Schlabach, took interest in becoming a jeweler and learned the trade from Joni while staying at their home. Abner had grown up on his parents' farm northeast of Bunker Hill and had apparently suffered from polio in his youth. The disease left him physically handicapped.

For a few years Abner operated the jeweler's trade in the J. J. Yoder house, until the property was sold to Arletus Miller in 1916. Then Abner and the Yoders moved onto the corner lot across the street from the butcher shop that was vacated by the John Keim family, who moved to Defiance County. At that time Mose J. Keim, a young carpenter who had the sawmill and planing mill in town, sold a .12-acre lot to Abner in 1916 for $100.00. A new watch repair shop was built on the lot that year. The original building still remains

there today, though it has undergone extensive remodeling. It is presently known as "The Watchman's Cottage Bed and Breakfast."

After the Yoders moved out of town, "Ab" stayed with Joseph Millers, who moved into the same house. In 1925 he bought the property on the adjacent street corner (today's bank lot) from William and Ada Mast, then stayed in one room of the house while renting to the Sylvia Oswalds. Two years later, in 1927, Abner married Lula D. Miller, and they began housekeeping on their Charm property.

"Ab" served the community's jeweler and repair needs for 22 years. Abner was ordained to the ministry in 1930 with the Conservative Amish Mennonite Church. By 1938 the Schlabachs had moved from Charm to Bunker Hill, where they were living when Abner died, November 5, 1948.

Earlier, in 1931, soon after his ordination, "Ab" had been thinking of quitting the repair work. It so happened that word got to Raymond L. Raber, who approached Schlabach about learning the trade. Abner was glad to help him get started and during the next year and a half Raymond looked on and helped the older gentleman in the watch shop. By 1933 he was able to take on the trade by himself. With "Ab" still living nearby, he could be readily summoned in difficult situations. The

284/
171/
50/2-
20-1896
100/2-
5-1911
137/
100/2-
23-1916
233/
97/
p.130
8/
𝒱84-
118-1916
𝒱84-
304-1916
100/9-
20-1916
𝒱92-
184-1925
263/
11/6-
1-1974
139/6-
11-1978

Raymond Raber's workbench at a busy hour.

V122-
47-1949
140/
85/

Schlabachs did keep their interest in the building and grounds, and after Abner's death it was transferred to Lula, in 1949.

Raymond, a son of Levi J. and Katie Ann Raber, was born a dwarf, March 5, 1914. Living 1¹/₂ miles southeast of Charm, he would ride his large-sized pony, Bessie, back and forth to work until the family moved to Charm in 1937.

Despite his 4' 1" height, he knew and exercised his knowledge of business well. Though he never advertised, he always had people bringing in their various timepieces in need of repair or oiling. He credited achievements to honesty and to treating his customers well, quoting Ben Franklin's saying, "Honesty is the best policy."

The repair shop was always a fascinating place to enter. Its shelves were lined with all sizes and shapes of clocks and watches ticking away in merry contentment while greeting the potential customer. A wide counter and showcase in the center of the single room set off the work area along the back of the building. On the repair desk could be seen the jeweler's tools, containers of cleaning solutions, and timepieces in their various states of repair. Boxes of candy bars which lined the front of the counter attracted the attention of those who entered. Not to be forgotten was the oft-used checker board in its familiar corner. The heavily worn glass-topped game board showed well the signs of use where locals like Harry Kauffman and John B. Kurtz honed their tactics and challenged anyone coming along to a game of checkers. The shop was a well known gathering place in town, with the attention focused on the game board.

139/6-
11-1978

Raymond, better known as as "Little Raymond," specialized in repairing complicated stopwatches which were brought or sent to him from his horseman friends. He fixed over 400 of these watches in a year, in addition to handling regular work coming into the shop. Encouraged by a horseman from Sunbury, Ohio to begin working on stopwatches, he eventually had horse owners, sulky drivers, and trainers from all over the United States send their broken watches to the "Ohio Amishman, Little Raymond" to be repaired.

Aside from his business in Charm, Raber's love for the harness horse developed into horse trading. He brought great numbers of former racehorses into the Amish community. Buying from horse sales or from the race tracks themselves, he resold the standardbreds at his brother Joe's farm, 1¹/₂ miles southeast of Charm. Many horses unable to stay in racing have done well pulling a buggy throughout the countryside, which was agreeable to Raymond's philosophy, "It's nice for the standardbreds that they can still have a useful life and do somebody some good."

V178-
451-
1971

The watch shop lot was transferred from Lula Schlabach and her second husband Norman D. Beachy to Raymond in 1971. In 1979, as his health was failing, the 65-year-old Charm resident died from an apparent heart attack in his house trailer on July 18.

V212-
127-
1980
284/

After his death most of the watch and clock materials, parts, and repairing tools were sold to his niece's husband, Mose E. Barkman, who had begun a jeweler's shop in Farmerstown. In 1980 the .12-acre lot and landmark jeweler building were transferred to Raymond's brother, Joe L. Raber. The structure was vacant a few years until it was leased to Ivan J. Miller of Berlin, who set up a town game room in it.

Thus ended the era of clock and watch repairing in town, but in remembrance of its existence, the present enterprise in the building has been named "The Watchman's Cottage Bed and Breakfast."

19/
p.36

A Mose Yoder is referred to in the writings of Clarence Troyer as also having been a watch repair man at Charm. His identity and time period of business is not known.

Post Office

As can be noted with the town's beginning, so also was the origin of the post office, in that they were both established later than the surrounding towns and offices. In 1875 the residents in and around Stevenson were receiving their mail from post offices at Berlin to the north, Farmerstown to the east, and Beck's Mills to the southwest.

201/
p.29

By 1885 the people of Stevenson (Stevensville) saw a need and began making arrangements for a local post office. The First Assistant Postmaster General of the Post Office Department at Washington, D.C. was contacted for assistance. The Postmaster General, A. E. Stevenson, accordingly sent out a location paper dated November 19, 1885 to a Mr. Oswald and Mr. Remington. We assume these men were Peter Oswald and Peter H. Remington. The men, with the help of the Berlin postmaster H. L. Giaugue, completed the questionnaire, dating it December 5, 1885, and returned it to Washington.

136/

According to a copy of the location paper, no mail route was traveling through the village and the postal outlet would need to be a "special office" supplied by the Berlin office, to which the mail was being carried three times a week. Remington is listed as the proposed postmaster.

Consequently the paper indicates another interesting fact regarding the naming of the small village. As previously noted, the town had been rec-

(No. 1011—New Series—January 1, 1884.)

(LOCATION PAPER.)

Post Office Department,

OFFICE OF THE FIRST ASSISTANT P. M. GENERAL,

WASHINGTON, D. C., _Nov 19_ , 188_5_.

SIR: Before the Postmaster General decides upon the application for the establishment of a post office at _____, County of _Holmes_, State of _Ohio_, it will be necessary for you to carefully answer the subjoined questions, get a neighboring postmaster to certify to the correctness of the answers, and return the location paper to the Department, addressed to me. If the site selected for the proposed office should not be on any mail route now under contract, only a "Special Office" can be established there, to be supplied with mail from some convenient point on the nearest mail route by a special carrier, for which service a sum equal to two-thirds of the amount of the salary of the postmaster at such office will be paid.

You should inform the contractor, or person performing service for him, of this application, and require him to execute the inclosed certificate as to the practicability of supplying the proposed office with mail, and return the same to the Department.

Very respectfully,

A. E. Stevenson

First Assistant Postmaster General.

To Mr. _Oswald & Remington_

care of the Postmaster of _Berlin_, who will please forward to him.

STATEMENT.

The proposed office to be called _Stevensville   Charm_

Select a short name for the proposed office, which, when written, will not resemble the name of any other post office in the United States.

It will be situated in the _S.E._ quarter of Section _Five_, Township _Eight_ (North or South).
Range _Five_ (East or West), in the County of _Holmes_, State of _Ohio_.
It will be near route No. _2.1491_, being the route from _Millersburgh_
Baltic, on which the mail is now carried _Three_ times per week.
The contractor's name is _Underwood_
Will it be directly on this route?—Ans. _No_
If not, how far from, and on which side of it?—Ans. _4 miles south of Berlin 3 miles west of Farmerstown 4 miles_
How much will it INCREASE the travel of the mail one way each trip?—Ans. _Three miles_
Where will the mail leave the present route to supply the proposed office?—Ans. _Berlin Ohio_
Where intersect the route again?—Ans. _Walnutcreek Ohio_
What post office will be left out by this change?—Ans. _None_
If not on any route, is a "Special Office" wanted?—Ans. _Yes_ To be supplied from _Berlin Ohio_
The name of the nearest one, on the same route, is _Farmerstown Ohio_
Its distance is _three miles_ miles in a _East_ direction from the proposed office.
The name of the nearest office on the same route, on the other side, is _Berlin Ohio_
Its distance is _Four_ miles in a _North_ direction from the proposed office.
The name of the nearest office to the proposed one, not on this route, is _Becks Mills Ohio_
Its distance by the most direct road _Three_ miles in a _Western_ direction from the proposed office.
The name of the most prominent river near it is _no river near_
The name of the nearest creek is _Doughty_
The proposed office will be _____ miles from said river, on the _____ side of it, and will be _one_ miles from said nearest creek, on the _East_ side of it.
The name of the nearest railroad is _____
If on the line of or near a railroad, on which side will the office be located; how far from the track; and what is, or will be, the name of the station?—Ans. _Not near a Rail Road - Seven miles from Rail Road_
What will be the distance from the proposed site to the nearest flag station?—Ans. _____
State name of station :—_____
What will be the distance from the proposed site to the nearest station at which mail trains make regular stops?—Ans. _____
State name of station? _____
If the proposed office is located where it can be supplied from a crane or flag station, or located over 80 rods from the station where mail trains make regular stops, will the mail be carried to and from the proposed office without expense to the Department?—Ans. _____
If it be a village, state the number of inhabitants.—Ans. _About Fifty_
Also, the population to be supplied by the proposed office.—Ans. _About Five hundred_
A diagram, or sketch from a map, showing the position of the proposed new office, with neighboring river or creek, roads, and other post offices, towns, or villages near it, will be useful, and is therefore desired.
A correct map of the locality might be furnished by the county surveyor, but this must be without expense to the Post Office Department.
ALL WHICH I CERTIFY to be correct and true, according to the best of my knowledge and belief, this _Fifth_ day of _December_, 188_5_.
(To Sign full name.) _P.M. Remington_, Proposed P. M.

I CERTIFY that I have examined the foregoing statement, and that it is correct and true, to the best of my knowledge and belief.

H. L. Giauque

Postmaster at _Berlin_

Ohio

(OVER.)

ognized earlier as Stevenson and by 1879 Stevensville is known to have been in usage. The form stated: "Select a short name for the proposed office, which, when written, will not resemble the name of any other post office in the United States." Apparently a discontinued office (April 15, 1830 to July 8, 1830) of Stark County, Ohio, named Stephensville, may have prevented the name Stevensville from being accepted when the application was made. This Stark County town has disappeared, so that today no hint remains of where it had been located in the county. However, the Stevensville name was not agreed upon for the post office site and, as can easily be seen on the document, the name "Stevensville" is crossed out and "Charm" inserted beside it. This is the first time the name "Charm" appears connected to the village. Other possible origins of the name chosen are further discussed in *Names Pertaining to Charm*.

On December 10, 1885 the town's credentials were accepted by the First Assistant General; the first postmaster, Peter H. Remington, was appointed for Charm on September 4, 1886. At the time he was the storekeeper of the small town. It is not known where the first post office was housed, although quite likely Peter would have had it in his store building, which was located across the street from today's store. When the Remingtons moved to Indiana in 1888, jeweler Joni J. Yoder was appointed on May 15. It is assumed that J. J. had the office in his jeweler's shop, which formerly stood where today's restaurant is located. In 1891 it is apparent that the building contained the post office, although Yoder was no longer in charge of the mail supply. On April 4, 1890 Isaac J. Miller, who was a merchandising retailing partner with Noah W. Hershberger, assumed postal duties.

The young Charm Post Office was met by disaster in 1894. On Saturday night of November 24 the office, which was by this time housed in the store building, was burned to the ground along with the store. Tramps had gained entrance and as a cover up had set the building on fire before making the getaway. (See *Store*.) When the smoke had cleared, everything from the post office was gone. Arrangements were soon made for the harness shop to serve as the postal center.

Meanwhile, the tramps were selling some of the stolen postage stamps below the face value, which aroused suspicion and led to their arrest near Coshocton, Ohio.

Also found on their persons were postage due stamps which, since they never got into the hands of individuals, would serve as strong evidence against them.

Postal Inspectors A. R. Holmes and S. T. Hooton

208/ p.92

253/

176/ 100/12- 17-1891

136/

100/11- 29-1894 50/12- 6-1894

50/12- 13-1894 50/3- 7-1895

questioned and arraigned the five prisoners. After a preliminary hearing at Coshocton, they were taken to Federal Court at Cleveland, Ohio on charges of robbing a post office. Two of the arrested, Joseph Quinn and Michael Grant, were sentenced to three years in prison with hard labor.

When the new store was built on the west side of the road, the building again housed the town's post office.

Isaac died at Charm in January, 1900, at which time his son Edward G. was commissioned, February 28, 1900.

Henry H. Hostetler became the next store owner and thus also served as postmaster, effective April 3, 1901.

According to government records, on October 1, 1908 an order was enacted by the Postal Department that the Charm office be inactive and the mail be taken to Sugarcreek. However, within a month, William A. Mast acquired the post office title, October 26, 1908. By October 31 the mail was to have been delivered to Charm again. Mast had acquired the merchandising business the year prior to his appointment and was known as a well respected citizen in the community. He served in the position for fifteen years until his business partner, William Perry Miller, took on postal duties May 24, 1923. When Miller quit the retailer business, the duties were resumed December 27, 1929 by Mrs. Cora E. Getz. She was the wife of Waldo Getz, who, along with two brothers, purchased the store in town.

The early mail boxes at the post office were closed along the front side. A small peek-in window allowed the box holder to see if any mail was present; if there was, the postmaster was asked to hand it out. However, around 1940 these were replaced by a lock-type mailbox. With a number combination on the small door, the individual could check and get his mail any time. This sec-

100/4- 8-1900 100/5- 3-1900 136/

100/4- 4-1907

171/

249/

The Post Office, housed in the Charm Center building. Charm branch of The Commercial Bank on right.

tion of 38 boxes was used until the post office was moved from the house trailer to the new Charm Center building in 1988. During the later years of the trailer–post office, a section of portable boxes was also used to supply local needs.

On May 26, 1931 Fannie Hummel (later married to Dey Troyer) was appointed by the postal department to serve at Charm. She was also employed at the Getz Brothers Store. Ralph E. Miller was confirmed as postmaster on September 27, 1944. He was a son of Arletus Miller, and had grown up in Charm.

In 1951 Ralph bought the store at Bunker Hill, *113/* and upon taking that responsibility, he resigned his post at the Charm office. Orie Oswald, who had purchased the store from Dennis Getz in 1942, took over postmaster duties August 25, 1952.

Inside the store, the postal service unit had formerly been placed along the north wall close to the front display windows. Later it was moved to the center of the building, along the top of the steps leading to the basement.

In March of 1972 the post office was moved out *19/p.39* of the store building and into a small house trailer. The trailer had earlier been used at Troyer's Hollow and was outfitted for overnight lodging on the campground. At Charm, Orie leased the ground immediately west of the harness shop, where he set the trailer for the newly located post office.

Oswald sold the store in 1970. Upon retirement, October 12, 1974, he transferred the post to his *𝒱175-* daughter Eleanor. Eleanor Gray had been a postal *131-1970* department clerk at Charm for five years before *116/* being commissioned to full postmaster duties.

By the late 1980s, plans were being carried out to move the post office to a new location. The new Charm Building was proposed to house a new post office facility offering 1200 square feet of floor space, compared to the 220 in the trailer. After an immense amount of "red tape" connected to U.S. Postal standards had been unraveled, the plan finally became a reality for the town. On July 23, *150/* 1988 the post office moved into the new building leased to the U.S. Postal Department. The updated office now houses 294 mail boxes, which are opened with a key lock. The large, expanded mail room greatly increased mail handling capabilities, and thereby serves local demands better.

Postmaster Eleanor Gray resides a mile northwest of town along TR 154 with her husband Larry. The couple have two children, Leah LaRayne and Shane Laramie.

At present Janet Sampsel is serving as clerk at the Charm office.

Since 1995 the mail is received at Charm from Canton. Earlier it was delivered by a rural route carrier from the Millersburg office. No mail is placed on a rural route from the Charm office. The surrounding community is served entirely by Millersburg carriers, except for residents who live a mile northeast of town and have a Sugarcreek address.

During the early to mid 1900s local mail was carried by rural delivery along some improved roads. Syl Gindlesberger brought the mail to *90/* Charm with his car from the Millersburg office. At the Andy J. Miller farm on the south edge of town, he stabled his two horses and buggy, which he would hitch and complete the mail route over stretches of early, unimproved roads. The circle to the southwest of town was begun with rural delivery in the early 1950s, with Mr. Mathie as carrier at the time.

The early Sugarcreek route to the northeast was *16/* delivered by Mr. Marshall with a team and buggy. He also had another set of horses at the Andy J. Millers, which he changed off when needed.

The local people of today served by the Millersburg office were all formerly of rural route number 3 and 4, respectively. During 1991 the route numbers were eliminated and only house and road number addresses are being used.

Cheese Factory

In light of the fact that the village of Charm is located within a cheese making area, due recognition may be credited to our immigrant Swiss cheese makers. Arriving in America from a country widely known for its cheese making abilities, they settled in dairying communities to share their expertise with the readily eager farmers in need of a milk market. In relation to its origina- *179/* tors, the famous dairy products was and is yet today known as "Swiss" cheese.

Because of the mountainous area of Switzerland, some of the dairy herds were taken to the high mountain pastures during the summer months. Thus, with each individual herd of cows, a cheese maker was present. This also contributes to the many Swiss cheese makers found in the country.

Prior to their appearance in the area, the farmers were processing their milk into butter which, in turn, could be sold to a ready market or bartered for necessities at stores. *306/*
p.2-1
Charm's first cheese maker was Frederick John *162/* Nickles, who was born at Bern, Switzerland on June 19, 1858 to Johann Friederick and Catherine (Sorgen) Nikles. (Note name change.) Frederick, married to Elizabeth Schott (who was born at Kappalen, Switzerland), had taken up the trade of a carpenter. Prior to his marriage he had begun his military training at age 20. With the Swiss government's compulsory "citizen army" requiring service for an extended period of years, he sought

❧

162/

164/

Nickles cheese factory built ca 1890. From left: son Fred, Fred Grossen, and Frederick Nickles. This building was removed in the early 1930s.

to leave his home country.

225/
1900

In 1885 Fred came to America in search of a new home, and took up residence at Barrs Mill, Ohio. By October, after the birth of their third child, the mother and children, ages 4 and 2 years and 6 weeks, made the journey by boat to the new country.

50/4-
4-1901

During 1887 the Nickles family moved to Charm, where he became the town's first cheese maker.

42/

The first cheese factory was built on the Emanuel Troyer farm at the south edge of the village. The small building had a single kettle for cheese processing and was located across the road from the present Levi A. Miller farm buildings. The late Mattie (Troyer) Miller (1885–1978) recalled that during her childhood she would run across the road to the cheese house, where the cheese maker gave her a handful of curds. Hurrying home again, she would sprinkle the curds with salt and eat the delicacy.

Apparently Troyer offered to build a factory on his farm in return for the Swiss emigrant's cheese making art being brought to the community, as no real estate transfer is related to this first dairy product venture.

With the increase in milk volume and the successful cheese making business, "Fritz" Nickles purchased 1.83 acre of land from Benjamin Helmuth in 1890 and built a new cheese factory the following year which measured approximately 24'

V56-
94-1890

x 30,' along with a two-story home immediately south of the blacksmith shop (east). This is the present Abe A. Mast home and property. The cheese factory was built with an overhanging roof on the front for unloading the milk wagons. Under it, on a platform, sat a scale with a tapered milk holding tub. Placed on the wall behind the

164/

scale was a chalkboard for recording the daily milk weights brought in from the farmers. A single kettle, hung from a swinging arm on the inside, could be swung to and from the fire. Butter was also made at the factory in a large, three-foot churn.

100/3-
23-1893

Within two years the business was manufacturing four wheels of cheese per day. By 1893 the

100/3-
2-1893

farmers of the community met and organized the Charm Cheese Company, hiring Fred Nickles as their cheesemaker. Serving on the committee were Levi D. Yoder, president; Benjamin Helmuth, treasurer; and Jacob E. Mast, committee man. In the

100/4-
12-1894

same year an addition was built onto the single story structure.

162/

During the summer of 1894 John C. Geib was employed to work in the cheese house. In 1897 Fred Grossen, who had come with the Nickles family from Switzerland, was helping out at the factory. In 1900 Jacob Binder, who emigrated that year,

225/
1900

was staying in the Nickles home and was engaged in the manufacturing of cheese.

At the Nickles home the basement was built to be used as a cheese cellar. After the wheels of cheese were boxed, they were brought to the coolness of the cellar, where they were fully cured under the close attention of the cheese maker until they were sold.

130/
100/5-
9-1901
100/11-
30-1889

Cheese was processed only between spring and fall at this time. No milking was done during the winter, except for the farm family's use. The dairy herds were arranged to freshen in the spring so they could soon be on pasture, and less winter feed supplies were needed for the dry cows. Cheesing was usually begun in May and lasted until November.

Though the manufacturing of cheese provided a welcomed and much needed capital for the farmers, the payments were not on a regular basis. Since no milk was brought to the creamery until spring, even then no payment could be expected until the cheese was sold later that year. Once the sale was made to distant markets, the farmers would come in and haul the wheels of cheese by wagon to the railroad station for shipment.

100/8-
23-1894
163/

In 1894 the company sold their cheese for ten cents per pound. In the early 1900s a price of fourteen cents per pound was paid for cheese. Around that time an area farmer, Peter C. Troyer, brought in 12,496 pounds of milk.

50/3-
16-1895
50/2-
20-1896

A local newspaper referred to Mr. Nickles as "an expert cheesemaker," noting that "what he doesn't know about cheesemaking isn't worth knowing." It also regarded him "as a professional storyteller."

V64-
531-1901
162/

In the summer of 1901 Fred Nickles sold the cheese factory and home to his former helper Fred Grossen. The Nickles household, now a family of nine, moved to Mt. Eaton, where they continued in the business of cheese making. Within a few years they moved onto a farm close to West Lebanon.

In 1930 Fred died after a bout with cancer. His wife, who suffered from hardening of the arteries, had a badly infected leg in her later years. However, because of a serious heart condition, her leg was not amputated. Suffering great pain, one night she heard a distinct crack; the next morning her leg was completely severed. Fortunately, it healed nicely under the care of her family members. Elizabeth died in 1946; she and her husband are buried in the Mt. Eaton, West Lawn Cemetery.

Fred Grossen took on the cheese making at the turn of the century. During the off season of 1902 he made a return trip to his native Switzerland. Grossen sold the property to Christian A. Hummel, the blacksmith, in 1909 and took on with the cheese industry at Riceland, Ohio, known as Grossen Cheese. Fred and his Swiss born wife, Rose, had only one daughter, who was born in 1904 at Charm. The girl remained single and left no further descendants of the Grossen family.
100/12
18-1902
𝒱77
114/
1909
162/

Alfred Laubster was employed by the cheese company as the next cheese maker. *8/*

By 1911 Gottfried Dapp, also Swiss, did cheese making at Charm, and was the last to be in business at the Nickles factory site. In 1914 he bought a quarter acre of land from Andrew J. Miller, along the edge of the school ground. Dapp built a new factory here along the west side of the road on today's cheese house ground. The building also had a roof extended over the front for the wagons to drive under when unloading the milk. The unloading dock was later cemented, and that is the only remaining evidence of this former structure, which is the slab used as a driveway at the Eric Guggisberg residence.
57/
225/
1910
𝒱78-
376-1914
42/

Along the north side of the building stood a framework hoisting a whey holding tank. The farmers coming in to dump milk could then refill their cans with the cheese by-product of whey to slop the hogs on the farm. The newer, updated factory now had sufficient floor space to set five kettles, which were heated by a Russel steam boiler. *164/*

When Gottfried first came to Charm, his accent was so Swiss that it was hard for him to converse with the local people. Learning this, the blacksmith, Christ Hummel, paid him a long visit, which was greatly appreciated by the lonely newcomer, who replied, "Now I have one friend."

Cheese maker Dapp was a big and heavily built person. Reportedly, he was able to remove the newly formed cheese curds from the kettle himself. Standing on a stool, he would grip the one end of the cloth mesh in his teeth, then scoop up
8/
166/

Gottfried Dapp's initials in the original Keim Lumber building.
249/

the heavy, dripping wet cheese and take it from the heated kettle.

Gottfried was single while living at Charm, though he had made a trip to Switzerland in hopes of finding a spouse. *8/*

Dapp left Charm in 1924, selling to Otto Stockli, and moved to Angels Camp, California. He ended up buying two gold mines at an abandoned mining camp, but it turned out they filled up with water. It would have been just as costly to remove the water from the mines as to produce gold.
𝒱94-
538-
1924
179/

At Charm, Gottfried's initials, which he carved on a post inside the old Keim Lumber planing mill, are a ready reminder of his former residency in town.

Otto Stockli came to America ca 1920 from Hergiswil, Canton Luzern, Switzerland. Hoping to learn the English language, aside from his already fluent Swiss, French, and Italian, he intended to return to his native country and seek employment on the Swiss railroad. He originally came to the dairying area of Wisconsin, but was attracted to the Tuscarawas Valley of Ohio by the growing demands for Swiss cheese makers. Otto was employed by Dapp at Charm and during this time he married Anna Pauli. Thereafter he worked at the Ragersville cheese factory until he was hired as the cheese maker at Charm.
8/

Anna and her five siblings were all born in Russia. The Russian government was employing Swiss cheese makers, and the Frederick Pauli family answered to that opportunity. Thereafter, they migrated to Sugarcreek, Ohio in 1922.
359/

As with most single Swiss men employed at cheese factories, his search for a wife also ended in his finding a Swiss girl. It was the Swiss ladies who understood the role of the cheese maker in their native country. It was their commitment to hard working and often busy husbands with an
179/

unusual work schedule six or seven days a week that the young gentlemen sought. Their role usually began at 5:00 A.M., by getting a fire set for hot water or steam. By 6:00 the milk wagons could be expected to arrive, which meant five hours of cheesing, and it would be past the noon hour before the cheese was set in molds. The afternoon work included the care of previously made cheese curing in the cellars. By suppertime the evening milk arrived, and another cheesing period meant that the day's work was over around midnight. Of course, then the dutiful woman of the house could be expected to prepare a hearty meal, even during the late hours of the night.

Thus, when the Swiss Frederick Pauli family came to Sugarcreek, it was no secret that the single cheese makers of the area, including Otto Stockli, took immediate interest in the marriageable daughter of the newly arrived family. Otto's foresight of initially securing permission from the parents paid off, and he was given the Pauli daughter in marriage at the Lutheran Reformed Church at Shanesville.

*V94-
538-
1924* In October of 1924 Otto, Anna, and three-month-old Calvin Otto moved to Charm and took residence in the house vacated by Gottfried Dapp, and Otto was hired as cheese maker of the Charm Cheese Company.

The small factory along the west side of the street at the south edge of town was powered, as previously mentioned, by a Russel steam engine still mounted on wheels. The engine was located in a lean-to built on the north side of the main building. A line shaft stretched the length of the factory, from which the water, milk, and whey pumps were run with belt power. Later, in the early 1930s, a newly invented milk agitator was added to the power source. The new milk stirrers were introduced by "Whitey" Beachy of Sugar Creek, and their advancement spread rapidly among the cheese houses of the time, doing away with the hand stirring of milk heating in the kettles.

*140/
179/* Two cellars were used to store the cheese, although earlier some was still stored in the former Nickles cellar. The cold cellar (approximately 50°) was underneath the house, where the wheels were placed in brine for three days, then dipped periodically throughout the next three weeks, to start a good, healthy rind and slowly get the culture working on the inside. From there the cheese was taken to the warm cellar (approximately 72°) located under the chicken house, immediately south of the living quarters. The two buildings were not connected at this time. Here they were cured and stored until shipment. A good, slowly cultured cheese would take about six months to fully mature.

When it was time to ship the cheese, the Keim Lumber Company of Charm made large wooden boxes which held four to six 200-pound cheeses that were hauled by local farmers to railroad shipping stations. During Stockli's 9-year stay at Charm, the first cheese began to be hauled away by semi truck. It is reported that the truck stood most of the day in the middle of the small, dusty road in front of the factory, while being loaded.

Also during the Stockli proprietorship, the first milk was brought in by truck. In the early 1930s Otto bought a small stake bed truck and would pick up milk from a few farmers northeast of Charm. The rest of the milk was brought in by wagons. The farmers dumped and weighed their own milk, and recorded it on the chalkboard. Later in the day, Otto would record the weights on a ledger. Cheesing, at this time, was done from March to the first Friday in December.

Milk prices were determined, and the payments made when the cheese was sold in the fall. Ten percent of the income was paid to the cheese maker for labor and coal to heat the boiler. Another five percent was paid for upkeep and improvements to whoever owned the factory. The 85 percent balance was then paid out by the cheese company committee to the farmers; that being determined solely by the weight of the milk brought in.

It was not uncommon to find young Swiss men employed by the cheese makers and working at the cheese factories.

Earlier, American farmers sponsored the Swiss immigrants who would, in turn, work for them as cheese makers for their sponsorship, and thereby also have a job. Later, the cheese makers would help men from their home country in the same way, while having the advantage of them working in the factory for repayment.

358/ At the Charm factory, Paul and John Ramseier were hired by Otto Stockli. In the early 1920s Stockli had advertised in a Swiss newspaper for help at Charm. Apparently Otto knew of the move to the Charm factory a year earlier, as Paul came to America in 1923, while the Stockli family moved to town the following year.

The Ramseier brothers were born at Grosshochstetten, Bern, Switzerland. Before leaving his homeland, Paul had promised his mother he would be back in five years. He kept his promise and did return. However, seeing opportunities in America, he came back to the United States. John came from Switzerland to Charm in 1925, and from there went to the Doughty factory at Emanuel J. Millers, two miles west of Charm.

*26/p.95
359/* Two Schmidt brothers, Ernest and John, were also hired by Otto. Ernie had come to America in 1921. From 1930 to 1932 he worked at Charm, then

Cheese maker John Mueller and wife Nina (Hershberger) on their fiftieth anniversary.

built the Sharp Run factory, west of Berlin, and was a cheese maker for an extended number of years.

These single hired hands would board with the Stockli family. The John Schmidts lived on the property across the road from the school. This was also owned by Stockli, and had been the former Nickles built home and factory. Otto sold it to Abe P. Troyer in 1933. The old Nickles cheese house was removed from the property in the mid 1930s. *V98- 571- 1930 V100- 482- 1933*

In 1933 Otto Stockli bade the Charm community goodbye, selling the factory to the farmer-owned Charm Cheese Company for $6,000.00. He then built a cheese factory at Mohicanville, located along the south edge of Ashland County, and later built the Stockli Cheese Factory at Warsaw. *V102- 139- 1934*

From a selection of ten applicants, John Mueller was hired by the committee as the next cheese maker. John was born at Arni Biglen, Canton Bern, Switzerland. In 1927 John was helping his father make wooden farm tools in his native country, when two of his brothers were thinking of going to America. With no original intentions of leaving his homeland, he nevertheless changed his mind when one of the brothers decided to stay home. He joined his brother Ernest on his departure for the United States. *164/ 100/5- 2-1990*

In America his initial venture in cheese making began at Ed Steiner Cheese of Baltic in 1929. From there he worked at Goose Bottom Cheese, north of Walnut Creek, from 1930 to 1932, before being employed at Charm. In 1934 John married Nina Hershberger, and they resided at the present Guggisberg house at the cheese factory along the south edge of town. The couple had four children born to them at Charm: Paul, Gladys, John Jr., and Alice. *283/*

In 1938 the older cheese factory was outdated and condemned. With building materials relatively cheap a few years after the Depression, the Cheese Company bought .2 acre from the neighboring farmer and built the present factory building adjoining the house and cheese cellar.

At this time the older factory structure was moved, by dozers, a mile south of town to the present Mose L. Troyer farm, and used as a hog shed. *283/*

The milk was all brought in with wagons, except for milk on the short route northeast of Charm; this milk was gathered with Mueller's 1947 Ford truck.

John retired from cheese making at Charm in 1959, though later on he assisted other cheese makers who needed his help. The elderly couple had resided along SR 39, east of Berlin. Prior to his death, April 6, 1992, John was one of oldest cheese makers in the area. One son, Paul, has continued in the cheese business and is owner of Mueller Cheese Factory of Sugar Creek. *164/*

With Mueller's retirement, Paul and Marilyn Hershberger purchased the business, real estate, and buildings from the cheese company in 1958. Paul took over as cheese maker in January of 1959. *165/ V139- 271- 1958*

However, with the dispersal of the cheese company, a three-member farmer's committee helped adjust the milk price. Over a few months of time, after that period's cheese and cream sales were received, the committee adjusted the milk price accordingly. With 14 percent received by the cheese maker, the balance was paid out by milk test and weight, respectively. The committee consisted of John P. Troyer, treasurer; Jacob D. Yoder; and Tobe *199/*

Charm cheese factory *178/*

M. Yoder. Tobe was succeeded by Levi D. Troyer, and later Levi was succeeded by Mose M. Miller. A yearly farmers' meeting was held around New Year's, and would end with ice cream and snacks furnished by the cheese maker—truly an enjoyable occasion.

Under Hershberger's ownership, milk truck routes were established and most of the canned milk brought in by truck. By 1968 the factory was expanded and modernized. Round copper cheese kettles were replaced by a rectangular stainless vat, and more milk could be processed. The summer of 1973 was their best year, producing 1,800 pounds of cheese per day. The factory was receiving milk from 64 farmers. Hershberger's product outlet was mainly with Warsaw Randles and the Biery Cheese Company of Louisville.

19/p.38

V186-
763-
1974

During his earlier years, Paul became interested in the industry while working for cheese makers John Lengacker and Merle Ladrach. Later he did the cheese making at the Mast Cheese Factory from 1951 to 1956. He came to Charm in 1959. Paul was the first native born proprietor at the Charm enterprise; his predecessors had all been of Swiss background. Even so, when the Hershberger family moved to Sugarcreek in 1974 and sold the business to Alfred Guggisberg, it was again under a Swiss emigrant's proprietorship.

Alfred Guggisberg, owner of Guggisberg Cheese of Doughty Valley 1^1/$_2$ miles northwest of Charm, was born in Switzerland in 1914 and married Margaret Fontanive in 1945. Arriving in America in 1947, they came to the Doughty Valley of Holmes County in 1950 to begin a long and suc-

178/

Swiss cheese maker Alfred Guggisberg and son Eric working newly formed blocks of cheese.

Original factory at Guggisberg Cheese

cessful cheese making career.   *26/p.95*

The Doughty Valley factory was built by Walter Eberhard in 1946.

After the purchase of the Charm factory, their oldest son, Eric, moved onto the premises. He took on cheese making along with the help of Charm resident Andy E. Raber.

The Charm factory has only manufactured the "Swiss" brand cheese. During competition at the

Ohio State Fair, Eric Guggisberg was awarded   *166/* grand champion honors in 1985, 1987, and 1988 for the Charm made cheese.

Much remodeling was done periodically at the Charm cheese factory during the Guggisberg ownership. Their main plant in the Doughty Valley was also expanding continually. Because of the introduction of more modern techniques and equipment at the plant, the Charm factory was eventually closed in 1984 and all its milk was transported to the Guggisberg plant.

A part of the Eric Guggisberg house and living quarters was possibly an early school building at Charm, from the 1800s, known as the "little red schoolhouse". The Guggisberg family built a commodious "Guggisberg Swiss Inn," 1¹/₄ miles north of Charm, in 1993.

Recent studies have noted that Ohio annually produces some 60 million pounds of cheese, which *100/5-* is more than a quarter of the total production in   *2-1990* the United States. Holmes and Tuscarawas Counties have contributed greatly to that yield. The area has been fortunate to attract the early attention of world renowned Swiss cheese makers, who have found the fertile farming area instrumental in their production of high quality cheeses.

Cider Press

The presence of an apple cider press contributes interest to the history of Charm. During the former days of the village, the   *109*

Swiss cheese factories – compiled by Alfred Guggisberg

pressed apple juice in various forms was greatly desired.

The freshly pressed juice was a pleasing drink in its own right. Stored in a wooden barrel in the coolness of fall, the "hard cider" could easily become a "mocker," with indiscriminate use. Given enough "barrel age," the extract would turn into a much needed apple cider vinegar, used as a condiment or preservative in early home life.

As most or all farms had sizeable orchards, the farmers were dependent on its production as part of their winter supply of food. Prior to the introduction of the fruit canning method (Civil War era), great quantities of apples were stored in the coolness of the "fruit cellar," while others were dried, then preserved in tightly closed containers until needed as a food, "snitz pie," or half-moon tarts. Apples and cider yields in excess of the home's needs could be sold as a much needed cash crop.

384/

It is assumed that the cider press, which was located 100 feet south of today's restaurant, was one of the early places of business in town, although there is no known proprietor until the late 1800s. In the fall of 1891 Joel Keim assisted Miller and Yoder with cider making. By 1894, on a single day, 58 teams had brought in apples yielding 2,673 gallons of cider. A few weeks later, a record 3,333 gallons were pressed. The next year Moses J. Miller also produced a high yield. Seth Erb had the business in 1899, and purchased a new gasoline engine to run the mill. Will Kaser helped Erb throughout the cider season.

100/11-5-1891
100/8-30-1894
100/9-13-1894
50/2-20-1896
100/8-3-1899
100/8-31-1899

The small pressing building sitting along the edge of the road had an elevator extending out the front, where the incoming wagons dumped their loads of apples. Inside, the apples were chopped into pulp, then leveled on numerous stacked, cloth-bound trays, which were pressed to extract the sweet juice.

57/

By 1903 Henry Aling was running the cider press, besides cooking apple butter and jellies. The Aling family lived in the former "little red school house" located at the later built cheese factory. Henry worked in the coal mines during the off season.

100/8-9-1906
100/8-16-1906
100/9-13-1906
100/8-1-1907
100/3-1-1911
100/8-

John J. Keim bought the business in 1906 and commenced the autumn occupation of pressing apples and boiling apple butter by the middle of August. By the second week of September the mill was running day and night from Tuesday morning until 12:00 Saturday night. The following year, 1907, he built a new cider press. In 1911 the trade was owned by the Keim Brothers, who started with the sawmill occupation that year and sold the press to Mose Yoder and John Schlabach.

A 1914 notice in *The Budget* stated that Ben H. Byler would make cider and apple butter every Tuesday and Thursday during the season. The following year Joseph D. Schlabach (DBH 1811)

5-1914
100/9-1-1915
100/9-19-1917
382/
90/

of Charm published a similar notice. Schlabach was still engaged with the press as of 1917. Around the 1920s, Lewis Kaser was running the press.

The cider press building was later used as a barn and included with the Isaac Bontrager harness shop lot, or the Harry Kauffman home. From this location the press was moved and set up between the Ervin Keim and Andy E. Raber residences, along the southwest edge of town, and it was operated by Sylvia Oswald and Abner Schlabach.

8/
356/

From there it was moved a mile northwest of Charm along TR 154, where, for some time, it was run again by a bachelor known as "Hungry Joe" Schlabach, who lived at what is known today as the Levi D. Schlabach property. Later Joe married Elizabeth Mast and moved to Oklahoma. After him, David S. Miller ("Cider Davy") was operator; he lived on the former farm at the Stark Wilderness lands. In the early 1930s the Millers moved west of Wilmot along SR 250. Despite the distance, for some time afterward Davy would drive the fifteen miles to Charm to run the press.

Dan D. Keim, who lived immediately north of the store at Charm, operated the press for years, until retired farmer Jacob D. Yoder bought the interest around 1970.

Presently John B. Yoder runs the apple cider operation with the old, aging press. The complicated gearing of the structure is still in reasonable condition, but it does require the attention, skill, and maintenance of a knowledgeable operator. Yoder received ownership in the early 1980s. A few years later he erected another building along his lane, then moved the cider press to his home, half a mile northwest of town. During the fall and winter season, pressing is usually done one day a week, usually on a Wednesday.

Stable

A stable in Charm was started during the years that doctors were present in the village.

In 1891 a new wagon shop was built in the town,

Butcher shop, store, and the Charm Flour Mills in background. Dated 1912–1916.

and sometime afterward the vacated building was used as a stable. It was located at the east edge of the present harness shop property.

Livery stables at this early time were welcome sites for the horse-using traveler. They provided a place to shelter and feed the weary animals. Usually they also had their own horses, which could be used for a fee.

William Hinkle of Mt. Hope moved to Charm in April of 1896 to take charge of the stable. William was the father-in-law of the town's practicing physician, Dr. Guittard. *251/4-16-1896*

In 1906 the .03-acre lot and building were transferred from William H. Hochstetler, the blacksmith, to John J. Keim. In 1911 Keim sold the tract ("being the ground on which the wagonmaker's shop stands and now being used as a stable") to Noah W. Hershberger for $290.00. Hershberger owned the parcel until his death. It was then transferred to his heirs, in 1918. However, it is known that the building was removed from the lot by 1916. *𝒱73-162-1906* *𝒱80-280-1911* *𝒱86-413-1918*

Meat Market and Charm Bologna

Early town meat markets were common in the area. Prior to and even after their appearance, frequent butchering on the farms was done, keeping the family and neighbors in a supply of meat. This meant not only a few extra cash dollars from selling meat, but also that the amount borrowed from the neighbor when they had butchered could be returned again. According to old ledgers, borrowing was extensive when money was not readily available.

At Charm, the first indication of a butcher shop is an April 14, 1892 newspaper article stating, "Price and Yoder have put up a building last week and are getting ready to butcher." Supposedly, this was the one located on the Andy E. Raber property at the south corner of the village. It had stood close to where the house is now built. Later, Brisban Kaser is known to have been butchering here. With previous experience at Millersburg and Berlin, he was also the first to operate a meat market at Charm. *100/4-14-1892*

Deed records indicate that two lots were transferred to Brisban in 1912, specifically the barn and jewelry shop ground immediately south of the store. On these lots a new three-story building, located in the center of town, was built as a place of business, along with living quarters. A part of the main floor and upstairs was used as a home, while the north side housed the meat market, locally known as the "butcher shop." A large, glass door showcase and cooler displayed the cuts and quarters of meat. Ice stored in the lower section of the case kept the meats fresh and cool until electricity became available. *8/*

Brisban and Arabell Kaser

In the basement, meat was cut up, and here Kaser also began making the widely known Charm Bologna. The finely ground, cooked, stuffed, and smoked bologna-type meat was a well seasoned and tasty variety at the market, as well as when it was made for custom work. The custom-made bologna of Charm would long be a contending business for this type of meat. *180/*

The main structure of the building, though greatly remodeled, still stands today—the present restaurant.

In back of the building stood a small smoke shanty and an ice storage building. During the winter months, ice would be cut and stored from a small pond 1/4 mile south of town, in the upper part of the Levi A. Miller pasture bottomland, then used as needed at the meat market. *181/*

Bris was a son of Elias and Amanda Kaser, who lived a mile west of Charm on the present Robert Barkman acreage. After marrying Arabell Jaberg, the Kasers resided at Berlin. Shortly thereafter, Bris and Ora moved to Charm, where they lived at the Abe Mast home a short time, until moving into the newly built butcher shop. *180/*

Roy and Ben Conkle of Beck's Mills worked in the meat market and stayed with the Kasers at Charm. Aden Desylvia Oswald, better known as Sylvia, was also employed by Bris.

Aside from meats, the small market carried a supply of canned goods, ice cream, soft drinks, and sandwiches. The sales counter along the center was

56/

Aden DeSylvia Oswald and jeweler Abner Schlabach.

also heavily stocked with candies, tobaccos, and varieties.

Around 1929, the Kasers moved to Brisban's home place, a mile southwest of Charm (Robert Barkman property), where he continued doing custom butchering. At this time Sylvia Oswald and Arletus Miller formed a partnership, taking on the business at Charm. The Oswald family lived in the market building. Sylvia was a son of Emanuel Oswald, who lived at the east edge of Charm. Arletus, a brother-in-law to his business partner, lived a few hundred yards north, on the property they had purchased from the jeweler Joni J. Yoder

19/p.37

𝒱84-
118-1916

122/

Arletus Miller family. Front: Lee and Priscilla. Back: Gerald, Ralph, Ruth, Edward, Forrest, and Robert.

in 1916.

182/ On January 6, 1934 Sylvia was badly burned or scalded on his leg while making bologna, and had to quit the business; he moved to the Andy N. Yoder farm, five miles south of town. Here his wife Emma (Conkle) died, and he moved to Berlin. The latter part of his life, he was confined to a wheelchair with multiple sclerosis, until his death in 1948.

Arletus, or Lee, went on with the market and bologna making, with the help of his son Forrest, who at 18 years of age had just finished high school. In 1950 the building was sold to Paul Hummel, who had the meat market and store in Berlin.

96/ The main floor living quarters were now completely eliminated and remodeled into an IGA grocery store and food counter. Brother-in-law Ray Mast, Jr. lived in the upstairs and took care of the new business.

122/ In 1953 Hummel sold the store to Forrest Miller, who, in the meantime, had worked at the Willard Miller butcher shop at Berlin and had built a new house and garage a mile northwest of town. Afterward, he built a bologna factory adjacent to the
19/p.37 store, where he continued with the business until 1971. He then purchased the general store and converted the former butcher shop building into a restaurant.

267/ The local people working for Miller in bologna
171/ making in-
cluded Ada
122/ Glick, Anna
Keim, Susie
Mast, Eliza-
beth Keim,
Fannie E.
Mast, Ivan
Miller, Ella
V. Hersh-
berger,
Amanda G.
Yoder, and
Mattie H.
Schlabach.
Interest-
ingly, peo-
ple from dif-
ferent walks

Forrest Miller making the Charm Bologna.

of life have made the old butcher shop and restaurant their home. It was originally occupied by Bris Kaser. Other occupants have been: Sylvia Oswald, Jacob I. Hershberger, Forrest Miller, Ray Mast Jr., Archie Carpenter, Ivan Miller, Perry Sampsel, Abe Mast, Ken Baker, Kenny Miller, Brian Miller, Jim Blue, Mel Kurtz, Olen Mast, Willard Miller, Mose Troyer, and Darrel Miller.

A look into the butcher shop living quarters would reveal an inside stairway to the third floor and a narrow porch with a hand railing attached to the outside front. After Hummel remodeled the building, an outside stairway led to the upstairs on the south side.

At Charm, bologna making ended under Forrest Miller's ownership. However, in 1980 Eli D. Miller of Beck's Mills took interest in butchering and, with the help of Forrest, got started in bologna making. Thus the recipe for the long standard Charm bologna is still used today by Miller's Custom Butchering.

During the 1940s Melvin B. Miller, who in 1939 purchased the corner lot property of today's bank location, did butchering in the barn on the lot. He specialized in hog butchering, which was done on the second floor of the building, while the lower part was used as with holding pens. A small smoke shanty set to the north of the barn was used in smoking the hams and sausages. 171/ V108- 324- 1939

In 1949 the Melvin Millers sold their corner lot property to Oren D. Keim and moved to Berlin.

Slate Roofing

As early as 1893, Gideon B. Helmuth, born in 1871 and a Charm native, was engaged in slate roofing. Between 1896 and 1912 he had owned several lots in Charm, which included the Joe D. Erb home of today on the east edge of town, and the store lot. 100/4- 24-1893 V61- 538-1896 V80- 233-1911

During 1896 Gideon acquired the wholesale slate dealership from J. M. Hostetler of Sugarcreek. 50/2- 20-1896

More extensively used as an earlier roofing material, slate is a metamorphic rock related to shale. The hard, fine-grained rock separated easily into thin, smooth layers, which were cut to size and widely used as a roofing material. A double layer slate roof is still recognized today as one of the most substantial roofing materials ever intro-

212/p.61

Gideon B. Helmuth

duced to the area.

At one time John Burkey, a brother-in-law of Gideon, had taken partnership in the company, which was known as the Helmuth–Burkey Slate Company. 26/p.22

Gideon Helmuth later moved six miles northwest of Charm along US 62, and eventually sold the business to A. S. Wengerd Slate Company, which continued the long standing slating business. 130/

Doctors

A medical practice in Charm sounds unreal and unheard of to most people. Nevertheless, three different doctors had located in the small town.

The first indication of the practice of medicine in Charm is from historian Clarence Troyer who, in 1975, published the *History of Villages – People – Places in Eastern Holmes County*. He was still able to talk with older residents like Mose Keim, Mrs. Louise Kaser, Henry Kauffmans, and Mrs. Mattie Miller. These people recalled a Dr. Guittard and a Dr. Whitmer as having practiced medicine at one time in Charm. Troyer indicates that if the Dr. Guittard whom these residents remember formerly practiced medicine in New Bedford, he had come to America from France and learned the English language while on board the boat coming to this country. Various records show that an F. J. Guittard immigrated to America in 1847, settled at New Bedford, and established a medical practice there in 1850. 19/p.35 61/ p.702 201/ p.29

The earliest reference found of a doctor is in a Beck's Mills newsletter in the *Holmes County Farmer* of February 28, 1895. The article states: "The new doctor at Charm seems to be well pleased with his location. He is busy practicing and with good results." Numerous later newsletters refer to a Dr. Guittard, but no given name is known, until a Charm article in *The Budget* gives his name as Al. This fits precisely into the family of Francis and Lydia Guittard of New Bedford as shown on the 1870 census, which lists a nine-year-old son Alwinch. With this and later evidence, Dr. Alwinch Guittard is identified as being the first medical doctor in Charm. 50/2- 28-1895 100/10- 17-1895 100/12- 19-1895

Al Guittard, the son of the French native, was born at New Bedford, December 9, 1860. After attending local school, he enrolled at Millersburg Normal School and Oberlin College. Thereafter he began the study of medicine with his father, and took his course of lectures at the Wooster University, graduating in 1885 at 24 years of age. The same year he married Lavina, daughter of William Hinkle of Mt. Hope, and opened his first office there. After only a short stay, they moved to Killbuck, where he built up a good practice. 61/ p.702

The young, rising physician moved again and

🍃

50/2-
28-1895
50/3-
12-1896
V61-
538-1896

brought his medical profession to Charm around the beginning of 1895. Newspapers from that time indicate that he had good success while in town and was well liked by all. In early 1896 he purchased the inventory of drugs and medicines from store owner Isaac J. Miller.

Dr. Guittard most likely had his office at the home which he purchased from Gideon B. Helmuth in 1896. The residence was located at the east edge of Charm and is owned today by Joe D. Erb.

100/7-
30-1896
100/4-
22-1897

Besides practicing medicine, he took on some farming and berry growing between calls, and also sold the famous "Rose's Beauty of Beauties" potatoes.

50/4-
15-1897

Under a newly established law, Dr. Guittard was employed as "physician to the poor" of German Township for a one-year term, beginning March 1, 1897.

50/4-
15-1897
50/10-
28-1897
100/7-
3-1902
100/5-
6-1897

The early doctor's stay at Charm was short lived and by May, 1897, after a two-year period, the 36-year-old doctor moved to Arthur, Illinois to resume medical duties there. Prior to leaving, on April 27, he had a public sale to dispose of personal property at his home in Charm. By 1902 he was living at San Francisco, California. Upon his departure, he was succeeded by his father, the Dr. Francis Joseph Guittard. The elderly Guittard was 69 the year he came to Charm, and a widower.

61/
p.702
201/
p.29

Francis came from France to America in 1847. Pursuing his interest, he attended the Cleveland Medical College, from which he later graduated, then moved to New Bedford. Within the last decade before locating in Charm, he had been one of the largest practitioners in the county. He rendered his services to medicine, as well as surgery. His wife, Lydia Myers, had died eight years before his move to Charm.

Their home at New Bedford was at the west edge of the village; it is now owned by Dan D. Miller. At her death in 1889, Lydia was buried in New Bedford, at the Zion United Church of Christ cemetery, adjacent to their residence. During 1891 a cut sandstone vault was erected for them on the church ground. The wrought iron, double gate structure bears the inscription: Dr. Francis Joseph Guittard, 1828–1902 and Lydia Myers Guittard, 1836–1889.

100/7-
26-1900
50/8-
2-1900
201/p.13

The third and last medical doctor at Charm was Dr. Joel E. Whitmar. He located here on July 26, 1900. Formerly he had practiced at Mt. Hope and Millersburg.

While at the village, his office was immediately south of the new store. This building also served

50/6-
7-1979

as their dwelling. The approximately 20' x 30,' gable roofed, simple framed structure was by no means an elaborate housing for medical practice, having served earlier as a jeweler's shop and post office. But it was undoubtedly adequate for the

❧

176/

The home and office of Dr. Joel Whitmar in the former jeweler's shop beside the store.

care of the community's needs at that time.

100/3-
19-1903
50/2-
7-1907

Dr. Whitmer discontinued his practice at Charm and moved to Millersburg in the spring of 1903. He died near Millersburg, February 4, 1907, at 65 years of age. At his death the body was shipped to Cleveland for cremation, then the ashes returned for burial at Millersburg, in accordance with his will.

Joel Whitmar was born near New Bedford, January 7, 1842. He was a veteran of the Civil War. Upon returning home, he taught school and afterward read medicine at the office of Dr. Francis J. Guittard in New Bedford. Joel graduated from the Wooster University of Cleveland in 1873, practicing at Walhonding, Mt. Hope, and Millersburg before coming to Charm. Two years before his death, he had a stroke, from which he never fully recovered.

Thus ended the short span of medical practice at Charm during the turn of the century, 1895 to 1903; it was entirely related to the French emigrant, Dr. Guittard.

Implement Dealer

After the disastrous fire left the early Charm store in ashes, in 1894 its owners, Isaac J. Miller and Noah W. Hershberger, dissolved partnership. Miller proceeded to rebuild a new store in order to continue with the trade, whereas

168/
50/2-
20-1896

Noah took on dealing in farm implements. By 1896 he was already busy selling agricultural machinery. Of the implements sold, the business was a dealer in Case equipment.

V64-
142-
1899

In 1899 Hershberger purchased 3.64 acres from former physician A. M. Guittard, who had moved to Illinois. The land was situated west from the main road in Charm and extended across the creek. Here Noah built a new house and barn, which today is owned by Noah and Ervin Raber.

264/
100/7-
4-1917

At Charm, Noah was regarded as an "all-around handyman." He was born in 1854 and had been married three times. He died June 30, 1917 of a heart attack, while doing the evening milking. He was buried at the Walnut Creek Mennonite Church cemetery. However, although Noah was a member of the Mennonite congregation, he never owned a car. *100/8-1-1917 100/1-30-1918*

After the appraisal in August, the home was sold to Albert J. Keim in January, 1918. *V86-414-1918*

Photography Studio

50/1-19-1899

In 1899 Charles Miller specialized in photography, offering some of the newest and latest styles in pictures. Assistant Johnny Hershberger was helping at the Miller studio.

Sources indicate that the business was located "...two doors east of Miller's store," which would possibly have been the former house on the corner lot, where today's Keim Lumber driveway is located.

The photographer was undoubtedly a son of the store owner Isaac Miller.

Stockyard and Auction

Before the days of community livestock auctions came into existence, the farmers would sell their stock to a stockyard proprietor who had access to outside markets.

Such a yard was located at Charm for many years. Livestock ready for market was brought to the Levi D. Yoder farm at the north edge of town; the farm is presently owned by Albert N. Schrock. At the Yoder farm, the livestock was weighed and accumulated in holding pens. A local buyer, Samuel D. ("Drover Sam") Miller of Martins Creek, would buy the stock. From the yard at Charm the animals were herded on foot or hauled to Millersburg, where they were shipped by railroad to distant markets. *89/ 16/*

After the Charm Flour Mill was built in 1912, the weigh station was moved to that location where the stock pens were erected south of the building in the summer of 1916. From there "Drover Sam," along with Charm resident Will Kaser, bought livestock, which was transported to Millersburg. Later Kaser and Lee Miller trucked livestock from the accumulation yard. *100/6-7-1916 71/*

In 1932 the Farmerstown Livestock Auction was founded. Both it and the Berlin Community Auction started by "Drover Sam" in 1911 were good livestock markets, and the small town stockyard faded from the scene. *26/p.93 56/*

Some records still exist of public livestock auctions held at Charm around the turn of the century. It is assumed these sales were held at the stockyard pens.

On Wednesday, May 1, 1901, the fourth monthly sale of the Charm Stock Sale Company was held at Charm. The auction was under the management of Emanuel D. Oswald, with J. Ab Finley as auctioneer. *50/4-25-1901*

In 1913 Samuel D. Miller and Gideon B. Helmuth were conducting the Charm sales. A bill of sale for Friday, May 9 consisted of two mares in foal, four colts, twenty dairy cows, one registered Guernsey bull, one registered Jersey bull, one Holstein bull, five yearling grade Guernsey calves, and fifteen Shropshire ewes with eighteen lambs. *100/5-9-1913*

After the stockyard was closed at Charm, another market frequently used was the stockyard and the Ohio Provision at Cleveland. A local trucker, Orie Oswald, would haul hogs directly from the farm to Cleveland with a single axle stock truck for 25 cents per hwt. *113/*

Keim Lumber Co.

The Keim Lumber Co., as it is known today, seems to be in continuous growth and expansion. As a building supply center committed to meeting consumer demands, its inventory is constantly increasing.

To the village of Charm, the company has been a valuable asset, with its ready flow of customers coming to town and patronizing other businesses as well. Equally important is the convenience of having a local supplier of building materials.

Their aim of being a one-stop building center has contributed to their being one of the leading suppliers in the state. By stocking a wide variety of framing material, finishing products, and plumbing and electrical supplies, along with free delivery service within a 150-mile radius, the company has been able to achieve that aim.

Now under its third generation of ownership, the company can rightly claim this success because of its continued effort of hard work, dedication, and honesty. Bill Keim, the present owner, maintained these qualities of excellence from his father Roman and grandfather Moses J. Keim.

Originally started at Charm, Keim Lumber Co. can trace its early beginning to the first part of the present century.

Mose J. Keim, son of Joseph Keim (OAG 2750), grew up on a farm—a mile northwest of Charm—now owned by Mrs. Jonas D. J. Miller. In young adulthood he learned the carpentry and woodworking trade along with working on the water-powered sawmill at the home. He married in 1906 to Sarah Kauffman, and the couple resided on the present Stark Wilderness farm adjacent to Troyer's Hollow. *8/ 107/*

In 1908 he purchased 1³/₄ acres at Charm from Henry Hochstetler and built a house a few hundred feet north of the store; this was the initial survey of the Keim Lumber grounds of today. *V77-107-1908*

Pursuing his interests further, he set up a sawmill in 1911. The mill had been located at the north end of the old Keim Lumber planing mill of today. Within the same year, Mose joined partner- *19/p.40*

❧

8 /
107 / ship with his brother John, and together they built a two-story planing mill for surfacing and molding finish lumber. The following year, 1912, Mose and his brother Abe, who was working for the partnership, went to Massillon by train and purchased a new 25HP Russel steam engine as a power unit.

The building, part of which is still standing today, was placed immediately south of the already existing sawmill, as can be seen on various prints of early Charm. The engine was set under the extended roof to the north, and there it could run both the sawmill and inside machinery.

19 / p.40   Mose Keim, later recalling his days with the sawmill, related how the big sawdust pile had to be removed. Since the streets of Charm were still dirt, dust, and mud, he loaded the sawdust on wagons and spread a four-inch layer across the road. He remarked, ". . . mixed with the mud and made a pretty good road."

The original early milling trade was known as Keim Brothers. Despite a successful undertaking, the partnership was short lived, as in 1916 John sold his share to his brother Mose and moved to Defiance County. The John Keims lived immedi-
V84-
309-1918 ately south of the mill building, and in 1918 also deeded this property to Mose.

Soon after the partnership was dissolved, the sawmill was discontinued. Mose still kept to carpentry work, even with the lumber business at home. His local help on the crew included Andy I. Miller and Joel Beiler, both bachelors living at Charm.

At home, Mose was making furniture as early as 1909. A secretary desk ($20.00) for John H. Miller
8 /
79 / is known to have been made that year. Later, in the shop, his work included the construction of solid wooden caskets, which were made and stored on the second floor of the mill. During the early years that the mill was in operation, Mose made a child's coffin and rough box for $5.25, while a regular size was $14.00.

8 /
42 /   During the early years of business, Mose Keim saw a need for expansion at the planing mill, and planned to tear off the south end of the mill.

At the time of the renovation, Lewis Kaser lived in Charm. He had no property, but saw an opportunity to acquire a house more quickly and cheaply
V92-
77-1923 than he could build one. After Andrew J. Miller sold him a quarter acre of ground immediately south of the cheese house in 1923, he moved a portion of the old planing mill to the site. The converted house is presently owned by Amanda A. Miller. The removed portion at the mill now left ample space for a driveway on the south side, while an addition was added to the far side of the original building for the needed work and storage area.

8 /   In 1918 one of the company's first owners, John Keim, returned from Defiance County and moved

171 /

🍂
116   The original Keim Brothers planing mill with a sawmill to the rear of the building. The Joni J. Yoder house and barn in background. From left: William A. Mast, Harvey Oswald, unknown. Note the spring-fed town watering trough in center. Ca 1920.

1¹/₂ miles northwest of Charm onto the present Joe M. Miller farm. The Keim family lived there five years, then in 1923 they moved again, to the Bowman Harness Shop acreage, three miles north of Bunker Hill. Here the Keims operated a lumber supply, with both a sawmill and planing mill.

During the beginning of the Depression era, John was seeking a new location to set up a mill. When he finally secured land at the south edge of Mt. Hope, construction was soon underway.

By 1932 the Depression had left Mose Keim substantially out of work, and making a living from lumber work looked bleak. His brother John needed help and wanted to give employment to Mose, so he offered him the opportunity to set up the shop machinery. When Mose accepted the offer, he sold his Charm acreage (in 1932), including the mill and home, to his brother Albert, who lived on the east edge of town. He began with doing the concrete work for the Mt. Hope building, then set up machinery, line shafts, and steam engine. Supposedly, the last steam engine made by the Russel Company of Massillon was purchased by Keim at a reduced price of $250.00 from $1,700.00, and set up by Mose as a power unit.

𝒱100-
241-1932
107/

At Charm, Al installed a feed grinder in the planing mill, and from this initial venture later built the feed mill at the south edge of the village.

43/

After a 1¹/₂-year stay at Mt. Hope, Mose Keim again bought the Charm investment, in 1934, and moved back to town. At this time, his son Roman took an interest in the company, and the business became known as M. J. Keim and Son. Slowly they saw their trade increase and prosper after the failing years of the Depression. Plywood was first sold by the lumber company in the early 1940s. A small dry kiln was attached to the planing mill, and in 1948 the first storage shed was built behind the mill. During the growth of the business, a new flooring machine was added in 1954, for manufacturing hardwood floors. By the middle of the century, the planing mill was expanded again, with a block building enclosing the original wooden structure on the front and north sides, as is still evident today. An office and hardware store were added on the south end of the reconstructed mill by town resident John Lahm. The north side housed a complete line of woodworking equipment now run by a Cummins diesel.

𝒱102-
365-
1934
19/p.40
295/

During the 1960s, the Keim house, to the south, was being used as an office for the growing company. The first pole building was added on the rising hillside to the east in 1962, by carpenters Coy Stevens, Darryl Weiss, Gordon Guthrie, and a Mr. Hall.

By this time the company had been joined by the present owner, Bill Keim, a son of Roman, and was now known as Keim Lumber Company. With

295/

Keim Lumber ca 1920

the grandson's involvement, the Charm-based lumber company now saw its third generation of ownership, with each contributing an active part to the business.

Grandfather Mose was still able to help with milling beyond his ninety years of age. His remark, "I work, not because I have to, but because I enjoy it," displayed his character well. With keen eyesight and an outstanding ability, he still honed a keen edge to the planer knives with a flat file without removing the set from the machine's head. Or, with the use of an antique folding pocket rule, he was able to maintain exacting lumber dimensions. Physically, the gray-haired gentleman was well, as his energetic, brisk walk could easily switch to a slow jog. Humorously, Mose would credit his good health to a breakfast of "coffee soup" each morning.

19/p.39

As previously mentioned, Mose grew up northwest of town. After marriage the couple lived a short time on the Stark Wilderness farm, then built the house in Charm immediately north of the planing mill. His first wife, Sarah Kauffman, died in 1948, and he remarried to Lizzie Schlabach in 1950. She died in 1969. Roman was their only child to reach adulthood. A daughter and two sons died in infancy. On April 2, 1974, at 93 years of age, Moses Keim was working on a step ladder and fell, suffering a broken hip and rib. While at the hospital, pneumonia set in, and he died April 15.

107/

𝒟ℬℋ
12756
218/

His son Roman married Mary Beachy in 1937 and resided in the same house with his father and stepmother. A hired girl, Susie E. Mast, also lived with the Keim families, and took care of household duties along with helping in mill work.

Aside from his business at Charm, Roman took great interest in big game hunting. His hunting trips took him across the western states and into Canada and Alaska, while collecting and bringing home trophy mounts of big game animals. However, his dream of getting the grand slam of bighorn rams was never accomplished. He still needed the Desert Bighorn, which was on a very limited permit drawing. With a trophy collection of the Rocky, Dall, and Stone rams, his hopes never diminished until ill health prevented him from traveling. Among other big game animals he can claim were moose, caribou, elk, Alaskan brown bear, black bear, cougar, antelope, and deer. Besides going on the hunt itself, Roman got great satisfaction from relating his experiences afterward.

A story of one of his excursions appeared in a local newspaper as told by Roman and is entitled *My Favorite Hunt*. It reads as follows:

100/2-
11-1987

"Can you imagine the smell and taste of walleye served golden brown with your favorite potatoes? You say it would be great, well, most of us nature lovers would agree. Something even greater are the memories that trickle through my mind as I recall one of my favorite hunting trips. It was the time I went way up north in the great Yukon Territory.

"I had done my first deer hunting in 1941. It took three seasons of hunting before I shot my first buck, a nice 8 pointer. I loved to hunt and decided to take a trip to Yukon. I made all the necessary arrangements and on a bright, sunny day in August during the 1960s, I started off to do some big game hunting in the northwest corner of Canada.

"As I recall the trip, it was a great hunt and I did some of the best lake trout fishing I ever did in my life. I just have to tell you more about fishing before we start our hunt. I pulled 18 to 22-inch fish out of the lake until my arms were tired. I recall one day I went out in our boat. The fishing was so good I had the bottom of the boat covered with fish in a short time. When I got back to camp I called the cook and asked him to come and take a look at all the fish. When he saw how many I caught, he got very upset with me. He went ahead and cleaned them and we all enjoyed fish for the next several days.

"It was an August day when I left Charm and took a bus to Canton. I boarded the train and headed for my destination, Whitehorse, Yukon. After three days travel I arrived at Whitehorse.

"The Yukon Territory lies in the northwest corner of Canada. The base rests on the northern border of British Columbia, and the peak on the Arctic Ocean. Alaska lies to the west and the Northwest Territories to the east.

"On arrival I met my head guide, a tall, slender Indian, Curley Desories. He told me I would be hunting with three other people. They were all three from West Germany. Two of them were of Royal descent. They turned out to be very nice people but not too good of hunters.

"We had a long way to go before we started our hunt. Each hunter had his own private guide. There were cooks and helpers. The helpers had the tents and all the necessary gear packed for the

hunting trip. With approximately 25 pack horses we started into the wilderness of the Yukon Territory.

"The white spruce reached for an endless sky. Smaller fir and poplar trees overshadowed the fireweed, which is the beautiful territorial flower. It grows to be 3 to 6 feet high and looks like a wand. In the summer clusters of rose–purple flowers bloom along the upper stalk.

"It was very exciting as we rode our horses for three days before we set up our permanent hunting camp for a three-week hunt.

"We had a license to hunt grizzly bear, caribou, sheep and moose.

"The weather was just great. The nights were cold and during the day you could roll up your shirt sleeves. We had some rain but mainly great weather.

"I was anxious to start hunting as we reached our campsite. The helpers set up the tents and got the camp in shape. I got my .270 and .30/06 hunting rifles ready and made plans with my guide for my first hunting day. Each hunter had his private guide and left camp on horseback in different directions for their hunt. The first [two] days no one got any game.

"On the third day of the hunt I connected. We spotted a large bull moose in the distance. The guide and I worked our way to within 150 yards. Using my 30/06 I brought him down. He had a 53 inch spread and weighed over 1400 pounds.

"The guide skinned the game on the spot. We packed the hide, meat and head on our horses. We had boxes called panniers strapped to the horses to take everything back to camp. At the camp the guide caped and salted the meat.

"Our meals consisted of everything you could imagine. Bacon and eggs, fresh fish and the meat of the game we shot. I like the sheep and caribou meat the best.

"I told my guide I would like to go after grizzly bear next. With our pack horses we started into grizzly territory. We rode all day before we found a spot where there were tracks everywhere. The blueberries were luscious and very plentiful.

"We didn't have a tent, so we picked a spot in the shelter of some trees and placed our sleeping bags on the ground and slept under the stars. I had my rifle beside me all night. The next morning as my guide was cooking breakfast, I spotted a good-sized grizzly on the nearby mountain side with my field glasses.

"We ate and started after him. The cover was fairly thick and suddenly I spotted him only 20 yards away. I fired and the old grizzly shrugged his shoulder and went on. Luckily he didn't attack. I shot two more times before I knocked him down. We dressed him out, loaded him on the pack horses and headed back to camp.

"We reached camp by late evening. One of the German hunters told us how he missed a full curl ram. It was possibly one of the nicest trophies ever seen in the area.

"My guide worked hard for me and as a result I shot all of my game animals within the first two weeks.

"I had a hard time finding a large ram. One day I decided to take a Fanni, which is a cross between a Dall and a Stone sheep. Now I had my license filled and had a week to relax. You remember I told you about all those fish I caught. I used the guide's rod and reel and he only had one lure but it sure did the job.

"The hunters from West Germany did not have a successful hunt. Only one of them shot two game animals and the other two went home empty-handed.

"I had some wonderful experiences and everyone treated me great.

"It's time to head south again, so I'll see you in the 'Back Woods' another time . . . on another trip."

Bill Keim, the third generation owner, has been instrumental in the lumber company's most sig-

nificant growth during its ³/₄ century history. As a teenager in the 1960s, Bill had already taken the responsibility of placing stock orders, because of his father's ill health. Roman's extended ordeal with health problems restricted his continual attention to business, and his son's help was well needed. Bill's years of solid commitment are truly an important factor in the company's growth of today.

Bill resides along SR 93 near Baltic. His wife, Carolyn Joy (Schlabach), passed away January 13, 1993. On May 21, 1994 he remarried to Eva Slabach.

By 1973 additional office, storage, and display areas were needed. A block storage and garage building had already been added by this time. Continuing plans finally developed into an extensive excavating project, with construction of the 80' x 160' steel beam building, beginning in 1973. Early the next year the new display store, warehouse, and office areas were opened. By now the building material retailer had also become an HWI (Hardware Wholesaler Inc.) distributor. Hundreds of hardware items were now readily available, which added greatly to the company's inventory. An expanded service desk island was added, along with a large selection of Rockwell and hand tools.

The Keim Lumber Company complex situated northeast of town, which originated in the building (bottom center) along SR 557. The latest addition was the planing mill facility in the right background. 1992.

The following year the first of the newer pole buildings, measuring 70' x 200', was erected. Later another one, of identical size, was added to the north end of the earlier shed. During the next decade, more storage buildings were added to the complex.

Renovation of the store building was begun in 1987. A two-story block addition was added along the east side, again greatly increasing store, warehouse, and office areas. Committed to the lumber industry, the big structure was then clad with a wooden lap siding. As of today, the company houses one of the largest displays of Delta tools in the state. A three-register checkout was added in the newer store, aiding the customer rush during special sales and busy seasons.

Three major annual sales are held throughout the year, namely: an Anniversary Sale in May, a Charm Merchant Days Sale in October, and a year-end Inventory Sale in December. Featured in the anniversary sales, since 1985, has been a free house giveaway that includes the framing material, windows, roofing, and siding to a house of specified size. Various other prizes are also awarded by drawings. Free food is served to customers and visitors attending the special sale. For example, in 1987 during their thirteenth anniversary appreciation, over 3,000 sandwiches were handed out, which included 250 pounds of Trail Bologna and over 100 pounds of Swiss cheese, 167 gallons of hand-dipped ice cream, 160 gallons of fruit punch, 220 dozen baked goods, close to 4,000 cups of cof-

50/5-7-1987

fee, and "oodles and oodles" of popcorn. The free houses are valued in excess of $10,000.00. The lucky winners have been:

295/

1985 – Roy Yoder Builders, Butler, Ohio
1986 – Ken Tomecko, Iberia, Ohio
1987 – C. R. Cotrell, Beloit, Ohio
1988 – Forrest Taylor, Howard, Ohio
1989 – Don Fondriest, North Canton, Ohio
1990 – Perry Carpenter, Howard, Ohio
1991 – Mel Grover, Medina, Ohio
1992 – Daniel P. Fry, Millersburg, Ohio
1993 – Karen Simpson, Mt. Vernon, Ohio
1994 – Chris Hensel, Strasburg, Ohio

Referring again to the planing mill, the machinery was eventually becoming outdated, and most of the company's trim and finish lumber supply was being purchased elsewhere. By the 1980s, significant changes were being made. Newer, electrical machinery was replacing the older, belt-driven equipment. Now, with increased capabilities and multiplying milling orders, the old building was rapidly becoming overcrowded. In 1985 the company acquired a number of acres of farm land from neighbor Crist U. Miller, and by the fall of 1989 work had begun on a 150' x 150' mill building along the east edge of the tract. That winter, during Christmas vacation, the machinery was transferred to the greatly expanded facility, and operations began by the second week of January, 1990. The operation is presently run by 25 to 30 employees, and they again manufacture most of their hardwood finish lumber inventory, along

295/

Delivery service—an important asset of Keim Lumber. Owner Bill Keim on far right. Ca 1990.

with custom orders. Custom mill work is in great demand.

A year later, in 1991, another storage building was put up adjacent to the mill. In 1993 more storage was added, and the milling machinery expanded accordingly.

At present the company has over 200,000 square feet of under-roof storage; it employs around 100 workers, which include three pole building carpenter crews; its office staff consists of 16 employees. It also operates a fleet of 22 vehicles.

295/

Despite its growth and prosperity, the company has not been free of misfortune. For instance, in 1991, when a new roof was being placed, an employee, Roman A. Hershberger, 37, misstepped and fell 24 feet; he was killed instantly.

Another misfortune struck the company on the evening of January 5, 1993, when the planing mill was discovered on fire. Employee Noah L. Yoder was on his way to the mill office around 9:00 P.M. when he noticed the light from the flames inside the building.

11/1-6-1993

With the intention of being gone a few days, Yoder had wanted to arrange orders for the coming week. Making a brief stop at the company's store, he talked with Junior Miller, who was doing office work there.

When Noah arrived at the mill office on the west side of the building, the fire was already blazing in the planing mill along the south inside office wall. At this time the windows had already broken from the intense heat. After a futile attempt to reach an outside phone line in the smoke-filled office, Noah called Junior at the front office on the intercom from the adjacent storage building, instructing him to call the fire department immediately!

In the meantime, employee Ivan Miller and Sara Ann Mast heard the emergency call on the loudspeaker system from Ivan's home in town. Racing to the office building, Ivan met Junior coming out the door, and was told to unlock the driveway gates. With that, Junior gathered fire extinguishers and raced to the scene with a golf cart, which was fortunately nearby. Twenty-five extinguishers were emptied by the time the first fire trucks arrived, and the flames had been subdued to four to five feet.

Apparently, the fire had somehow started at an electric fork lift that was plugged in for overnight charging. The immedate area had many sanding belts hanging on the wall, which created a hot base from the glued product.

After the main fire was extinguished and smoke was vacuumed from the building, some truss rafters were found still smoldering. Holes were cut in the roof with chain saws to find the burning spots; the last was found at 7:00 the next morning.

Eight fire departments had responded to the call, but with the flame-retardant insulation and drywall used on the inside of the mill, the fire was greatly contained.

Cleanup was begun the next week. Though structural injury was at a minimum, the high heat and heavy smoke had done considerable damage throughout the building. Along with extensive cleaning, completely new electrical wiring was needed. Bearing replacements had to be made, and, of course, some machinery which was damaged beyond repair needed replacement.

By the middle of February, some machinery was being run again, and the mill was gradually put back in production.

Charm Flour Mills

Today the feed mills of Charm have disappeared and are replaced with a furniture and craft store. They have added the mill name to their businesses—"Ole Mill Crafts" and "Ole Mill Furniture," respectively.

During the fateful role in their history at Charm, the once prosperous places of business have been eliminated. While no grinding and mixing are being done in Charm today, the harness shop does act as a branch outlet of Maysville Elevator and sells a complete line of feeds and health care products, doing a substantial business.

The first grinding mill established in Charm was the Charm Flour Mills, established in 1912. Presently this three-story building is being used as a plumbing shop, craft shop, and an apartment.

In order to understand why the mill was built at Charm, a look into the history of earlier area milling would be helpful.

Gristmills in the days of our pioneer forefathers were primarily run by water power. There is found in the writings of historian George Newton, of 1889, that an Abraham Gerber (GB1a) of Walnut Creek township had the first "corn cracker" in the settlement. This was run by oxen on a treadmill. As stated, the chief power source was water. Since the gristmill was a year-round business, a sizeable stream was needed to furnish the water power even in dry seasons. In this locality, or even in the whole southeast part of Holmes County, the only stream to offer this amount of water was the Doughty Creek. Flowing from Berlin through Clark enroute to the Killbuck Creek, this, naturally, is where the mills appeared. The farthest upstream was known as the Wise Grist Mill, a mile northwest of Charm between SR 557 and TR 335.

68/p.83

26/p.20

A short distance below the Wise location, at the head of the Doughty Glens, Peter Nowels built a mill around 1820. The gears and millstones for this

❧

mill were to have been made by Jacob Korns, who was a blacksmith at Berlin. After a short proprietorship, Nowels sold the quarter section (Sec. 1 Twp. 8 R. 6) on which this mill was located to
308/ Jonathan Miller in 1825. Miller was taxed for this land the following year.

309/ Early mills in Holmes County were taxed and
1834 Miller is listed as paying taxes for a grist mill on the 1834 records. This mill was of importance to
70/5- the young pioneering community; in 1825, when
1825 Holmes County was organized and commissioners began to lay out roads, the second of the first four roads to be petitioned for was to extend to "... the Jonathan Miller mill on the Doughty fork of the Killbuck." This is the route of today's SR 557 from its beginning two miles southeast of Farmerstown to the Mrs. Jonas D. J. Miller farm a mile northwest of Charm. (See *Roads*.) By 1837 the grist mill was operated along with a sawmill. Probably because of the flourishing establishment of the later Wise grist mill, a short distance upstream, the Miller grist mill, in due time, was closed down. However, the sawmill continued in operation until the early part of the twentieth century. (See *Sawmilling*.)

50/2- One mile west of Charm, in the Doughty Glens,
14-1924 Isaac Aultman built a grist mill in the 1830s, soon
19/ after settling in the hollow which came to be
p.154 known as Aultman's Hollow. (See *Troyer's Hollow of the Doughty*.) A mile farther downstream, Benjamin Beck erected a mill in 1864, and installed the Aultman grist mill equipment, each using the renewable source of water power. Benjamin also established businesses that would carry on his name, that of Beck's Mills.

201/p.29 Concerning the earlier mentioned Wise Mill, in
𝒱4- 1834 Peter Wise settled on Lot #16, Berlin Town-
166-1837 ship, two miles northwest of Charm along the
213/ stream of the Upper Doughty Valley. This tract of
p.35 land was a part of the school lands set aside by
309/ the federal government for the maintenance of public schools in the Connecticut Western Reserve of northeastern Ohio. These lands were originally leased for seven to fifteen years, and the lessee was required to improve the property by clearing, fencing, and planting 100 apple trees.

By an act of the state legislature, along with Congressional and local consent, the school land was offered for sale in 1831. In 1837 Peter Wise bought from the state of Ohio Lot #16, on which was located the Wise homestead (the Andy M. Yoder farm today), a short distance south of their namesake, the "Wise School."

Peter, along with his family, who were Virginians, in due time built a sawmill (taxed for sawmill, 1839) and woolen mill along the Doughty stream.

Peter has also been regarded as having built the Wise Grist Mill; however, conflicting evidence would indicate otherwise. A 1932 Holmes County
108/ history, by W. S. Hanna, states, "Moses Nowels
p.133 built the Wise mill in 1822." This may indicate his placement of a dam across the creek at the location of interest and his setting up of a sawmill, as by 1834 the only mill taxed here was a sawmill owned by George Myers.

In 1837 Myers bought Lot #21 from H. Rice, the
𝒱4- State of Ohio's agent for school lands. This con-
426- sists of the Merle Miller, Eli Mullet, Dan N. Yoder,
1837 and Guggisberg Cheese acreages today. In 1839
309/ George is taxed for both a sawmill and a grist mill,
321/ with this lot the only one of five which he owned
p.12 that the Doughty stream passed over. From a family history we also note: "The flour and grist mill on the Doughty Creek, which was known formerly as the Wises Mills, was built by a Mr. Myers many years ago ..."

𝒱13- In 1847 George Myers sold 214 acres, of Lot #17
598- and #21, which included the mill grounds, to John
1847 and Bazalel Maxwell. Two years later Bazalel as-
𝒱15- sumed sole ownership. Maxwell then sold 130
131-1849 acres of Lot #21 to Peter Wise in 1858, with men-
𝒱23- tion on the deed of "... reserving and excepting
252- (forever) privileges to back the water on said pre-
1858 mises on the south side to the distance of 41 perches (north) from the south line to a mark on a rock on the bottom of the creek (Douty's fork)."
22/p.23 This was a water right for the "Jonathan Miller" mill, immediately downstream. In due time the "Wise Grist Mill," a sawmill and woolen mill at the homestead, and the "Jonathan Miller" sawmill were all operated by the Wise family. A son, Hiram, apparently operated these lower two mills for some time.

320/p.64 Jefferson Varns had possession of the milling
𝒱46- trade, ca 1880, with Peter Wise, and for some time
213-1882 employed Pete Weidner as miller. Jefferson, a step-
350/p.6 son to Peter, was later a farmer at Beck's Mills.

In 1882 the mill acreage was transferred from Wise and Varns to Jeremiah Miller, whose father Joni Miller and grandfather Jonathan had operated the mills at the head of the glens. Jeremiah moved to Indiana in 1874, then returned to Ohio four years later. At the mill, William Loudenslager operated the business, and in the meantime Jeremiah erected the house and barn on the farm along SR 557.

104/ The mill was a three-story building with a rope on the outside to hoist barrels of grain to the top floor. The milling machinery was a four-foot Burr for grinding feed and a four-foot Burr and one Reel for grinding and bolting the flour. When the equipment was remodeled a few years after the Miller purchase, a roller system was added. Simon Syler

71/

Smoldering remains of the Wise Grist Mill. The steam boiler is in the foreground and the large water wheel is seen on the right.

helped run the mill a short time until Jeremiah took care of the whole operation.

Earlier, mill stones were used in the grinding process, but by now they had been replaced with more modern machinery. In order to supply the community with their grinding needs, Miller often had to run the mill day and night. During dry seasons when the water supply was low, a steam engine, and later a diesel, were used for power. A dam wall spanned the creek from its east bank to the raised opposite side, where a culvert headed the mill race. The water wheel was the largest of its kind along the Doughty—eight feet high and twelve feet wide, newly placed in July of 1902. The wall along the width of the creek was a wooden structure of posts, braces, and planks. The posts were set in square holes mortised into the solid rock creek bed. After placing the posts and braces in a triangular form, planks were then nailed on the upstream side to hold the water. With occasional high water and flooding, the dam would break. However, with this wooden construction, the wall could be replaced more easily than if stones and dirt had been used to build the dam.

100/7-10-1902

307/
p.30

During the 1800s a Jeremiah Miller and his brother-in-law Shem Miller took a contract to build a stone wall for the dam, and twice the partly built wall was washed out by high water, so that finally a wooden frame was used again. Remains of this water project are still visible today.

321/
p.13

A heavily bound, two-inch-thick ledger records the mill activity of Jeremiah. The earliest entries are of April, 1894, twelve years after the Upper Doughty purchase. In it he records 534 different customers until 1911. His business was highly patronized, as he supplied the flour, corn meal, stock feed, oils, seeds, and "Pratts" brand feeds to the community. Aside from these, he also made a breakfast cereal, "Jerry's Creamo."

133/
97/
p.236

People coming to the mill would often trade for items of need, as cash was not always readily available. Trades mentioned in the account ledger include lumber, labor, cider making, bull dog, hogs, clover hulling, fish, posts, and pills.

Jeremiah, better known as "Meel Yammie," used "The Doughty Roller Mill" as a business name, although it was still widely known as the Wise Grist Mill.

133/

Letterhead of J. J. Miller.

Apparently Miller turned over the milling trade to his son-in-law Daniel J. Mast in 1911, followed by a deed transfer in April of 1912. The Mast proprietorship at the Doughty was shortlived, as on Saturday afternoon, July 6, 1912, tragedy struck when the old landmark caught fire and was completely destroyed. Supposedly, the fire was caused by spontaneous combustion. The day was an unusually hot summer day. Circulating reports indicate that the sun shining through an upstairs window pane might have ignited the dust accumulation. From Charm the fire was first noticed by the high column of black smoke which ascended to a great height on the wind-free day and was seen for miles.

V 81-48-1912
50/7-11-1912

8/
16/

The community was now without a nearby mill. The vital importance of a feed mill to the farming population influenced Levi D. Yoder to offer a small parcel of his farm land as a site for a new building. In the same year, 1912, he sold 1.45 acre of land, at the northwest corner of Charm, to Daniel Mast for $290.00. The new construction was soon underway by foreman Joe Keim. His help included Al Keim, John Keim, Harry Kauffman, and John Erb.

V81-46-1912

It has been said that the logs to provide the lumber were cut close to Farmerstown and hauled to

75/

167/

71/

The newly built Charm Flour Mills. The main structure bore a close resemblance to the Wise Grist Mill.

Charm with eight or ten teams. At the steep hill two miles east of town, three extra teams helped the log wagons up the muddy grade.

With commendable progress, the new grist mill at Charm took shape. A cut sandstone foundation was placed for the wooden structure. The Keim Brothers sawmill in town provided a ready supply of dimensional lumber. Six months after the fire had destroyed the former mill along the Doughty, its proprietor, D. J. Mast, was ready to

100/12-
11-1912 begin with flour and grist milling, the second week of December, 1912.

57/ The three-story mill bore a close resemblance to its forerunner, except the new one had a roof extending over the driveway on the south side. The mill was furnished with needed equipment, including a "Little Midget Maid Flour Mill."

79/11-
13-1912 The initial power was furnished by steam. In 1919 Mast installed two new diesel engines, a 30
100/2- hp. to do grinding and an 11 hp. to run the flour
10-1919 mill.

The newly established grist mill was now ready for a progressive future during the next sixty years.
99/ Mast was already shipping loads of sacked flour to Millersburg, delivering it with team and wagon.

Within a short time, the Daniel J. Masts built a new house and barn on the lot in Charm. This is,

today, the Miller's Dry Goods property, adjacent to the former grist mill building.

As a remembrance of their former mill along the
149/ Doughty, the Masts brought along a cut sandstone and placed it as a landing for the front porch steps. The stone is still in place today, bearing the holes where a diesel engine had been bolted, along with a cut groove for oil drainage.

V89-
477-1920 In 1920 the Daniel J. Masts sold the mill to nephew Jeremiah E. Miller and moved to Orrville
V93- soon thereafter. Later, in 1922, Jeremiah sold one-
51-1922 half undivided interest to Arletus Miller, who lived
99/ across the street. "Lee" had been employed by
100/4- Mast when the family moved to Charm in 1916.
12-1916 In 1924 the mill was sold to Jeremiah's father,
V93- Emanuel J. Miller, who was a brother of Mrs. Dan
389-1924 Mast.

The Emanuel J. Millers, better known as "Meel Monys," had a long history of milling experience.
101/ Brought up at the Doughty mill, they had oper-
55/ ated mills at Benton, Sugarcreek, and Trail before coming to Charm. They moved to Charm in November of 1923 and did a remarkable business. During their years at Charm, the mill at Sugarcreek was dismantled and some of the equipment brought to the Charm mill.

Deliveries were made with team and wagon, and neighbor Lee Miller also made delivery runs with his truck. Most of the Charm-made "Flavo
85/ Flour" was sold locally and at nearby towns.
75/ During the daytime the flour would be ground, and by evening the storage bin needed to be emptied, which at times meant sacking flour late into the night. The bags were all weighed individually, which made for a time-consuming job. "Mony" employed some local boys to help get all the flour
168/ sacked on the same day.
56/ During Miller's ownership, he installed a 55 hp.
148/ slow speed Buckeye diesel. The single cylinder engine was set at 325 rpms, with a 12-inch bore and 5-foot flywheel. To get the huge engine started, compressed air was forced into the cylinder. The large flywheel had timing marks, and when they came to position, a valve was opened manually to force the air into the cylinder head, thereby get-

189/

☙

ting the needed rpms to start the engine.

Aside from grinding operations, they sold *101/* "Purina" brand feeds.

By 1934 reports were circulating that "Meel Mony" would consider selling the flour mill. This *56/* news eventually reached the attention of Fannie *𝒱102-* Troyer, who was working at the Getz Brothers' *339-1934* store at Charm. Hearing this, she immediately called her husband Dey, who was working for his uncle at Bolivar. The same evening, he stopped at Charm to see Emanuel about buying the mill. Within a short time, details were taken care of and the Charm Flour Mill was transferred to Dey Troyer in 1934.

During the years of the Troyer ownership, the Charm enterprise experienced its greatest flour sales. Their major customers included Nickles Bakery, Norman's Bakery, McLane Groceries, and McGowen Brothers Wholesale. Aside from these *148/* sales, a weekly route was taken through the area towns. Orders were compiled one day and deliveries made the next. Local resident Orie Oswald did a lot of these delivery runs with his small truck.

A whole wheat cereal, "Midget Maid Cremo," was also made at the Flour Mill.

At this time the feed mill was also selling Master Mix Feeds; Dey Troyer at Charm was the first *56/* to have this brand of feed shipped into Holmes County when a carload arrived at Millersburg in 1936 or 1937. Dey had a building in Millersburg where carload shipments could be stored and then distributed from there. Most of the trucking was *105/* done by their own fleet of trucks, which included *148/* a tractor-trailer rig and a $2^1/_2$-ton truck, both Reos.

Dey also sold field tile and the Finzer building block at the Charm location.

Jonas Kauffman, who had been working for Emanuel J. Miller, continued to work for Dey at the mill, and was soon joined by his brother Mose. Others employed by Troyer were Gerald Mast, Wayne Spielman, Edward Miller, Glen Lorentz, Joe L. Raber, Adrian Scheetz, Andy Mast, and Roman A. Raber.

The Gerald Masts moved to Charm soon after being married in 1941, while he worked at the mill. *103/* Around 1945, Dey placed Gerald at the New Bedford mill, which he also owned, to take on duties there.

The long history of flour milling came to an *56/* abrupt end in 1947. Government regulations required that only stainless steel equipment be used in manufacturing flour. Troyer was not interested in making this major change, and therefore the production of the highly regarded Charm-made flour was discontinued.

In 1950 Dey chose to operate the New Bedford *𝒱123-* Feed Mill himself, and accordingly sold the Charm *331-1950*

business to Jacob A. Miller and Noah A. Raber.

Jake and Noah continued selling the Master Mix *168/* feed, and in 1956 sold the business to Carl, Wayne, *102/* and Merle Weinman of Wooster, who also owned the feed mill at Mt. Hope at the time. During this ownership, five different kinds of feed were offered: Master Mix, Honeggers, Murpheys, Larro, and Bart's Mix. The latter was made from a formula obtained at Michigan. The feed formula was blended together at Charm and sold as Bart's Mix.

During the Weinman proprietorship, the "Charm Flour Mills" was renamed to "Charm Feed Mill."

Delbert Harmon of Charm was working for Miller and Raber, and also continued to work for *𝒱145-* the Weinmans until he and Eli M. Miller eventu- *32-1961* ally bought the feed mill in 1961. Three of the feeds were soon discontinued, while Master Mix and Honeggers brands were still sold. Delbert, who owned a small truck, made pickups and deliveries at area farms for their feed and grinding needs. The steady hum of the mill engine was a familiar sound throughout town as the necessary business continued.

By 1969 Eli was preparing to move to Indiana *𝒱172-* to his wife's home community, and Delbert wanted *95-1969* to step down from the strain of management. At this time the mill was transferred to Oren D. and his son, Daniel O. Keim. The Keims had been in the feed milling trade for an extended period of time, as Oren also owned the mill on the south side of town known as the Keim Feed Mill.

After three years of business at the former flour mill, the Keims sold the acreage and building to *𝒱181-* Ed Raber and Abe A. Mast in 1972. After this trans- *337-1972* fer, the milling equipment was removed from the structure, which was then sold at a public auction held on the grounds.

The last engine used to run the mill was a 6–71 *168/* GM diesel. This motor was installed in 1954 by Raber and Miller after the misfortune of a cracked

328/ *p.22*

Charm Feed Mill – 1964

🐝

head on the well known, slow speed Buckeye.

Since the mill had now ceased to operate, it was converted into an auction barn, where Charm Auctions were periodically held over the next few years.

Funeral Directors and
Casket and Tombstone Makers

Within the Amish community, the interment of their deceased is still being carried out independently. With the exception of legal matters and a mortician's care, the viewing and burial are arranged by the church members and neighbors.

The funeral directors and casket makers have charge over a designated area within the community. This capacity is usually fulfilled until the appointed person is no longer able to perform that duty, in which case another person is appointed.

79/1912 In the Charm area the position is currently filled by Joe D. Yoder and Mose M. Yoder, both of Farmerstown. Earlier, during the first quarter of the century, the Keim Brothers at Charm made the wooden caskets. Within this period and also later,
191/ Seth M. Erb of Charm and Noah J. Raber, who lived two miles southeast of town, attended to funeral responsibilities.

During the flu epidemic of 1918 to 1920, when many people died, Raber was making caskets and had to make numerous ones at night and even on Sunday in order to have them ready when needed. Noah was succeeded by John F. Raber, a cabinet maker at Farmerstown. From Raber, it was passed on to Joe D. Yoder of that area in 1981.

197/ Succeeding Erb at Charm was Levi J. M. Miller
76/ (1887–1971), who was involved with casket making. From him, Crist B. Miller of Charm became director, and thereafter (ca1963) Crist G. Yoder of Beck's Mills made caskets and served as director. From Yoder, the caretaker position passed to Monroe L. Yoder of Farmerstown. After Monroe's sudden death in 1988, his son Mose continued the practice, along with the elderly Joe D. Yoder, who, since 1984, constructs the caskets at his home workshop.

At Charm, white sand and mortar tombstones were made for quite a number of years. Mose L. Yoder, who came to Charm from Kansas in 1907, made the cast grave markers until the mid 1900s. After Yoder, they were made by Charm resident Harry Kauffman during his retirement years, until his death in 1974. Thereafter, Tobias M. Yoder, a retired farmer living at the north edge of town, continued with the work into the early 1980s. Since then, the Charm-made markers have been replaced mainly with the longer lasting marble stones. However, the third generation marker

making was continued briefly by Levi T. Yoder of Troyer Valley.

Fur and Wool Buyers

8/
V91-
356-
1922
Amos Helmuth was a well known fur buyer during the first quarter of the present century. He lived in the former Joel Beiler house immediately east of the present harness shop which he acquired in 1922.

Amos was killed in a single car accident on US 62, a mile east of Millersburg, on January 3, 1923.

Harry Kauffman, living at the former wagon shop and Isaac Bontrager harness shop (1944–1974), bought wool at his residence in Charm. The fleece was purchased by the pound, and he weighed and stored it in his small barn on the property that had earlier been the cider press building.

Harry died in 1974 at 83 years of age.

Kaser Furniture Shop

42/
169/
50/
3-?-
1920
Lewis Kaser is remembered by older residents of today as a furniture maker in early Charm. The older couple, Lewis and Lydia Kaser, moved onto the former Fred Nickles property in 1920. Not owning a property in town, Mr. Kaser took the opportunity to make use of the south part of the old Keim Lumber planing mill,
V92-
77-1923 when remodeling was done there. Securing a quarter acre of ground from Andrew J. Miller at the south edge of Charm in 1923, he moved the mill building to the lot. After remodeling, the dwelling was used as a home and workshop by the Kasers. The north end of the small building was used as a workshop for furniture making.

V109-
487-
1940
Lewis Kaser died November 23, 1929 and was buried at the New Bedford, Lutheran Reformed Cemetery.

V109-
591-
1940
384/
p.15
At the time of the estate settlement in 1940, the lot was transferred to his son Victor, who had also been living there. Victor was a well driller. The same year that Vic acquired the property, he resold it to neighboring farmer Andrew J. Miller.

V. J. Kaser and Co. Well Drilling

90/ Victor Kaser was known in the area as a water well driller. He lived in the remodeled part of the old Keim Lumber planing mill which his parents, Lewis and Lydia Kaser, had moved ca 1923, immediately south of the cheese factory. After his father's death in 1929, Vic and his wife Myrtle moved into the Charm residence with his widowed mother.

In well drilling, Kaser had some form of partnership with Abe P. Troyer. Together the men also sold and serviced Aermotor wind operated pumps.

From Charm, Vic moved to Holmesville, where he was living in 1940 at the time of the estate settlement, and the small lot on the south edge of town was sold to Andrew J. Miller. After the move, Kaser continued drilling water wells in the area.

V109-
487-
1940

In remembering Vic Kaser, the well driller, the livelihood of his stepson, Russel Donley, is often recalled. Russel had enrolled at Charm School in 1930.

Troyer's Windmill Sales

Windmill pumps have long been used in the area, and are still a common sight throughout the community. From almost any panoramic view of the countryside, a number of these towered wheels may be seen readily turning to the command of wind currents.

94/

David J. Troyer, living a mile east of Charm, is presently a dealer with the Aermotor Windmill Company. The century old company was established in 1888, when it introduced the first all steel windmill made in America. With efficiency tests of up to 87% greater than the wooden wheel of the time period, the Aermotor mills gained fast popularity across the world.

Locally, the wind pump was already sold in the 1930s by Victor Kaser and Abe P. Troyer. Vic lived at Charm and was a water well driller. He had a dealer partnership with Troyer, and they sold, set up, and serviced the Aermotor mills. When Kaser left town ca 1940, Abe continued in the sales with the help of his brother John. After Abe's death in 1952, the brother assumed sole responsibility of the dealership. The Troyer farmer then sold and serviced the pumps until 1978, when the business transferred to a son, David, who is now engaged in the sales. Today, along with the help of his sons, the business is a third generation involvement.

Troyer specializes in 8-foot and 10-foot diameter wheel mills which are capable of pumping a 300-foot well. Earlier, a 20-foot wheel was made; however, a 16-foot is the largest available today. Towers commonly range in height from 20 feet to 40 feet. The tallest tower placed in service by the Troyers was 107 feet high.

Throughout a forty-mile area, he annually services around 300 windmills, which operate on low maintenance and upkeep.

Threshing

Charm is located in a fertile farming community, where most of the hay and grain needed on the farm are cultivated and raised on farms consisting of 80 or over 100 acres. During the 1800s and up into the middle 1900s, the fall harvesting of grains would bring visiting threshing machines to the farm. These were powered by steam engines and later with gasoline or diesel tractors and were clumsy pieces of machinery to be taken over hilly country roads, let alone the earlier unimproved roads they also had to travel.

The rigs were often owned by a party of two or three people. Some parties had a few threshing outfits that were dispatched in separate courses throughout the area.

The threshers attending to these machines had demanding responsibilities—maneuvering and keeping the rig in running order. Such examples of expertise may be noted by the fact that these early steam engine–threshing machine combinations were crossing down the steep grades of Troyer's Hollow, across the Doughty Creek and up the equally steep opposite slope. Often, along with threshing, the proprietor also did clover hulling, sawmilling, and picket milling with his power unit.

108/
p.131

Prior to the advancement of threshing machines, much more of the hard harvesting labor was done by hand. The ripened fields of grain were cut manually with a scythe and neatly tied in sheaves for drying. Once cured, the grain was beaten from the straw with sticks or a flail, or was tramped out by horses or cattle. After the straw was shaken with wooden forks for separating, the grains were placed on large pieces of cloth and tossed into the air to blow the chaff away, a process known as winnowing.

Around 1835, the first "bob tailed thresher" was used in the county. The cylinder beating the straw from the grain was run by oxen or horse power, but then had to be separated by hand. Within a few years, windmills were introduced that blew out the straw and chaff. Not long afterward, threshing machines were built which had a cylinder and separator that would now thresh, separate, and clean the grain, making it ready for the mill or market.

On the farm during harvest time, the dry, unthreshed grains were formerly brought into the barn and stacked until the threshing parties appeared. Early barns did not have the attached straw sheds—these began to appear at the turn of the century—so the grain was hauled back outside and threshed where the straw stack would be placed.

Stacking the straw on a neat, well-balanced stack was an art in itself. The work was often done in a sense of competition. The hard labor involved could easily be a futile attempt if the stack happened to topple over.

168/

One such incident is related, where the farmer on top of the stack hollered down, "How does it look?" The helper down below returned a shout,

❧

"Just as straight as an egg . . . oops, there it goes," while, much to their displeasure, the stack toppled down.

When the later sheds were built onto the farm barns, the threshing was done inside the barn and the straw was blown into the inside straw storage area.

Because of the wide range of territory that had to be covered, the rigs were kept busy late into the fall or even early winter.

A list compiled of known threshers operating within a two-mile radius of Charm indicates the following:

208 /

	1860	John Kneb – Eli Klinetschmidt
100 / 11-	1861	David Beachy – David Miller
12-1891	1862	Beck – Steve Mullet
100 / 12-	1863	Steve Mullet – J. Raber – A. Farver
17-1891	1864	Jonas Stutzman
388 /	1867	Peter Hershberger – Christian Gingerich
100 / 6-	1868	Zook – Porr – Mullet
28-1894	1869	Mike and Daniel Erb – Daniel Oswald
50 / 2-		
20-1896	1870	Mike Levengood – Ed Lawer
100 / 6-	1871	Jacob Schlabach – Tobias Kuhns
20-1901	1872	John Frey – D. Miller – Jonathan Miller
100 / 6-		
12-1902	1873	D. D. Miller – Jonathan Miller – J. Frey
100 / 8-		
2-1906	1874	D. D. Miller – Jonathan Miller – Bendict Miller
	1875	Mike Levengood
	1876	John Miller – Jacob Schlabach
	1877	Brenly – Kerstetler – Kaser – Eli Schlabach – Chris Yoder – Peter Berkman
	1878	Wilhelm Deetz
	1879	Christian Farmwald
	1880	Kaser – Christian Farmwald
	1881 to 1889	Bill Deetz
	1891	Miller – Joel Keim
	[1894	Joel Keim sold half interest of his threshing outfit to Joni M. Hershberger and hired Jonas D. Miller and Noah Schlabach to assist them]
	1896	Joel Keim
	1901	Peter Erb – Miller – Flinner
	1902	Miller – Flinner [they purchased a new traction engine]
	1906	Peter Erb

The Erb involvement in threshing, clover hulling, and picket milling was a long-time family occupation. The Erbs grew up two miles south-

207 /
p.147

west of Charm and were involved in four generations of threshing, from Millersburg to Baltic. As noted, brothers Daniel and Mike were already threshing in 1869. When Daniel moved to Oregon

≈

178 /

Early threshing rig

in 1899, the younger brother, Mike, continued in the business, passing it to his sons and grandsons and the earlier mentioned son-in-law, Joel Keim. Sons Peter and David were local threshers from the turn of the century until around the 1930s, whereas David's son Joe was involved in threshing from 1944 until the 1960s. Another of Mike's grandsons, John V. Erb, was also a thresher in the area, as was his son Valentine, thus accounting for four generations of Erb threshers.

100 / 6-
14-1910

Other threshers owning or operating the local threshing rigs during the early to mid 1900s were

169 /
192 /

Mast Brothers, Russel Shenemen, Ben C. Miller, Emanuel J. Yoder, Jacob D. Yoder, Levi Keim, Perry S. Miller, and Al Keim.

Steam engines were a common sight at Charm. Perry S. would park his Russel engine behind the blacksmith shop during the 1920s when the Millers lived at the present Abe Mast property.

Al Keim, also of Charm, had steam engines engaged in threshing and sawmilling, and for a short time powered his feed mill with one. When the Keim family lived on the farm at the east edge of town, it was a common sight to see his engines and tractors parked in a neat row along the bank of a creek that flowed through his pasture. Ear-

100 / 11-
12-1891

lier, in the fall of 1891, Joel Keim had built a roundhouse to store the engines. Joel lived a mile north-west of Charm on the present John S. Miller farm.

81 /
170 /

During the early 1930s, steam engines were disappearing fast, and numerous ones were driven on the fateful journey to Baltic, where they were loaded onto railroad cars as junk. The first tractor to replace the cumbersome steam engine in the area was a Rummley Oil Pull owned by thresher Peter Erb.

After the earlier mentioned Perry S. Miller moved from the Charm area to the farm two miles east toward Farmerstown in the 1930s, he still remained active with threshing. Miller was involved

185 /

with a partnership that included John Schlabach, Jonas A. Troyer, Mose Mast, and John Shetler.

193 /

In 1932 Al Keim sold a threshing rig to John J. Yoder, who was also in sawmill partnership, with

This 16 HP Russel steam engine was one of two purchased by Perry S. Miller in 1927 when the Russel company of Massillon went out of business. The engine was used in Miller's threshing operation. Later, when it became outdated, it was junked. Ray Conn, a John Deere dealer of Wooster, happened to come by just as the governor was beginning to be knocked to pieces with a sledgehammer, as it sat in a Coshocton junkyard. Recognizing the engine as one like his own, he quickly halted the destruction and purchased the rusting steamer. Later, Conn sold it to Allen Weidman, who restored it to its original condition; it is now owned by Allen's son Carl, of Wooster. Years after the Miller ownership, sons Perry and Sam found a receipt of their father's purchase of the engine, and luckily found this restored steamer on display by Weidman at the Dover Power Show, with the corresponding serial number, 17145.

Jonas D. Troyer and Abe P. Troyer. This rig ownership later consisted of Abe P. and John's brother, Abe J. Yoder, who took on threshing when John continued with sawmilling. Both Troyer and Yoder lived at Charm. Later, they sold the rigs, which consisted of four threshing machines, silo fillers, corn huskers, and tractors, to Noah A. Raber and Joe D. Erb. Noah bought Troyer's share in 1942, and Joe bought Yoder's share in 1944. *168/*
129/

With the four machines going in different directions, they did around 100 jobs per season. Their hired help operating rigs included Levi J. Troyer, Henry A. Mast, and Valentine J. Erb.

At the beginning of the Raber–Erb partnership in the early 1940s, most of the farmers were leaving the shocked grain in the fields until the rig arrived for threshing. Earlier, the grain was brought into the barn or stacked on a large stack on the outside, and there awaited the arrival of the threshing machine. This later practice resulted in a higher quality grain and straw, even though the previous custom had been considered a must in grain farming.

In 1947 Noah and Joe built a storage shed a half mile southeast of Charm, along SR 557, to house the numerous pieces of equipment. Their threshing partnership continued until 1950, when Raber took share in the feed mill at Charm. *𝒱121-*
596-
1948

By this time, neighboring farmers were securing their own rigs. This reduced the number of jobs required per outfit and resulted in an earlier finish for the threshing season.

At the time of Noah and Joe's dissolving of partnership, the equipment was divided between the two, then sold off. The threshing machines consisted of two Keck Gonnermans, one Huber, and one John Deere. A local farmer, Levi D. Troyer, bought a Keck Gonnerman from Raber and continued working one of the threshing rings a few miles south of Charm. This was probably one of the last large community rings operated in the area. *168/*

Clover Hulling

Along with grain farming, the propagation of clover was previously practiced throughout the area. After the clover was cut and dried, the hay was run through the clover huller to extract the tiny seeds, which could be sold to a ready market. Hulling was an occupation that went with threshing, and a business could be made traveling from farm to farm rendering such service.

The Erb family from the area were long contenders in the hulling of clover. In 1895 Michael Erb and sons produced 800 bushels of seeds, and the following year totaled over 850. The season lasted from August until late fall.

During such an engagement in 1902, David M. Erb frequently did some squirrel hunting in the early morning, until the dew had lifted and the clover was dry enough to hull. On the Saturday morning of August 31, Dave had gone to the woods, and while climbing through a fence, he accidentally discharged the gun, which severed his left thumb. The wound was dressed with the help of Dr. Whitmer of Charm.

In the spring of 1906, he again badly cut the same hand while working on a picket mill.

100/11-
26-1896

8/

100/9-
4-1902

Sawmilling

Within the Charm area, farming and sawmilling have provided steady means of employment since the early days of the pioneer forefathers. Sawmills have been an important asset to the community. In the pioneering period, their existence was largely welcomed for the initial building needs throughout a settlement.

Chief means of power for the mills originated with water power, and have advanced thereafter by the use of steam, gasoline, diesel, and electric. Steam powered sawmills and gristmills were first set up in the county by 1858.

108/
p.133

The first sawmills to appear in the immediate area, run by water power, were built along the Doughty Creek. Pioneer Michael Beck settled at Beck's Mills in Mechanic Township in 1822. A few years after coming to the valley, he built a dam across the creek and erected a sawmill as his first business venture. Incidentally, the small town was later named after him because of his flourishing enterprises of milling and merchandising along the Doughty. (See *Troyer's Hollow of the Doughty*.)

22/
p.30

A mile upstream from the Becks, Isaac Aultman was also establishing places of business in the narrow confines of the Doughty Glens in the 1830s. The settlement was 1 1/2 miles west of Charm, and also included a sawmill, along with a gristmill and woolen mill.

50/2-
14-1924

Farther upstream, at the head of the Doughty Glens, Peter Nowels erected a gristmill, around

❧

130

1820. Within a few years, Jonathan Miller was operating this mill, and by 1837 was also being taxed for a sawmill. The mill was located on the west bank of the stream and north of present TR 123 on the Jonas D. J. Miller farm. Historians differ in their views of early proprietorship of this sawmill. The most widely accepted view is that it was originally built by Peter Wise, a prominent land and business owner of the 1800s. However, local records reveal a different point of view: 1. The gears and mill stones for the Peter Nowels mill were made by Jacob Korns, a blacksmith of Berlin; 2. Jonathan Miller was deeded this quarter section of land (Sec. 1 Twp. 8 R. 6) from Peter Nowels in January, 1825; 3. By May, when a new road was reviewed by the commissioners of Holmes County, it was to extend to ". . . Jonathan Miller's mill on [Doughty's] Fork of the Killbuck." (See *Roads*); 4. A Holmes County history written by W. S. Hanna in 1932 states that Jonathan Miller erected a mill in 1825. (This contradicts the No. 1 statement. However, the brief Nowels involvement could easily have been forgotten); 5. Peter Wise settled in 1834; 6. Jonathan Miller was taxed for a gristmill in 1834 and for a grist and sawmill in 1837. Thus credit appears due to Miller for operating the early sawmill at this location. During the pioneering period, it was not unusual to find a gristmill and sawmill being operated at one location, as is evident here.

26/
p.20
V5-
377-
1825
70/
5-1825

108/
p.133
201/
p.29
309/

The recognized sawmill builder Jonathan Miller (ML 613) was born in Somerset County, Pennsylvania. His father was the widely known Christian (Schmidt) Miller, who, a blacksmith by trade, was undoubtedly instrumental in the son's mechanical ability. Another son, Daniel, also had a mill in the Charm vicinity—an oil extracting mill.

Jonathan married Magdalena Kauffman, and they arrived at the Holmes County settlement in 1819 with their family of seven children, originally settling on the present Jacob A. Hershberger farm (Lot #21), 1 1/2 miles southeast of Berlin.

320/p.3
V TR-
62-1819

The mentioned sawmill was later owned by a son, Joni, who sold it to Peter Wise in 1865 and moved to Indiana two years later along with his aged and widowed father. Jonathan died that fall and is buried in Indiana. Peter's son, Hiram, in turn operated the mill, which was later transferred to Daniel J. Miller, who owned it by 1875. Daniel, known as "John Dannie," still operated the sawmill at the turn of the century. The mill had a vertical jigsaw-type blade, and sawing was a slow process. Locally, it has been said that he had a cot at the mill to take a nap while making a cut on a log. Later in life, Daniel moved to Geauga County. The last proprietor of this mill was the Joseph Keim family. This water wheel setup was one of the numerous dams washed out during the flood of 1911. At the time, the mill was also washed downstream,

V27-
369-
1865
22/
p.33

142/
8/
50/9-
21-1911

Early steam powered sawmill

and part of the building came to rest on top of a nearby bridge. Today a level spot and some indication of a dam wall along the creek bank are the only reminders of the once prominent place of business.

A short distance upstream, across Mechanic Township's northern border in Lot #21 of Berlin Township, Moses Nowels built a mill in 1822. In 1835 George Myers was being taxed for a sawmill at this location, which was between SR 557 and TR 335, a short distance south of today's Guggisberg Cheese. This is where the later known Wise Grist Mill had stood. Within the next quarter mile, Peter Wise, formerly of Virginia, set up another sawmill soon after settling in the valley in 1834. The Wise mill was two miles northwest of Charm on the farm now owned by Andy M. Yoder. Peter also later built, at this location, a woolen mill, which was operated until his death in 1900.

Two and a half miles east of Charm, in Sec. 2 Twp. 8 R. 5, John Christner was being taxed for a sawmill in 1839. This was along the Walnut Creek on the Dan M. Miller or Aden R. Miller farms of today.

From such early water driven sawmills, the milling needs were supplied for a young and developing settlement until the introduction of steam power. As noted, in 1858 the first steam sawmills

108 /
p.133
309 /

22 /
p.33
201 /

309 /

108 /
p.133

were being set up in the county. Interestingly, on an 1861 atlas, one such mill is shown as located to the south of TR 167 on today's Enos D. Raber farm, which is two miles east of Charm.

An important aspect with steam engines coming into use was the fact that the sawmills could now be moved to where they were needed on the farms. It is evident that by this time sawmilling and threshing went hand in hand, as during the off threshing season, the steam engines (or later, tractors) could be applied to the milling trade.

Locally, during the early 1900s, the Hostetler Brothers, along with Hershberger and Oswald, were engaged in custom sawing. In 1911 at Charm, the Keim Brothers set up a sawmill across from the road, and 500 feet north of the store. The employment of a sawmill in town by the brothers, Mose and John, marked the beginning of today's widely operated Keim Lumber Company. Undoubtedly the brothers had been involved with their father's water-powered sawmill which was washed out the same year they set up the mill at Charm.

100 / 12-
19-1901
100 / 5-
3-1906
19 / p.40

Yoder Lumber Company Inc.

As previously mentioned, the sawmilling industry is still evident today, as two well established businesses are located within our area of interest—Yoder Lumber Company Inc. and Raber Lumber Company. Both companies are locally owned, with the ownerships presently extended to the second generations.

193/ The Yoder company originated ca 1932 when John J. Yoder (OAG 3014) took up the sawmilling trade with partners Abe P. Troyer and Jonas D. Troyer. At the time they were also local threshers.

𝒱103- John had grown up three miles south of Charm.
408-1936 In 1936, shortly after marriage, he bought the prop-
𝒱107- erty immediately east of the harness shop in town.
353-1938 John and his wife Lizzie resided here until 1938.
𝒱108- Selling their half interest to his brother Crist, they
324-1939 bought the Melvin B. Miller farm one mile east of Charm. The Millers then bought the Abner Schlabach property in town, where the bank is today.

193/ By 1937 John and Crist were in business to-
171/ gether. As noted, he bought the farm in 1938, and
279/ at that time sold the mill to Atlee D. Schlabach.

After a few years on the farm, John again became involved in sawmilling. In 1944 he bought
176/ woods from neighboring farmer Albert N. Raber and began sawing in partnership with John P. Troyer. Shortly thereafter, Yoder resumed full responsibilities at the mill. At this time sawing was done in between the farm work, and was done mostly during fall and winter.

193/ In 1947 Crist again joined his brother John in
145/2- the sawmilling venture, which they operated by
26-1991 going from farm to farm, cutting and sawing marketable timber. Acquiring a vendor's license in that year also, the company was beginning to buy more of their own timber, rather than doing only custom sawing. Quality grade lumber and veneer logs were sought from premium trees, while secondary material was cut up for railroad ties, bridge beams, building material, and blocking.

In 1954 the partnership was dissolved and John continued the trade, while Crist resumed farming on the earlier purchased Snell farm at the SR 557–US 62 intersection.

During the next year or two (1955–1956), John brought the mill home to the farm and made a permanent setup in his pasture field along CR 70. He had, by this time, hired about six employees. Two of them, John O. Miller and Roy J. Miller, operated the saw and log carriage.

198/ In 1962 the first pallets were made in the newly built shop at the lumber yard, and in 1963 a new 50' x 136' structure was added to house a fully automatic Enterprise mill.

Recent figures indicate that over four million board feet of lumber are cut annually by the mill operation at the yard. During the fall of 1994, the circular mill was replaced with a 6' vertical band head-rig. At the time, the setup was also greatly altered and updated. Production resumed in early 1995. With the company's increasing pallet pro-

351/

The original Yoder Lumber Co. sawmill operation at the present location, ca 1960.

duction, new buildings have been added in 1969, 1986, and 1992, respectively.

As new fields of interest were pursued, the company acquired its first lumber drying kilns in 1978, which consist today of a branch plant adjacent to the Hiland High School, along SR 39. In 1981 full ownership was acquired of a lumber dimension plant at the dry kilns. The company today has branched out from timber and pulpwood harvesting and sawing to the utilization of green lumber as pallets or of dry lumber in the production of many different wood specialties.

John J. Yoder, the company's original owner, died in 1974. Sons Eli, Roy, Mel, and Syl have ownership at present, while employing around 100 employees throughout their operation.

Raber Lumber Company

168/
𝒱142-
325-
1960
Raber Lumber Company originated in 1958 when Noah A. Raber, a former thresher and feed mill operator, bought the acreage and set up a sawmill a mile southeast of Charm. The original mill, along SR 557, was closer to the road than today's arrangement. During 1966 a new setup was made behind the earlier location.

In due time the operation expanded to the production of pallets. During the 1980s the assembling of wooden pallets was eliminated, as the blocking lumber was cut up and sold as a ready-cut material to other pallet shops.

The two Raber sons, Ed and Ervin, have taken a position of significance in the company, along with their semi-retired father.

In January of 1990 the older mill, building, and shop were completely torn away and replaced with a new and expanded facility that spring. The following year another addition was added. In June of 1990 production resumed with a rebuilt Cleereman carriage setup. The company employs around six workers, while the younger brother Ervin operates the headrig and Ed maintains the

Picket mill

timber supply, besides overseeing their family operation.

Miller's Custom Sawing

Miller's Custom Sawing is located at the Yoder Lumber sawmill yard east of Charm, along CR 70. This business is owned by Roy E. Miller, who is primarily engaged in cutting the surplus log inventory for Yoder Lumber. The five-man operation mill was set up in 1983.

248

K and B Lumber

During the fall of 1993, K and B Lumber began sawing at their newly located business. Construction of the mill began that summer and continued into the early winter. Although construction was not completed, the mill was set up well enough that they began sawing that fall. The business, owned by Martin Kuhns and Robert Barkman, is situated on Barkman's acreage along CR 19, a mile west of Charm. The partner ownership focuses on grade lumber production at their small scale operation.

Picket Milling

Picket fences, in their respective time, encircled the home, garden, or yard, created an appearance of neatness, along with being useful.

A picket mill was a specially designed, small sawmill for cutting up the short length pickets.

Some of the mills are known to have had two cutting blades. Mounted on the same mandrel, the one side had the bigger saw for cutting up the initial log, while the opposite side used a smaller blade to cut the picket to desired dimensions.

Records indicate some early milling activities which no longer exist today. Locally, thresher Joel J. Keim, along with Jacob L. Miller and Jonas D. Miller, went to Shreve to buy a picket mill in June, 1892. Keim's occupation of picket milling with his Erb brothers-in-law had been longstanding and well respected in the area.

100/6-14-1892 50/2-20-1896

"Farming Out" the Snyder Horses

From 1876 until 1926, area farmers took advantage of the draft horse market created by Henry D. Snyder and Sons of Millersburg. The Snyder horses of Holmes County were considered among the finest animals to be shipped to large urban markets. Aside from his own 300-acre farming operation, Snyder "farmed out" horses to be fed and conditioned until ready for resale.

343/

Among Charm area farmers who kept Snyder's animals were Jacob E. Mast, S. C. Miller, Christian Yoder, and Benjamin Raber. The farmer assumed all care, furnished the feed, and brought the horses to Millersburg when ready and approved. Though different payment arrangements were considered, fifty cents a day per head was usually agreeable.

Mr. Snyder would make periodic visits to farms

🕭

to ensure that proper care was being given to his animals. He would have each horse brought individually from the stall, then decide if they were ready for market. Upon approval, the farmers would lead them to Millersburg; the animals were often led there as a long string of horses, tied at the tails and halters.

Most of the reputable work horses were shipped to New York City by railroad. So prosperous was Mr. Snyder's business that in 1899, 612 horses, mostly Percherons, were sent to New York. The following year, in January, another 25 (valued at $9,000.00), arrived at the New York Horse Company. The constant need for horses to be used in city delivery wagons kept the market open until the advancement of the motor age.

During this early period, all goods and supplies sold by stores and retailers were brought in from the shipping station with heavy wagons, known as "dray wagons." At that time, delivery wagons for milk and ice cream were also horse drawn. These home deliveries were the last to disappear in the city with the coming of motor vehicles.

Taxi and General Hauling

A taxi and general hauling service with car, van, pickup, or truck has been a longstanding business venture, either partial or full time. Since a large percentage of the area's population has been Amish, advantage has been taken of such an availability of customers.

Quite a few local residents have rendered such a service since the first half of the century. Presently Olen Mast, who has resided in Charm since 1978, is providing van service. With a fourteen-passenger van, he provides full service in local or long distance hauling.

173/ Olen was born in 1931 to Joe and Ida (Christner) Mast at Goshen, Indiana. After growing up in Mercer County, Pennsylvania, he had various and interesting employments across the country. During 1959 and 1960, Olen was a taxi driver at Fairbanks, Alaska, then served there for another year as a cab dispatcher. From 1962 to 1966 he worked on and operated a drilling rig throughout the North Slope of the Brooks Mountain Range in Alaska. The purpose of the venture was to run seismographic surveys across the vast stretches of the slope in the development of the Alaskan oil fields. For ten years, beginning in 1968, he was involved in the thoroughbred horseracing circuit across the country.

Olen came to Charm on October 18, 1978 and stayed a few weeks at the Jonas R. Yoder home, then moved to the upstairs of the restaurant. In 1985 he set up a trailer behind Charm Plumbing,

on the lot owned by Amanda Miller, and he has resided there ever since.

299/ David Farver, owner of a local milk truck route, and brother-in-law Perry Sampsel, living a half mile northwest of town, do general hauling with pickups. Perry retired from long distance trucking in 1986.

Eugene "Poogy" Schlabach began taxi work in the fall of 1993, continuing the well patronized service of his late father, Levi D. Schlabach.

113/ Will Kaser, a Charm resident and stock buyer, hauled livestock for area farmers during the first half of the present century. In the 1930s, Orie Oswald acquired a truck and did livestock trucking.

8/

Amos Helmuth, the fur buyer and taxi driver at Charm, was killed while taking a passenger to Millersburg in his Dodge touring car. On January 3, 1923 he was taking Isaac Bontrager to the train depot. The roads were icy that day, and along the golf course area on US 62, he lost control of his car, which resulted in his instant death.

112/ Jonas E. Troyer, better known as "Jay Lynn," lived in Charm and made taxiing his livelihood. Troyer lived in the two-story building that had earlier been built onto the Christ Hummel house for "Isaac Andy," located across the street from the restaurant. Jonas lived here until his death in 1942.

V84- Between storekeeping and bologna making,
118-1916 Forrest Miller (1916–1981) was often called upon for hauling, as was his father Arletus, who moved
190/ to Charm in 1916.

Clarence Scherer, who lived a half mile northwest of town, did general hauling in the 1950s.

Homer Farver did light trucking, and his wife Vera was also engaged in hauling local people with her small sized car.

In 1950 Jacob A. Keiffaber built a home on a small lot, a mile northwest of town along SR 557. Jake did trucking with a single axle, stake bed dump truck until his health began to fail during the late 1970s. He died July 13, 1981 as a retired farmer and trucker.

John S. and Ella Lahm built onto their property purchased in 1955 at the northwest edge of Charm. After John's retirement from carpentry and masonry work, he engaged in light hauling with a
385/ pickup along with being a township trustee.
V134-
479- On January 1, 1955, Archie Carpenter moved
1957 into the living quarters above the restaurant, and did taxiing. In 1957 he purchased a half acre lot half a mile south of town, where he built a home.

Interestingly, his service started a business connection with local lumberman, V. J. Erb, after Archie began working for him as a pallet salesman. As the pallet business increased, Archie became part owner of the Pallet All and Semac Industries lumber works.

During 1958 Melvin C. and Esther (Weaver) Domer purchased the Ervin Keim property located immediately south of the Lahm lot. Melvin did hauling with car and light truck up into the 1970s. He passed away September 13, 1978.

Living a mile southeast of Charm, Lester Scherer did taxing during his retirement in the 1970s and 1980s.

A pair of drivers, Mel Kurtz and Jim Blue, took residence in the living quarters over the restaurant during the middle 1970s. Though the two shared one apartment, they independently took care of their own business. Their stay in town was shortlived; Kurtz returned to Geauga County and Blue to Pennsylvania.

Levi D. Schlabach, who lived a mile and a half west of town, was very active as a driver. The widowed, semi-retired gentleman began hauling with a pickup, then later drove a gray and maroon *150 /* Chevy van. Levi passed away March 15, 1993.

Gary Keim and his brother LaVern, along with their spouses, did some taxi service during their stay at the village. Garys lived on the lot between the restaurant and Ole Mill Furniture, then moved to Killbuck in the fall of 1990. Laverns lived on his parents' property a half mile southeast of town until they moved in 1991.

Retired storekeeper and postmaster Orie Oswald did some amount of passenger service during the late 1980s and early 1990s for the local community.

Presently Albert A. Keim is engaged in a trucking business known as Keim Trucking. Local trucking, lime and fertilizer distribution, and transporting coal has been an expanding business in the Keim family. Their recent interest in a small fleet of tractor–trailer rigs has greatly increased their *100/7-* trucking activities. *29-1992*

The Keims, formerly living in Charm, to the west *𝒱163-* of the schoolhouse, have been in the trucking busi- *231-1967* ness since 1945. During the late 1960s the business was moved to their newly built home a short distance southeast of town. In the early 1990s a son, Harold, moved onto the property to eventually take on responsibilities.

For years a bus line has connected Charm to other towns along the route. The three-day-a-week service is provided today by Edward Atkins. Towns along the scheduled routes include Dover, Sugarcreek, Farmerstown, New Bedford, Charm, Berlin, Millersburg, and Beck's Mills. The often used service is provided on Mondays, Tuesdays, and Fridays, along with special runs on off days when there are sales or other events.

Keim Hatchery

A hatchery at Charm, in connection with a *37 /* feed mill, was a family operated business. *188 /* Charm resident Dan J. Keim died during the flu epidemic of 1919–1920, leaving his wife with four young children.

The family resided immediately northwest of the store in the three-story home built by the newly married Keim. After Dan's death, four small incubators were set up in the basement of the home. The four children continued the business after the mother passed away in 1935.

In 1938 the two boys, Oren and Dan, bought a much larger incubator, which was installed by Mike S. Erb. With a capacity of 8,600 eggs on 48 drawers, they could set chicken, duck, or geese hatches. The setup was heated by a hard coal boiler that was fired two times a day. At the time the small hatchery was set up, it provided a means for the young, widowed mother to make a living.

With the later feed mill purchase in town by son Oren, the two businesses were known as Keim Feed Mill and Hatchery. The hatchery was discontinued in 1948.

Keim Feed Mill

T he second feed mill at Charm originally be- *8 /* gan at the old Keim Lumber planing mill. During the Depression of 1932, the lumber company's owner, Mose J. Keim, moved to Mt. Hope for one and a half years, as work was very slow at Charm.

About this time, a brother, Albert, who was a *106 /* noted thresher and sawyer, set up a grinder and *107 /* mixer in the planing mill. As this was a dusty pro- *179 /* cess, it was not advisable to have the mill in the *98 /* same building as the lumber works. Accordingly, Al built a new mill across the road from the schoolhouse. Apparently the mill was erected in 1933, where the present "Ole Mill Furniture" is today. The business was known as "Keim's Mills."

This building was originally erected on cement-filled barrel pillars as a precaution during high water levels, as it sat close to the Charm creek.

Feeds highly associated with feed milling at Charm.

Early in its establishment, the mill did have some water damage, at the time of the 1935 flood.

At first the grinding operation was powered with a Baker traction steam engine, which sat on the south side of the mill. Within a few years, an addition was put on the back side and an Allis-Chalmers engine installed as a power unit.

237 /
𝒱107-
429-
1938

In 1938 the mill was sold to a nephew, Oren D. Keim, who operated it along with sons and his brother Dan and continued an extended business under the name of "Keim Feed Mill."

Different brands of feed sold by the Keims were Old Ford, Wayne, Conkeys, Gold Star, and Eshleman, along with Globe fertilizer, advertised as "The World's Best." Because of their later ownership of the Charm Feed Mill, they eventually also brought the Master Mix feed supplies to this mill, when Charm Feed was shut down in 1972.

𝒱172-
95-1969

The elderly Keim, along with his son Daniel, purchased the other town milling business from Delbert Harmon and Eli M. Miller in 1969. For three years the family operated both locations until it was resold in 1972, when milling discontinued in the town's first feed mill, the Charm Flour Mills.

𝒱190-
509-
1975

Oren Keim, upon retirement, chose to sell the mill he had operated close to forty years. The mill was sold to Charm resident Abe A. Mast only a short period before Oren's unexpected stroke-related death, May 8, 1975.

126 /
127 /

Under the Mast ownership, the mill was greatly redesigned and expanded. A new addition on the west end housed the horizontal mixer, grinding equipment, and bins. Up-to-date elevators were installed, towering high above the roof, and the original building was then used for storage and office space. A basement was added underneath the mill, providing more essential floor space. A new engine was installed at this time to replace the older Allis-Chalmers, which gave out at this point.

At the time the Masts acquired the mill, Eshleman and Master Mix feeds were sold, and the mill name was changed to Charm Feed Mill. Within their first years, Eshleman was discontinued and Wayne Feeds brought in. These two, along with the mill's own blends of "Charming"—horse feed, dairy and poultry feed, calf starter, and mineral

mixes—were sold until the time of their closing in 1986.

With the employment of Roy A. Miller, the Masts did a substantial amount of business. Roy had worked at the New Bedford mill, so his experience in milling was highly important to the new ownership. In 1982 Miller bought the harness shop inventory, while the Mast family business was continued by siblings Sara Ann and Leon.

With the Masts' involvement in the earlier Charm Auctions, they had felt an urge to become involved in the furniture business.

In due time, in April of 1986, the Charm Feed Mill discontinued its services. However, a limited amount of feed was still kept on hand for the next few months, while the east part of the building was completely remodeled for the anticipated furniture store. The two-story furniture outlet was completed by June, as the feed milling activity in town came to an abrupt end. After 74 years of mill activity in town, the Mast-owned mill was the last to operate as a grinding and mixing service.

Interestingly, even though there was no extended line of a family-owned mill, the Mast family was the fourth generation of descendants of Daniel J. Mast, who had originally brought the milling trade to Charm in 1912.

Cane Press

The cane pressing operation at Charm began on the Christian B. Miller farm when the family lived two miles west of town. The farm is owned today by Joe H. Miller. The first press used by Crist was one with vertical rollers.

43 /

Cane pressing is one of the latter steps in preparing the final product of cane molasses. As is the case with corn, cane is planted in the spring. By fall, when the slender stalks are fully matured and ripened, the leaf foliage is stripped, the stalks cut, and the red seed pod at the top removed. At the press, the stalks are run through the tightly set rollers that squeeze the sweet sap water into a holding tank. Once enough water is accumulated, it is run into large, rectangular pans set over a fire pit, where it is boiled down to a dark, heavy cane molasses syrup.

𝒱108-
132-
1938

The Miller family moved to the east edge of Charm (Vernon A. Kline farm) in 1938, and brought along with them the cane pressing interest. Crist built a new building and also at that time bought a horizontal roller press. The operation, located at the CR 70–TR 369 intersection, consisted of a low-roofed, open-side press and tractor structure, while the cooking shanty was a small, gable-roofed building set at a lower level.

𝒱121-
157-
1947

The farm was transferred from "Benedict Crist" to son Levi in 1947; then in 1955, Levi D. Troyer,

327 /
p.6

❧

Cane press at the east edge of Charm

his brother-in-law, bought the farm. Troyer oper- *U130-* ated the long-known Charm cane press until it was *403-* sold in the early 1970s to Eli D. Miller of Beck's *1955* Mills. In 1989 the former Charm press was bought *387/* by Henry J. C. Yoder, also of Beck's Mills, who farms some acres of cane himself, along with doing custom pressing and molasses cooking.

Joe Erb Excavating

Joe Erb bought his first bulldozer in 1945. The *129/* previous year he had joined in partnership with Noah A. Raber and acquired the local threshing rig from Abe P. Troyer and Abe J. Yoder. Getting involved in excavating allowed him more full time occupation when threshing was in the off season.

A bulldozer in the Charm area in 1945 was quite a new undertaking. At this time no other dozers were to be found in the vicinity. As excavating work increased for Erb, more earthmoving equipment was acquired and the threshing work eventually eliminated.

By 1968 the firm was doing local strip mining for coal, and became known as Charm Mining. The Erb involvement with strip mining, then reclaiming the land afterward, was one of the first of such practices in the state of Ohio.

Charm Mining merged with Holmes Limestone

Company in 1971 and is a division of their extensive strip mining operation.

Joe Erb retired from excavating in 1991, and today he is owner of Erb's Sports and Archery in Charm.

Restaurant

Initially, the restaurant at Charm had its begin- *9/* ning in 1950, when Paul Hummel, a former *19/p.37* town resident, purchased and completely re- *96/* modeled the meat market structure. It had previously been a small store which sold meat and a few groceries, and it had living quarters attached to it.

Under Paul's renovation, a food counter and a well supplied IGA grocery store came into existence. An addition along the south side of the building had been added to house a bar stool counter, grill, French fryer, soda fountain, and ice cream. With Hummel's ownership of the meat market and store at Berlin, his brother-in-law, Ray Mast Jr., took care of management at Charm. Junior and Gladys lived above their place of business while he was engaged in carpentry work along with the storekeeping and food service.

In 1953 the business and lot were sold to Forrest Miller, who had previously worked for his father in the same building while it was still a meat mar-

327 /
p.26

IGA store and food counter – 1965

ket and bologna factory. Forrest and his wife Margaret (Ely) had made this their home for ten years after their marriage in 1939. The Millers, living in their newly built home a mile northwest of town, continued with the small food bar and groceries until 1970. By this time Forrest had also acquired the general store in town and, along with son Ivan, remodeled the aging meat market structure into the modern Amish Corners Restaurant.

19 / p.37   In 1973 the restaurant was sold to Thurston Ralph, who took charge of the business on December 3. By this time they could accommodate approximately eighty people in the small country town business.

Ralph also owned the IGA store in Walnut Creek at this time.

During the next decade the restaurant was transferred to numerous owners and managers. In 1975 the business was sold to Dave Lappen, who, in turn, transferred it to Emanuel Mullet and Levi Beachy the following year. Under this ownership the venture was managed successively by Bruce Cooker and Thurston Ralph.

𝒱192-
255-
1975
𝒱195-
110-1976
259 /

In 1978 Levi Beachy sold his interest to his brother Noah, who, along with his wife Silvia, took over management duties.

88 /   On August 1, 1979 Henry Troyer and Albert M. Miller joined partnership and received the business interest. The following July (1980), Troyer sold his share to Albert. With the Miller family now assuming full possession, they hired Mark Miller to help in business duties. Levi "Shorty" Schrock came in as manager on January 19, 1981, until the concern opened under new ownership in January of 1983.

During the Millers' proprietorship, an "all you can eat, Friday Fish Special" was introduced on the menu, which continued under later managements and attracted large numbers of people. Another highlight during this time was the widely known "shirttail board" displayed in the restaurant throughout the deer gun season. The follow-

🌤
138

ing year at the Charm Days auction a quilt would be sold which was made from the previous year's collected shirttails.

𝒱219-
958-1983
46 /
150 /
𝒱227-
963-1985

Willard Miller received title and took on responsibilities January 13, 1983, then sold it in 1985 to Mose Troyer, who changed the name to "Troyer's Homestead Restaurant." Troyer came in as manager February 6, 1985.

Over the course of several ownerships, various remodeling and updating projects were carried out. Dave Lappan enclosed the area between the kitchen and former bologna-making building. This had previously been connected by only an open wooden walkway. Albert Miller added a facelift

234 /   of new paint to the outside. Willard Miller remodeled the upstairs living quarters by lowering the ceilings, installing a new floor and paneling the walls. Mose Troyer installed a modern and enlarged sewage system during his two years of business in Charm.

Troyer sold the business to Ann DeHass in April of 1987. In the same year extensive remodeling was done on the aging structure. The bologna factory building that in past years had been used as a food and storage area was now fully connected to the older building. The wall between the dining rooms was removed, and a completely new seating arrangement was introduced. The combined structures were resided with a dark brown siding, attractively adding to the well patronized business.

Since the DeHass ownership, the place of dining was renamed "The Homestead Restaurant." During tourist seasons, it is not unusual to find a line of people outside waiting to be seated.

50 / 12-
10-1987

Prior to their appearance at Charm, the DeHass family spent eight years at Lynchberg, Virginia. While the husband, Dan, was involved in evangelism, Ann operated her own restaurant. Ann, inspired by her mother's home cooking, promotes the well-patronized business with the idea of "homemade, quality, and heaping;" thus advertising, "Grandma Esther's Recipe."

The family resides a mile west of Walnut Creek,

249 /

The Homestead Restaurant – 1991

where they have an extensive bed and breakfast facility.

At Charm the DeHasses also provide a bed and breakfast room. This single room facility is located in the former jeweler's shop across the road. From 1991 to 1994, two upstairs rooms of the restaurant were also used as a bed and breakfast.

Farver Milk Transport

366 /

After graduating from high school, David Farver began hauling milk for the Charm Cheese Factory. The can milk was picked up at area farms, then brought to the factory, where it was processed into cheese. In February of 1962, Farver bought his first milk truck, from cheese maker Paul Hershberger. For 32 years David hauled milk to the Charm factory. He continued to transport milk to the Doughty Valley–Guggisberg Cheese when the Charm plant was closed down in 1984.

Sharpening Service

131 /
161 /

During his retirement, Ben J. Troyer of Charm was engaged in saw and mower sharpening. In the early 1960s Troyer had bought a Foley handsaw filer and operated a small business, until ill health compelled him to quit the service.

In 1965 the trade was passed to Andy M. Hershberger, who lived a short distance east of town. In the early 1970s the sharpening equipment was moved to his brother-in-law, Eli E. Hershberger, who lived a mile from Charm. In 1974 his father, Emanuel, began working in Eli's shop.

During 1976 the elder Hershberger, who had retired from farming, moved to the immediate neighborhood, bought the tools, and made the setup in the former Charm Plumbing building. In 1982 Emanuel added a carbide saw sharpener and the needed welding equipment to better supply the community's needs. Today the semi-retired grandfather has built a steady business which required a day-to-day schedule. He is located a mile southeast of Charm along SR 557.

Saw Hammering

John Oren Miller began hammering circular sawmill saws approximately thirty years ago. The art of saw hammering involves maintaining the proper dish and tension in accordance with the speed of the blade. The sawyer has seen millers throughout the state come to Charm to have their saw problems taken care of.

During the 1970s and 1980s John was a distributor for the Hoe Saw Company, selling saws, shanks, and bits to the sawmilling industry.

Andy's Craft Shop

V149-
184-
1962
360 /

In 1962 Andy L. Miller purchased a small acreage a mile southeast of Charm from Moses E. Mast, and built a home and shop building. Employed as a carpenter, Miller set up woodworking machinery in his new shop. By the late 1960s he was making truck bed floors, and he eventually began making wooden wheelbarrow handles. The handles were fully made, drilled, and varnished at the location, then shipped in semi load quantities. Broker Roy Runion had a machinist from Wooster custom make the automated machine to accurately produce the handles. The business and handle machine was later sold to Berlin Wood Inc.

From Charm the Miller family moved to the McConnelsville, Ohio area.

Miller's Dry Goods

The dry goods store in Charm is owned by Mrs. Aden (Amanda) Miller, who, along with her two daughters, has built a substantial business at their home. The store, which has been remodeled numerous times, offers one of the largest displays of dry goods, quilts, and sewing *19 / p. 37* supplies in the area. The business was started in *149 /* 1966, when they bought the Sam E. Miller inventory and began a dry goods outlet of their own. At first the store was located in their kitchen and living room, until a room was added along the back of the house, which in due time was outgrown because of added supplies.

On the property, immediately south of the house, was the former harness shop building, which was remodeled and later used as a house. Amanda's parents, the John V. Erbs, moved here in the mid 1960s and her mother, Katie, died here in 1968. Her father continued to live in the house with a hired maid, Fannie L. Raber, until 1978, when he moved into the dry goods storeroom of the Miller house and the store was moved into the remodeled home. Since the dry goods outlet was

249 /

Miller's Dry Goods – 1991

moved here, the building has been extensively remodeled to house the ever expanding inventory. An enclosed walkway was built to connect the store and house. In 1981 a large addition was added on the back. More recently, in 1990, an expanded and updated quilt room was attached to the north end. The quilts were now displayed individually on a rack for the customer's satisfaction. During 1994 the barn adjacent to the store was greatly renovated to house the expanding quilt display and sales.

Miller's Dry Goods hires local women to piece, mark, quilt, and bind quilts that may be deeply appreciated by the interested buyer. Custom made quilts may also be ordered at the store. A designated area for quilting allows visiting women to enjoy a relaxing pastime.

Recent years have brought an extensive amount of tourist trade to the store.

In addition to the Millers as clerks, they employ a few additional workers as needed.

Amanda, daughter of John V. Erb (OAG 3976) resides with her youngest daughter, Mary, in a newly constructed log home. Her husband, Aden E. Miller, died October 26, 1978. In 1988 a log home, manufactured by Doughty Wood Products, was built across the creek and west of the store. The *150/* unique house features a slate roof complete with copper valleys and ridges. Prior to their placement, the century old slate was removed from the Central Christian Church of Coshocton, Ohio and the old Keim barn, a mile southwest of Beck's Mills. A wooden covered bridge spanning the creek between the home and her place of business adds a touch of distinction to the home as well as to the town itself.

In 1991 the Millers and the neighboring com-*149/* munity were startled and shocked when an armed *171/* break-in took place at the dry goods store. Early Saturday morning on April 13, at 1:50 A.M., a car with a loud muffler slowly made its way through the sleeping town and parked behind petroleum tanks on the Albert N. Schrock farm a short distance north of town. It occupants, Matthew B. Miller, 21, and Timothy E. McFadden, 30, both of Holmesville, returned to the village and dry goods store on foot. Gaining entrance through a locked outside basement door, the men were later apprehended at the scene by sheriff's deputies. Further investigation revealed their loaded handgun hidden in the store and cash money thrown everywhere in their haste to dispose of the stolen goods once the authorities arrived.

During the following weeks Matt pleaded guilty in a "plea bargain" and admitted to numerous other break-ins in which the two men were in-

370/
#91-
CR26-
9-738

volved. On July 24 and 25 a jury trial was held at Millersburg for Timothy McFadden, who finally changed his plea from innocent to guilty on the second day of the proceedings. On July 31 he was sentenced to 8 to 25 years in prison by Judge Thomas White. By the second week of October, Miller was sentenced to 5 to 15 years in prison for his involvement with the crime. However, in June of 1992 he was granted 5 years probation and his previous sentence was suspended.

Miller deeply regrets his involvement with the incident and has since turned to a family life.

Hershberger Gun Shop

344/

Hershberger Gun Shop had its beginning in early 1967. At the time, Jonas V. Hershberger took interest in gun trading and set up a shop in his father's vacant house and wood shop on the farm, 1¹/₂ miles south of Charm. Pursuing his interest further, he bought the gun shop inventory of Levi L. Yoder on January 1, 1968. Attached to this transfer was the dealership to major firearms: Remington, Winchester, Ithaca, Marlin, Savage, and Harrington and Richardson.

This early gun shop originally stood southwest of the main house and was later extensively remodeled for living quarters; it was moved a short distance to its present location. In 1973 a new pole structure was placed along CR 600 on the Hershberger farm to house the gun shop. With expanded floor space, business increased. By now it consisted of new sales, used gun trading, repairing, custom reloading, and bow hunting equipment.

In 1979, a year after he married, Hershberger decided to place a new brick building on the acquired property, along the north edge of the farm.

Jonas experienced a flourishing trade from a wide territory, while also becoming a master gunsmith. At the present location, a mile south of Charm, handgun and bowhunting inventories were discontinued in due time. The bowhunting supplies were purchased by East Holmes Archery in 1983. Later this archery business was sold to Erb's Sports and Archery of Charm.

By the 1990s the U.S. government was increasing its attention to crime prevention and focused on gun control as a corrective measure. The passage of the Brady Gun Law of 1993 made significant inroads in regulation and control, while adding paperwork and restrictions to the already burdensome legal matters. This, along with numerous break-ins (the last occurring on March 7, 1994, when twenty guns were stolen), moved Hershberger to decide to close down the business. In accordance with that decision, inventory was reduced in 1994, and the well-patronized store was closed on May 14.

Miller's Tax Service

Emanuel M. Miller has added a tax service specialty to the town's businesses. After an initial course with H & R Block, Emanuel began offering the service to his clients in 1971. Over the years a steady increase in volume has been evident. Today over 200 customers visit the Miller residence annually for income tax purposes. *277 /*

Later home courses with Revised Tax Services and Professional Bookkeeping have expanded Miller's capabilities in the business.

Charm Engine

Today's well-established Charm Engine began as a small business on the farm of Melvin A. Barkman, a short distance northwest of Charm. A back injury had forced Barkman to quit farming, and he became involved in tractor mechanics and pressure sprayer setups in the late 1960s. Eventually his first introduction to small engines was the sales and service of the McCulloch chain saws during 1972. *187 /*
11 / 4-
13-1987

After a number of years of increasing business in the small shop, a new building was put up along SR 557, in 1976. The new location, a mile northwest of Charm, now offered a wider selection of brand name chain saws, mowers, and weed eaters.

During the thirteen years the engine and repair shop was operating, most of the employees were of the immediate family.

In June of 1989 the business end of the operation was sold to the five shareholders of Charm Engine Corporation. Later that year, a new and greatly enlarged 60'x160' building was erected at the present location, $1/2$ mile north of town. The building, owned by Charm Center Corporation, was then leased to the engine corporation, which opened its newly located business on December 18, 1989.

Stocking a reputable selection of engines, saws, and mowers, they were distributors of Stihl, Toro, Wheelhorse, Homelite, Jacobsen, Lawn-Boy, Tanaka, Honda, Kohler, Kawasaki, Briggs & Stratton, and Tecumseh products. The extensive inventory of new merchandise and parts has provided satisfaction and high quality serve to the community.

On June 1, 1993 the demanding business was transferred to Paul D. Shetler, long time employee and son-in-law of the business' founder. Soon after the business changed hands, the line of riding garden tractors was eliminated. Chain saws have remained a heavy part of the well-patronized service stemming from a large radius in the area of today's timber and logging industry.

Charm Plumbing

Charm Plumbing originated as Raber's Plumbing in 1969 when Melvin H. Raber took on his father's well-established business, with Andy N. Miller as partner. The business was located three miles south of Charm at this time. *269 /*
285 /

In 1970 Raber purchased the Andy L. Miller property, which included a shop building formerly used in making wooden wheelbarrow handles. During January of 1972 Raber and Miller moved the business to this location, a mile southeast of Charm. Incorporating soon thereafter, the business was renamed Charm Plumbing. *71175-*
42-1970

In due time an inventory of electrical products was added and an electrician was hired; the venture became Charm Plumbing and Electric.

During 1979, after the former Charm Feed Mill building was acquired, the plumbing and electrical business was moved to Charm. The outlet was now more centrally located among other places of business.

During this first year of relocation, on September 14, flooding brought over two feet of water into the basement of the building. This was six inches lower than the high water mark of the 1935 flood. A red-painted, steel post in the former feed mill building shows this early flood water level.

The following year, 1980, the partnership was dissolved. Raber continued in the plumbing trade, while Miller took on well drilling, which he had been involved with since 1974.

During 1982 the upstairs of the old mortise and tenon-framed building was remodeled into an apartment. In 1985 the plumbing inventory was greatly reduced and the business moved to the basement. The main floor was now changed into a craft store known as "Ole Mill Crafts."

The plumbing business was then turned over

171 /

Charm Plumbing situated in the former feed mill building.

completely to Ivan Kline. Kline had worked for Charm Plumbing since 1977. He took partnership with the company in 1983, then became its sole owner in 1985.

Today's plumbing service offers new and repair work on almost any plumbing-related job: water systems, hot water heating, well setups, and sewage.

Charm Rocker Shop

326/

Charm Rocker began with the construction of a bent hickory rocking chair in 1972. Owner Henry B. Yoder began making the all-wood rocker in his home workshop. The rocker consists of dormant hickory twigs and mostly oak or walnut finished lumber. It is not only a well-fitting and contoured easy chair, but an attractive addition to a living room, as well. During recent years the chairs have been built by another shop, with Charm Rocker supplying all of the material.

Construction of an oak porch swing was begun in the early 1980s, along with a wooden glider a few years later. In 1993 the swing was discontinued and more attention was focused on living room gliders and dining chairs. The family-operated business specializes in a retail mail order business which advertises the oak living room glider, various oak dining chairs, and a select number of quality furniture.

In 1993 a display room was opened in a recently built gristmill replica on the property. A visit to the rocker shop is highlighted by the numerous species of exotic animals found on the grounds, including llamas, ostriches, and emus.

The Yoder family also owns the Charm Tank Sales business located at their home, a half mile east of Charm.

Charm Auction

125/

The Charm Auctions of the 1970s were conducted with the enthusiasm of its owners and to the entertainment of the often overflowing crowds. A Friday night auction, it consisted of unclaimed merchandise, store closeouts, factory select furniture, and consignments. At the auctions almost anything could turn up, from toys and gifts to tools and furniture. A quality spring and mattress was also sold at the sales.

V181-
337-
1972

The auction originated in 1972 when the Charm Feed Mill was purchased by Ed Raber and Abe A. Mast. After the feed milling equipment was sold at public auction, the beam framed structure was remodeled to accommodate the auction barn.

218/

Upon completion, old church benches were brought in for seating. The first auction was held on March 16, 1973.

❧

In the late 1970s these evening sales were discontinued and the building was used for storage, until it was sold to Charm Plumbing in 1979.

Charm Drilling

285/

Andy N. Miller bought his first drilling rig while in joint ownership with Melvin H. Raber of Charm Plumbing. The cable rig, purchased in 1974, was a Cyclone #40. The first well placed by Miller was on the Eli A. Yoder farm, two miles west of Beck's Mills. The business was located at the Raber property, a mile southeast of Charm. In 1979 the plumbing and drilling works were moved to Charm, to the former Charm Feed Mill building. In 1980 their partnership was dissolved and Andy took on Charm Drilling, with the business still housed at that location.

A new Bucyrus-Erie 22W rig was acquired in 1980; it was also a drum and cable type of machine.

Charm Drilling was involved mainly in water well drilling and reactivating in Holmes, Wayne, Tuscarawas, and Stark Counties. During its span of existence, the company explored the possibilities of a shallow Berea gas well drilled to a depth of 1,100 feet, on the Melvin H. Raber farm, $1^1/_2$ miles southeast of Charm.

Miller closed down the drilling venture in 1984.

Ivan Yoder Builders

261/

Ivan Yoder Builders started in 1977 with construction of new housing, and since this has been their number one occupation. Substantial and continual growth to the present has resulted from their reputation for high quality workmanship.

The Yoder family moved a mile north of Charm in 1980 and since then have erected woodworking shops to build and finish custom cabinetry and trim work. During 1980 Ivan joined partnership with fellow carpenter John Henry Yoder.

The Yoder carpenters are able, with subcontracting, to offer a completed house from start to finish, to the homeowner's specifications. Presently three crews are employed by Yoder, who does most of his own drafting and estimates. At present their main work is being done in Holmes County and the Dover–New Philadelphia area, where they average 25 new houses a year.

Pine Pallet

177/

A mile north of Charm, Pine Pallet has been in continued growth since its beginning in 1977. The business, owned by the Jacob Hochstetler family, originated with the construction of wooden box-spring frames and pallets. As the frame trade increased, the pallets were canceled out of the operation. By 1991 the company began fabricating complete box-springs, which are sold mainly under the brand name of Therapedic.

The well-established local business presently employs twelve workers at its location on TR 369.

Charm Tractor

Monroe C. Yoder began with tractor mechanics southwest of Sugarcreek in 1975. The following year he moved to a small shop along SR 557, three miles southeast of Charm. In 1977 he purchased an acre of land a mile northwest of town and built a larger shop on the triangle-shaped lot for tractor overhauling and repair work.

369/
𝒱199-
598-
1977

Considerable damage was done to the shop by a fire in 1983 resulting from an electrical short in connection with a bridge replacement adjacent to the property.

The owner specializes in rebuilding older and antique-type tractors.

Charm Bulk Foods

A bulk food store had been the dream of Mary Ann Schlabach for quite some time. Because she was handicapped, the occupation could provide her with means of income while having a supporting business at home.

The welcomed opportunity came up unexpectedly in 1978. On July 20 the Charm General Store was destroyed by fire, which left the community without a grocery supply in the immediate area. Shortly after the disaster, the Schlabach family readied a small room in the house to accommodate the new store. Originally the store was known as "Mary Ann's Bulk Food Store." The outlet was located on TR 156, overlooking the Charm village from the west.

176/

During 1990 a sister, Ada, took interest in the store, and the name was changed to "Charm Bulk Foods."

In 1991, when the Schlabach family was preparing to move to their property on the west edge of town, a new building was put up for the store and warehouse. The inventory was brought to the new facility and opened to the public on February 14, 1991. The small store has done well for the women who operate a neat, well-stocked, and well-established place of business.

Pine Grove Camping

Joe and Elizabeth Erb offer a place of relaxation to picnickers, campers, and fishermen on their private property, 1/2 mile east of Charm. On the secluded spot is a 3/4-acre pond which was

129/

189/

Pine Grove Camping

built in 1969, a newly built log cabin, an open pavilion, and a picnic area. Fishing in the well-stocked pond is permitted for those leasing the campground facilities.

The Erbs had been involved earlier with a fishing pond adjoining their camping acreage.

𝒱128-
238-1953

In 1953 Joe, Atlee D. Schlabach, and Levi D. Schlabach bought six acres of land and built a 3 1/2-acre lake, known as the Charm Dam. Fishing was open to the public until 1966, when the acreage was sold to Fender's Fish Hatchery.

𝒱128-
239-
1953
𝒱158-
363-1966

J. R. Yoder Nylon

J. R. Yoder Nylon is located on TR 159, a mile northeast of Charm. Jonas R. Yoder, along with his son Leroy, owns and operates the nylon harness shop. When the Yoders' son-in-law continued with farming in 1978, Jonas started a harness-making operation in his implement shop on the farm.

175/

A new feature in harness making was introduced to the community here, that of using a bioplastic coated nylon instead of leather. The new product makes a neat, long-lasting harness, which is used locally among the horse and buggy population, as well as among horsemen in the horse show rings.

In 1988 the business moved to the newly erected shop at its present location. The constant growth of sales and increasing range of marketing are evidence of the quality, workmanship, and commitment applied to harness making at the newly founded nylon harness works.

Charm Woodcraft

John A. Miller purchased a property on the north edge of Charm in 1978. Along with the main house on the half-acre lot was a double story garage and tenant house. The following year John converted the building into a shop area, and has since modified and added onto the woodworking facility. The main work of the business is the

380/
𝒱203-
497-
1978

❧

construction of wooden wishing wells and wooden steam shovel toys for youngsters.

Charm Greenhouse

174/

The Jacob J. Yoder family, living along TR 369, a half mile north of Charm, began the Charm Greenhouse in 1982 as a sideline income and as a means of whetting the "green thumb" inclination of its family members. Despite the small scale operation, the business grew sufficiently to provide high quality vegetable plants and flower beds for the area's residents.

The "growing" trade was discontinued after the 1993 growing season was over.

Charm Tank Sales

326/

Charm Tank Sales is located one half mile east of Charm at the Charm Rocker Shop (the Henry B. Yoder residence). Yoder added the tank sales to his well-established hickory rocker business in the mid 1980s. At the residence, the former propane tanks are converted to usable and long lasting air tanks, ranging in size from 120 to 30,000 gallons. The readied and repainted tanks are sold and distributed over a wide territory, both within the state and beyond.

Ole Mill Furniture

126/

A furniture store in Charm became a reality in 1986, when the introduction of furniture retailing in the village became a success. In 1986 the Charm Feed Mill was closed and the building extensively remodeled into a three-story furniture outlet. The business property at the south edge of Charm was owned by Abe A. Mast, then transferred to his son Leon during the year of remodeling. With the mill closing to most of its business operations in April of 1986, the new structure rapidly took shape. By June, Charm's first furniture store was opened, with a large selection of high quality furnishings.

V230-954-1986

Among leading manufacturers who supply the ever-increasing inventory are King Hickory, Tim

berline, Leick, Tell City, and Richardson Brothers. Locally made items are also sold. Various displays of living room and bedroom suites, dinettes, recliners, rockers, bookcases, china cabinets, coffee tables, and more can be found in the homelike atmosphere of the store. High quality mattresses, box springs, and water beds, along with lawn furniture and craft specialties, are also on display.

As a service to customers, home deliveries can be arranged when needed.

In 1988 and 1993, respectively, more floor space and a warehouse area were added to the expanding business, so that today no hint, except its name, remains of its having been a place of milling.

From fall of 1988 to spring of 1989, Ole Mill Furniture II operated as a factory select outlet to the business in the basement of the Charm Center Building.

Along with trade with today's increasing tourist flow, the reputable firm does a substantial amount of business, both local and distant.

The owners, Leon and Lois Mast, reside 2½ miles east of Charm. They employ Sara Ann (Mast) Miller as their only full-time employee.

Ole Mill Crafts

150/

The Olde Flour Mill Craft Shoppe became Charm's first craft shop to open while further promoting the tourist trade to the village.

332/

The business is located, as designated by its name, in the former feed mill building that later housed the Charm Auction and plumbing shop. The store was originally opened by the Melvin H. Raber family in 1986, and soon thereafter its name was changed to Ole Mill Crafts.

Mel had been a partnership owner of Charm Plumbing. During 1985 the plumbing inventory was reduced. The remaining wares were moved to the basement, and the main floor of the build-

249/

249/

Ole Mill Furniture – 1991

Ole Mill Crafts – 1994

ing was remodeled for a craft store facility.

In the fall of 1990, Ole Mill Crafts was discontinued until the summer of 1991, when one of the Raber daughters, Rhoda, assumed ownership and continued with the craft business. The following year (1992), a line of bulk food was added to its heavily stocked inventory, which includes hand painted items and appliqued hoops as specialties. The store has a small woodworking shop where cutouts are made during store hours and can be readily observed by customers.

Ye Old Gift Shoppe

During the years of 1986 and 1987, Aretta Keim operated a craft and gift store in the house formerly located where the bank is today. *271/*

At this time, the Keim family lived in Charm on the lot between the restaurant and Ole Mill Furniture.

Hickory rockers, hickory doll furniture, and consignment items were to be found at Aretta's place of business.

A guest book kept at the store reveals that people have visited the shoppe from as far a distance as Germany.

The outlet was closed in 1987 when plans were made to renovate the lot for the Charm Center Building.

Commercial and Savings Bank

For a number of years, town merchants and residents pursued the idea of locating a bank in Charm. During 1980, storeowner Ed Raber presented a petition to the people of Charm for their opinion on having a bank located in town. Since the residents responded favorably, local banks were contacted; they, too, expressed interest. However, a suitable location had to be found for the proposed bank. An appropriate site became available in 1985, when the lot on the southeast street corner in town was offered for sale. On August 29, 1985 the former Oren Keim property was sold at public sale to Ed Raber and Bill Keim. *218/*

Stemming from that purchase was the formation of the Charm Center Corporation, consisting of nine shareholders, namely: Ed Raber, President–Treasurer; Bill Keim, Vice President; Ivan Miller, Secretary; Roy Miller, Mel Yoder, Jake Hochstetler, Erma Miller, Ervin Raber, and Jim Gause.

During 1987 the century-old house on the property was removed, and in its place a two-story commercial building was erected. The structure, known as the Charm Center Building, was originally designed to house a bank and post office, with additional space in the basement for other business enterprises.

249/

The Charm branch of the Commercial and Savings Bank, situated in the Charm Center Building.

As construction progressed on the building, the west part was rapidly completed, so that by December 14, 1987 the Commercial and Savings Bank of Millersburg opened a branch office at Charm.

The Commercial Bank has had an extended history of banking in Holmes County, established in 1879 at Millersburg. In Charm the bank was a welcome asset to the community. Upon opening, Ervin Yoder was appointed as Branch Manager. Presently, Martha Weaver, Loretta Gray, and Lisa Kauffman serve as bank tellers. The Charm banking facility features a safe deposit box rental and a drive-through window. The steep driveway at the window is of unique construction; it is heated for safe wintertime driving. *144/*

Brookline Antiques

Brookline Antiques originated at the old barn building on the Charm Center lot in 1987. The owners, Brooks and Kathleen Harris, both retirees, find dealing in antiques both interesting and rewarding in their retirement. The older couple of Killbuck take great interest in items of local interest and history. They have contributed greatly in that respect with their preservation and displays of local history at the antique store. *189/* *50/10-22-1987*

They opened the shop at Charm on Labor Day in association with Gallery East, operated by artist Claude Ruston "Rusty" Baker. The antique wares were displayed among the collection of Baker's paintings until the following year, 1988, when the gallery moved to a different location.

Since the store was begun, numerous additions and changes have been made to the old mortise and tenton-framed barn. In the spring of 1990 a 27-foot mural of Charm (dating ca 1895–1925) was placed along the south wall of the building. The historical painting was painted during the winter of 1989 by Rusty Baker under the supervision of Brooks Harris. Along with the mural, a museum of Charm and related areas was added, beginning in 1992. Visitors to the store can now glimpse an

❧

actual part of the history of the town and community. Interestingly, displayed below the painting's early businesses is a collection of tools of trades that were used during earlier time periods of the village.

Mr. and Mrs. Harris are natives of West Virginia and are both retired from teaching at West Holmes High School. Their long interest in antiques can be easily seen in their past careers, for Brooks was a teacher of history and also the originator of the school's historical displays.

Mr. Harris frequently attends public sales throughout the area, where he purchases most of the items offered at his store.

Gallery East

50/10-
22-1987
A young and active artist, Claude Ruston "Rusty" Baker, briefly opened an art gallery at Charm in September, 1987. The new art display was located on the second floor of the barn owned by Charm Center Corporation. Baker's gallery shared occupancy of the floor with Brookline Antiques.

The bright-eyed and talkative artist from Killbuck, Rusty Baker, could often be seen at work at his Charm location. During his short stay in town, Rusty worked mostly on silhouette paintings with natural-setting backgrounds.

Gallery East moved out in 1988.

The young artist has also done numerous historical murals. Among them is an 8' x 27' painting of early Charm, displayed in the Brookline Antique store. More of his murals are exhibited at *189/* Killbuck, Millersburg (Pizza Hut), and Roscoe Village, Ohio, and at New Martinsville, West Virginia.

Chiropractor and Massotherapist

150/
A chiropractic practice at Charm began soon after the completion of the Charm Center Building in 1987. Dr. John J. Octave, a chiropractic physician, opened an office on March 29, 1988, in the basement of the building. His practice turned out to have a short stay in town.

At the same time, a foot specialist shared the office with Dr. Octave. Both men were from the Columbus area, where they also had practices.

The part-time business at Charm was short lived and in the late summer of that year, both doctors moved out.

270/
By September a massotherapist, Dr. Larry Andrews, opened office at the same place. This also began as a part-time business at Charm, as he had an established practice at Brewster. After arriving in town, Dr. Andrews, Charm Therapy Clinic, extended office hours to three days per week to better accommodate patients' needs. Meanwhile, the Brewster location has been discontinued.

Dr. Andrews graduated from Ohio College of Massotherapy at Akron.

The Andrews family resides at Atwood Lake.

E and E Woodcraft

275/
As the tourist craft business began to increase at Charm, Ervin and Ella Raber set up a store in 1988. Because of earlier experience in the craft trade, they were able to establish a small and appealing tourist shopping place in the lower portion of the barn on the Charm Center lot.

The store specializes in unfinished pine products. Excelling in this type of craft has demanded expansion of their woodworking facilities at their residence two miles south of Beck's Mills. Among items on display at the store are shelves, shadow boxes, magnets, souvenirs, old advertising reproductions, and crafts.

The Rabers also market their products at two other localities, along with wholesaling.

Ole Mill Furniture II

150/
As an annex to Ole Mill Furniture, a store outlet of factory second merchandise was opened in the basement of the Charm Center Building in August of 1988. On April of the following year, the Mast-owned business closed down. The store's main selection consisted of furniture and chairs, with the supply dependent on availability.

A Bit of Charm

150/
During July, 1988 a craft shop opened in the former jeweler's shop. The building and lot are owned by Ann DeHass. More recently the single room structure was used as a game room. The shop was managed by Jean Hartley, who sold a variety of small, locally made crafts. A Bit of Charm closed in the fall of 1990 because of the upcoming remodeling of the building for a bed and breakfast.

Arvada's With Charm

349/
Attracted to the increasing tourist trade of Holmes County, Bob and Arvada Everhart opened a gift and craft shop at Berlin, Ohio. In 1989 a second store was opened at Charm.

During early 1989, Mrs. Everhart made a stop at Charm and quite unexpectedly ended up leasing a basement room of the Charm Center Building. In April of that year their new outlet of gifts and crafts was opened.

The neat, single-room business is a storehouse of interest to visiting tourists, who can find there: Paige pottery, pewter items, tin ware, rugs, dolls, and a collection of framed and matted pictures.

The Everharts live at Berlin and are kept active with their places of business.

Barkman's Bed and Breakfast

The first bed and breakfast located at Charm was Barkman's Bed and Breakfast. The four-bedroom rentals were furnished in the upstairs of the Ivan R. Barkman house, located adjacent to Miller's Dry Goods. The business was open to overnight guests from April, 1989 to the spring of 1990.

386/

Erb's Sports and Archery

Originally opening as Erb's Sports and Antiques, the business of Erb's Sports and Archery is located in the second story of the harness shop. Joe Erb, the owner, built a new addition to the harness shop when the post office moved to its new location, across the street, in 1988. Since then, an upstairs part of this new building has been used for the Erbs' store. An outside stairway ascends to the upper level, where Joe and his wife Elizabeth attend to customers' needs.

150/

The store was opened part-time in the spring of 1989, and offered a variety of sporting goods and antiques. By the fall of 1991, the antique trade was discontinued. Earlier that year, the inventory of East Holmes Archery was purchased, and the shop now specialized in bowhunting equipment. With the increase in sporting goods supplies, the store became a dream house to the outdoorsman. At this time the business was renamed "Erb's Sports and Archery." In early spring of 1992, an indoor bow range and storage addition were built onto the store.

Joe Erb, a long time big game hunter and outdoorsman, finds the new business of great interest to him. His earlier hunting excursions have enabled him to bring home trophy mounts of numerous big game across America and Canada.

Since 1991, the location has been set up as a checking station during the Ohio deer hunting season.

Charm Furniture

Charm Furniture originated as a sideline business and has since grown, beyond expectations, to a full time business. Owners Emanuel M. and Mary Miller opened the new venture, originally named Charm Furniture and Such, in their recently constructed barn–storage building on August 21, 1989. They began with selling factory-select furniture, but now they are offering merchandise mainly of superior quality. Inventory includes oak dining room suites, gliders, hickory rockers, clocks, china cabinets, tables, chairs, cof-

277/

fee tables, and end tables.

The outlet is located at their residence, off SR 557 in Charm, at the rear of Charm Plumbing or Ole Mill Crafts.

Old Blacksmith Gift Shop

Added to the extended line of businesses is the Old Blacksmith Gift Shop. In 1989 the blacksmith shop, owned by Jonas Yoder, was closed when he retired. The building was then completely renovated to house a gift shop. A son, Jacob J. Yoder, is the owner of the newly located outlet, which opened in September of that year. In their well-established place of business the Yoder family offers a variety of kitchen wares, games, crafts, and locally made items.

156/

Bertha Yoder Quilts

In 1990 Mrs. Syl (Bertha) Yoder began selling quilts at her home, at the northwest edge of town. She had been an avid quilter since moving into town in 1981. Pursuing her interest at home, she was able to care for her young family while bringing in an additional income.

276/

Eventually, other women were piecing, quilting, and binding quilts for Bertha, which gave her the needed inventory for retailing the locally made handiwork. Specializing in single hand stitching in a variety of patterns, she offered her customers quilts of uniform and superb quality.

In August of 1992 the Yoders moved out of Charm and into their newly built house, northwest of Sugarcreek.

J and M Rocker

Taking interest in producing a long time favorite—a child's hickory rocker—Jonas and Emanuel Miller set up shop in early 1990 on the Miller farm, a mile south of Charm. The scaled down version of a full size rocker is truly appealing to a young child. With a bent hickory design, the remainder of the chair is finished out in oak, ash, cherry, or walnut.

150/
277/

The chair was previously made by members of the Mose Troyer family living immediately east of the Jonas Millers, from whom the initial equipment of the business was purchased.

By 1992 other interests caused the production at the location to close down.

Charm Bicycle

Charm Bicycle is located at Miller's Dry Goods, and is owned by Amanda Miller's son-in-law, Ivan R. Barkman. Originally, the bike shop was located behind the dry goods store. The new business took a gradual start, when it

386/

🍂

opened in the fall of 1990 by repairing a few bicycles, along with selling parts and accessories. A year later, a distributorship was finalized for the dealership to Raleigh and Nishiki bicycles, which greatly increased sales. Since then, the high quality Diamond Back bicycle has also been stocked. Barkman offers a full line of service to his customers.

By early 1994, an addition was put onto the barn–quilt shop, which now houses the new bicycle facility.

The Watchman's Cottage Bed and Breakfast

150/ With the increasing tourism in Holmes County, bed and breakfasts became rapidly expanding enterprises in the late 1980s and early 1990s. One such enterprise is "The Watchman's Cottage Bed and Breakfast" at Charm.

The new business was located on the corner lot across the street from the restaurant, in the former watch repair shop, as the name itself suggests. After the closing of the craft shop "A Bit of Charm" in the fall of 1990, the building and grounds were extensively remodeled. A brick fireplace and chimney erected on the south side of the building enhanced the feeling of coziness and warmth within the single-room quarters. Along its front, the old

72/ cement hitching rail (a common landmark in town), erected in 1924, was removed and replaced with a new Mast poured wall during December

260/ and January of 1991. Soon afterward, Johann Schlabach and Nathan Martin added the neatly laid rows of brick facing.

The small lot, enclosed by picket and wrought iron fencing, is a neat and cozy spot in the village of Charm. The stark white-painted cottage was opened for business February 20, 1991.

The following summer, the upstairs of the Homestead Restaurant was also remodeled for expanded bed and breakfast housing. A long

249/

❧
148

The Watchman's Cottage Bed and Breakfast – 1991.

wooden stairway, added to the north side of the building when the restaurant was remodeled earlier, led to the three bedrooms overlooking Charm and SR 557. These rooms were closed in 1994.

The owner of the unique bed and breakfast, Ann DeHass, serves the occupants to their satisfaction in her nearby restaurant. The restaurant's placemat menu described these places of business in neat little poems.

151/
Bed and Breakfast #1
Gaze across the street to find
A place that will take you back in time—
The Victorian Age; cozy, peaceful, unique, serene;
Visit this place to see what I mean.

Bed and Breakfast #2
Not only across the way, but above your head,
You'll find rest and a snug antique bed.
The rooms are three, none of them the same;
Forever in your memory they'll remain.

Troyer's Arrow and Supply

When Erb's Sports and Archery began specializing in bowhunting equipment in 1991, archery was a widely practiced sport in the area. With the constant demand for arrow supplies and repair work, Delbert Troyer began this service at his home workshop at the east edge of town. He carries the full line of equipment for arrow alignment, nocking, and fledging, to fill the customer's needs. From the broad range of available arrow supplies and components, new arrows can be constructed to specifications.

Country Parlor Crafts and Gifts

135/ Country Parlor Crafts and Gifts was a craft shop that operated during the 1991 tourist season. The business was owned by Don and Barb Hines and was located in the basement of the Charm Center Building. The small store was initially opened in April, 1991, and after the tourist season ended that fall, it was closed.

The middle-aged Hines couple was from Mansfield and made the hour-long drive to Charm each business day. Don, who had retired from work because of multiple sclerosis, helped make the wooden cutouts at their home. These and other items were handpainted by Barb at their place of business. The inventory in the basement room display included handcrafted miniatures, country collectibles, and woodcrafts.

Shady Maple Crafts

372/ Shady Maple Crafts began as a business in 1991 and is located at the north edge of the village. The small home workshop vocation allows its proprietor, Eli E. Miller, to remain active despite open heart surgery a number of years ago (1983). The work involved at the location is partially manufacturing oak porch swing and glider seats. Along with this, he also makes cloth, Log Cabin-style keychains. All work is done for wholesaling.

Just the Two of Us

Appearing at Charm as a craft store, Just the Two of Us operated at the Charm Center Building basement from August, 1992 until late that fall. The small store was furnished by proprietors Nancy Kalinowski and Mary Yoder with much of their own handiwork. Most of the items displayed featured the women's artistic touch in handpainted wooden crafts. Also included among the wooden products were a variety of dried flower arrangements.

Mrs. Kalinowski resided in the Tiverton Center area, and Mary lived 2¹/₂ miles northeast of Charm. After closing, the Kalinowskis moved to Florida.

Charm Wood Shop

As area woodworkers found increasing demands from the furniture and craft industry, numerous small shops opened producing the crafted products which the area is noted for. These "cottage industries" have been mainly family-operated businesses.

The Charm Wood Shop originated in 1992 at the east edge of town, when owner and farmer Vernon Kline needed to change his farming pattern. In a woodworking facility which they had converted from a storage building, the family is now engaged in making lazy susan turntables, shelves, and cutting boards.

Hillside Crafts

Hillside Crafts originated in the early part of 1993 at the former Hillside Carriage and Buggy Shop. The business, owned by James Yoder, is located a mile northwest of Charm along TR 154. Its display room is stocked with a variety of inventory, including oak furniture, unfinished pine furniture, hickory rockers, quilt racks, baskets, shelves, and crafts. Situated in an area heavily dotted with craftsmen, their items can be correctly termed, "locally made."

Ridge View Furniture

Samuel Yoder placed a new set of buildings and a woodworking shop along TR 154, a mile west of Charm, in 1993. Earlier, before marriage, Samuel operated a well-established business known as Long Lane Furniture, on his parents' farm in the New Bedford area. The business was briefly interrupted until the new facility was ready, then the furniture venture was continued and renamed Ridge View Furniture. Yoder does custom woodworking which includes quality oak or walnut bedroom suites.

Miller Dimensions

Jacob R. Miller began a glue clamp operation in late 1993 on his father-in-law Vernon Kline's farm, at the east edge of Charm. Miller does custom, dimensional wood gluing, for which there is a great demand in the area. As the business became established, it soon outgrew the initial building on the farm, and in December of 1994 was moved to the former Charm Engine building, a mile west of Charm. At this time, Jacob was joined in partnership by a brother, Paul.

MFB Repair and Supply

After retiring from the management of Charm Engine, Melvin A. Barkman built a shop at his property, a mile northwest of Charm, in 1993. Although Barkman hopes to stay within the limits of a hobbyist, he has equipment for both steel and woodworking. Mel anticipates having furniture making and restoring woodwork a high priority. His experience with metal work also enables Barkman to excel in that type of work.

Country Charm

As spring arrived, following the record cold winter of 1993–1994, Larry and Sally Hockenberry were preparing to open "Country Charm" in March of 1994. Located in the basement of the Charm Center Building, the small shop specializes in sugar-free chocolates. Cake and candy molds, as well as gifts, may also be found at the neat little store.

Most of the chocolates are made by the Hockenberrys from their own recipe. The middle-aged couple resides at Dover, Ohio.

Sunshine Antiques

In October of 1994, Sunshine Antiques was opened in the second story of the Homestead Restaurant. The upstairs rooms, which had been most recently used as a bed and breakfast, were now refurnished as an antique store.

Sunshine DeHass, the owner, displays glassware and furniture in her new place of business. DeHass has closed the store over winter and expects to open again in the spring.

School History

From the early pioneers to the present day society, schools and education can be considered a cornerstone of the building of our nation. Though the methods of teaching and studying have varied greatly in past centuries, education is still intended to prepare students to meet the future in all walks of life.

As the early lawmakers saw the importance of education, they accordingly made provisions for the states to support their schools.

29/ 213/ p.35 224/ V-J p.141

The basis for Ohio school laws stemmed from the 1785 and 1787 Land Ordinances, which required that the revenues of Section 16 of each township of the Northwest Territory be used to maintain schools. Encouragement to schools and good government is provided on this 1787 document: Article 3 – "Religion, morality and knowledge, being necessary to good government and the happiness of mankind, schools and the means of education shall be forever encouraged." The financial support for early Ohio public schools was computed completely from "school land" monies. In 1803 the Ohio Legislature provided for the leasing of these lands and in 1826 permitted the sale of the school sections. Up until 1930 school support was based entirely on the real property taxes and revenues that the Section 16 school lands provided. By this time the rise in industrialization made the Land Ordinance school law obsolete, as some of the sections may never have been developed, thus netting very little revenues; and legal changes were made accordingly.

The history of the early Charm, or Stevenson, school is very dim so far, but we can form some idea of its former establishment. As noted in Henry Howe's *Historical Collections of Ohio* (1902), Ohio had no laws governing its first schools and since the state's settlement was made by many different classes of people, schools were set up among these groups or communities. Education depended mainly on the previous training and habits of the pioneers. As little state monies were available and school levies were unheard of, the early school was more or less a private school. With the teacher agreeing to "keep school" for a certain length of time, the parents agreed to pay from one to three dollars per child enrolled for the teacher's services. The buildings were extremely simple, and all ages were taught in one room. Apparently there were no grades; students advanced through classes when they were "through the book." When children were needed at home or on the farm, they went to school only when their work duties permitted.

Charm School No. 3

19/ p.35

There is found in Clarence Troyer's *History of Villages – People – Places in Eastern Holmes County* (1975), of his interviews with Ray Hummel, Louise Kaser and Mrs. Andy (Mattie) Miller, that a "little red" schoolhouse had existed at the turn of the century in Charm. Hummel had stated that his parents used to live in it after it was converted to a dwelling. The old school had stood adjacent to the cheese factory and a short distance south of the present schoolhouse. Ray's parents, Christ and Amanda Hummel, were married October 28, 1894, so the building was still standing at that time. No exact date is known when it was built. The county's oldest map, of 1861, shows that a school was already located in the village at that time (See map, p. 24). Deed records indicate that the lands immediately outlying Charm were all acquired from the government between 1815 to 1835. Since no other school is known to have been within two miles, it would seem logical that a young community needed a local school. Thus it would appear reasonably safe to assume that the one-room schoolhouse was built ca. 1830 at the countryside crossroad. Henry Howe's *Historical Collections of Ohio* (1902) describes the typical early school as a building ". . . fifteen to eighteen

224/ V-J p.141

Charm School No. 3

feet wide and twenty-four to twenty-eight feet long . . ." with the benches principally rude and having no backs. Desks were sometimes furnished for the "big boys and girls."

There is some indication that the present Eric Guggisberg house contains the structure (present at the turn of the century) of the "little red schoolhouse" within its walls.

The second school building was a two-story wooden frame structure built on the site of the present schoolhouse.

No actual date is known when the second one was built to replace the former one-room building. In the growing community the first schoolhouse was eventually overcrowded and provisions had to be made accordingly. Here again we may use history to determine the approximate date of its formation. Around 1843 an enumeration was taken of the school-age children and parents in Holmes County. From this data the townships were divided into school districts. Within each district a "place of learning" was built and individually numbered. From various recordings and early school records we find that Charm School was School No. 3.

The closest date found on the building of the "two story" is a deed of 1855. A Christian and Katherine Miller of the S.W.Qtr. Sec. 4 (Vernon Kline farm) sold .4 acre of land to School District No. 3 of German Twp. on April 16, 1855.

This transaction points to a very important fact about the two early schoolhouses. Incidentally, a section line runs between the sites of the two buildings. With the '55 deed from Sec. 4 where the "two story" had stood, the older "little red," though close by, was actually located across the section line in Sec. 7. This would definitely put a dividing line between the two school buildings, as each had set on separate parcels of land.

It would seem logical to believe that the new building would have been built the same year, after the April, 1855 transfer, though the deed was

171/

33/Nov. 1989 p.6

V21- 511- 1855

not recorded until October 27, 1856. The deed also indicated Michael Domer as being Chairman of the Board of Education of German Township and that the purchase cost of the land was $15.90.

At the school, primary lessons were taught on the first floor and grammar in the upper room. The terms *primary* and *grammar*, to designate the classes, was still used on Charm school records in 1951. An inside stairway and outside fire escape steps led to the top floor. The school bell hung in the tower on the east end of the building and proclaimed the school's sessions. A coal shanty standing between the school and the road was kept supplied with coal from local underground mines while the privies were located a short distance to the south.

Many memories still linger among the former pupils of the "two story schoolhouse." Among them is the death of a highly respected teacher, William Perry Miller, during the school term; wintertime sledding on the Schlabach hill road; hiding in the crawl space underneath the building; carrying drinking water from a nearby well; jumping out the window during class to play ball; flying down the outside steps with a sled; playing in the brush thickets close by; and, of course, hurrying to the "john" in all "climates." Roman Keim, recalling his school days, says, "We didn't leave a stone unturned," and apparently the days of the "two story" were not dull.

However, once again Charm was in need of a school replacement, which it received in 1938.

At this time plans were being made to erect a new brick fireproof school building. With the combined effort of the state, the school board, and an architect, the project was put underway.

At the close of the school term in 1938 the old wooden two story structure was moved a short distance from the site so that construction could begin immediately on the new one. At the time, the building was sold at auction to Gideon Troyer

67/ 75/ 107/ 288/

71/

333/

The two-story school with a full width porch.

for a few hundred dollars; Troyer then disassembled the old landmark and used the lumber to build a house and shop on the farm (the Dan E. Mast farm today). To his amazement, the ceiling joist space had been laid full of boards to act as a sound barrier between the upper and lower rooms. Today the farm workshop still bears reminders of the early schoolhouse at Charm. The three original glass and wood panel doors readily bring back memories of its former pupils. On the wooden siding can still be seen clearly the etched initials *HEO*, most likely those of turn-of-the-century students, Herbert or Harvey Oswald. Also, the slate roof was used for the Troyers' new house on the farm.

30/

The *"Specifications of the materials and labor to be used and employed in the erection of a fireproof School Building, Charm, Ohio; for the Board of Education; Clark Rural School District; Holmes County, Ohio"* were drawn up by Fred D. Jacobs, a registered architect of Coshocton, Ohio.

31/
103/
288/
296/
297/

The general contractor for the new building was Manass J. Miller. His employees included a brother Jake and two sons, Lloyd and Edward, along with Robert R. Troyer, Jonas P. Miller, and Crist C. Miller. The brick work was done by Rudy and Bobby Neff, Max Smith, Rudy Miller, and Dyke Gerber. Local resident Jake I. Hershberger helped with cement mixing and brick tending. The roof was laid by Omer Blough, whose enterprise developed into the company known today as Sugar Creek Roofing. Among Blough's workers were James Hershberger and Oris Miller. While placing the flat roof, Oris was backing along and accidentally tripped out over the two-foot-high rim along the south side. Landing on a sandpile twenty-five feet below, he luckily suffered only broken ribs. Miller recuperated at home the rest of the summer, thus being unable to help with the remaining school roofing job.

32/

As the construction progressed there was an apparent shortage of funds. With not enough money to finish the building before school started in the fall, the contractor said the building would be locked, with no school beginning until monies

36/

Charm School, built in 1938.

we secured. Under this dilemma the board sought the advice of W. W. Badger, a lawyer of Millersburg. He recommended that they try to get a tax levy passed. A special election was accordingly held on August 9, 1938 to decide on a two year, two mill levy for the purpose of general construction and equipping the Charm School. After the votes were cast, the levy had passed by a slim margin. The banks were now willing to finance the remaining costs, knowing that funds would be available.

50/
7-14-
1938

By late September of 1938 the new Charm School building was completed at a cost of $15,000 and classes were held on schedule.

100/
10-22-
1938

At this time a school bus was already bringing children to the Charm School.

Compulsory Attendance

24/
p.55
336/p.2
23/

Enforcement of the compulsory school attendance law of Ohio did not receive much attention until the 1940s and '50s. Earlier, in 1921, the provisions of the Bing law, Section 3321.01, Revised Code, stated that "A child between six and eighteen years of age is of compulsory school age." The law further provided (Section 3221.03 Revised Code), "Every child of compulsory school age shall attend a school or participate in a special education program that conforms to the minimum standards prescribed by the state board of education until the child either: (A) Receives a diploma . . . successfully completing high school; (B) Receives an age and schooling certificate . . .; (C) Is excused from school . . . or if in need of a special education . . . ."

336/
p.2-3

For a long time the one room, public country school had been in use, where most or all of the Amish pupils from the area were enrolled, from grades one through eight. The non-Amish students graduating from these schools would then attend consolidated high schools. However, the Amish were satisfied with the eighth grade education provided, and students would quit schooling at that time. When the Amish were pressured to abide by the state's ruling, an Amish pupil would remain in school until he or she reached sixteen years of age, simply repeating the eighth grade. But when the one room schools became overcrowded, these extra pupils could not be accommodated. Eventually, with more consolidated public schools being attended by non-Amish, the single room school buildings began fading from the scene. Throughout the Amish community of Holmes, Wayne, and Tuscarawas Counties, these schools remained in use longer because of Amish resistance to the consolidation movement.

It is not certain what compelled the county school boards to attempt to strictly enforce the law regarding Amish school children during the middle 1900s. In neighboring Wayne County, beginning in 1942, the issue created great controversy. Eventually this resulted with an Amish student being confined to a children's home and a father being jailed as they resisted education beyond the eight grade. County officials reasoned that the Amish parents were negligent by not providing the proper education for their children, as required by state law.

336/
p.4

This law caused much concern among the Amish. They felt that schooling should end with the eighth grade or when a child reached fourteen years of age. The child could thereafter be brought up in the home under the influence of the parents, with training in social and religious obligations.

25/

With this concern the Holmes County Amish drew up and presented to the Holmes County Board of Education an explanation of their views.

A copy is recorded along with the Board's minutes of September 11, 1954 and reads as follows:

Reasons for not Sending our Children to School Beyond the Elementary Eighth Grade

We believe that our children should be properly educated and trained for manhood and womanhood. We especially [believe] they need to be trained in those elements of learning which are given in the elementary schools.

We believe that our children have attained sufficient schooling when they have passed the eighth grade of elementary school, and that in our circumstances, way of life, and religious belief, we are safeguarding their home and church training in secular and religious belief and faith by keeping them at home under the influence of their parents.

We believe farming, and housekeeping on the farm, to be the best vocations for our children in order to have them follow our way of life and belief. Therefore being free from the many evils which attend many other occupations which of necessity employ persons of uncertain and evil character and habits. Continual associations with such characters, we believe will contribute to loose morals, and intemperate and [undesirable] habits, which are not consistent for any Christian, nor edifying to the church.

In addition to the training in farming and housekeeping, we believe that our children should be well and properly trained in the Scriptures, and the understanding thereof. Under the doctrines of our church, this duty is being placed on the parents, and only they can discharge this duty if their children are under their full supervision; a situation which

does not exist if they are attending school.

We believe that such time [spent] in the classroom, beyond the eighth grade or the age of fourteen, will often lead to indolence and an inclination for types of work which require less manual labor, without regard for spiritual and sometimes physical welfare; often resulting in becoming entangled with things that are not edifying.

It is our belief that the teaching of the German language as it is used in our church services, can only be adequately given to our children, once they are freed from attending public school. This is a responsibility for the parents, and is [usually] done in the home.

Further attending school, we feel has the inclination to make our youth more athletic minded, of which we are continually endeavoring to avoid. As we feel a true Christian can not [participate] in such sports activities.

We are only giving praise to those in authority, but we feel the compulsory [a]ttendance law was created without due respect to persons having religious scruples against attendance beyond the eighth grade, or after a child reaches puberty, in accordance with the religious rights and liberties as provided in our Constitution. Such a law would hardly be justified, so we are kindly asking to be granted leniency in its enforcement. If we are found guilty of violating the law, it is only so for religious reasons. May the Grace of God be with you.

Statement and Resolution of the Amish Church of Holmes County Regarding Public School Attendance

Since the Old Order Amish of America are using the Articles of the Confession of Faith, established at Dortrecht, Holland in 1621, as their foundation of their belief in establishing certain church doctrines; we Amish people feel it necessary [from time to time] to further establish such regulations in order to maintain the Christian standards of our belief.

Through the enforcement of the Compulsory School Attendance law, we Amish people are thereby molested and prejudiced as evildoers in our religious persuasion, practice and custom. We are stern believers in a Supreme Being, and recognize God as an object of worship and love. Therefore we feel his obedience cannot be burnt out of a man, nor scourged into him, "for as a man thinketh in his heart so is he."

Be it therefore resolved, by the undersigned

Bishops and Ministers of our respective church districts; that no parents of our faith shall cause his or her child to attend school of an advanced grade in the Public School System, other than the elementary schools. This resolution was voiced [sic] upon by the membership and same was [approved; as an ordinance it] has no reflection on any other church group or denomination and is only adopted for the membership of Holmes County. Signed by Bishops, Ministers and Deacons: Jacob J. Mast, Gideon E. Troyer, Andrew J. Weaver, Dan N. Miller, Albert J. Beachy, Andrew N. Troyer, Jonas A. Keim, Dan N. Stutzman, Eli E. Hershberger, Andy J. Mast, David P. Troyer, Abe N. Miller, David L. Raber, Crist A. Troyer, Eli M. Miller, Joe P. Miller, Aden A. Yoder, Noah I. Yoder, Wm. T. Weaver, Emanuel E. Miller, John D. Fry, Noah R. Troyer, Abe E. Miller, John A. Troyer, Dan N. Yoder, Melvin A. Raber, Amos Raber, Roman J. Miller, Joe J. Miller, Roy L. Schlabach, Abe E. Miller, Ben E. Weaver, Martin A. Miller, and David J. Miller.

Afterward the Holmes County Amish parents who were not complying with the law were sent letters of warning by the county school officials. Daniel E. Wolboldt, the Holmes County Attendance Officer, issued a letter of similar nature in *The Daily Record* (Wooster, Ohio) which stated:

"To the parents of the East Holmes County District and surrounding townships.

"I am making this final appeal to you parents to send your children who have passed the 8th grade and are not 16 years old, to school. The East Holmes school district has provided a 9th grade special school for any Amish or English speaking children to attend. They have worked hard, with the county board of education and the state board of education to get approval of this special school with a promise by parents to comply with the state school laws: such school was established.

"The children must be in school until they have passed the [8th] grade, then they can get a work permit at the age of 16 years, but if no work permit is obtained, they must be in school until they have reached the age of 18 years.

"There are being prepared in the office of the county superintendent, complaints against from 25 to 30 parents, which will be turned over to the Prosecuting Attorney for action. Please do not force me to ask for prosecution. I have sent letters of instruction to 26 parents with a card for enrollment in this special school. I again ask you, please comply with the request of school authorities before I am forced to prosecute."

24/
p.57-58

154

76/
26/
p.65
341/

In January of 1955 the doors were opened for the special ninth grade enrollment. Pupils in the Charm area attended the Meadow Valley School east of New Bedford and the Baptist Church building being used as a school at Berlin. The old church no longer remains today; it had been located immediately south of present Berlin Baptist Church on the corner of South Market and Oak streets.

The Berlin classes were taught by John Maxwell; Sturgis Miller (Arithmetic); Edythe Boyd (English) and Thomas Coulter (German).

At this time also the school year was extended from eight months to nine.

After the 1955–1956 school year the classes were discontinued as school officials were relaxing their pressure. A ninth grade class, meeting one day a week, was arranged, with the teachers being Amish farmers.

11/1-9-
1959

Locally the schools were held at five different places. At Flat Ridge the teachers were Lizzie Nisley, Ben R. Miller – Ben J. Raber, and Simon J. Miller. Teachers at Troyer Ridge were Henry Shetler and Fannie Nisley, and at Graber School were Jacob Graber and Roy J. Raber. Mose M. Miller and Alvin I. Yoder taught this special class at their residence.

Meanwhile, in neighboring Wayne County, the school officials could not reach a satisfactory compromise with the Amish community and charges were brought against those who refused to comply with the minimum standards. After months of delay the State Department of Education set new standards for one room schools.

24/
p.59

An article in *The Daily Record* (Wooster, Ohio) of January 28, 1959 discussed the new law indicating that beginning in the 1959–60 school year, no more than two grades per classroom could be taught by one teacher. The aim of this measure was to bring "sudden death" to one room schools in which eight grades were taught by one teacher. State funds were to be discontinued if the minimum standard was not met.

OHIO Form IV 3331.02 R.C. SCHOOL RECORD OF APPLICANT FOR EMPLOYMENT CERTIFICATE SCHOOL DISTRICT

I certify that Vernon J. Miller FULL NAME OF PUPIL
who resides at Charm, Ohio EXACT ADDRESS
whose age is 16 years and _____ months, attended school 160 days the current year, and 173 days last school year.
This pupil has successfully completed the 9th grade and is presently enrolled in the 10th grade.
This pupil ☐ is ☐ is not enrolled in the State Approved work program.
Comments: (INCLUDING STANDING IN STUDIES AND RATING IN CONDUCT) Good
Jacob R. Graber SIGNATURE OF PRINCIPAL
Graber School NAME OF SCHOOL
Feb 18, 1971 DATE

Copy of work permit.

Charm School, which was enrolling four grades within one classroom, made its changes accordingly during the next two years. The area's school attendance was rearranged mainly between the Charm and Flat Ridge schools.

211/
p.XV

Stemming from this compulsory education issue, the concern among the Amish resulted in their establishing their own schools. Today's widespread parochial school movement originated in Wayne County in 1944 followed by the first school built in Holmes County in 1954. These one-room schools, dotting the countryside, are church-funded, entirely free of state support. Present schools number around one hundred, and have seen a steady increase. The schools are governed by state requirements along with their own school committee standards.

In 1972 the one-day-a-week ninth grade was discontinued when the U.S. Supreme Court ruled that Amish parents could not be forced by state authorities to send their children to high school.

143/
Aug.
Sept.
1972
p.21-22

This ruling stemmed from measures taken against a group of Wisconsin Amish who were brought to court following their refusal to send their children beyond the eighth grade. The U.S. Supreme Court finally ruled on the issue. The decision of the high court was announced on May 15, 1972.

Chief Justice Warren Burger delivered the Court's forty-page opinion, stating that "the Amish religion pervades and determines virtually their entire way of life." The court apparently realized that "to believe is to act," which can be referred to the Anabaptist forefathers who suffered severe persecution in order to live out their beliefs.

The opinion also referred to the First Amendment recognizing freedom of religion as a religious belief, not a personal preference, and indicated that compulsory attendance for the Amish would "force them to give up their belief" or "to migrate to some more tolerant region," which the Amendment was intended to prevent.

Testifying at the hearing was Dr. John A. Hostetler, who pointed out that to force high school attendance upon Amish children could undermine and might eventually destroy the Old Order Amish church community as we know it today. His testimony declared compulsory attendance to be psychologically harmful to Amish children.

The Court recognized that the Amish do not object to elementary education but that they "believe that higher learning tends to develop values . . . that alienate man from God."

After the Supreme Court's ruling in 1972, special ninth grade education ceased in Holmes County.

Clark Township Local School District

The Charm School was one of four two-room schools located in the Clark Township Local School District. The four schools within the township provided for first through eighth grade education. With no high school in the township, the board paid a tuition fee to surrounding districts for pupils seeking a high school education.

During the 1950s the small township districts were urged by the State Department of Education to consolidate, thus forming larger districts to be capable of providing high school facilities and education.

Efforts were made in 1954 to unite Clark, Berlin, Saltcreek, Walnut Creek, and Paint Townships. This bid to form a larger school district had failed as the result of a petition rejected a second time during that year. In November of 1955 the consolidation issue was put to a vote and again soundly defeated.

26/
p.65

After the county's efforts for consolidation had failed, Berlin, Walnut Creek, and Paint Districts united to form the East Holmes Local School District in 1956. They subsequently built the high school at Hiland, as their own schools had overflowing attendances.

During 1968, in a renewed attempt to have Clark and Saltcreek districts join with East Holmes Local School District, the county board stressed the fact that the state required each district to have a high school; otherwise it was to be dissolved and its territory joined with another school district. Under the state's ruling (Sec. 3311.29 Ohio Revised Code), such action was to take place by July 1, 1968 or state funds could be withheld. The local board, in its own defense, stated that they were paying tuition to other districts for each pupil needing high school education, which has worked out satisfactorily.

49/
2-8-
1968

A public meeting with county and Clark Local board members was held at the Charm School to discuss the issue. The community, mostly Amish, was largely not in favor of consolidation. Since the Amish favored not sending their children to high school and yet they would have to carry a heavier tax burden, the idea did not seem appropriate.

The County Board's minutes of October 12, 1967 indicated that "no action will be taken on the dissolution of Clark and Salt Creek Township until a later date."

At the February 8, 1968 meeting the Clark and Salt Creek boards were invited (and present) to participate in a course to follow with the transfer of the two township districts to a district providing an educational program for grades one to

❧

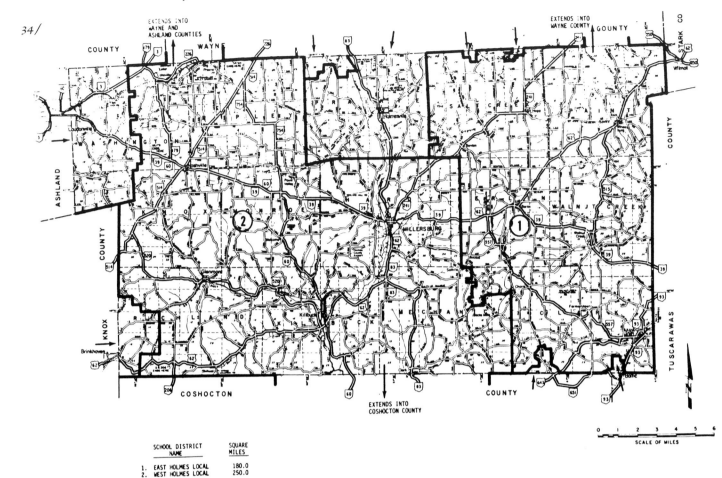

SCHOOL DISTRICT NAME	SQUARE MILES
1. EAST HOLMES LOCAL	180.0
2. WEST HOLMES LOCAL	250.0

Holmes County school district divisions.

twelve, or East Holmes Local. After a full discussion of Ohio Revised Code Section 3311.29, a conclusion was reached at the end of the meeting that each township board was to further consider the proposed action in their regular meeting to make the transfer of territory at the County Board's March 14 meeting.

Later, after counseling with two county board members, the local boards brought the case to the attention of the State Board. From "The Statement of Position of Clark Township Local School District and Salt Creek Township Local School District," filed with the board's minutes, more details are found. "Section 3311.29, Ohio Revised Code, provides for elimination of school districts which do not provide twelve grades of school, but is subject to the exception; The State board of education may authorize exceptions to school districts where topography, sparcity of population, and other factors make compliance impracticable."

Since both districts were paying tuition for sending their students to other districts and most of the students were Amish and did not plan to attend high school, the township boards felt it constituted "an unusual and special situation." The representatives of Clark and Salt Creek districts

375/ 3-1968

acting on these matters informed the president and a member of the Holmes County Board of Education on March 8 of their intention to appear before the Ohio State Board on March 11 to request an exception. The county members, contacted by the local board representatives, promised that the county board would wait one month (April 1968) before taking any action in dissolving the Clark and Saltcreek districts. On March 11 the state board was informed by the township school representatives of their case. The state board agreed they would vote on the issue at the April meeting. Because of the promises of the county members, the local boards intentionally stayed away from the March 14 County Board meeting to see what action would be taken by the state. But the County Board, contrary to its promises, adopted a resolution dissolving Clark Township Local School District and Salt Creek Township Local School District on that meeting date. Because of this action the township boards felt that the county board had acted in bad faith and misled them so as to prevent them from presenting their claim for exemption and status of their matter before the State Board. They requested that the Board of Education of Holmes County cancel its resolution of

375/ 6-25- 1968 42/

March 14, 1968, which was to dissolve the two districts on the effective date of June 30, 1968, and wait for the State Board's ruling.

With no change in referendum from the state board, the final special business meeting of the Clark Township Local School Board before consolidation was held June 25, 1968. The last members to serve on the board were Noah A. Raber (President), Ben Beachy, Albert A. Raber, Monroe Beachy, and LaRue Oswald (Clerk).

Among the local people serving in school-related positions were board members John Lahm, Albert A. Keim, Paul Hershberger, and Noah A. Raber; LaRue Oswald (Clerk); janitors Albert Keim, Abe P. Troyer, Emanuel Miller, Bena Miller, Mrs. Abe P. Troyer, Ben Troyer, Amanda A. Miller, Mattie Raber and Ervin Raber; and enumerators Albert Keim and Albert Kaser.

The teachers of Clark Local Schools had adopted a school philosophy for their aim and guideline in teaching. A revision of the 1964 copy was submitted by the teachers on September 30, 1966 and reads as follows:

"We, the teachers of Clark Local Schools believe that the chief aim and duty of our schools is to develop in the life of each individual to the extent that he may become an intelligent, useful, and well adjusted citizen of this great nation.

"We believe that the pupils in the schools of Clark Township need more thorough training in the basic fundamental subjects of education, namely; reading, writing, English, arithmetic and spelling.

"We aim to be living examples of what we consider to be happy, progressive and christian members of our homes, schools, and citizens of our country.

"We will try our utmost to provide an atmosphere in our classrooms where our pupils will feel happy and secure.

"We intend to accept each child as he is, and try to provide opportunities for individual differences in work and play, teaching him the lessons of sharing responsibilities in the hope that it will lead to the art of living peaceably with all men.

"We teachers should practice and insist on good manners being practiced in the schools. Friendliness, courtesy, respect for each other, and for older people should be empathetically stressed.

"We will teach each child (according to his ability) to speak, read, write and spell the English language, this being their chief means of communication.

"We aim to develop in each child a love for home, a love for beauty and all of God's creations that they may become honored and respected citizens.

35/

"Through this type of instruction, we believe that our students will be qualified to accept the responsibilities, necessary for good citizenship, and thereby a better America."

The teachers and the pupils both share a similarity after leaving the classroom and walking in their separate paths through life, in that they all recall affectionately the memories of the years devoted to school. The student's guidance from his teacher will often leave an impression, be it good or otherwise, throughout his entire life. Reminiscing over bygone schooldays is enlightening to old and young alike as happenings and events are shared from their respective time.

Special Classes

A vocational agriculture class was begun at Charm in 1969. For some time the class was held in the basement of the school. Later a bus was remodeled to facilitate the needs of the program. The shop bus would visit the various schools participating in the vocational agriculture class. In 1988 the special bus was discontinued and a classroom was set up at Chestnut Ridge for that purpose. Great interest has been shown in the program. Teachers for the vocational agriculture class have included Tom Andrews, Bob Reed, and Dave Woodring.

Since 1974 a special federal program has been implemented at Charm to provide the slow learner with the opportunity to reach the intended class level. The program has also been known as Remedial or Title I Reading and Math. A portable classroom was erected adjacent to the school building for this purpose in 1982. Since, some of the classes have been held in the basement of the Charm school building.

1/

In the 1986–87 school year a Readiness class was begun at Charm to prepare preschool children for their enrollment in first grade the following year. In 1992 the class was discontinued at Charm and has since been held at Flat Ridge.

Teachers for these programs have been:

1974–75	Joyce Miller – Reading
1975–76	Rachel Kaufman – Reading
1976–77	Debbie (Lytle) Schrock – Reading
	Laura (McCombs) Coblentz – Math
1977–78	Debbie (Lytle) Schrock – Reading
	Laura (McCombs) Coblentz – Math
1978–79	Debbie Schrock – Reading
	Laura Coblentz – Math
1979–80	Elizabeth Gerber – Reading
	Laura Coblentz – Math
1980–81	Elizabeth Gerber – Reading
1981–82	Elizabeth Gerber – Reading

1982–83	Elizabeth Gerber – Reading	
1983–84	Elizabeth Gerber – Reading	
1984–85	Elizabeth Gerber – Reading	
	Karen Reiss – Art	
1985–86	Connie Byler – Reading	
1986–87	Marcia Miller – Readiness	
	Linda Amstutz – Reading	
1987–88	Marcia Miller – Readiness	
	Linda Amstutz – Reading Recovery	
	Susan Lingler – Reading	
1988–89	Marcia Miller – Readiness	
	Susan Lingler – Reading Recovery/Reading	
1989–90	Marcia Miller – Readiness	
	Susan Lingler – Reading Recovery/Reading	
1990–91	Marcia Miller – Readiness	
1991–92	Marcia Miller – Readiness	
	Susan Lingler – Reading	
1992–93	Susan Lingler – Reading	
1993–94	Susan Lingler – Reading	
	Linda Slease – Reading	
1994–95	Susan Lingler – Reading	
	Kim Youngen – Reading	

Elementary Records

The following teachers and enrollments for Charm School have been compiled from various records, including the holdings of the Holmes County Office of Education, East Holmes Local Administrative Office and Charm School. Along with these local newspapers, newsletters, teachers, and students have also been consulted. The Charm School's enrollment history is not complete, as recordings have been lost and their information mislaid or forgotten. Perhaps future researchers may uncover additional documents, so that the records may be more complete.

19/p.35 From historian Clarence Troyer's writing we learn of more early Charm teachers but are unable to give the dates of their teaching. They are George Miller, Irene Kaser, Nita Fair, and William Kaser (William Kaser was teaching ca. 1915).

311/ **1878–79**
L. J. Dietz

100/
8-14-1891 **1891–92**
Mary Schuler
100/ L. E. Funk (Grammar)
11-5-1891

50/4- **1893–94**
19-1894 S. B. Fair
Mary Schuler

100/5- **1894–95**
10-1894 Cora I. Miller (Primary)

The great art of learning is to undertake but little at a time.
1919 school souvenir

⁎

178/ **1895–96**
Ed Fair
Cora Miller
Blanch Guittard
Irene Guittard
Fannie Helmuth
Albert E. Hershberger
Boyd E. Hershberger
Eddie Hershberger
Erice Hershberger
Ida Hershberger
Nettie Hershberger
Sovilla Hershberger
Jacob Kaser
Katie Kaser
Sovilla Kaser
Will Kaser
Henry Klinegnecht
John Klinegnecht
Will Klinegnecht
Abe J. Mast
Eli J. Mast
Eli J. Mast
Jacob Mast
Lizzie J. Mast
Menno J. Mast
Mose J. Mast
Sarah Mast–Yoder
Amanda D. Miller
Andrew J. Miller
Anna Miller
Charlie Miller
Dan D. Miller
Daniel or Samuel Miller
David D. Miller
Fannie Miller
Frank Miller
Henry N. Miller
Jacob J. Miller
James Miller
John D. Miller
John N. Miller
Nettie Miller
Fritz Nickles
Marie Nickles
Amanda Price
William Price
Jeff Troyer
John A. Troyer
Jonas E. Troyer
Mattie E. Troyer
Ben E. Yoder
Henry E. Yoder
Joe E. Yoder

100/ **1896–97**
12-31-1896 *Virgil Guittard*
M. I. Miller

50/ **1898–99**
4-13-1899 *Henry P. Ledrich*

100/ **1899–1900**
11-16-1899 *Henry P. Ledrich*

50/ **1900–01**
4-4-1901 *William D. Fisher*
Ida Kersteller
Henry Ledrich
178/ Howard Aling
Eddie N. Hershberger
Ida Hershberger

Joseph Hershberger
Brisban Kaser
Sovilla Kaser
Will Kaser
Rob Klinegnecht
Amos Ladrich
Joe Ladrich
Katie Ladrich
Eva Lanzer
Myrtle Lanzer
Rob Lanzer
Dan J. Mast
Jacob J. Mast
Mose J. Mast
Albert S. Miller
Charlie Miller
D/o Ed Miller
Frank Miller
Henry N. Miller
Joe S. Miller
John S. Miller
Jonas D. Miller
Mose S. Miller
Nettie Miller
Son of Ed Miller
Emma Nickles
Fritz Nickles
Ida Nickles
Rosa Nickles
Albert Oswald
Herb Oswald
Mart Oswald
Priscilla Oswald
Walter Oswald
Albert Scherer
Levi L. Schlabach
Jacob Snyder
Sam Snyder
Andrew Styer
David P. Troyer
John A. Troyer
Mose P. Troyer
Fanny L. Yoder
30/ Mary L. Yoder

1903–04
W. L. Miller
(All Grammar)
Ida Hershberger
John Hershberger
Lydia Hershberger
Lizzie Hostetler
Mary Hostetler
Sadie Hostetler
Brisban Kaser
Albert Keim
Mary Keim
Eva Lanzer
Myrtle Lanzer
Robert Lanzer
Eli Mast
Barbara Miller
Charles Miller
Levi Miller
Moses Miller
Ben Oswald
Herbert Oswald
Walter Oswald
Sarah Schlabach
Harvey Swonger
Fanny Yoder

30/ **1904–05**
A. W. Oswald
Ida Hershberger
John Hershberger
Lydia Hershberger
Atlee Hochstetler
Maray A. Hochstetler
Sadie L. Hochstetler
Mary E. Hostetler
Maggie Jones
Clara Kaser
Ellen Kaser
Erma Lanzer
Eva Lanzer
Myrtle Lanzer
Robert Lanzer
Adam A. Miller
Barbara Miller
Charles J. Miller
Moses S. Miller
Benjamin Oswald
Herbert Oswald
Walter Oswald
Sarah Schlabach
John A. Troyer
John S. Troyer
Fanny L. Yoder
Mary E. Yoder
Mary L. Yoder

30/ **1905–06**
Jno. S. Miller
Anna Bontrager
Katie Erb
Mattie Erb
Ida Hershberger
John Hershberger
Lydia Hershberger
Atlee Hochstetler
Clara Kaser
Ellen Kaser
Andy Keim
Joseph Keim
Levi Keim
Bessie Lanzer
Erma Lanzer
Eva Lanzer
Myrtle Lanzer
Robert Lanzer
Ammon Miller
Andy Miller
Barbara Miller
Dan Miller
Eli Miller
Emma Miller
Joe Miller
Moses S. Miller
Perry Miller
Herbert Oswald
Lydia Oswald
Sanford Oswald
Walter Oswald
Dewey Reidenbach
Fanny Reidenbach
Alvin Schlabach
Eli Schlabach
Elizabeth Schlabach
Gideon Schlabach
Levi Schlabach
Sarah Schlabach
Anna Troyer

Barbara Troyer
Cornelius Troyer
David Troyer
Jno. A. Troyer
John S. Troyer
Lizzie A. Troyer
Lizzie S. Troyer
Mary Troyer
Moses Troyer
Simon P. Troyer
Amanda Yoder
David Yoder
Eli J. Yoder
Jacob J. Yoder
Mary Yoder
Mary L. Yoder
Moses Yoder

30/ **1906–07**
W. D. Fisher
Annie Bontrager
Abraham Erb
Vina Erb
John Hershberger
Atlee W. Hostetler
May Hummel
Ray Hummel
Andy J. Keim
David J. Keim
Joseph J. Keim
Levi Keim
Ammon N. Miller
Andy J. Miller
Andy M. Miller
Daniel M. Miller
Eli Miller
Emma Miller
Fanny A. Miller
Joe Miller
Mary J. Miller
Moses S. Miller
Perry Miller
Sarah A. Miller
Herbert Oswald
Lydia Oswald
Sanford Oswald
Walter Oswald
Dewey Reidenbach
Fanny Reidenbach
Daniel Schlabach
Eli Schlabach
Levi L. Schlabach
Lydia Schlabach
Annie Troyer
Barbara S. Troyer
Cornelius Troyer
David P. Troyer
Elizabeth A. Troyer
Elizabeth S. Troyer
John A. Troyer
John S. Troyer
Mary A. Troyer
Moses P. Troyer
Albert L. Yoder
Amanda L. Yoder
David J. Yoder
Eli J. Yoder
Jacob J. Yoder
Mary J. Yoder
Mary L. Yoder

355/

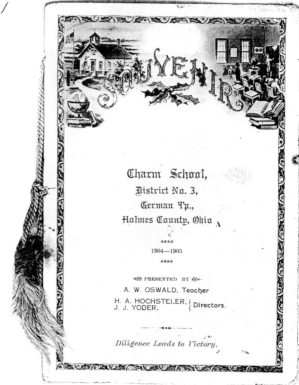

Charm School,
District No. 3,
German Tp.,
Holmes County, Ohio

****
1904—1905
****

❊ PRESENTED BY ❊

A. W. OSWALD, Teacher

H. A. HOCHSTELER,
J. J. YODER, } Directors.

Diligence Leads to Victory.

241/ **1907–08**
Percy Gerber

30/ **1908–09**
241/ *Jacob Schlarb*
Percy Gerber
Anna Bontrager
Abraham Erb
David Erb
Lavina Erb
May Hummel
Ray Hummel
Verna I. Hummel
Alma Kauffman
Andy J. Keim
Annie Keim
Henry Keim
Joseph J. Keim
Levi J. Keim
Sanford S. Keim
Harold Mast
Ammon N. Miller
Andy Miller
Andy J. Miller
Daniel M. Miller
Eli Miller
Emma Miller
Joe Miller
Joseph M. Miller
Katie A. Miller
Mary Miller
Mary J. Miller
Perry S. Miller
Lydia Oswald
Sanford Oswald
Sylva Oswald

Dewey Reidenbach
Fanny Reidenbach
Oscar Reidenbach
Alvin Schlabach
Eli Schlabach
Gideon S. Schlabach
Johnny Schlabach
Levi S. Schlabach
Mary Ann Schlabach
Sarah C. Schlabach
Amanda
    Swartzentruber
John Swartzentruber
Katie Swartzentruber
Abraham Troyer
Anna P. Troyer
Barbara Troyer
Cornelius S. Troyer
David Troyer
Emanuel Troyer
Emma Troyer
Katie M. Troyer
Mary A. Troyer
Mattie Troyer
Moses P. Troyer
Phineas Troyer
Simon P. Troyer
Albert Yoder
Amanda S. Yoder
Annie Yoder
Eli J. Yoder
Jacob Yoder
Mary J. Yoder
Mary S. Yoder
Tobias Yoder

A little too late is much too late. ❧
1900 Charm School writing exercise

189/

1909–10
16/
26/p.72 *Elva Brown*
Louise Engle
    (All Primary)
Abraham Erb
Lovina Erb
Esther Hummel
May Hummel
George Kaser
John Kaser
Tava Kaser
Anna Keim
Henry Keim
Harold Mast
Ande J. Miller
Andy Miller
Eli Miller
Joe Miller
Mary Miller
Desylvia Oswald
Lydia Oswald
Oscar Reidenbach
Alvin Schlabach
Daniel Schlabach
Joas Schlabach
Johnny Schlabach
Jonas Schlabach
Lydia Schlabach
Mary Ann Schlabach
Katie Swartzentruber
Abraham Troyer
Barbara Troyer
Dan Troyer
Emanuel Troyer
Emma Troyer
Katie Troyer
Mary A. Troyer
Mattie Troyer
Phineas Troyer
Albert Yoder
Katie Yoder
Tobias Yoder

1909–10
30/
Carl A. Miller
    (All Grammar)
Anna Borntrager
Abraham Erb
May Hummel
❧ Ray Hummel
Verna Hummel
160 Andy J. Keim

Henry Keim
Joe Keim
Levi Keim
Sanford Keim
Ammon N. Miller
Andy Miller
Daniel M. Miller
Emma Miller
Joseph M. Miller
Mary J. Miller
Perry S. Miller
Herbert Oswald
Lydia Oswald
Sanford Oswald
Dewey Reidenbach
Fanny Reidenbach
Alvin J. Schlabach
Gideon L. Schlabach
Levi Schlabach
Amanda
    Swartzentruber
John Swartzentruber
Anna P. Troyer
Cornelius S. Troyer
David P. Troyer
Moses P. Troyer
Simon Troyer
Albert Yoder
Amanda Yoder
Jacob J. Yoder
Mary Yoder
Mary Yoder

1910–11
Louise Engle
    (All Grammar)
Anna Bontrager
Abraham Erb
May Hummel
Ray Hummel
Andrew Keim
Henry Keim
Levi Keim
Sanford Keim
Ammon Miller
Andrew Miller
Joe Miller
Perry S. Miller
Lydia Oswald
Sanford Oswald
Alvin Schlabach

Gideon Schlabach
Amanda
    Swartzentruber
26/p.72 John Swartzentruber
30/   Anna Troyer
Moses Troyer
Simon P. Troyer
Albert Yoder
Amanda Yoder
Jacob J. Yoder

1911–12
16/
Louise Engle

1912–13
16/
159/ *Louise Engle*
Walter Oswald

1913–14
16/
Louise Engle

1914–15
30/
Louise Engle
    (All Primary)
Atlee Keim
Willie Keim
Grace Mast
Adam Miller
Amanda Miller
Henry Miller
Lizzie Miller
Monroe Miller
Oren Oswald
Gideon Schlabach
Mattie Schlabach
Amanda Troyer
Andrew A. Troyer
Andy J. Troyer
Daniel Troyer
Johnny Troyer
Katie Troyer
Mary Troyer
Peter Troyer
Bernice Unger

Abner Yoder
Dana Yoder
Jeremiah Yoder
John Yoder
Lizzie Yoder
Lovina Yoder
Nela Yoder
Susan Yoder

1914–15
8/
A. B. Huprich
    (Grammar)

1915–16
30/
Louise Kaser
Joseph Miller (1)
Andrew Troyer (1)
John Troyer (1)
Christ Yoder (1)
Atlee Keim (2)
Willie Keim (2)
Manda Miller (2)
Monroe Miller (2)
Gideon Schlabach (2)
Andrew Troyer (2)
Eli Troyer (2)
Katie Troyer (2)
Bernice Unger (2)
Lizzie Yoder (2)
Lovina Yoder (2)
Grace Mast (3)
Abner Miller (3)
Adam Miller (3)
Henry Miller (3)
Lizzie Miller (3)
Mattie Schlabach (3)
Daniel Troyer (3)
Mary Troyer (3)
Oren Oswald (4)
Amanda Troyer (4)
Peter Troyer (4)
Daniel Yoder (4)
John Yoder (4)
Manela Yoder (?)

95/

SCHOOL DISTRICT NO. 3
1924
Teacher, ESTHER MAYER
School Officers

James Schutt
        Albert Fair
                    Cyrus Dauer
Albert Nirote

PUPILS

Sarah Schlabach   Joseph Miller
Anna Schlabach   Levi Yoder
Ida Yoder   Katie Y. Miller
Mary Ann Miller   Atlee Schlabach
Mary Mast   Tena Keim
Malinda Miller   John Troyer
Edna Oswald   Eli Troyer
Fannie Oswald   Katie A. Miller
Katie J. Miller   Susan Yoder
Mattie Bontrager   Violet Kaser
Howard Kaser   Fannie Hummel
Roman Keim   Truman Oswald
Henry Miller   Levi Oswald
Moses Yoder   Fannie Miller
Lena Mast   Katie E. Miller
            Eli Mast

30/ **1915–16**
A. B. Huprich
Abraham Keim (5)
Joseph Miller (5)
Simon J. Schlabach (5)
Abraham Troyer (5)
Andrew Yoder (5)
David Yoder (5)
Mary Ann Yoder (5)
Fred Hershberger (6)
Anna Keim (6)
John Schlabach (6)
Mattie Troyer (6)
Noah Yoder (6)
Henry Keim (7)
Harold Mast (7)
A. DeSylva Oswald (7)
Katie Swartzentruber (7)
Albert L. Yoder (7)
Tobias Yoder (7)

8/
30/ **1916–17**
Louise Kaser
Floyd Fraelich (1)
Garnet Fraelich (1)
Andrew Mast (1)
Eli D. Mast (1)
Henry Miller (1)
Johnny Miller (1)
Atlee Schlabach (1)
Andy A. Troyer (1)
Johnny Troyer (1)
Martha Troyer (1)
Christian Yoder (1)
Gideon Schlabach (2)
Andrew J. Troyer (2)
Eli P. Troyer (2)
Katie Troyer (2)
Bernice Unger (3)
Lizzie Yoder (3)
Lovina Yoder (3)
Susian Yoder (3)
Grace Mast (4)
Abner Miller (4)
Adam Miller (4)
Henry Miller (4)
Lizzie Miller (4)
Mattie Schlabach (4)
Daniel Troyer (4)
Mary Troyer (4)
Peter Troyer (4)
John Yoder (4)
Manilius Yoder (4)

30/ **1916–17**
A. B. Huprich
Abraham Keim (5)
Oren Oswald (5)
Amanda Troyer (5)
Daniel Yoder (5)
Mary Ann Yoder (5)
Joseph Miller (6)
John Schlabach (6)
Simon Schlabach (6)

Abraham Troyer (6)
Andrew Yoder (6)
David Yoder (6)
Harold Mast (7)
Silvia Oswald (7)
Noah Yoder (7)
Tobias Yoder (7)
Bellemeda Aling (8)
Katie Swartzentruber (8)

30/
158/ **1917–18**
Louise Kaser
Harold Fraelich (1)
Ben J. Miller (1)
David Miller (1)
Fannie Miller (1)
John Miller (1)
Katie Miller (1)
Moses Miller (1)
Levi Oswald (1)
Atlee Schlabach (1)
Martha Troyer (1)
Christian Yoder (1)
Susan Yoder (1)
Floyd Fraelich (2)
Garnet Fraelich (2)
Andrew Mast (2)
Eli Mast (2)
Henry Miller (2)
Andrew A. Troyer (2)
John Troyer (2)
Giddie Schlabach (3)
Andrew Troyer (3)
Eli Troyer (3)
Lizzie Yoder (3)
Lovina Yoder (3)
Marie Aling (4)
Adam Miller (4)
Henry Miller (4)
Lizzie Miller (4)
Manilius Yoder (4)

30/ **1917–18**
A. B. Huprich
Grace Mast (5)
Mattie Schlabach (5)
Amanda Troyer (5)
Daniel Troyer (5)
Mary Troyer (5)
Peter Troyer (5)
John Yoder (5)
Abraham Keim (6)
Joseph Miller (6)
Oren Oswald (6)
Simon Schlabach (6)
Abraham Troyer (6)
Andrew Yoder (6)
Daniel Yoder (6)
David Yoder (6)
Bellemeda Aling (8)
Harold Mast (8)
Silvia Oswald (8)
Noah Yoder (8)

16/ The school is out vacation's come
The bell has ceased to sound
The old schoolhouse has lost its hum
And silence broods around.
        1909 Charm School souvenir

30/
130/ **1918–19**
132/ *Mae Fisher*
Ruth Cox
Minnie Stingel
Lester Miller
Albert Keim (1)
Amanda Keim (1)
Deniah Keim (1)
Noah Keim (1)
Roman Keim (1)
Helen Mast (1)
Arletus E. Miller (1)
Ben J. Miller (1)
Katie Miller (1)
Lizzie Miller (1)
Moses Miller (1)
Atlee Schlabach (1)
Mattie Troyer (1)
Eli Yoder (1)
Levi Yoder (1)
Moses Yoder (1)
Eli Mast (2)
Fannie Miller (2)
Katie Miller (2)
Levi Oswald (2)
Christ Yoder (2)
Susan Yoder (2)
Andy Mast (3)
Henry Miller (3)
John Troyer (3)
John Miller (4)
Gid Schlabach (4)
Andrew Troyer (4)
Eli Troyer (4)
Lizzie Yoder (4)
Henry Miller (5)
Mary Troyer (5)
Peter Troyer (5)
John Yoder (5)
Manilius Yoder (5)
Grace Mast (6)
Oren Oswald (6)
Daniel Yoder (6)
David Yoder (6)

30/ **1919–20**
Minnie Stingel
Ruth Cox
Lester Miller
Saloma Erb (1)
Amanda Keim (1)
Noah Keim (1)
Roman Keim (1)
Fannie Mast (1)
Helen Mast (1)
Lena Mast (1)
Lydia Mast (1)
Mary Mast (1)
Daniel Miller (1)
Henry A. Miller (1)
Joseph Miller (1)
Katie Miller (1)
Katie Y. Miller (1)
Mary Ann Miller (1)
Simon Miller (1)
Sarah Schlabach (1)
Levi Yoder (1)
Moses Yoder (1)
Deniah Keim (2)
Moses Miller (2)
Atlee Schlabach (2)
Mattie Troyer (2)
Eli Mast (3)
Fannie Miller (3)
Katie Miller (3)
Levi Oswald (3)
John Troyer (3)
Susan Yoder (3)
Andrew Mast (4)
Gideon Schlabach (4)
Eli Troyer (4)
Mary Bontrager (5)
Albert Kaser (5)
Andrew Troyer (5)
Mary Troyer (5)
Peter Troyer (5)
John Yoder (5)
Grace Mast (6)
David Yoder (6)
Oren Oswald (7)
Silvia Oswald (8)
Noah Yoder (8)

130/ From 1918 to 1920, school was not operating fully because of the flu epidemic. Teacher Mae Fisher boarded at Al Keims and was replaced by Minnie Stingel early in the school year. Lester Miller lived at the Em. J. Yoder farm along SR 39 and walked to school from there, going in a "direct straight line." Ruth Cox
130/ and Minnie Stingel were replaced by Lester Miller when they got the flu around New Year of 1920. In 1990 Minnie still recalled her teaching at Charm during an interview with her. She resided at Sagamore Hills, Ohio at 88 years old. Since 1991 she is a resident at Walnut Hills Nursing Home – Walnut Creek, Ohio. 🍂

Those can conquer who think they can.
        1901 Charm School writing exercise.

30/ **1920–21**
Elmer Kner
Saloma Erb (1)
Mary Mast (1)
Ada Mast (1)
Fannie Mast (1)
Lydia Mast (1)
Albert Miller (1)
Benjamin Miller (1)
Elizabeth Miller (1)
Katie Miller (1)
Mary Ann Miller (1)
Simon Miller (1)
Edna Oswald (1)
Fannie Oswald (1)
Sarah Schlabach (1)
Ida Yoder (1)
Sarah Bontrager (2)
Howard Kaser (2)
Amanda Keim (2)
Roman Keim (2)
Helen Mast (2)
Lina Mast (2)
Ben Miller (2)
Daniel Miller (2)
Henry Miller (2)
Joseph Miller (2)
Katie Miller (2)
Annie Schlabach (2)
Martha Troyer (2)
Levi Yoder (2)
Moses Yoder (2)
Tena Keim (3)
Katie Miller (3)
Moses Miller (3)
Atlee Schlabach (3)

337/ **1920–21**
Lee Fair
Lora Miller (8)
Grace Mast (Grammar)
Oren Oswald
    (Grammar)
Bernice Unger
    (Grammar)

30/ **1921–22**
Ivan Hostetler
Irene Keim (1)
Oren Keim (1)
John Mast (1)
Forrest Miller (1)
Henry Miller (1)
Raymond Oswald (1)
Katie Troyer (1)
Joseph Wagner (1)
Saloma Erb (2)
Amanda Keim (2)
Lydia Mast (2)
Mary Mast (2)
Albert Miller (2)
Benjamin Miller (2)
Katie Miller (2)
Mary Ann Miller (2)
Edna Oswald (2)
Fannie Oswald (2)
Sarah Schlabach (2)
Nettie Wagner (2)
Ida Yoder (2)
ఆ Sarah Bontrager (3)
162 Howard Kaser (3)

Roman Keim (3)
Helen Mast (3)
Lena Mast (3)
Daniel Miller (3)
Henry Miller (3)
Joseph Miller (3)
Katie Miller (3)
Anna Schlabach (3)
Martha Troyer (3)
Mollie Wagner (3)
Levi Yoder (3)
Moses Yoder (3)

169/
30/ **1921–22**
Ervin Hostetler
Irene Mayer
Paul Hummel (1)
Anna Keim (1)
Oren Keim (1)
Mary Ann Mast (1)
Bena Miller (1)
Edna Miller (1)
Mattie Miller (1)
Richard Miller (1)
Roman Miller (1)
Amanda Keim (2)
Irene Keim (2)
John Mast (2)
Albert Miller (2)
Benjamin Miller (2)
Forrest Miller (2)
Henry Miller (2)
Raymond Oswald (2)
Saloma Erb (3)
Lydia Mast (3)
Mary Mast (3)
Katie Miller (3)
Mary Ann Miller (3)
Edna Oswald (3)
Fannie Oswald (3)
Anna Schlabach (3)
Sarah Schlabach (3)
Ida Yoder (3)

30/ **1923–24**
Irene Mayer
Henry Erb (1)
Anna Keim (1)
Susan Keim (1)
Anna Miller (1)
Bena Miller (1)
Edna Miller (1)
Mattie Miller (1)
Roman Miller (1)
Ruth Miller (1)
Sarah Miller (1)
Violet Oswald (1)
Phineas Yoder (1)
Paul Hummel (2)
Oren Keim (2)
John Mast (2)
Mary Ann Mast (2)
Eli Miller (2)
Richard Miller (2)
Raymond Oswald (2)
Saloma Erb (3)
Amanda Keim (3)
Irene Keim (3)
Lydia Mast (3)
Albert Miller (3)
Aden Miller (?)

178/

Fall Harvest Display – ca 1915

Elmer Miller (3)
Forrest Miller (3)
Henry Miller (3)

95/ **1923–24**
Esther Mayer
    (All Grammar)
Mattie Bontrager
Fannie Hummel
Howard Kaser
Violet Kaser
Roman Keim
Tena Keim
Eli Mast
Lena Mast
Mary Mast
Fannie Miller
Henry Miller
Joseph Miller
Katie A. Miller
Katie E. Miller
Katie J. Miller
Katie Y. Miller
Malinda Miller
Mary Ann Miller
Edna Oswald
Fannie Oswald
Levi Oswald
Truman Oswald
Anna Schlabach
Atlee Schlabach
Sarah Schlabach
Eli Troyer
John Troyer
Ida Yoder
Levi Yoder
Moses Yoder
Susan Yoder

30/ **1924–25**
Irene Mayer
Henry S. Erb (1)
Daniel D. Keim (1)
Susan D. Keim (1)
Anna L. Miller (1)
Emanuel A. Miller (1)
John H. Miller (1)

Levi M. Miller (1)
Ralph Miller (1)
Roman H. Miller (1)
Sarah J. Miller (1)
Phineas M. Yoder (1)
Anna D. Keim (2)
Bena A. Miller (2)
Edna H. Miller (2)
Mattie J. Miller (2)
Richard Miller (2)
Ruth Miller (2)
Paul Hummel (3)
Amanda J. Keim (3)
Oren D. Keim (3)
John E. Mast (3)
Mary Ann Mast (3)
Eli J. Miller (3)
Elmer J. Miller (3)
Henry A. Miller (3)

30/ **1925–26**
Irene Mayer
Daniel D. Keim (1)
Ervin A. Keim (1)
Jacob E. Mast (1)
Ada J. Miller (1)
Levi M. Miller (1)
Lydia Miller (1)
Martha J. Miller (1)
Samuel M. Miller (1)
Lizzie M. Yoder (1)
Henry S. Erb (2)
Susan D. Keim (2)
Anna L. Miller (2)
Emanuel A. Miller (2)
John H. Miller (2)
Ralph Miller (2)
Richard Miller (2)
Roman H. Miller (2)
Sarah J. Miller (2)
Phineas M. Yoder (2)
Anna D. Keim (3)
Bena A. Miller (3)
Edna H. Miller (3)
Henry Miller (3)
Mattie J. Miller (3)
Ruth Miller (3)

30/

1926–27
Eva Steiner
Lizzie D. Erb (1)
Moses S. Erb (1)
Amanda A. Mast (1)
Eli A. Mast (1)
Ada J. Miller (1)
Ammon H. Miller (1)
Billy Miller (1)
Gerald Miller (1)
Lydia E. Miller (1)
Peter L. Miller (1)
Samuel M. Miller (1)
Lizzie M. Yoder (1)
Henry S. Erb (2)
Daniel D. Keim (2)
Ervin A. Keim (2)
Jacob E. Mast (2)
John H. Miller (2)
Levi M. Miller (2)
Martha J. Miller (2)
Sarah J. Miller (2)
Anna L. Miller (3)
Emanuel A. Miller (3)
Mattie J. Miller (3)
Ralph Miller (3)
Roman H. Miller (3)
Susan D. Miller (3)
Ada A. Troyer (3)
Phineas M. Yoder (3)
Elizabeth Bontrager (4)
Anna D. Keim (4)
Amanda B. Kurtz (4)
Bena A. Miller (4)
Edna H. Miller (4)
Henry Y. Miller (4)
Ruth Miller (4)

4/

1926–27
William Perry Miller
(Grammar)

30/

1927–28
Irene Kaser
Joseph D. Erb (1)
Mary A. Keim (1)
Eli A. Mast (1)
Verna A. Mast (1)
Albert H. Miller (1)
Benny Miller (1)
Elizabeth A. Miller (1)
Fannie A. Miller (1)
Moses M. Miller (1)
Nancy A. Miller (1)
Sarah A. Miller (1)
Eli Raber (1)
Eli M. Troyer (1)
Lizzie D. Erb (2)
Amanda A. Mast (2)
Ammon H. Miller (2)
Billy Miller (2)
Gerald Miller (2)
Henry A. Miller (2)

Lydia E. Miller (2)
Peter L. Miller (2)
Samuel M. Miller (2)
Lizzie M. Yoder (2)
Daniel D. Keim (3)
Ervin A. Keim (3)
Jacob E. Mast (3)
John H. Miller (3)
Levi M. Miller (3)
Martha J. Miller (3)
Phineas M. Yoder (3)

4/

1927–28
William Perry Miller
(Grammar)

1928–29
Albert N. Fair
Samuel D. Erb (1)
Dorothy Kaser (1)
Mary A. Keim (1)
Katie Ann Kurtz (1)
Ivan A. Mast (1)
Abraham Miller (1)
Benny Miller (1)
Jacob A. Miller (1)
Nancy A. Miller (1)
Sarah A. Miller (1)
Eli J. Raber (1)
Levi D. Schlabach (1)
Peter M. Troyer (1)
Katie Ann Yoder (1)
Mattie M. Yoder (1)
Joe D. Erb (2)
Susie Kurtz (2)
Eli A. Mast (2)
Susie E. Mast (2)
Verna A. Mast (2)
Albert H. Miller (2)
Elizabeth A. Miller (2)
Fannie A. Miller (2)
Moses M. Miller (2)
Lizzie D. Erb (3)
Amanda A. Mast (3)
Abe A. Miller (3)
Ammon H. Miller (3)
Billy Miller (3)
Eli A. Miller (3)
Gerald Miller (3)
Henry A. Miller (3)
Katie Miller (3)
Katie A. Miller (3)
Lydia J. Miller (3)
Peter L. Miller (3)
Samuel M. Miller (3)
Lizzie M. Yoder (3)
Noah D. Yoder (3)
Daniel D. Keim (4)
Ervin A. Keim (4)
Jacob E. Mast (4)
Christian Miller (4)
John H. Miller (4)
Levi M. Miller (4)
Martha J. Miller (4)
Phineas M. Yoder (4)

2/
30/

1928–29
William Perry Miller
Elizabeth Borntrager
 (5)
Anna L. Miller (5)
Emanuel A. Miller (5)
Ralph Miller (5)
Roman H. Miller (5)
Ada A. Troyer (5)
Anna D. Keim (6)
Susie D. Keim (6)
Amanda B. Kurtz (6)
Bena A. Miller (6)
Edna H. Miller (6)
Ruth Miller (6)
Edgar Ott (6)
Mattie Troyer (6)
Oren D. Keim (7)
Fannie B. Kurtz (7)
John E. Mast (7)
Mary Ann Mast (7)
Albert L. Miller (7)
Eli J. Miller (7)
Elmer J. Miller (7)
John E. Yoder (7)
Irene A. Keim (8)
John B. Kurtz (8)
Forrest Miller (8)

2/
30/

1929–30
Albert N. Fair
Samuel D. Erb (1)
Katie Ann Kurtz (1)
Albert A. Mast (1)
Ivan A. Mast (1)
Annie M. Miller (1)
Damos A. Miller (1)
Lizzie L. Miller (1)
Mattie H. Miller (1)
Levi D. Schlabach (1)
Katie Ann Yoder (1)
Verna R. Yoder (1)
Joe D. Erb (2)
Dorothy Kaser (2)
Mary A. Keim (2)
Susie E. Mast (2)
Verna A. Mast (2)
Abe A. Miller (2)
Albert H. Miller (2)
Benny Miller (2)
Jacob A. Miller (2)
Moses M. Miller (2)
Nancy A. Miller (2)
Sarah A. Miller (2)
Peter M. Troyer (2)
Mattie M. Yoder (2)
Susie B. Kurtz (3)
Eli A. Mast (3)
Fanny A. Miller (3)
Mattie Miller (3)
Lizzie D. Erb (4)
Amanda A. Mast (4)
Ammon H. Miller (4)
Billy Miller (4)
Gerald Miller (4)
Katie A. Miller (4)
Lydia J. Miller (4)
Peter L. Miller (4)
Samuel M. Miller (4)
Lizzie M. Yoder (4)

2/
30/

1929–30
William Perry Miller
Richard Miller (?)
Daniel D. Keim (5)
Ervin A. Keim (5)
Jacob E. Mast (5)
John H. Miller (5)
Levi M. Miller (5)
Martha J. Miller (5)
Phineas M. Yoder (5)
Anna L. Miller (6)
Emanuel A. Miller (6)
Ralph Miller (6)
Roman H. Miller (6)
Ada A. Troyer (6)
Susie D. Keim (7)
Amanda B. Kurtz (7)
Bena Miller (7)
Edna H. Miller (7)
Ruth Miller (7)
Edgar Ott (7)
Roman E. Yoder (7)
Oren D. Keim (8)
John E. Mast (8)
Mary Ann Mast (8)
Eli J. Miller (8)

1930–31
Albert Kaser
Eli E. Mast (1)
Albert M. Miller (1)
Henry A. Miller (1)
Lovina A. Miller (1)
Robert Miller (1)
Calvin Stockli (1)
Katie M. Troyer (1)
Emma M. Yoder (1)
Moses T. Yoder (1)
Albert A. Mast (2)
Annie M. Miller (2)
Damos A. Miller (2)
Elizabeth L. Miller (2)
Mattie H. Miller (2)
Levi Schlabach (2)
Katie Ann Yoder (2)
Verna R. Yoder (2)
Samuel D. Erb (3)
Dorothy Kaser (3)
Katie Ann Kurtz (3)
Ivan A. Mast (3)
Susan E. Mast (3)
Abraham A. Miller (3)
Jacob A. Miller (3)
Nancy A. Miller (3)
Sarah A. Miller (3)
Peter M. Troyer (3)
Mattie M. Yoder (3)
Joseph D. Erb (4)
Mary A. Keim (4)
Susan B. Kurtz (4)
Eli A. Mast (4)
Verna A. Mast (4)
Albert H. Miller (4)
Bennie Miller (4)
Fannie H. Miller (4)
Moses M. Miller (4)

16/

Not for school but for life we learn.

1930–31

William Perry Miller
Russel Donley (5)
Lizzie Erb (5)
Amanda A. Mast (5)
Ammon H. Miller (5)
Gerald Miller (5)
Katie Miller (5)
Lydia Miller (5)
Peter L. Miller (5)
Samuel M. Miller (5)
William Perry Miller (5)
Lizzie M. Yoder (5)
Daniel Keim (6)
Ervin Keim (6)
Jacob E. Mast (6)
John H. Miller (6)
Levi M. Miller (6)
Phineas M. Yoder (6)
Anna D. Keim (7)
Emanuel A. Miller (7)
Ralph Miller (7)
Roman H. Miller (7)
Ada A. Troyer (7)
Susan Keim (8)
Amanda Kurtz (8)
Bena A. Miller (8)
Ruth Miller (8)
Edgar Ott (8)

1931–32

Albert Kaser
Albert D. Erb (1)
Eli E. Mast (1)
Fannie E. Mast (1)
Henry H. Miller (1)
Katie L. Miller (1)
Celesta A. Schlabach (1)
Abe M. Troyer (1)
Sarah P. Troyer (1)
Eli D. Yoder (1)
Fannie T. Yoder (1)
Katie Ann Mast (2)
Albert M. Miller (2)
Henry A. Miller (2)
Lovina A. Miller (2)
Robert Miller (2)
Calvin Stockli (2)
Katie M. Troyer (2)
Emma M. Yoder (2)
Maggie Yoder (2)
Moses T. Yoder (2)
Katie Ann Kurtz (3)
Susan E. Mast (3)
Anna M. Miller (3)
Dames A. Miller (3)
Elizabeth L. Miller (3)
Mattie H. Miller (3)
Levi D. Schlabach (3)
Katie Ann Yoder (3)
Verna R. Yoder (3)
Samuel D. Erb (4)
Dorothy Kaser (4)
Abraham A. Miller (4)
Albert H. Miller (4)
Jacob A. Miller (4)
Nancy A. Miller (4)
Sarah A. Miller (4)
Wilbur Orion Miller (4)
Peter M. Troyer (4)
Mattie M. Yoder (4)

1931–32

William Perry Miller
Joseph D. Erb (5)
Mary A. Keim (5)
Susan B. Kurtz (5)
Eli A. Mast (5)
Verna A. Mast (5)
Ben Miller (5)
Fanny A. Miller (5)
Moses M. Miller (5)
Russel Donley (6)
Lizzie D. Erb (6)
Amanda A. Mast (6)
Jacob E. Mast (6)
Ammon Miller (6)
Eli Miller (6)
Gerald Miller (6)
Katie A. Miller (6)
Lydia Miller (6)
Peter L. Miller (6)
Samuel M. Miller (6)
Wm. Perry Miller (6)
Lizzie Yoder (6)
Ervin A. Keim (7)
John H. Miller (7)
Levi M. Miller (7)
Phineas M. Yoder (7)
Emanuel A. Miller (8)
Ralph Miller (8)

1932–33

Albert Kaser
Albert A. Keim (1)
Anna M. Mast (1)
Henry A. Mast (1)
Anna A. Miller (1)
Elizabeth H. Miller (1)
Katie L. Miller (1)
Perry M. Miller (1)
Esta Corrine Oswald (1)
Aden M. Troyer (1)
Sarah R. Yoder (1)
Albert D. Erb (2)
Eli E. Mast (2)
Fannie E. Mast (2)
Henry H. Miller (2)
Celesta A. Schlabach (2)
Abe M. Troyer (2)
Sarah Troyer (2)
Eli D. Yoder (2)
Fannie T. Yoder (2)
Katie Ann Mast (3)
Albert M. Miller (3)
Henry A. Miller (3)
Lovina A. Miller (3)
Robert Miller (3)
Calvin Stockli (3)
Katie Troyer (3)
Emma Yoder (3)
Moses T. Yoder (3)
Verna R. Yoder (3)
Katie Ann Kurtz (4)
Susan E. Mast (4)
Annie M. Miller (4)
Dames A. Miller (4)
Elizabeth L. Miller (4)
Mattie H. Miller (4)
Levi D. Schlabach (4)
Katie Ann Yoder (4)

1932–33

William Perry Miller
Sam D. Erb (5)
Dorothy Kaser (5)
Abie A. Miller (5)
Albert H. Miller (5)
Jacob A. Miller (5)
Nancy A. Miller (5)
Sarah A. Miller (5)
Peter M. Troyer (5)
Mattie M. Yoder (5)
Joseph D. Erb (6)
Mary A. Keim (6)
Susan B. Kurtz (6)
Eli A. Mast (6)
Verna A. Mast (6)
Ben Miller (6)
Fannie A. Miller (6)
Moses M. Miller (6)
Russel Donley (7)
Elizabeth D. Erb (7)
Daniel D. Keim (7)
Amanda A. Mast (7)
Jacob E. Mast (7)
Ammon H. Miller (7)
Gerald Miller (7)
Katie A. Miller (7)
Lydia Miller (7)
Peter L. Miller (7)
Samuel M. Miller (7)
William P. Miller (7)
Lizzie M. Yoder (7)
Ervin A. Keim (8)
Levi M. Miller (8)

1933–34

Albert Kaser
Albert A. Keim (1)
Mattie E. Mast (1)
Amanda A. Miller (1)
Benjamin M. Miller (1)
Mattie L. Miller (1)
Elizabeth P. Troyer (1)
John S. Troyer (1)
Mary M. Yoder (1)
Anna M. Mast (2)
Henry A. Mast (2)
Anna A. Miller (2)
Elizabeth H. Miller (2)
Katie L. Miller (2)
Perry M. Miller (2)
Aden M. Troyer (2)
Sarah R. Yoder (2)
Albert D. Erb (3)
Eli E. Mast (3)
Fannie E. Mast (3)
Henry H. Miller (3)
Celesta A. Schlabach (3)
Abraham M. Troyer (3)
Sarah P. Troyer (3)
Eli D. Yoder (3)
Fannie T. Yoder (3)
Katie Ann Mast (4)
Albert M. Miller (4)
Henry A. Miller (4)
Lovina A. Miller (4)
Robert Miller (4)
Katie M. Troyer (4)
Emma M. Yoder (4)
Katie Ann Yoder (4)
Moses T. Yoder (4)
Verna R. Yoder (4)

1933–34

William Perry Miller
Katie Ann Kurtz (5)
Susie E. Mast (5)
Anna M. Miller (5)
Dames Miller (5)
Lizzie L. Miller (5)
Mattie H. Miller (5)
Levi D. Schlabach (5)
Samuel D. Erb (6)
Dorothy Kaser (6)
Albert H. Miller (6)
Jacob A. Miller (6)
Lizzie A. Miller (6)
Nancy A. Miller (6)
Sarah A. Miller (6)
Peter M. Troyer (6)
Mattie M. Yoder (6)
Joseph D. Erb (7)
Mary A. Keim (7)
Eli A. Mast (7)
Verna A. Mast (7)
Ben Miller (7)
Fannie A. Miller (7)
Moses M. Miller (7)
Gerald Miller (8)
Peter L. Miller (8)
Samuel M. Miller (8)
William Miller (8)

1934–35

Albert Kaser
Donald Dale Kaser (1)
Edna M. Mast (1)
Anna L. Miller (1)
Clavin Miller (1)
Levi A. Miller (1)
Raymond Schlabach (1)
Anna S. Troyer (1)
Eli A. Yoder (1)
Henry D. Yoder (1)
Noah T. Yoder (1)
Albert A. Keim (2)
Mattie E. Mast (2)
Amanda A. Miller (2)
Benjamin M. Miller (2)
Mattie L. Miller (2)
Elizabeth P. Troyer (2)
John S. Troyer (2)
Mary M. Yoder (2)
Anna M. Mast (3)
Henry A. Mast (3)
Anna A. Miller (3)
Blaine Miller (3)
Elizabeth H. Miller (3)
Katie L. Miller (3)
Perry M. Miller (3)
Ruby I. Miller (3)
Aden M. Troyer (3)
Sarah R. Yoder (3)
Albert Yutzy (3)
Albert Erb (4)
Eli E. Mast (4)
Fannie E. Mast (4)
Henry H. Miller (4)
Celesta A. Schlabach (4)
Abraham M. Troyer (4)
Katie M. Troyer (4)
Sarah P. Troyer (4)
Eli D. Yoder (4)
Emma M. Yoder (4)
Fannie T. Yoder (4)

1934–35

William Perry Miller
Katie Ann Mast (5)
Albert M. Miller (5)
Henry A. Miller (5)
Lawrence Miller (5)
Lovina A. Miller (5)
Robert Miller (5)
Katie Ann Yoder (5)
Moses T. Yoder (5)
Verna R. Yoder (5)
Katie Ann Kurtz (6)
Susie E. Mast (6)
Anna M. Miller (6)
Dames Miller (6)
Lizzie L. Miller (6)
Mattie H. Miller (6)
Levi D. Schlabach (6)
Samuel D. Erb (7)
Dorothy Kaser (7)
Albert H. Miller (7)
Jacob A. Miller (7)
Lizzie J. Miller (7)
Nancy A. Miller (7)
Sarah A. Miller (7)
Peter M. Troyer (7)
Mattie M. Yoder (7)
Joseph D. Erb (8)
Mary A. Keim (8)
Eli A. Mast (8)
Verna A. Mast (8)
Ben Miller (8)
Fannie A. Miller (8)
Moses M. Miller (8)

1935–36

Olive Mast
Anna J. Hershberger (1)
Jonas A. Keim (1)
Abbie A. Miller (1)
Ada A. Miller (1)
Edward Ray Miller (1)
Myrtle Mae Miller (1)
Robert Keith Miller (1)
Alvin A. Schlabach (1)
Anna S. Troyer (1)
John E. Troyer (1)
Abe M. Yoder (1)
Jonas R. Yoder (1)
Katie M. Yoder (1)
Donald Dale Kaser (2)
Sarah A. Keim (2)
Edna M. Mast (2)
Anna L. Miller (2)
Calvin J. Miller (2)
Levi A. Miller (2)
Mattie L. Miller (2)

Raymond A. Schlabach (2)
Eli A. Yoder (2)
Henry D. Yoder (2)
Noah T. Yoder (2)
Albert A. Keim (3)
Mattie E. Mast (3)
Amanda A. Miller (3)
Benjamin M. Miller (3)
Elizabeth P. Troyer (3)
John S. Troyer (3)
Mary M. Yoder (3)
Anna M. Mast (4)
Henry A. Mast (4)
Anna A. Miller (4)
Elizabeth H. Miller (4)
Harold Blaine Miller (4)
Katie L. Miller (4)
Perry M. Miller (4)
Ruby I. Miller (4)
Aden M. Troyer (4)
Sarah R. Yoder (4)

1935–36

William Perry Miller
Lawrence Miller (?)
Albert D. Erb (5)
Eli E. Mast (5)
Fannie E. Mast (5)
Henry H. Miller (5)
Celesta A. Schlabach (5)
Abe M. Troyer (5)
Katie M. Troyer (5)
Sarah P. Troyer (5)
Eli D. Yoder (5)
Emma M. Yoder (5)
Fannie T. Yoder (5)
Katie Ann Mast (6)
Albert M. Miller (6)
Henry A. Miller (6)
Lovina A. Miller (6)
Katie Ann Yoder (6)
Moses T. Yoder (6)
Verna R. Yoder (6)
Katie Ann Kurtz (7)
Susie E. Mast (7)
Damas Miller (7)
Lizzie L. Miller (7)
Mattie H. Miller (7)
Robert Jay Miller (7)
Levi D. Schlabach (7)
Samuel D. Erb (8)
Dorothy Jean Kaser (8)
Jacob A. Miller (8)
Lizzie J. Miller (8)
Nancy A. Miller (8)
Peter M. Troyer (8)
Mattie M. Yoder (8)

Many good purposes lie in the graveyard.

1900 Charm School writing exercise

The Owl — Be wise, learn to read by reading.

Teacher Florence Shafer –
1967 Charm classroom motto

1936–37

Olive Mast
Katie J. Hershberger (1)
Abe L. Miller (1)
Amanda M. Troyer (1)
Eli A. Troyer (1)
Abe M. Yoder (1)
Amanda A. Yoder (1)
Sarah T. Yoder (1)
Ada J. Hershberger (2)
Anna J. Hershberger (2)
Jonas A. Keim (2)
Abbie A. Miller (2)
Ada H. Miller (2)
Calvin J. Miller (2)
Edward Ray Miller (2)
Robert Keith Miller (2)
Alvin A. Schlabach (2)
Anna S. Troyer (2)
John E. Troyer (2)
Jonas R. Yoder (2)
Donald Dale Kaser (3)
Sarah A. Keim (3)
Edna M. Mast (3)
Anna L. Miller (3)
Levi A. Miller (3)
Mattie L. Miller (3)
Raymond J. Schlabach (3)
Eli A. Yoder (3)
Henry D. Yoder (3)
Noah T. Yoder (3)
Katie J. Hershberger (4)
Albert J. Keim (4)
Mattie E. Mast (4)
Amanda A. Miller (4)
Benjamin M. Miller (4)
John S. Troyer (4)
Mary M. Yoder (4)

1936–37

William Perry Miller
Albert Fair
Cyrus O. Stengel
Anna M. Mast (5)
Anna A. Miller (5)
Harold Blaine Miller (5)
Katie L. Miller (5)
Lizzie H. Miller (5)
Perry M. Miller (5)
Aden M. Troyer (5)
Sarah R. Yoder (5)
Albert D. Erb (6)
Eli E. Mast (6)
Fannie E. Mast (6)
Henry A. Mast (6)
Henry H. Miller (6)

Celesta A. Schlabach (6)
Abe M. Troyer (6)
Katie M. Troyer (6)
Eli D. Yoder (6)
Emma M. Yoder (6)
Fannie T. Yoder (6)
Clara J. Hershberger (7)
Katie Ann Mast (7)
Albert M. Miller (7)
Henry A. Miller (7)
Lovina A. Miller (7)
Katie Ann Yoder (7)
Moses T. Yoder (7)
Verna J. Yoder (7)
Robert Jay Miller (8)
Levi D. Schlabach (8)

1937–38

Olive Mast
David Miller (1)
Noah M. Miller (1)
Robert L. Miller (1)
Irene A. Schlabach (1)
Eli A. Troyer (1)
Jonas M. Troyer (1)
Raymond A. Troyer (1)
Amanda J. Yoder (1)
Jacob D. Yoder (1)
Katie Hershberger (2)
Abe L. Miller (2)
Doris Miller (2)
Amanda M. Troyer (2)
Abe M. Yoder (2)
Amanda A. Yoder (2)
Sara T. Yoder (2)
Ada J. Hershberger (3)
Anna J. Hershberger (3)
Jonas A. Keim (3)
Abbie A. Miller (3)
Ada H. Miller (3)
Calvin J. Miller (3)
Edward Ray Miller (3)
Robert Keith Miller (3)
Alvin A. Schlabach (3)
Anna S. Troyer (3)
Jonas R. Yoder (3)
Donald Dale Kaser (4)
Sarah A. Keim (4)
Monroe Kuhns (4)
Edna M. Mast (4)
Anna L. Miller (4)
Levi A. Miller (4)
Mattie L. Miller (4)
Raymond Schlabach (4)
Eli A. Yoder (4)
Henry D. Yoder (4)
Noah T. Yoder (4)

Teacher Perry Miller died in the spring of 1937 and the school term was finished by Albert Fair and Cyrus O. Stengel.

❧

1937–38

Albert Kaser

2/
30/

Katie J. Hershberger (5)
Albert A. Keim (5)
Arletta Lahm (5)
Mattie E. Mast (5)
Amanda A. Miller (5)
Benjamin M. Miller (5)
John S. Troyer (5)
Mary M. Yoder (5)
Anna M. Mast (6)
Henry A. Mast (6)
Anna A. Miller (6)
Harold B. Miller (6)
Katie L. Miller (6)
Lizzie H. Miller (6)
Perry M. Miller (6)
Aden M. Troyer (6)
Sarah R. Yoder (6)
Albert D. Erb (7)
Grace Lahm (7)
Eli E. Mast (7)
Fannie E. Mast (7)
Henry H. Miller (7)
Celesta A. Schlabach (7)
Abe M. Troyer (7)
Katie M. Troyer (7)
Eli D. Yoder (7)
Emma M. Yoder (7)
Clara J. Hershberger (8)
Katie Ann Mast (8)
Albert M. Miller (8)
Fannie T. Yoder (8)
Moses T. Yoder (8)
Verna R. Yoder (8)

1938–39

Olive Mast

2/
30/

Violet D. Erb (1)
Edwin A. Keim (1)
Amanda H. Miller (1)
Fannie M. Troyer (1)
Raymond A. Troyer (1)
Ella R. Yoder (1)
Joe M. Yoder (1)
Mary T. Yoder (1)
David A. Miller (2)
Noah M. Miller (2)
Robert L. Miller (2)
Eli A. Troyer (2)
Jonas M. Troyer (2)
Amanda J. Yoder (2)
Jacob D. Yoder (2)
Katie J. Hershberger (3)
Abe L. Miller (3)
Doris M. Miller (3)
Amanda M. Troyer (3)
Abe M. Yoder (3)
Amanda A. Yoder (3)
Sarah T. Yoder (3)
Ada J. Hershberger (4)
Anna J. Hershberger (4)
Jonas A. Keim (4)
Abbie A. Miller (4)
Ada H. Miller (4)
Calvin J. Miller (4)
Edward Ray Miller (4)
Robert Keith Miller (4)
Anna S. Troyer (4)
Jonas R. Yoder (4)

1938–39

Albert Kaser

2/
30/

Donald Dale Kaser (5)
Sarah A. Keim (5)
Edna M. Mast (5)
Anna L. Miller (5)
Levi A. Miller (5)
Mattie L. Miller (5)
Eli A. Yoder (5)
Henry D. Yoder (5)
Noah T. Yoder (5)
Katie J. Hershberger (6)
Albert A. Keim (6)
Arletta Lahm (6)
Mattie E. Mast (6)
Amanda A. Miller (6)
Benjamin M. Miller (6)
John S. Troyer (6)
Mary M. Yoder (6)
Anna M. Mast (7)
Henry A. Mast (7)
Annie H. Miller (7)
Harold Blaine Miller (7)
Katie L. Miller (7)
Lizzie H. Miller (7)
Perry M. Miller (7)
Aden M. Troyer (7)
Sarah R. Yoder (7)
Albert D. Erb (8)
Grace Lahm (8)
Eli E. Mast (8)
Atlee C. Miller (8)
Celesta Schlabach (8)
Abe M. Troyer (8)
Katie M. Troyer (8)
Eli D. Yoder (8)
Fannie T. Yoder (8)

1939–40

Olive Mast

2/

Levi Miller Jr. (1)
Joe Miller (1)
Katie Ann Raber (1)
Ada Troyer (1)
Katie Troyer (1)
Elmina Yoder (1)
Moses Yoder (1)
Susie Yoder (1)
Violet Erb (2)
Edwin Keim (2)
Amanda Miller (2)
Fannie Troyer (2)
Raymond Troyer (2)
Joe Yoder (2)
Mary Yoder (2)
David Miller (3)
Noah Miller (3)
Robert Miller (3)
Amanda Troyer (3)
Eli Troyer (3)
Jonas Troyer (3)
Amanda Yoder (3)
Jacob Yoder (3)
Katie Hershberger (4)
Abe Miller (4)
Doris Miller (4)
Noah Raber (4)
Abe Yoder (4)
Amanda Yoder (4)
Sarah Yoder (4)

In 1937–38 the last classes were held in the old two story wooden schoolhouse.

1939–40

Albert Kaser

2/

Ada Hershberger (5)
Anna Hershberger (5)
Jonas A. Keim (5)
Abbie Miller (5)
Ada Miller (5)
Edward Miller (5)
Keith Miller (5)
Anna Troyer (5)
Jonas Yoder (5)
Donald Kaser (6)
Sarah Keim (6)
Edna Mast (6)
Levi Miller (6)
Mattie Miller (6)
Susana Raber (6)
Eli A. Yoder (6)
Henry Yoder (6)
Noah Yoder (6)
Katie Hershberger (7)
Albert Keim (7)
Arletta Lahm (7)
Mattie Mast (7)
Amanda Miller (7)
Benjamin Miller (7)
John Troyer (7)
Mary Yoder (7)
Anna Mast (8)
Henry Mast (8)
Annie Miller (8)
Blaine Miller (8)
Katie Miller (8)
Perry Miller (8)
Aden Troyer (8)
Sarah Yoder (8)

1940–41

Olive Mast

2/

Donald Hagans (1)
Levi Miller (1)
Roman Miller (1)
Anna Raber (1)
Saloma Troyer (1)
Levi Yoder (1)
Melvin Yoder (1)
Moses Yoder (1)
Joe Miller (2)
Levi Jr. Miller (2)
Katie Ann Raber (2)
Ada Troyer (2)

Katie Troyer (2)
Elmina Yoder (2)
Susie Yoder (2)
Edwin Keim (3)
Amanda Miller (3)
Raymond Troyer (3)
Joe Yoder (3)
Mary Yoder (3)
David Miller (4)
Noah Miller (4)
Robert Miller (4)
Eli Troyer (4)
Amanda Yoder (4)
Jacob Yoder (4)

1940–41

Gerald Miller

2/
30/

Katie J. Hershberger (5)
Abe L. Miller (5)
Doris Miller (5)
Noah J. Raber (5)
Edna D. Schlabach (5)
Abe M. Miller (5)
Amanda A. Yoder (5)
Sara T. Yoder (5)
Ada J. Hershberger (6)
Anna J. Hershberger (6)
Jonas A. Keim (6)
Abbie A. Miller (6)
Ada H. Miller (6)
Edward Miller (6)
Keith Miller (6)
Anna S. Troyer (6)
Jonas R. Yoder (6)
Donald Kaser (7)
Sarah A. Keim (7)
Edna M. Mast (7)
Levi A. Miller (7)
Mattie L. Miller (7)
Susann Raber (7)
Eli A. Yoder (7)
Henry D. Yoder (7)
Noah T. Yoder (7)
Katie J. Hershberger (8)
Albert A. Keim (8)
Arletta Lahm (8)
Mattie E. Mast (8)
Amanda A. Miller (8)
Benjamin M. Miller (8)
John S. Troyer (8)
Mary Ann Yoder (8)

We are not fully clothed until we wear a smile.
Teacher Elson Sommers –
1989 Charm classroom motto

39/ Albert Kaser lived in Charm at the time of teaching. Albert died July 6, 1973. He had undergone heart surgery five years prior to his death.

2/ **1941–42**
Ethel Miller
Malinda Mast (1)
Abigail Miller (1)
Fannie Miller (1)
Paul Mueller (1)
LaRue Oswald (1)
Andy Raber (1)
Mose L. Troyer (1)
Mary Yoder (1)
Melvin Yoder (1)
Mose D. Yoder (1)
Donald Hagans (2)
Roman Miller (2)
Anna Raber (2)
Katie Ann Raber (2)
Saloma Troyer (2)
Levi Yoder (2)
Mose J. Yoder (2)
Joe Miller (3)
Levi Miller Jr. (3)
Ada Troyer (3)
Katie Troyer (3)
Elmina Yoder (3)
Susie Yoder (3)
Edwin Keim (4)
Amanda Miller (4)
Eli Troyer (4)
Raymond Troyer (4)
Joe Yoder (4)
Mary Yoder (4)

30/ **1941–42**
Gerald Miller
Anna L. Miller (5)
David D. Miller (5)
Noah M. Miller (5)
Robert L. Miller (5)
Amanda J. Yoder (5)
Jacob D. Yoder (5)
Abe L. Miller (6)
Doris Miller (6)
Noah J. Raber (6)
Abe M. Yoder (6)
Amanda A. Yoder (6)
Sarah T. Yoder (6)
Abe J. Hershberger (7)
Jonas A. Keim (7)
Abbie A. Miller (7)
Ada H. Miller (7)
Edward Miller (7)
Keith R. Miller (7)
Anna S. Troyer (7)
Andrew A. Yoder (7)
Jonas R. Yoder (7)
Donald Dale Kaser (8)
Sarah Mae Keim (8)
Edna M. Mast (8)
Levi A. Miller (8)
Mattie L. Miller (8)

Susann J. Raber (8)
Eli A. Yoder (8)
Henry D. Yoder (8)
Noah T. Yoder (8)

30/ **1942–43**
Priscilla Miller
Abigail Miller (1)
Levi A. Miller (1)
Gladys Mueller (1)
Henry M. Raber (1)
David J. Troyer (1)
Fannie S. Troyer (1)
Annie T. Yoder (1)
Malinda M. Mast (2)
Fannie L. Miller (2)
Paul Mueller (2)
LaRue Oswald (2)
Andrew M. Raber (2)
Moses L. Troyer (2)
Mary A. Yoder (2)
Melvin J. Yoder (2)
Moses A. Yoder (2)
Moses J. Yoder (2)
Donald Hagans (3)
Roman L. Miller (3)
Anna M. Raber (3)
Katie Ann Raber (3)
Levi T. Yoder (3)
Joe M. Miller (4)
Levi L. Miller Jr. (4)
Ada J. Troyer (4)
Katie S. Troyer (4)
Ella R. Yoder (4)
Susie A. Yoder (4)

30/ **1942–43**
Gerald Miller
Edwin A. Keim (5)
Amanda H. Miller (5)
Raymond A. Troyer (5)
Amanda J. Yoder (5)
Joe M. Yoder (5)
Mary T. Yoder (5)
David A. Miller (6)
Noah M. Miller (6)
Robert L. Miller (6)
Jacob D. Yoder (6)
Abe L. Miller (7)
Doris Lucille Miller (7)
Noah J. Raber (7)
Abe M. Yoder (7)
Amanda A. Yoder (7)
Sarah T. Yoder (7)
Ada J. Hershberger (8)
Jonas A. Keim (8)
Abbie A. Miller (8)
Ada H. Miller (8)
Anna S. Troyer (8)
Jonas R. Yoder (8)

315/ A liar is sooner caught than a cripple.

1900 Charm School writing exercise

2/ **1943–44**
Priscilla Miller
Ada Miller (1)
Ida Miller (1)
Henry Raber (1)
Roman Yoder (1)
Abigail Miller (2)
Levi A. Miller (2)
Gladys Mueller (2)
David Troyer (2)
Fannie Troyer (2)
Annie Yoder (2)
Melvin Yoder (2)
Fannie Mast (3)
Malinda Mast (3)
Paul Mueller (3)
LaRue Oswald (3)
Andy Raber (3)
Mose L. Troyer (3)
Mary Yoder (3)
Mose D. Yoder (3)
Mose J. Yoder (3)
Roman Miller (4)
Anna Raber (4)
Katie Ann Raber (4)
Levi T. Yoder (4)

30/ **1943–44**
Gerald Miller
Joe M. Miller (5)
Levi L. Miller (5)
Ada J. Troyer (5)
Katie S. Troyer (5)
Elmina R. Yoder (5)
Susie A. Yoder (5)
Edwin A. Keim (6)
Amanda H. Miller (6)
Raymond A. Troyer (6)
Joe M. Yoder (6)
Mary T. Yoder (6)
David A. Miller (7)
Noah M. Miller (7)
Robert L. Miller (7)
Jacob D. Yoder (7)
Abe L. Miller (8)
Doris Lucille Miller (8)
Noah J. Raber (8)
Abe M. Yoder (8)
Sarah T. Yoder (8)

2/ **1944–45**
Priscilla Miller
Mattie Hershberger (1)
Levi A. Keim (1)
John Mueller Jr. (1)
Daniel Troyer (1)
Fannie A. Troyer (1)
Mattie Troyer (1)
Fannie Yoder (1)
Roman Yoder (1)
Ada Miller (2)
Ida Miller (2)
Henry Raber (2)
Abigail Miller (3)
Levi A. Miller (3)
Gladys Mueller (3)
Andy Raber (3)
David Troyer (3)
Fannie S. Troyer (3)
Annie Yoder (3)

Melvin Yoder (3)
Malinda Mast (4)
Fannie Miller (4)
Roman Miller (4)
Paul Mueller (4)
LaRue Oswald (4)
Moses Troyer (4)
Mary Yoder (4)
Moses D. Yoder (4)
Moses J. Yoder (4)

2/ **1944–45**
Gerald Miller
Anna Raber (5)
Katie Ann Raber (5)
Levi Yoder (5)
Joe Miller (6)
Levi Miller (6)
Ada Troyer (6)
Katie Troyer (6)
Raymond Troyer (6)
Elmina Yoder (6)
Susie Yoder (6)
Edwin Keim (7)
Amanda Miller (7)
Joe Yoder (7)
Mary Yoder (7)
Abe Miller (8)
David Miller (8)
Noah Miller (8)
Robert Miller (8)
Abe Yoder (8)
Jacob Yoder (8)

2/
30/ **1945–46**
Ethel L. Miller
Lovina R. Hershberger (1)
Verna J. Kurtz (1)
John L. Miller (1)
Susan Miller (1)
Eli M. Raber (1)
Daniel L. Troyer (1)
Levi J. Troyer (1)
Mattie R. Hershberger (2)
Levi A. Keim (2)
Dan N. Miller (2)
John Mueller Jr. (2)
Fannie A. Troyer (2)
Mattie S. Troyer (2)
Fannie J. Troyer (2)
Roman J. Yoder (2)
Ada A. Miller (3)
Fannie N. Miller (3)
Ida L. Miller (3)
Henry M. Raber (3)
Melvin J. Yoder (3)
Abigail Miller (4)
Levi A. Miller (4)
Gladys Mueller (4)
Andy Raber (4)
David Troyer (4)
Fannie Troyer (4)
Annie T. Yoder (4)
Moses J. Yoder (4)

293/   It takes an unselfish man to plant a tree.
                                        Charm schoolteacher Howard Kaser

---

2/   **1945–46**
Venus Zuercher
Malinda Mast (5)
Fannie L. Miller (5)
Roman L. Miller (5)
Paul J. Mueller (5)
LaRue Oswald (5)
Moses L. Troyer (5)
Mary Yoder (5)
Moses D. Yoder (5)
Anna M. Raber (6)
Katie Ann Raber (6)
Elmina R. Yoder (6)
Levi T. Yoder (6)
Ada N. Miller (7)
Joe M. Miller (7)
Levi L. Miller (7)
Ada J. Troyer (7)
Katie S. Troyer (7)
Raymond A. Troyer (7)
Susie A. Yoder (7)
Edwin A. Keim (8)
Abe L. Miller (8)
Amanda Miller (8)
Abe M. Yoder (8)
Joe M. Yoder (8)
Mary T. Yoder (8)

30/   **1946–47**
Ethel L. Miller
D. D. Miller
Willie Keim (1)
Anna L. Miller (1)
Ivan Miller (1)
John L. Miller (1)
Susan L. Miller (1)
Elinor Oswald (1)
Roy Schlabach (1)
Mary S. Troyer (1)
Katie T. Yoder (1)
Lovina R. Hershberger
   (2)
Verna J. Kurtz (2)
Eli M. Raber (2)
Daniel L. Troyer (2)
Levi J. Troyer (2)
Roman J. Yoder (2)
Mattie R. Hershberger
   (3)
Levi A. Keim (3)
Daniel N. Miller (3)
John Mueller Jr. (3)
Henry M. Raber (3)
Fannie A. Troyer (3)
Mattie S. Troyer (3)
Fannie J. Yoder (3)
Ada A. Miller (4)
Fannie N. Miller (4)
Ida Miller (4)
Andy Raber (4)
Melvin J. Yoder (4)

2/   **1946–47**
Venus Zuercher
❧   Malinda Mast (5)

Abigail L. Miller (5)
Levi A. Miller (5)
Roman L. Miller (5)
Gladys Mueller (5)
David J. Troyer (5)
Fannie S. Troyer (5)
Moses L. Troyer (5)
Anna T. Yoder (5)
Moses J. Yoder (5)
Fannie L. Miller (6)
Paul J. Mueller (6)
LaRue Oswald (6)
Anna M. Raber (6)
Mary A. Yoder (6)
Moses D. Yoder (6)
Elmina R. Yoder (7)
Levi T. Yoder (7)
Ada N. Miller (8)
Joe M. Miller (8)
Levi L. Miller Jr. (8)
Ada J. Troyer (8)
Katie S. Troyer (8)
Raymond A. Troyer (8)
Susie A. Yoder (8)

30/   **1947–48**
Ethel L. Miller
Vernon A. Keim (1)
Melvin M. Raber (1)
Fannie A. Schlabach (1)
Atlee L. Troyer (1)
Edgar Allan Troyer (1)
Willie Keim (2)
Anna L. Miller (2)
Ivan Miller (2)
John L. Miller (2)
Susan L. Miller (2)
Elinor Oswald (2)
Roy A. Schlabach (2)
Mary S. Troyer (2)
Katie T. Yoder (2)
Lovina R. Hershberger
   (3)
Verna J. Kurtz (3)
Eli M. Raber (3)
Daniel L. Troyer (3)
Levi J. Troyer (3)
Roman J. Yoder (3)
Mattie R. Hershberger
   (4)
Levi A. Keim (4)
Daniel L. Miller (4)
John Mueller Jr. (4)
Henry M. Raber (4)
Fannie A. Troyer (4)
Mattie S. Troyer (4)
Fannie J. Yoder (4)

2/   **1947–48**
D. D. Miller
Malinda M. Mast (5)
Ada A. Miller (5)
Fannie N. Miller (5)
Ida L. Miller (5)
Levi A. Miller (5)

Andy M. Raber (5)
Melvin J. Yoder (5)
Moses J. Yoder (5)
Abigail Miller (6)
Roman L. Miller (6)
Gladys Mueller (6)
David J. Troyer (6)
Moses L. Troyer (6)
Anna T. Yoder (6)
Fannie L. Miller (7)
Paul J. Mueller (7)
LaRue Oswald (7)
Anna M. Raber (7)
Mary A. Yoder (7)
Moses D. Yoder (7)
Raymond A. Troyer (8)
Ella R. Yoder (8)
Levi T. Yoder (8)

2/   **1948–49**
30/   *Ethel Stutzman*
Ruth Willems
David Farver (1)
Sarah Keim (1)
Susie Keim (1)
Mary J. Kurtz (1)
Christian L. Miller (1)
Dorothy A. Schlabach
   (1)
Abe S. Troyer (1)
Ada S. Troyer (1)
Anna J. Troyer (1)
Anna J. Yoder (1)
Anna M. Yoder (1)
Mary A. Yoder (1)
John L. Miller (2)
Melvin Raber (2)
Fannie A. Schlabach (2)
Atlee Troyer (2)
Edgar Troyer (2)
William Keim (3)
Anna L. Miller (3)
Ivan Miller (3)
Susan L. Miller (3)
Elinor Oswald (3)
Roy A. Schlabach (3)
Mary S. Troyer (3)
Katie T. Yoder (3)
Lovina Hershberger (4)
Verna Kurtz (4)
Eli Raber (4)
Daniel Troyer (4)
Levi J. Troyer (4)
Roman J. Yoder (4)

2/   **1948–49**
D. D. Miller
Mattie R. Hershberger
   (5)
Daniel N. Miller (5)
John Mueller Jr. (5)

Henry M. Raber (5)
Fannie A. Troyer (5)
Mattie S. Troyer (5)
Fannie J. Yoder (5)
Ada A. Miller (6)
Fannie N. Miller (6)
Ida L. Miller (6)
Levi A. Miller (6)
Andy M. Raber (6)
Melvin J. Yoder (6)
Mose J. Yoder (6)
Malinda M. Mast (7)
Abigail Miller (7)
Roman L. Miller (7)
David J. Troyer (7)
Fannie S. Troyer (7)
Mose L. Troyer (7)
Annie T. Yoder (7)
Fannie L. Miller (8)
Annie M. Raber (8)
Ella R. Yoder (8)
Mary A. Yoder (8)
Moses D. Yoder (8)

2/   **1949–50**
Ethel Stutzman
Janet Farver (1)
Roy Keim (1)
Elaine Miller (1)
Sarah Miller (1)
Alice Mueller (1)
Anna Raber (1)
Mary Raber (1)
Amanda Troyer (1)
Anna J. Yoder (1)
Mary M. Yoder (1)
David Farver (2)
Sarah Keim (2)
Susie Keim (2)
Mary J. Kurtz (2)
Crist Miller (2)
Anna M. Raber (2)
Mahlon Raber (2)
Dorothy Schlabach (2)
Abe Troyer (2)
Ada Troyer (2)
Anna Troyer (2)
Mary Yoder (2)
Anna L. Miller (3)
Ivan Miller (3)
John L. Miller (3)
Simon Miller (3)
Melvin Raber (3)
Fannie Schlabach (3)
Atlee Troyer (3)
Edgar Troyer (3)
Willie Keim (4)
Susan Miller (4)
Elinor Oswald (4)
Roy Schlabach (4)
Mary S. Troyer (4)
Katie T. Yoder (4)

5/   David D. Miller lived in Berlin after moving there from Protection, Kansas in 1941. He was bishop of Mennonite churches
at Martin's Creek, Berlin, and Millersburg, and served as mis-
sion bishop of Ohio. David died in January of 1976 at Goshen,
Indiana, where he moved a few years prior to his death. He is
buried at Elkhart Prairie Cemetery.

2/ **1949–50**
Howard Kaser
Lovina Hershberger (5)
Verna Kurtz (5)
Eli Raber (5)
Daniel Troyer (5)
Levi Troyer (5)
Roman Yoder (5)
Mattie Hershberger (6)
Daniel N. Miller (6)
John Mueller Jr. (6)
Henry Raber (6)
Fannie A. Troyer (6)
Fannie J. Troyer (6)
Ada A. Miller (7)
Fannie N. Miller (7)
Ida Miller (7)
Levi A. Miller (7)
Andy Raber (7)
Melvin Yoder (7)
Malinda Mast (8)
Abigail Miller (8)
Roman L. Miller (8)
Gladys Mueller (8)
David Troyer (8)
Fannie S. Troyer (8)
Mose L. Troyer (8)

2/ **1950–51**
Elsie Miller
Susie Hershberger (1)
Barbara Kurtz (1)
Mahlon Miller (1)
Ervin Schlabach (1)
Sarah Troyer (1)
Esther Yoder (1)
Janet Farver (2)
Roy Keim (2)
Elaine Miller (2)
Sarah Miller (2)
Alice Mueller (2)
Mary Raber (2)
Amanda Troyer (2)
Anna Yoder (2)
David Farver (3)
Sarah Keim (3)
Susie Keim (3)
Mary Kurtz (3)
Christian Miller (3)
Dorothy Schlabach (3)
Abe Troyer (3)
Ada Troyer (3)
Anna Troyer (3)
Anna Yoder (3)
Mary Yoder (3)
Anna Miller (4)
Ivan Miller (4)
John Miller (4)
Simon Miller (4)
Melvin Raber (4)
Fannie Schlabach (4)
Atlee Troyer (4)
Mattie Yoder (4)

2/
30/ **1950–51**
Howard Kaser
Willie Keim (5)
Susan L. Miller (5)
Elinor Oswald (5)
Roy A. Schlabach (5)
Mary S. Troyer (5)

Katie T. Yoder (5)
Lovina R. Hershberger (6)
Verna J. Kurtz (6)
Eli M. Raber (6)
Daniel L. Troyer (6)
Levi J. Troyer (6)
Roman J. Yoder (6)
Mattie R. Hershberger (7)
Daniel N. Miller (7)
John Mueller Jr. (7)
Henry M. Raber (7)
Fannie A. Troyer (7)
Mattie S. Troyer (7)
Fannie J. Yoder (7)
Ada A. Miller (8)
Fannie N. Miller (8)
Ida Miller (8)
Andy Raber (8)
Annie Yoder (8)

2/ **1951–52**
30/ *Elizabeth Beyeler*
Clara O. Keim (1)
Andy N. Miller (1)
Eli L. Miller (1)
Mahlon L. Miller (1)
Eli S. Troyer (1)
Albert M. Yoder (1)
Susie R. Hershberger (2)
Barbara J. Kurtz (2)
Ervin A. Schlabach (2)
Sarah J. Troyer (2)
Janet Farver (3)
Roy O. Keim (3)
Elaine Miller (3)
Sarah L. Miller (3)
Alice Mueller (3)
Mary M. Raber (3)
Robert E. Raber (3)
Amanda L. Troyer (3)
Anna J. Yoder (3)
Mary M. Yoder (3)
David Farver (4)
Sarah Keim (4)
Susie Keim (4)
Mary Kurtz (4)
Crist Miller (4)
Ivan Miller (4)
Sandra Raber (4)
Dorothy Schlabach (4)
Abe Troyer (4)
Ada Troyer (4)
Anna J. Troyer (4)
Anna Yoder (4)

2/ **1951–52**
Howard Kaser
Anna Miller (5)
John Miller (5)
Simon Miller (5)
Melvin Raber (5)
Fannie Schlabach (5)
Atlee Troyer (5)
Willie Keim (6)
Susan Miller (6)
Elinor Oswald (6)
Roy Schlabach (6)
Mary Troyer (6)

76/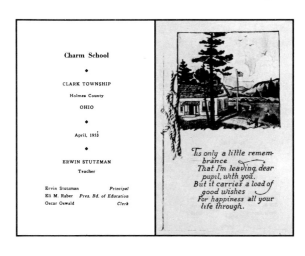

Charm School

CLARK TOWNSHIP
Holmes County
OHIO

April, 1953

ERWIN STUTZMAN
Teacher

Ervin Stutzman   Principal
Eli M. Raber   Pres. Bd. of Education
Oscar Oswald   Clerk

'Tis only a little remembrance
That I'm leaving, dear pupil, with you.
But it carries a load of good wishes
For happiness all your life through.

Katie Yoder (6)
Lovina Hershberger (7)
Verna Kurtz (7)
Eli Raber (7)
Daniel Troyer (7)
Levi Troyer (7)
Roman Yoder (7)
Mattie Hershberger (8)
Daniel Miller (8)
John Mueller Jr. (8)
Henry Raber (8)
Fannie Troyer (8)
Mattie Troyer (8)
Fannie Yoder (8)

30/ **1952–53**
Elizabeth Beyeler
Anna R. Hershberger (1)
Clara O. Keim (1)
Andy J. Kurtz (1)
Fannie M. Raber (1)
Mary L. Troyer (1)
Andy N. Miller (2)
Eli L. Miller (2)
Mahlon L. Miller (2)
Eli S. Troyer (2)
Albert M. Yoder (2)
Susie R. Hershberger (3)
Barbara J. Kurtz (3)
Ervin A. Schlabach (3)
Janet Farver (4)
Roy O. Keim (4)
Elaine Miller (4)
Sarah L. Miller (4)
Alice Mueller (4)
Mary M. Raber (4)
Robert Raber (4)
Amanda L. Troyer (4)
Sarah J. Troyer (4)
Anna J. Yoder (4)
Mary M. Yoder (4)

30/ **1952–53**
Erwin Stutzman
David Farver (5)
Sarah R. Keim (5)
Susie O. Keim (5)
Mary J. Kurtz (5)
Christian L. Miller (5)
Ivan Miller (5)

Sandra J. Raber (5)
Dorothy A. Schlabach (5)
Abe S. Troyer (5)
Ada S. Troyer (5)
Anna J. Troyer (5)
Anna M. Yoder (5)
Anna L. Miller (6)
John L. Miller (6)
Simon L. Miller (6)
Melvin Raber (6)
Fannie A. Schlabach (6)
Atlee L. Troyer (6)
William R. Keim (7)
Susan L. Miller (7)
Roy A. Schlabach (7)
Mary S. Troyer (7)
Katie T. Yoder (7)
Lovina R. Hershberger (8)
Verna J. Kurtz (8)
Eli M. Raber (8)
Daniel L. Troyer (8)
Levi J. Troyer (8)
Roman J. Yoder (8)

2/ **1953–54**
30/ *Elizabeth Beyeler*
Roy E. Mast (1)
Lizzie M. Miller (1)
Mary Ann Miller (1)
Gary Scherer (1)
Jacob J. Yoder (1)
Anna Hershberger (2)
Clara Keim (2)
Andy Kurtz (2)
Andy Miller (2)
Fannie Raber (2)
Mary Troyer (2)
Eli Miller (3)
Mahlon Miller (3)
Eli Troyer (3)
Albert Yoder (3)
Susie R. Hershberger (4)
Barbara J. Kurtz (4)
Ervin A. Schlabach (4)
Sarah J. Troyer (4)

❧

Live with the lame and you will limp.
1900 Charm School writing exercise

30/ **1953–54**
Howard Kaser
Janet Farver (5)
Roy O. Keim (5)
Elaine Miller (5)
Sarah L. Miller (5)
Alice Mueller (5)
Mary M. Raber (5)
Amanda L. Troyer (5)
Anna J. Yoder (5)
Mary M. Yoder (5)
David Farver (6)
Sarah R. Keim (6)
Susie O. Keim (6)
Mary J. Kurtz (6)
Christian L. Miller (6)
Ivan Miller (6)
John L. Miller (6)
Dorothy A. Schlabach (6)
Abe Troyer (6)
Ada S. Troyer (6)
Anna J. Troyer (6)
Anna M. Yoder (6)
Anna L. Miller (7)
Simon L. Miller (7)
Melvin Raber (7)
Fannie A. Schlabach (7)
Atlee L. Troyer (7)
William Keim (8)
Susan L. Miller (8)
Roy A. Schlabach (8)
Mary S. Troyer (8)
Katie T. Yoder (8)

1954–55
110/ *Betty Miller (1–4)*
290/ *Howard Kaser (5–8)*

1955–56
110/ *Elizabeth Beyeler (1–4)*
290/ *Howard Kaser (5–8)*

1956–57
110/ *Darlene Oswald (1–4)*
290/ *Howard Kaser (5–8)*

1957–58
110/ *Darlene Oswald (1–4)*
290/ *Howard Kaser (5–8)*

1958–59
110/ *Darlene Oswald (1–4)*
125/ *Howard Kaser (5–8)*

30/ **1959–60**
Darlene Oswald
Vickie Carpenter (1)
Ada S. Erb (1)
Steve Hershberger (1)
Harold Keim (1)
Kenny Miller (1)
Jonas D. Raber (1)
Lucinda Raber (1)
Mary Ann Schlabach (1)
Andy Troyer (1)
Donnie Weaver (1)
Ronnie Keim (2)
Eli Mast (2)
Abe Miller (2)
Mose Miller (2)
Mattie Schlabach (2)
Ronnie Schlabach (2)
Verna Schlabach (2)
Ella Troyer (2)
Ida Troyer (2)
Alma Yoder (2)
Andy Yoder (2)
John Erb (3)
Marie Raber (3)
Bobby Schlabach (3)
Ada Mae Troyer (3)
Violet Weaver (3)
Elizabeth Yoder (3)
Susie Erb (4)
Ben Kurtz (4)
Dena Miller (4)
Jonas Miller (4)
Rebecca Miller (4)
Edward Raber (4)
Roman Raber (4)
Roy Raber (4)

30/ **1959–60**
Howard Kaser
Danny O. Keim (5)
Gary A. Keim (5)
Katie O. Keim (5)
Irvin A. Miller (5)
Ben D. Raber (5)
Leroy J. Raber (5)
Gary C. Scherer (5)
Karen C. Scherer (5)
Ida P. Yoder (5)
Joe J. Yoder (5)
George A. Carpenter (6)

Levi M. Hershberger (6)
Annie M. Miller (6)
Mary G. Schlabach (6)
Bertha J. Yoder (6)
Clara O. Keim (7)
Lizzie M. Miller (7)
Jacob J. Yoder (7)
Katie P. Yoder (7)
Annie R. Hershberger (8)
Andy J. Kurtz (8)
Barbara A. Raber (8)
Fannie M. Raber (8)
Mary L. Troyer (8)
Melvin J. Yoder (8)

30/
110/ **1960–61**
Florence Shafer (2–3)
Howard Kaser (6–7)

30/
110/ **1961–62**
Florence Shafer (2–3)
Howard Kaser (6–7)

30/
110/ **1962–63**
Florence Shafer (2–3)
Howard Kaser (6–7)

30/ **1963–64**
Florence Shafer
Eli J. Hershberger (3)
Alden Keim (3)
Randall Keim (3)
Ben M. Miller (3)
Effie Miller (3)
Rebecca Miller (3)
Vernon J. Miller (3)
Steven Scherer (3)
Alvin Schlabach (3)
Katie Mae Schlabach (3)
Atlee M. Shetler (3)
Betty J. Yoder (3)
Melvin A. Yoder (3)
Mary D. Burkholder (4)
Donna Lou Hershberger (4)
Betty J. Kurtz (4)
Esther M. Miller (4)
Melva A. Miller (4)
Verba E. Miller (4)
Edna M. Nisley (4)
Abe A. Raber (4)
Fannie P. Raber (4)
Harvey P. Raber (4)
Lizzie A. Raber (4)
Eli M. Shetler (4)
Amanda N. Yoder (4)

Katie Ann Yoder (4)
Ronnie Yoder (4)

30/ **1963–64**
Howard Kaser
John V. Erb (7)
Susie S. Erb (7)
Jonas V. Hershberger (7)
Sam E. Hershberger (7)
Dan A. Nisley (7)
Junior M. Nisley (7)
Marie B. Raber (7)
Sylvanus M. Raber (7)
Henry M. Shetler (7)
Ada Mae Troyer (7)
Elizabeth M. Yoder (7)
Dan O. Keim (8)
Ben J. Kurtz (8)
Dena A. Miller (8)
Jonas M. Miller (8)
Aden B. Raber (8)
Amanda A. Raber (8)
Andy M. Raber (8)
Annie M. Raber (8)
Edward N. Raber (8)
Eli P. Raber (8)
Roman A. Raber (8)
Roy M. Raber (8)
Fannie A. Yoder (8)
Joe J. Yoder (8)

30/ **1964–65**
Florence Shafer
Ella S. Erb (3)
Alden Keim (3)
Roy R. Kline (3)
Henry M. Miller (3)
Moses J. Miller (3)
Nelson E. Miller (3)
Alta M. Raber (3)
Henry E. Troyer (3)
Lydia Mae Yoder (3)
Eli J. Hershberger (4)
Esther V. Hershberger (4)
Randall Keim (4)
Ben M. Miller (4)
Effie Miller (4)
Rebecca Ann Miller (4)
Vernon J. Miller (4)
Steven Scherer (4)
Alvin Schlabach (4)
Katie Mae Schlabach (4)
Atlee M. Shetler (4)
Betty J. Yoder (4)
Melvin A. Yoder (4)

30/
110/ Due to an Ohio law going into effect limiting two grades per classroom (See Compulsory Attendance), the Charm enrollment was divided during the 1959–60 school year with Flat Ridge. The following were included with the transfer to Charm: Sam Hershberger, Dan A. Nisley, Melvin J. Nisley, Eli E. Hershberger, Andy M. Troyer, Raymond D. Miller, Melvin H. Raber, Andy M. Nisley, Marvin Schrock, Sylvanus Raber, Marie B. Raber, Jonas V. Hershberger, Atlee Raber, Mose V. Hershberger, Mary M. Troyer, Erma H. Raber, Emma L. Miller, and Sarah N. Yoder.

41/ By Christmas of the 1965–66 term, Howard was noticeably sick and more forgetful with his duties. He was still teaching at Charm School until Wednesday, March 23, 1966, then on Friday the 25th he went to Columbus for tests and x-rays. He had surgery to remove part of a brain tumor soon thereafter. Howard died October 7, 1966. He had married Lorene Mast in 1937. After marriage he had taught school at South Mt. Hope, Benton, and Wise, and was at Charm, where he had grown up, a total of sixteen years. Many pupils remember Howard's firm, sound, and respected teaching practice.

30/ **1964–65**
Howard Kaser
Ronald Lynn Keim (7)
Abe M. Miller (7)
Mose A. Miller (7)
Vernon M. Nisley (7)
Marie J. Raber (7)
Mattie H. Schlabach (7)
Verna H. Schlabach (7)
Esther M. Shetler (7)
Lydia Ann Stutzman (7)
Ella L. Troyer (7)
Emma L. Troyer (7)
Ida E. Troyer (7)
Alma J. Yoder (7)
Andy P. Yoder (7)
Menno A. Yoder (7)
Susie S. Erb (8)
Jonas V. Hershberger (8)
Sam E. Hershberger (8)
Junior M. Nisley (8)
Marie B. Raber (8)
Sylvanus M. Raber (8)
Henry M. Shetler (8)
Ada Mae Troyer (8)
Elizabeth M. Yoder (8)

30/ **1965–66**
Florence Shafer
Fannie O. Keim (3)
John R. Kline (3)
Edna A. Miller (3)
Sarah J. Miller (3)
Viola H. Schlabach (3)
Arlene J. Troyer (3)
Jonas L. Troyer (3)
Mose E. Troyer (3)
Jonas J. Yoder (3)
Katie J. Yoder (3)
Malinda A. Yoder (3)
Ella S. Erb (4)
Roy R. Kline (4)
Henry M. Miller (4)
Moses J. Miller (4)
Nelson E. Miller (4)
Alta M. Raber (4)
Henry E. Troyer (4)
Lydia Mae Yoder (4)

30/
28/ **1965–66**
Howard Kaser
Otto S. Regula
Oscar Fender
Ada S. Erb (7)
Alvin V. Hershberger (7)
Sara Ann Hershberger (7)
Steven Hershberger (7)
Harold Keim (7)
Wayne A. Miller (7)
Jonas D. Raber (7)
Mary Ann Schlabach (7)
Andy E. Troyer (7)
Mose A. Yoder (7)
Ronald Lynn Keim (8)
Abe M. Miller (8)
Mose A. Miller (8)
Vernon M. Nisley (8)
Marie J. Raber (8)

Verna H. Schlabach (8)
Esther M. Shetler (8)
Lydia Ann Stutzman (8)
Ella L. Troyer (8)
Emma L. Troyer (8)
Ida E. Troyer (8)
Alma J. Yoder (8)
Andy P. Yoder (8)
Menno A. Yoder (8)

30/ **1966–67**
Florence Shafer
Lydia Ann Erb (3)
LaVern Keim (3)
Linda Mae Kline (3)
Ervin N. Miller (3)
Paul M. Miller (3)
Sarah E. Miller (3)
Roman M. Nisley (3)
Emma H. Raber (3)
Erma A. Raber (3)
Henry D. Raber (3)
Noah E. Raber (3)
Ida H. Schlabach (3)
Katie Mae Schrock (3)
Alma M. Shetler (3)
Eli C. Yoder (3)
Monroe A. Yoder (3)
Sylvanus J. Yoder (3)
Fannie O. Keim (4)
John R. Kline (4)
Edna A. Miller (4)
Sarah J. Miller (4)
Viola H. Schlabach (4)
Jonas L. Troyer (4)
Mose E. Troyer (4)
Arlene J. Troyer (4)
Jonas A. Yoder (4)
Katie J. Yoder (4)
Malinda A. Yoder (4)

30/ **1966–67**
Otto S. Regula
Oscar Fender
Mary D. Burkholder (7)
Betty J. Kurtz (7)
Esther M. Miller (7)
Melva A. Miller (7)
Verba E. Miller (7)
Edna M. Nisley (7)
Fannie P. Raber (7)
Eli M. Shetler (7)
Ronnie Gene Yoder (7)
Ada S. Erb (8)
Alvin V. Hershberger (8)
Sara Ann Hershberger (8)
Harold Ray Keim (8)
Wayne A. Miller (8)
Jonas D. Raber (8)
Mary Ann Schlabach (8)
Andy E. Troyer (8)
Mose A. Yoder (8)

30/ **1967–68**
Florence Shafer
Roy J. Hershberger (3)
Mary J. Mast (3)
Sara Ann Mast (3)
Delbert M. Nisley (3)

30/ December 17, 1968

Copy of the letter sent to President Richard Nixon along with a portrait drawing of the president sketched by Betty J. Yoder, an eighth grade student at Charm School.

Ada A. Raber (3)
Eli Raber Jr. (3)
Marie A. Raber (3)
Mary Esther Raber (3)
Aden M. Troyer (3)
Anna R. Troyer (3)
Annie A. Yoder (3)
Lydia Ann Erb (4)
LaVern Keim (4)
Linda Mae Kline (4)
Ervin N. Miller (4)
Mary N. Miller (4)
Paul M. Miller (4)
Sarah E. Miller (4)
Roman M. Nisley (4)
Emma H. Raber (4)
Erma A. Raber (4)
Henry D. Raber (4)
Ida H. Schlabach (4)
Katie Mae Schrock (4)
Alma M. Shetler (4)
Eli C. Yoder (4)
Monroe A. Yoder (4)
Sylvanus J. Yoder (4)

30/ **1967–68**
Donald DeHass
Eli J. Hershberger (7)
Esther V. Hershberger (7)
Randall Keim (7)
Aden L. Miller (7)
Ben M. Miller (7)
Vernon J. Miller (7)
Mary D. Burkholder (8)
Betty J. Kurtz (8)
Esther M. Miller (8)
Melva A. Miller (8)
Verba E. Miller (8)
Edna M. Nisley (8)
Fannie P. Raber (8)
Eli M. Shetler (8)

Emma P. Raber (7)
Alvin H. Schlabach (7)
Atlee M. Shetler (7)
Betty J. Yoder (7)
Melvin A. Yoder (7)

1968–69
Florence Shafer
Mary Ann Barkman (3)
30/ Fannie D. Burkholder (3)
Roy J. Hershberger (3)
Mary Ellen Kline (3)
Naomi A. Mast (3)
Fannie E. Miller (3)
Miriam A. Miller (3)
Moses H. Miller (3)
Anthony Earl Parks (3)
Amanda A. Raber (3)
Ervin N. Raber (3)
Marvin J. Raber (3)
Celesta H. Schlabach (3)
Esta A. Schrock (3)
Anna M. Shetler (3)
Amanda R. Troyer (3)
John E. Troyer (3)
John Henry Troyer (3)
Levi M. Troyer (3)
Andy L. Yoder (3)
LaVern Keim (4)
Mary J. Mast (4)
Sara Ann Mast (4)
Ada A. Raber (4)
Marie A. Raber (4)
Mary Esther Raber (4)
Aden M. Troyer (4)
Anna R. Troyer (4)
Annie A. Yoder (4)

❧

30/ **1968–69**
Donald DeHass
Ella S. Erb (7)
Roy R. Kline (7)
Henry M. Miller (7)
Moses J. Miller (7)
Nelson E. Miller (7)
Alta M. Raber (7)
Henry E. Troyer (7)
Eli J. Hershberger (8)
Esther V. Hershberger (8)
Randall Keim (8)
Aden L. Miller (8)
Ben M. Miller (8)
Vernon J. Miller (8)
Emma P. Raber (8)
Alvin H. Schlabach (8)
Atlee M. Shetler (8)
Betty J. Yoder (8)

1/
284/ **1969–70**
Kathy Miller
Anna Jean Kline (3)
Ivan J. Miller (3)
Reuben H. Miller (3)
David A. Raber (3)
Paul Raber Jr. (3)
Jacob M. Shetler (3)
Ivan R. Troyer (3)
Mabel D. Troyer (3)
Effie M. Yoder (3)
Mary Ann Barkman (4)
Fannie D. Burkholder (4)
Roy J. Hershberger (4)
Mary Ellen Kline (4)
Naomi A. Mast (4)
Fannie E. Miller (4)
Miriam A. Miller (4)
Moses H. Miller (4)
Anthony Earl Parks (4)
Amanda A. Raber (4)
Ervin N. Raber (4)
Marvin J. Raber (4)
Celesta H. Schlabach (4)
Esta A. Schrock (4)
Anna M. Shetler (4)
Amanda R. Troyer (4)
John E. Troyer (4)
John Henry Troyer (4)
Levi M. Troyer (4)
Andy L. Yoder (4)

30/ **1969–70**
Donald DeHass
Fannie O. Keim (7)
John R. Kline (7)
Edna A. Miller (7)
Sarah J. Miller (7)
Abe P. Raber (7)
Viola H. Schlabach (7)
Jonas L. Troyer (7)
Arlene J. Yoder (7)
Jonas A. Yoder (7)
Katie J. Yoder (7)
Ella S. Erb (8)
Roy R. Kline (8)
Henry M. Miller (8)
Mose J. Miller (8)

Nelson E. Miller (8)
Alta M. Raber (8)
Henry E. Troyer (8)

1/ **1970–71**
284/ *John Miller*
Dale Kreisher
Esther Barkman (3)
Anna Mae Miller (3)
Esther A. Miller (3)
Noah H. Miller (3)
Robert R. Miller (3)
Roy A. Miller (3)
Daniel A. Raber (3)
Emma A. Raber (3)
Katie A. Raber (3)
Ada H. Schlabach (3)
Delbert M. Shetler (3)
Atlee A. Troyer (3)
Atlee M. Troyer (3)
Mary Ann Troyer (3)
Susan D. Troyer (3)
Atlee A. Yoder (3)
Anna Jean Kline (4)
Ivan J. Miller (4)
Reuben H. Miller (4)
Paul Raber Jr. (4)
Jacob M. Shetler (4)
Ivan R. Troyer (4)
Mabel D. Troyer (4)
David A. Yoder (4)
Effie M. Yoder (4)

1/ **1970–71**
Linda Miller
Lydia Ann Erb (7)
Fannie O. Keim (7)
Linda Mae Kline (7)
Sarah E. Miller (7)
Roman M. Nisley (7)
Henry D. Raber (7)
Katie Mae Schrock (7)
Alma M. Shetler (7)
Paul M. Shetler (7)
Sylvanus J. Yoder (7)
John R. Kline (8)
Edna A. Miller (8)
Sara J. Miller (8)
Abe P. Raber (8)
Viola H. Schlabach (8)
Jonas L. Troyer (8)
Arlene J. Yoder (8)
Jonas A. Yoder (8)
Katie J. Yoder (8)

1/ **1971–72**
Dale Kreisher
Reuben R. Beachy (5)
Anna L. Erb (5)
Christina M. Erb (5)
Anna Jean Kline (5)
Ivan J. Miller (5)
Linda Mae Miller (5)
Patricia A. Miller (5)
Reuben H. Miller (5)
Miriam Raber (5)
Paul Raber Jr. (5)
Jacob M. Shetler (5)
David N. Troyer (5)
Ivan R. Troyer (5)
Mabel D. Troyer (5)

315/ They are rich who have a friend.
1900 Charm school writing exercise

Annie L. Yoder (5)
Dennis J. Yoder (5)
Effie M. Yoder (5)
Isaac Yoder (5)
Marlene A. Yoder (5)
Noah L. Yoder (5)

1/ **1971–72**
James Lowery
Mary Ann Barkman (6)
Lester M. Beachy (6)
Ruth D. Beachy (6)
Fannie D. Burkholder (6)
Mary L. Erb (6)
Roy J. Hershberger (6)
Mary Ellen Kline (6)
Naomi A. Mast (6)
Anna M. Miller (6)
Esther N. Miller (6)
Fannie E. Miller (6)
Miriam A. Miller (6)
Moses H. Miller (6)
Wilbur J. Miller (6)
Anthony Earl Parks (6)
Amanda A. Raber (6)
Arlene M. Raber (6)
Ervin N. Raber (6)
Marvin J. Raber (6)
Celesta Schlabach (6)
Esta Schrock (6)
Anna M. Shetler (6)
Amanda R. Troyer (6)
Esther B. Troyer (6)
Esther N. Troyer (6)
John E. Troyer (6)
John Henry Troyer (6)
Levi M. Troyer (6)
Andy L. Yoder (6)
Jonas L. Yoder (6)
Norman L. Yoder (6)

1/ **1972–73**
Elson Sommers
Aden Raber (1)
Arlene Ann Raber (1)
Elsie Mae Raber (1)
Jonas H. Raber (1)
Wilma H. Raber (1)
Wayne A. Schrock (1)
Ervin D. Troyer (1)
Katie R. Troyer (1)
Wilma D. Troyer (1)
Leroy J. Yoder (1)
Marvin L. Yoder (1)
Mabel M. Barkman (2)
Daniel R. Keim (2)
David E. Miller (2)
Esther C. Miller (2)

Mose B. Miller (2)
Allen M. Raber (2)
Alma E. Raber (2)
Cinda Sue Raber (2)
Erma A. Raber (2)
Katie Mae Raber (2)
Roy M. Troyer (2)
Anna L. Yoder (2)
Robert M. Barkman (3)
Paul S. Erb (3)
Daniel A. Hershberger (3)
Leon Ray Mast (3)
John Oren Miller Jr. (3)
Katie A. Miller (3)
Ada Mae Raber (3)
Ben A. Raber (3)
Clara A. Raber (3)
Linda H. Raber (3)
Mary M. Shetler (3)
Cinda D. Troyer (3)
Eli Troyer Jr. (3)
Laura R. Troyer (3)
Lizzie Mae Troyer (3)

1/ **1972–73**
James Lowery
Aden D. Burkholder (4)
Patricia Keim (4)
Dennis J. Miller (4)
John E. Miller (4)
Robert B. Miller (4)
Benjamin A. Raber (4)
Edward M. Raber (4)
Erma A. Schrock (4)
Ada Mae Troyer (4)
Levi Troyer Jr. (4)
Sara E. Troyer (4)
Sarah D. Troyer (4)
Saloma L. Yoder (4)
Esther M. Barkman (5)
Anna Mae Miller (5)
Esther A. Miller (5)
Roy A. Miller (5)
Emma A. Raber (5)
Ada H. Schlabach (5)
Delbert M. Shetler (5)
Atlee A. Troyer (5)
Atlee M. Troyer (5)
Mary Ann Troyer (5)
Susan D. Troyer (5)
Robert L. Yoder (5)
Ivan J. Miller (6)
Paul Raber Jr. (6)
Jacob M. Shetler (6)
Ivan R. Troyer (6)
Mabel D. Troyer (6)
Abe L. Yoder (6)
Effie M. Yoder (6)

284/ In 1972–73 the seventh and eighth grade classes were held in the basement.

1/

1972–73
Henry Troyer
Mary Ann Barkman (7)
Fannie D. Burkholder (7)
Roy J. Hershberger (7)
Naomi Mast (7)
Fannie E. Miller (7)
Miriam A. Miller (7)
Anthony Earl Parks (7)
Ervin N. Raber (7)
Marvin J. Raber (7)
Celesta H. Schlabach (7)
Esta A. Schrock (7)
Anna M. Shetler (7)
Amanda R. Troyer (7)
John E. Troyer (7)
John Henry Troyer (7)
Levi M. Troyer (7)
Andy L. Yoder (7)
Mary J. Mast (8)
Sara Ann Mast (8)
Delbert M. Nisley (8)
Ada A. Raber (8)
Dan P. Raber (8)
Junior E. Raber (8)
Mary Esther Raber (8)
Ida H. Schlabach (8)
Aden M. Troyer (8)
Anna R. Troyer (8)
Anna A. Yoder (8)
Sarah L. Yoder (8)

1/
284/

1973–74
Elson Sommers
Danny Edward Gaugel (1)
Alma A. Hershberger (1)
Dorothy A. Mast (1)
Ivan R. Mast (1)
Atlee C. Miller (1)
Dennis J. Miller (1)
Erma A. Raber (1)
Esta E. Raber (1)
Lena E. Raber (1)
Wayne M. Shetler (1)
Clara A. Troyer (1)
Jonas M. Troyer (1)
Marie D. Troyer (1)
Adam L. Yoder (1)
Ben J. Yoder (1)
Eli A. Yoder (1)
Mary Ann Yoder (1)
Mary W. Yoder (1)
Aden A. Raber (2)
Arlene A. Raber (2)
Elsie Mae Raber (2)
Wilma H. Raber (2)
Jonas H. Schlabach (2)
Wayne A. Schrock (2)
Ervin D. Troyer (2)
Katie R. Troyer (2)
Wilma D. Troyer (2)
Leroy J. Yoder (2)
Marvin L. Yoder (2)

1/

1973–74
Dale Kreisher
Mabel Barkman (3)
Gregory James Gaugel (3)
David E. Miller (3)
Esther C. Miller (3)
Mose B. Miller (3)
Allen M. Raber (3)
Alma E. Raber (3)
Cinda Sue Raber (3)
Erma A. Raber (3)
Katie Mae Raber (3)
Roy M. Troyer (3)
Anna L. Yoder (3)
Robert M. Barkman (4)
Paul S. Erb (4)
Daniel A. Hershberger (4)
Leon Ray Mast (4)
John Oren Miller Jr. (4)
Katie A. Miller (4)
Ada Mae Raber (4)
Ben A. Raber (4)
Clara A. Raber (4)
Linda H. Raber (4)
Mary M. Shetler (4)
Cinda D. Troyer (4)
Eli Jr. Troyer Jr. (4)
Laura R. Troyer (4)
Lizzie Mae Troyer (4)
Saloma L. Yoder (4)
Aden D. Burkholder (5)
Patricia Keim (5)
Dennis J. Miller (5)
John E. Miller (5)
Robert B. Miller (5)
Benjamin A. Raber (5)
Edward M. Raber (5)
Erma A. Schrock (5)
Ada Mae Troyer (5)
Sara E. Troyer (5)
Sarah D. Troyer (5)
Levi Yoder Jr. (5)

1/

1974–75
Elson Sommers
Samuel Hershberger (1)
Ivan R. Mast (1)
Katie R. Mast (1)
Edward C. Miller (1)
Mary B. Miller (1)
Nancy B. Miller (1)
Edward H. Raber (1)
John Henry Troyer (1)
Lizzie E. Troyer (1)
Norman F. Troyer (1)
Adam L. Yoder (1)
Erma H. Yoder (1)
Ervin A. Yoder (1)
Katie M. Yoder (1)
Danny Edward Gaugel (2)
Alma A. Hershberger (2)
Leroy V. Kline (2)
Dorothy A. Mast (2)
Atlee C. Miller (2)
Dennis J. Miller (2)

Erma A. Raber (2)
Esta E. Raber (2)
Lena E. Raber (2)
Wayne M. Shetler (2)
Clara A. Troyer (2)
Jonas M. Troyer (2)
Marie D. Troyer (2)
Ben J. Yoder (2)
Eli A. Yoder (2)
Mary Ann Yoder (2)
Mary W. Yoder (2)

1/

1974–75
Christina Davis
Aden A. Raber (3)
Arlene Ann Raber (3)
Elsie Mae Raber (3)
Wilma H. Raber (3)
Jonas H. Schlabach (3)
Wayne A. Schrock (3)
Ervin D. Troyer (3)
Katie R. Troyer (3)
Wilma D. Troyer (3)
Leroy J. Yoder (3)
Marvin L. Yoder (3)
Mabel M. Barkman (4)
Gregory Gaugel (4)
David E. Miller (4)
Esther C. Miller (4)
Mose B. Miller (4)
Allen M. Raber (4)
Alma E. Raber (4)
Cinda Sue Raber (4)
Erma A. Raber (4)
Katie Mae Raber (4)
Roy M. Troyer (4)
Anna L. Yoder (4)

1975–76
Elson Sommers
Vernon J. Hershberger (1)
Allen J. Miller (1)
Erma B. Miller (1)
Lucinda C. Miller (1)
Annie H. Raber (1)
Barbara Ann Raber (1)
Edward H. Raber (1)
Mervin A. Raber (1)
David Troyer Jr. (1)
Katie J. Yoder (1)
Laura W. Yoder (1)
Miriam H. Yoder (1)
Mose A. Yoder (1)
Wayne J. Yoder (1)
Wyman L. Yoder (1)
Samuel A. Hershberger (2)
Ivan R. Mast (2)
Katie R. Mast (2)
Edward C. Miller (2)
Mary B. Miller (2)
Nancy B. Miller (2)
Norman F. Troyer (2)
Adam L. Yoder (2)
Erma H. Yoder (2)
Ervin A. Yoder (2)
Katie M. Yoder (2)

1/

1975–76
Christina Davis
Danny Gaugel (3)
Alma A. Hershberger (3)
Leroy V. Kline (3)
Dorothy A. Mast (3)
Atlee C. Miller (3)
Dennis J. Miller (3)
Erma A. Raber (3)
Esta E. Raber (3)
Wayne M. Shetler (3)
Marie D. Troyer (3)
Mary W. Troyer (3)
Ben J. Yoder (3)
Eli A. Yoder (3)
Mary Ann Yoder (3)
Aden A. Raber (4)
Arlene Ann Raber (4)
Elsie Mae Raber (4)
Wilma H. Raber (4)
Jonas H. Schlabach (4)
Wayne A. Schrock (4)
Ervin D. Troyer (4)
Katie R. Troyer (4)
William D. Troyer (4)
Leroy J. Yoder (4)
Marvin L. Yoder (4)

1/

1976–77
Elson Sommers
Ivan J. Burkholder (1)
Leon J. Hochstetler (1)
Mary D. Keim (1)
Mabel V. Kline (1)
Sara R. Mast (1)
Bruce V. Miller (1)
Edward J. Miller (1)
Maynard E. Miller (1)
Ray E. Miller (1)
Wayne J. Miller (1)
Ivan M. Raber (1)
Marion Lynn Raber (1)
Wayne H. Raber (1)
Edna R. Troyer (1)
Eldon D. Troyer (1)
Esther D. Troyer (1)
Katie L. Yoder (1)
Lizzie H. Yoder (1)
Miriam J. Yoder (1)
Vernon J. Hershberger (2)
Allen J. Miller (2)
Erma B. Miller (2)
Lucinda C. Miller (2)
Annie H. Raber (2)
Barbara Ann Raber (2)
Edward H. Raber (2)
Mervin A. Raber (2)
Miriam Raber (2)
David Troyer Jr. (2)
Katie J. Yoder (2)
Laura W. Yoder (2)
Miriam H. Yoder (2)
Mose A. Yoder (2)
Wayne J. Yoder (2)
Wyman L. Yoder (2)

❧

1976–77
Christana Davis
Samuel A. Hershberger (3)
Ivan R. Mast (3)
Katie R. Mast (3)
Edward C. Miller (3)
Mary B. Miller (3)
Nancy B. Miller (3)
Norman F. Troyer (3)
Adam L. Yoder (3)
Erma H. Yoder (3)
Ervin A. Yoder (3)
Alma A. Hershberger (4)
Leroy V. Kline (4)
Dorothy A. Mast (4)
Atlee C. Miller (4)
Dennis J. Miller (4)
Esther E. Miller (4)
Erma A. Raber (4)
Esta E. Raber (4)
Wayne M. Shetler (4)
Marie D. Troyer (4)
Ben J. Yoder (4)
Eli A. Yoder (4)
Mary W. Yoder (4)

1977–78
Elson Sommers
Aden J. Burkholder (1)
Loyel E. Hershberger (1)
Mary A. Hershberger (1)
Mary J. Hershberger (1)
Duane J. Hochstetler (1)
Elsie R. Mast (1)
Alma J. Miller (1)
Atlee B. Miller (1)
Stephen Ray Miller (1)
Bert E. Raber (1)
Bryan M. Raber (1)
Lovina A. Raber (1)
Lucy L. Raber (1)
Myron A. Raber (1)
Robert E. Raber (1)
Atlee H. Yoder (1)
Ervin W. Yoder (1)
Mervin J. Yoder (1)
Ivan J. Burkholder (2)
Leon J. Hochstetler (2)
Mary D. Keim (2)
Mabel V. Kline (2)
Sarah R. Mast (2)
Bruce V. Miller (2)
Edward J. Miller (2)
Maynard E. Miller (2)
Ray E. Miller (2)
Wayne J. Miller (2)
Ivan M. Raber (2)
Marion Lynn Raber (2)
Wayne H. Raber (2)
Edna R. Troyer (2)
Eldon D. Troyer (2)
Esther D. Troyer (2)
Katie L. Yoder (2)
Lizzie H. Yoder (2)
Miriam J. Yoder (2)

1977–78
Christina Davis
Vernon J. Hershberger (3)
Allen J. Miller (3)
Erma B. Miller (3)
Lucinda C. Miller (3)
Annie H. Raber (3)
Barbara Ann Raber (3)
Edward H. Raber (3)
Mervin A. Raber (3)
Miriam Raber (3)
David Troyer Jr. (3)
Katie J. Yoder (3)
Laura W. Yoder (3)
Miriam H. Yoder (3)
Mose A. Yoder (3)
Wayne J. Yoder (3)
Wyman L. Yoder (3)
Samuel A. Hershberger (4)
Ivan R. Mast (4)
Katie R. Mast (4)
Edward C. Miller (4)
Mary B. Miller (4)
Nancy B. Miller (4)
Norman F. Troyer (4)
Adam L. Yoder (4)
Erma H. Yoder (4)
Ervin A. Yoder (4)

1978–79
Elson Sommers
David Allen Erb (1)
Lizzie D. Keim (1)
Atlee B. Miller (1)
Marvin E. Miller (1)
Miriam V. Miller (1)
Leroy E. Raber (1)
Miriam H. Raber (1)
Emma D. Troyer (1)
Adah J. Yoder (1)
Ivan A. Yoder (1)
Mary J. Yoder (1)
Peter L. Yoder (1)
Susie W. Yoder (1)
Aden J. Burkholder (2)
Ivan J. Burkholder (2)
Loyel E. Hershberger (2)
Mary A. Hershberger (2)
Mary J. Hershberger (2)
Duane J. Hochstetler (2)
Elsie R. Mast (2)
Alma J. Miller (2)
Stephen Ray Miller (2)
Albert E. Raber (2)
Bryan M. Raber (2)
Lovina A. Raber (2)
Lucy L. Raber (2)
Myron A. Raber (2)
Robert E. Raber (2)
Eldon D. Troyer (2)
Atlee H. Yoder (2)
Ervin W. Yoder (2)
Mervin J. Yoder (2)

But the soul is not the body,
And the breath is not the flute;
Both together make the music,
Either marred and all is mute.
          —Browning
     Charm School Pupils Annual Record

———————————————

1978–79
Christina Hayes
Leon J. Hochstetler (3)
Mary D. Keim (3)
Mabel V. Kline (3)
Sarah R. Mast (3)
Bruce V. Miller (3)
Edward J. Miller (3)
Maynard E. Miller (3)
Ray E. Miller (3)
Wayne J. Miller (3)
Edward H. Raber (3)
Ivan M. Raber (3)
Marion Lynn Raber (3)
Wayne H. Raber (3)
Edna R. Troyer (3)
Esther D. Troyer (3)
Katie L. Yoder (3)
Lizzie H. Yoder (3)
Miriam J. Yoder (3)
Vernon J. Hershberger (4)
Allen J. Miller (4)
Erma B. Miller (4)
Lucinda C. Miller (4)
Annie H. Raber (4)
Barbara Ann Raber (4)
Mervin A. Raber (4)
Miriam E. Raber (4)
David Troyer Jr. (4)
Katie J. Yoder (4)
Laura W. Yoder (4)
Miriam H. Yoder (4)
Mose A. Yoder (4)
Wayne J. Yoder (4)
Wyman L. Yoder (4)

1979–80
Elson Sommers
Dennis J. Burkholder (1)
Vernon A. Hershberger (1)
Oren D. Keim (1)
Judy Ann Kline (1)
Mary V. Kline (1)
Ivan E. Mast (1)
Allen E. Miller (1)
Mary A. Miller (1)
Roy J. Miller (1)
Verba B. Miller (1)
Wayne J. Miller (1)
Ada A. Raber (1)
Laura A. Raber (1)
Linda A. Raber (1)
Miriam H. Raber (1)
Rhoda M. Raber (1)
Susan A. Schrock (1)

Joseph R. Troyer (1)
Alma H. Yoder (1)
Peter L. Yoder (1)
Sara Ann Yoder (1)
David Allen Erb (2)
Lizzie D. Keim (2)
Atlee B. Miller (2)
Marvin E. Miller (2)
Miriam V. Miller (2)
Leroy E. Raber (2)
Emma D. Troyer (2)
Adah J. Yoder (2)
Ivan A. Yoder (2)
Mary J. Yoder (2)
Susie W. Yoder (2)

1979–80
Christina Hayes
Aden J. Burkholder (3)
Ivan J. Burkholder (3)
Loyel E. Hershberger (3)
Mary A. Hershberger (3)
Mary J. Hershberger (3)
Duane Hochstetler (3)
Leon Hochstetler (3)
Elsie R. Mast (3)
Alma J. Miller (3)
Stephen Ray Miller (3)
Albert E. Raber (3)
Bryan M. Raber (3)
Lovina Raber (3)
Lucy L. Raber (3)
Myron A. Raber (3)
Robert E. Raber (3)
Eldon D. Troyer (3)
Atlee H. Yoder (3)
Ervin W. Yoder (3)
Mervin J. Yoder (3)
Mary D. Keim (4)
Mabel V. Kline (4)
Sarah R. Mast (4)
Bruce V. Miller (4)
Edward J. Miller (4)
Maynard E. Miller (4)
Ray E. Miller (4)
Wayne J. Miller (4)
Edward H. Raber (4)
Ivan M. Raber (4)
Marion Raber (4)
Wayne H. Raber (4)
Edna R. Troyer (4)
Esther D. Troyer (4)
Katie L. Yoder (4)
Lizzie A. Yoder (4)
Miriam J. Yoder (4)

1/

1980–81
Elson Sommers
Dennis J. Burkholder (1)
Emma Lou Erb (1)
Ada A. Hershberger (1)
Marie A. Kline (1)
Carol A. Mast (1)
John Henry Mast (1)
Allen R. Miller (1)
Marvin A. Miller (1)
Karen Sue Raber (1)
Linda A. Raber (1)
Ray L. Raber (1)
Melody Ann Schrock (1)
Leroy D. Troyer (1)
Levi D. Troyer (1)
Abe J. Yoder (1)
Betty J. Yoder (1)
Betty L. Yoder (1)
Ella A. Yoder (1)
Ruth W. Yoder (1)
Vernon A. Hershberger (2)
Oren D. Keim (2)
Judy Ann Kline (2)
Mary V. Kline (2)
Ivan E. Mast (2)
Allen E. Miller (2)
Joseph A. Miller (2)
Mary A. Miller (2)
Roy J. Miller (2)
Verba B. Miller (2)
Wayne J. Miller (2)
Ada A. Raber (2)
Laura A. Raber (2)
Miriam H. Raber (2)
Rhoda M. Raber (2)
Susan A. Schrock (2)
Joseph R. Troyer (2)
Alma H. Yoder (2)
Peter L. Yoder (2)
Sara Ann Yoder (2)

1/

1980–81
Kimberly Torgler
David Allen Erb (3)
Lizzie D. Keim (3)
Atlee B. Miller (3)
Marvin E. Miller (3)
Miriam V. Miller (3)
Paul A. Miller (3)
Leroy E. Raber (3)
Emma D. Troyer (3)
Adah J. Yoder (3)
Ivan A. Yoder (3)
Mary J. Yoder (3)
Susie W. Yoder (3)
Aden J. Burkholder (4)
Ivan J. Burkholder (4)
Loyel E. Hershberger (4)
Mary A. Hershberger (4)
Mary J. Hershberger (4)
Duane J. Hochstetler (4)
Leon J. Hochstetler (4)
Elsie R. Mast (4)
Alma J. Miller (4)
Miriam A. Miller (4)
Steven Ray Miller (4)

Albert E. Raber (4)
Bryan M. Raber (4)
Lovina A. Raber (4)
Lucy L. Raber (4)
Myron A. Raber (4)
Robert E. Raber (4)
Eldon D. Troyer (4)
Atlee H. Yoder (4)
Ervin W. Yoder (4)
Mervin J. Yoder (4)

1/

1981–82
Elson Sommers
Erma J. Burkholder (1)
Ina D. Keim (1)
Barbara V. Kline (1)
Susie B. Miller (1)
Betty E. Raber (1)
David M. Raber (1)
Marilyn M. Raber (1)
Naomi A. Raber (1)
Abe H. Yoder (1)
Esther J. Yoder (1)
Floyd L. Yoder (1)
Jacob A. Yoder Jr. (1)
Marlene J. Yoder (1)
Ruth W. Yoder (1)
Wayne J. Yoder (1)
Dennis J. Burkholder (2)
Emmy Lou Erb (2)
Ada A. Hershberger (2)
Marie A. Kline (2)
Carol A. Mast (2)
John Henry Mast (2)
Allen R. Miller (2)
Marvin A. Miller (2)
Karen Sue Raber (2)
Linda A. Raber (2)
Ray L. Raber (2)
Leroy D. Troyer (2)
Levi D. Troyer (2)
Abe J. Yoder (2)
Betty J. Yoder (2)
Betty L. Yoder (2)
Ella A. Yoder (2)

1/

1981–82
Kim Gerber
Vernon A. Hershberger (3)
Oren D. Keim (3)
Judy Ann Kline (3)
Mary V. Kline (3)
Ivan E. Mast (3)
Allen E. Miller (3)
Joseph A. Miller (3)
Mary A. Miller (3)
Roy J. Miller (3)
Verba B. Miller (3)
Wayne J. Miller (3)
Ada A. Raber (3)
Laura A. Raber (3)
Miriam H. Raber (3)
Rhoda M. Raber (3)
Susan A. Schrock (3)
Joseph R. Troyer (3)
Alma H. Yoder (3)
Peter L. Yoder (3)
Sara Ann Yoder (3)
David Alan Erb (4)
Lizzie D. Keim (4)

Atlee D. Miller (4)
Marvin E. Miller (4)
Miriam V. Miller (4)
Emma D. Troyer (4)
Adah J. Yoder (4)
Ivan A. Yoder (4)
Mary J. Yoder (4)
Susie W. Yoder (4)

1/

1982–83
Elson Sommers
Ina D. Keim (1)
Martha D. Keim (1)
Rhoda A. Kline (1)
Marlene B. Kurtz (1)
Fannie E. Mast (1)
Betty J. Miller (1)
Katie Mae Miller (1)
Leroy E. Miller (1)
David Allen Nisley (1)
Dorothy L. Raber (1)
Edna A. Raber (1)
Karen M. Raber (1)
Verna A. Raber (1)
Aden A. Yoder (1)
David J. Yoder (1)
Edward J. Yoder (1)
Floyd L. Yoder (1)
Rhoda J. Yoder (1)
Roy W. Yoder (1)
Erma J. Burkholder (2)
Barbara V. Kline (2)
Susie B. Miller (2)
Betty E. Raber (2)
David M. Raber (2)
Marilyn M. Raber (2)
Mary Esther Raber (2)
Naomi A. Raber (2)
Ada H. Yoder (2)
Esther J. Yoder (2)
Jacob A. Yoder (2)
Marlene J. Yoder (2)
Ruth W. Yoder (2)
Wayne J. Yoder (2)

1/

1982–83
Kim Gerber
Dennis J. Burkholder (3)
Emma Lou Erb (3)
Ada A. Hershberger (3)
Marie A. Kline (3)
Carol A. Mast (3)
John Henry Mast (3)
Allen R. Miller (3)
Marvin A. Miller (3)
Karen Sue Raber (3)
Linda A. Raber (3)
Ray L. Raber (3)
Leroy D. Troyer (3)
Levi D. Troyer (3)
Abe J. Yoder (3)
Betty J. Yoder (3)

Betty L. Yoder (3)
Ella A. Yoder (3)
Vernon A. Hershberger (4)
Oren D. Keim (4)
Judy Ann Kline (4)
Mary V. Kline (4)
Ivan E. Mast (4)
Allen E. Miller (4)
Joseph A. Miller (4)
Mary A. Miller (4)
Peter L. Miller (4)
Roy J. Miller (4)
Verba B. Miller (4)
Wayne J. Miller (4)
Ada A. Raber (4)
Laura A. Raber (4)
Miriam H. Raber (4)
Rhoda M. Raber (4)
Susan A. Schrock (4)
Joseph R. Troyer (4)
Alma H. Yoder (4)
Sara Ann Yoder (4)

1/

1983–84
Elson Sommers
Jerry Ray Erb (1)
Mabel A. Hershberger (1)
Ervin B. Kurtz (1)
Leroy Mast (1)
Aden Ray Miller (1)
Anna Mae Miller (1)
Kathy Miller (1)
Paul J. Miller (1)
Susan R. Miller (1)
Vernon B. Miller (1)
David Allen Nisley (1)
Ruth Marie Raber (1)
Melvin D. Troyer (1)
Reuben F. Troyer (1)
Susan R. Troyer (1)
Amanda A. Yoder (1)
Emma H. Yoder (1)
Reuben J. Yoder (1)
Ina D. Keim (2)
Martha D. Keim (2)
Rhoda A. Kline (2)
Marlene B. Kurtz (2)
Fannie E. Mast (2)
Betty J. Miller (2)
Katie Mae Miller (2)
Leroy E. Miller (2)
Dorothy L. Raber (2)
Edna A. Raber (2)
Karen M. Raber (2)
Verna A. Raber (2)
Aden A. Yoder (2)
David J. Yoder (2)
Edward J. Yoder (2)
Floyd Yoder (2)
Rhoda J. Yoder (2)
Roy W. Yoder (2)

315/ No man is always wise.
1900 Charm School writing exercise ❧

1983–84
Kim Gerber
Erma J. Burkholder (3)
Barbara V. Kline (3)
Susie B. Miller (3)
Betty E. Raber (3)
David M. Raber (3)
Marilyn M. Raber (3)
Mary Esther Raber (3)
Naomi A. Raber (3)
Abe H. Yoder (3)
Esther J. Yoder (3)
Jacob A. Yoder Jr. (3)
Marlene J. Yoder (3)
Ruth W. Yoder (3)
Wayne J. Yoder (3)
Dennis J. Burkholder
    (4)
Emma Lou Erb (4)
Ada A. Hershberger (4)
Marie A. Kline (4)
Carol A. Mast (4)
John Henry Mast (4)
Allen R. Miller (4)
Marvin A. Miller (4)
Karen Sue Raber (4)
Linda A. Raber (4)
Ray L. Raber (4)
Leroy D. Troyer (4)
Levi D. Troyer (4)
Abe J. Yoder (4)
Betty J. Yoder (4)
Betty L. Yoder (4)
Ella A. Yoder (4)

1984–85
Elson Sommers
Jay Brian Hershberger
    (1)
Ruby E. Hershberger
    (1)
Emanuel D. Keim (1)
Cindy V. Kline (1)
Jacob E. Mast (1)
Duane J. Miller (1)
Marilyn E. Miller (1)
Miriam B. Miller (1)
Vernon B. Miller (1)
Joseph A. Raber (1)
Joseph L. Raber (1)
Lorene H. Shetler (1)
Naomi D. Troyer (1)
Adrian L. Yoder (1)
Cindy M. Yoder (1)
John Ray Yoder (1)
Katie J. Yoder (1)
Paul H. Yoder (1)
Susie J. Yoder (1)
Jerry Ray Erb (2)
Mabel A. Hershberger
    (2)
Leroy R. Mast (2)
Aden Ray Miller (2)
Anna Mae Miller (2)
Kathy Miller (2)
Paul J. Miller (2)
Susan R. Miller (2)
Ruth Marie Raber (2)
Melvin D. Troyer (2)
Reuben F. Troyer (2)
Susan R. Troyer (2)

Amanda A. Yoder (2)
Emma A. Yoder (2)
Reuben J. Yoder (2)

1984–85
Catherine Snyder
Ina D. Keim (3)
Martha D. Keim (3)
Fannie E. Mast (3)
Betty J. Miller (3)
Katie Mae Miller (3)
Leroy E. Miller (3)
Dorothy L. Raber (3)
Edna A. Raber (3)
Karen M. Raber (3)
Verna A. Raber (3)
Aden A. Yoder (3)
David J. Yoder (3)
Edward J. Yoder (3)
Floyd L. Yoder (3)
Rhoda J. Yoder (3)
Roy W. Yoder (3)
Erma J. Burkholder (4)
Barbara V. Kline (4)
Susie B. Miller (4)
Betty E. Raber (4)
David M. Raber (4)
Marilyn M. Raber (4)
Mary Esther Raber (4)
Naomi A. Raber (4)
Abe H. Yoder (4)
Esther J. Yoder (4)
Jacob A. Yoder Jr. (4)
Marlene J. Yoder (4)
Ruth W. Yoder (4)
Wayne J. Yoder (4)

1985–86
Elson Sommers
Lena J. Burkholder (1)
Arlen D. Erb (1)
David A. Hershberger
    (1)
Marie E. Hershberger
    (1)
Arie R. Mast (1)
Ervin J. Miller (1)
Linda V. Miller (1)
Marlene Miller (1)
Matthew A. Miller (1)
Ruby J. Miller (1)
William Ray Miller (1)
Naomi E. Raber (1)
Rachel A. Raber (1)
Tobias M. Raber (1)
Mabel H. Shetler (1)
Mervin H. Shetler (1)
Owen E. Shetler (1)
David F. Troyer (1)
Adrian L. Yoder (1)
Jay Brian Hershberger
    (2)
Ruby E. Hershberger
    (2)
Emanuel D. Keim (2)
Cindy V. Kline (2)
Jacob E. Mast (2)
Duane J. Miller (2)
Marilyn E. Miller (2)
Miriam B. Miller (2)
Vernon B. Miller (2)

Joseph A. Raber (2)
Joseph L. Raber (2)
Lorene H. Shetler (2)
Naomi D. Troyer (2)
Cindy M. Yoder (2)
John Ray Yoder (2)
Katie J. Yoder (2)
Paul H. Yoder (2)
Susie J. Yoder (2)

1985–86
Catherine Snyder
Jerry Ray Erb (3)
Mabel A. Hershberger
    (3)
Leroy R. Mast (3)
Aden Ray Miller (3)
Anna Mae Miller (3)
Kathy V. Miller (3)
Paul J. Miller (3)
Susan R. Miller (3)
Ruth Marie Raber (3)
Melvin D. Troyer (3)
Reuben F. Troyer (3)
Susan R. Troyer (3)
Amanda A. Yoder (3)
Emma H. Yoder (3)
Reuben J. Yoder (3)
Ina D. Keim (4)
Martha D. Keim (4)
Fannie E. Mast (4)
Betty J. Miller (4)
Katie Mae Miller (4)
Leroy E. Miller (4)
Dorothy L. Raber (4)
Edna A. Raber (4)
Karen M. Raber (4)
Verna A. Raber (4)
Aden A. Yoder (4)
David J. Yoder (4)
Edward J. Yoder (4)
Floyd L. Yoder (4)
Rhoda J. Yoder (4)
Roy W. Yoder (4)

1986–87
Elson Sommers
Esther J. Burkholder (1)
Naomi R. Herhsberger
    (1)
Arie R. Mast (1)
Clara E. Mast (1)
Allen R. Miller (1)
Katie Mae Miller (1)
Mary B. Miller (1)
Matthew P. Miller (1)
Fannie Mae Raber (1)
James Andrew Raber
    (1)
Mahlon D. Raber (1)
Alma A. Yoder (1)
Jonas J. Yoder (1)
Leroy J. Yoder (1)
Rosanna M. Yoder (1)
Lena J. Burkholder (2)
Arlen D. Erb (2)
David A. Hershberger
    (2)
Marie E. Hershberger
    (2)
Ervin J. Miller (2)

Linda V. Miller (2)
Marlene M. Miller (2)
Matthew A. Miller (2)
Ruby J. Miller (2)
William Ray Miller (2)
Naomi E. Raber (2)
Rachel A. Raber (2)
Tobias M. Raber (2)
Mabel H. Shetler (2)
Mervin H. Shetler (2)
Owen E. Shetler (2)
David F. Troyer (2)
Adrian L. Yoder (2)

1986–87
Cynthia Short
Jay Brian Hershberger
    (3)
Ruby E. Hershberger
    (3)
Cindy V. Kline (3)
Jacob E. Mast (3)
Duane J. Miller (3)
Marilyn E. Miller (3)
Miriam B. Miller (3)
Vernon B. Miller (3)
Joseph A. Raber (3)
Joseph L. Raber (3)
Lorene H. Shetler (3)
Naomi D. Troyer (3)
Cindy M. Yoder (3)
John Ray Yoder (3)
Katie J. Yoder (3)
Paul H. Yoder (3)
Susie J. Yoder (3)
Jerry Ray Erb (4)
Mabel A. Hershberger
    (4)
Leroy R. Mast (4)
Aden Ray Miller (4)
Anna Mae Miller (4)
Kathy V. Miller (4)
Paul J. Miller (4)
Susan R. Miller (4)
Ruth Marie Raber (4)
Melvin D. Troyer (4)
Reuben F. Troyer (4)
Susan R. Troyer (4)
Amanda A. Yoder (4)
Emma H. Yoder (4)
Reuben J. Yoder (4)

1987–88
Elson Sommers
Dennis M. Hershberger
    (1)
Ruby E. Hershberger
    (1)
David M. Miller (1)
Leroy B. Miller (1)
Mary J. Miller (1)
Rhoda R. Miller (1)
Marlin Jay Raber (1)
Rhoda Marie Raber (1)
Jacob E. Shetler (1)
Robert P. Shetler (1)
Ruby D. Troyer (1)
Cindy Sue Yoder (1)
Linda J. Yoder (1)
Mary Esther Yoder (1)
(continued)

Naomi J. Yoder (1)
Rosanna N. Yoder (1)
Esther J. Burkholder (2)
Andrew M.
Hershberger (2)
Naomi R. Hershberger
(2)
Arie R. Mast (2)
Clara E. Mast (2)
Allen R. Miller (2)
Katie Mae Miller (2)
Mary B. Miller (2)
Fannie Mae Raber (2)
James Andrew Raber
(2)
Mahlon D. Raber (2)
Mervin H. Shetler (2)
Alma A. Yoder (2)
Jonas J. Yoder (2)
Leroy J. Yoder (2)
Rosanna M. Yoder (2)

1/ **1987–88**
Judy Mann
Lena J. Burkholder (3)
Arlen D. Erb (3)
David A. Hershberger
(3)
Marie E. Hershberger
(3)
Ervin J. Miller (3)
Linda V. Miller (3)
Marlene M. Miller (3)
Matthew A. Miller (3)
Ruby J. Miller (3)
Naomi E. Raber (3)
Rachel A. Raber (3)
Tobias M. Raber (3)
Mabel H. Shetler (3)
Owen E. Shetler (3)
David F. Troyer (3)
Adrian L. Yoder (3)
Jay Bryan Hershberger
(4)
Ruby E. Hershberger
(4)
Cindy V. Kline (4)
Jacob E. Mast (4)
Duane J. Miller (4)
Marilyn E. Miller (4)
Miriam B. Miller (4)
Vernon B. Miller (4)
Joseph A. Raber (4)
Joseph L. Raber (4)
Lorene H. Shetler (4)
Naomi D. Troyer (4)
Cindy M. Yoder (4)
John Ray Yoder (4)
Katie J. Yoder (4)
Paul H. Yoder (4)
Susie J. Yoder (4)

1/ **1988–89**
Elson Sommers
Clara R. Hershberger
(1)
David M. Hershberger
(1)
Dennis M. Hershberger
(1)
Lizzieann V. Kline (1)

Ada Mae Miller (1)
Daniel J. Miller (1)
David J. Miller (1)
Susan V. Miller (1)
Willis J. Miller (1)
Jason Lee Raber (1)
Wayne E. Raber (1)
Leona H. Shetler (1)
Alan M. Yoder (1)
Duane Alan Yoder (1)
Ruby E. Hershberger
(2)
David M. Miller (2)
Leroy B. Miller (2)
Marlin Jay Miller (2)
Mary J. Miller (2)
Rhoda Marie Miller (2)
Rhoda R. Miller (2)
Jacob E. Shetler (2)
Robert P. Shetler (2)
Ruby D. Troyer (2)
Cindy Sue Yoder (2)
Linda J. Yoder (2)
Mary Esther Yoder (2)
Naomi J. Yoder (2)
Rosanna N. Yoder (2)

1/ **1988–89**
Judy Mann
Andrew M.
Hershberger (3)
Esther J. Hershberger
(3)
Naomi R. Hershberger
(3)
Arie R. Mast (3)
Clara E. Mast (3)
Allen R. Miller (3)
Katie Mae Miller (3)
Mary B. Miller (3)
Fannie Mae Raber (3)
James Andrew Raber
(3)
Mahlon D. Raber (3)
Mervin H. Shetler (3)
Alma A. Yoder (3)
Jonas J. Yoder (3)
Leroy J. Yoder (3)
Rosanna M. Yoder (3)
Lena J. Burkholder (4)
Arlen D. Erb (4)
David A. Hershberger
(4)
Marie E. Hershberger
(4)
Ervin J. Miller (4)
Linda V. Miller (4)
Marlene M. Miller (4)
Matthew A. Miller (4)
Ruby J. Miller (4)
Naomi E. Raber (4)
Rachel A. Raber (4)
Tobias M. Raber (4)
Mabel H. Shetler (4)
Owen E. Shetler (4)
David F. Troyer (4)
Adrian L. Yoder (4)

30/ **1989–90**
Elson Sommers
Marlene Kay Barkman
(1)

Allen E. Hershberger
(1)
Cheryl Ann
Hershberger (1)
James E. Hershberger
(1)
Joseph E. Hershberger
(1)
Milan M. Hershberger
(1)
Johnny R. Mast (1)
Junior E. Mast (1)
Esther L. Miller (1)
Leanna R. Miller (1)
Leroy R. Miller (1)
Ivan P. Shetler (1)
Wayne F. Troyer (1)
Cindy J. Yoder (1)
Marilyn N. Yoder (1)
Sara Ann Yoder (1)
Wayne A. Yoder (1)
Clara R. Hershberger
(2)
David M. Hershberger
(2)
Dennis M. Hershberger
(2)
Lizzieann V. Kline (2)
Ada Mae Miller (2)
Daniel J. Miller (2)
David J. Miller (2)
Susan V. Miller (2)
Willis J. Miller (2)
Jason Lee Raber (2)
Wayne E. Raber (2)
Leona H. Shetler (2)
Alan M. Yoder (2)
Duane Alan Yoder (2)

30/ **1989–90**
Judy Mann
Ruby E. Hershberger
(3)
David M. Miller (3)
Leroy B. Miller (3)
Mary J. Miller (3)
Rhoda R. Miller (3)
Marlin Jay Raber (3)
Rhoda Marie Raber (3)
Jacob E. Shetler (3)
Robert P. Shetler (3)
Ruby D. Troyer (3)
Cindy Sue Yoder (3)
Linda J. Yoder (3)
Mary Esther Yoder (3)
Naomi J. Yoder (3)
Rosanna N. Yoder (3)
Esther J. Burkholder (4)
Andrew M.
Hershberger (4)
Naomi R. Hershberger
(4)
Arie R. Mast (4)
Clara E. Mast (4)
Allen R. Miller (4)
Katie Mae Miller (4)
Mary B. Miller (4)
Fannie Mae Raber (4)
James Andrew Raber
(4)
Mahlon D. Raber (4)

Mervin H. Shetler (4)
Alma A. Yoder (4)
Jonas J. Yoder (4)
Leroy J. Yoder (4)
Rosanna M. Yoder (4)

30/ **1990–91**
Elson Sommers
Robert E. Barkman (1)
Mervin Ray
Hershberger (1)
Betty L. Miller (1)
Jacob J. Miller (1)
Jonas B. Miller (1)
Myron R. Miller (1)
Marlene M. Raber (1)
Rachel E. Raber (1)
David E. Shetler (1)
Rachel M. Yoder (1)
Rebecca I. Yoder (1)
Marlene Kay Barkman
(2)
Allen E. Hershberger
(2)
Cheryl Ann
Hershberger (2)
James E. Hershberger
(2)
Joseph Hershberger (2)
Milan Hershberger (2)
Johnny R. Mast (2)
Junior E. Mast (2)
Esther L. Miller (2)
Leanna R. Miller (2)
Leroy R. Miller (2)
Ivan P. Shetler (2)
Wayne F. Troyer (2)
Cindy J. Yoder (2)
Marilyn N. Yoder (2)
Sara Ann Yoder (2)
Wayne A. Yoder (2)

30/ **1990–91**
Judy Mann
Clara R. Hershberger
(3)
David M. Hershberger
(3)
Dennis M. Hershberger
(3)
Lizzieann V. Kline (3)
Ada Mae Miller (3)
Daniel J. Miller (3)
David J. Miller (3)
Susan V. Miller (3)
Willis J. Miller (3)
Jason Lee Raber (3)
Wayne E. Raber (3)
Leona H. Shetler (3)
Alan M. Yoder (3)
Duane Alan Yoder (3)
Ruby E. Hershberger
(4)
David M. Miller (4)
Leroy B. Miller (4)
Mary J. Miller (4)
(continued)

ᑫ

Rhoda R. Miller (4)
Marlin J. Raber (4)
Rhoda Marie Raber (4)
Jacob E. Shetler (4)
Robert P. Shetler (4)
Ruby D. Troyer (4)
Cindy Sue Yoder (4)
Linda J. Yoder (4)
Mary Esther Yoder (4)
Naomi J. Yoder (4)
Rosanna N. Yoder (4)

30/

1991–92
Elson Sommers
Junior Kline (1)
Mary E. Mast (1)
Carol V. Miller (1)
David Albert Miller (1)
Rosie J. Miller (1)
Laura A. Raber (1)
Randy Jay Raber (1)
David Alan Troyer (1)
Dennis A. Yoder (1)
Marie J. Yoder (1)
Paul A. Yoder (1)
Robert E. Barkman (2)
Mervin Ray
   Hershberger (2)
Betty L. Miller (2)
Jacob J. Miller (2)
Jonas B. Miller (2)
Myron R. Miller (2)
Rachel M. Miller (2)
Marlene M. Raber (2)
Rachel E. Raber (2)
David E. Shetler (2)
Rebecca Yoder (2)

30/

1991–92
Judy Mann
Marlene Kay Barkman
   (3)
Allen E. Hershberger
   (3)
Cheryl Ann
   Hershberger (3)
James E. Hershberger
   (3)
Joseph E. Hershberger
   (3)
Milan M. Hershberger
   (3)
Johnny R. Mast (3)
Junior E. Mast (3)
Esther L. Miller (3)
LeAnna R. Miller (3)
Leroy R. Miller (3)
Ivan P. Shetler (3)
Wayne F. Troyer (3)
Cindy J. Yoder (3)
Marilyn N. Yoder (3)
Sara Ann Yoder (3)
Wayne A. Yoder (3)
Clara R. Hershberger
   (4)
David M. Hershberger
   (4)
Dennis M. Hershberger
   (4)
❧ Lizzieann V. Kline (4)
178   Ada Mae Miller (4)

Daniel J. Miller (4)
David J. Miller (4)
Susan V. Miller (4)
Willis J. Miller (4)
Jason Lee Raber (4)
Wayne E. Raber (4)
Leona H. Shetler (4)
Alan M. Yoder (4)
Duane Alan Yoder (4)

1992–93
Elson Sommers
Kristina Sue Barkman
   (1)
Myron E. Barkman (1)
Emma Sue
   Hershberger (1)
Marvin M. Hershberer
   (1)
John Henry Miller (1)
Joseph J. Miller (1)
Leon R. Miller (1)
LeRoy R. Miller (1)
Linda Sue Miller (1)
Mary Esther Miller (1)
Mary Ann Schlabach
   (1)
Michael D. Troyer (1)
Clyde R. Yoder (1)
Daniel J. Yoder (1)
Marie J. Yoder (1)
Robert E. Barkman (2)
Junior Kline (2)
Mary E. Mast (2)
Carol V. Miller (2)
David Albert Miller (2)
Rosie J. Miller (2)
Laura A. Raber (2)
Randy Jay Raber (2)
David Alan Troyer (2)
Dennis A. Yoder (2)
Paul A. Yoder (2)

30/

1992–93
Judy Mann
Mervin Ray
   Hershberger (3)
Betty L. Miller (3)
Jacob J. Miller (3)
Jonas B. Miller (3)
Myron R. Miller (3)
Rachel M. Miller (3)
Marlene M. Raber (3)
Rachel E. Raber (3)
David E. Shetler (3)
Rebecca I. Yoder (3)
Marlene Kay Barkman
   (4)
Allen E. Hershberger
   (4)
Cheryl Ann
   Hershberger (4)
James E. Hershberger
   (4)
Joseph E. Hershberger
   (4)
Milan M. Hershberger
   (4)
Johnny R. Mast (4)
Junior E. Mast (4)
Esther L. Miller (4)

LeAnna R. Miller (4)
Leroy R. Miller (4)
Ivan P. Shetler (4)
Wayne F. Troyer (4)
Cindy J. Yoder (4)
Marilyn N. Yoder (4)
Sara Ann Yoder (4)
Wayne A. Yoder (4)

30/

1993–94
Elson Sommers
James Aden Barkman
   (1)
Steven R. Barkman (1)
David V. Miller (1)
Mary Ann Miller (1)
Naomi J. Miller (1)
Cindi E. Raber (1)
Linda W. Schrock (1)
Irene W. Shetler (1)
Verna E. Shetler (1)
Brian R. Yoder (1)
Clyde R. Yoder (1)
David J. Yoder (1)
Edward J. Yoder (1)
Joseph J. Yoder (1)
Matthew E. Yoder (1)
Ray N. Yoder (1)
Kristina Sue Barkman
   (2)
Myron E. Barkman (2)
Emma Sue
   Hershberger (2)
Marvin M.
   Hershberger (2)
John Henry Miller (2)
Joseph J. Miller (2)
Leon R. Miller (2)
Leroy R. Miller (2)
Linda Sue Miller (2)
Mary Esther Miller (2)
Mary Ann Schlabach
   (2)
Michael D. Troyer (2)
Daniel J. Yoder (2)
Marie J. Yoder (2)

30/

1993–94
Judy Mann
Robert E. Barkman (3)
Junior Kline (3)
Mary E. Mast (3)
Carol V. Miller (3)
David Albert Miller (3)
Rosie J. Miller (3)
Laura A. Raber (3)
Randy Jay Raber (3)
David Alan Troyer (3)
Dennis A. Yoder (3)
Paul A. Yoder (3)
Mervin Ray
   Hershberger (4)
Betty L. Miller (4)
Jacob J. Miller (4)
Jonas B. Miller (4)
Myron R. Miller (4)
Rachel M. Miller (4)
Marlene M. Raber (4)
Rachel E. Raber (4)
David E. Shetler (4)
Rebecca I. Yoder (4)

30/

1994–95
Audrey Schlabach (1)
Michelle Miller (2)
Arlene E. Barkman (1)
Eugene Roy Barkman
   (1)
Lavern A. Burkholder
   (1)
Mark E. Hershberger (1)
Robert R. Hershberger
   (1)
Christina A. Miller (1)
Daniel L. Miller (1)
David R. Miller (1)
Erma J. Miller (1)
Mary Ellen Miller (1)
Emily Raber (1)
Leanna A. Raber (1)
Myron P. Shetler (1)
James E. Troyer (1)
Lisa Ann Troyer (1)
Brian R. Yoder (1)
Maria Ann Yoder (1)
Paul Andrew Yoder (1)
Ray A. Yoder (1)
James Aden Barkman
   (2)
Steven R. Barkman (2)
David V. Miller (2)
Mary Ann Miller (2)
Naomi J. Miller (2)
Cindi E. Raber (2)
Linda W. Schrock (2)
Irene W. Shetler (2)
Verna E. Shetler (2)
Clyde R. Yoder (2)
David J. Yoder (2)
Edward J. Yoder (2)
Joseph J. Yoder (2)
Matthew E. Yoder (2)
Ray N. Yoder (2)

30/

1994–95
Judy Mann
Kristina Sue Barkman
   (3)
Myron E. Barkman (3)
Emma Sue
   Hershberger (3)
Marvin M.
   Hershberger (3)
John Henry Miller (3)
Joseph J. Miller (3)
Leon R. Miller (3)
LeRoy R. Miller (3)
Linda Sue Miller (3)
Mary Esther Miller (3)
Mary Ann Schlabach (3)
Michael D. Troyer (3)
Daniel J. Yoder (3)
Marie J. Yoder (3)
Robert E. Barkman (4)
Junior Kline (4)
Mary E. Mast (4)
Carol V. Miller (4)
David Albert Miller (4)
Rosie J. Miller (4)
Laura A. Raber (4)
Randy Jay Raber (4)
David Alan Troyer (4)
Dennis A. Yoder (4)
Paul A. Yoder (4)

Teacher – William L. Miller

10/

Teacher – Albert Fair

223/
p.105

Teacher – Louise (Engle) Kaser

26/
p.73

Teacher – Irene Mayer

182/

Teachers – Ruth Cox and Minnie Stingel – 1919

64/

Teacher – Esther Mayer

182/

39/

Teacher – Albert Kaser

5/

Teacher – David D. Miller

5/

Teacher – Ethel (Miller) Stutzman

36/

Teacher – Priscilla (Miller) Falb

134/

Teacher – Gerald Miller

41/

Teacher – Howard Kaser

373/

Teacher – Venus Zuercher

13/

3/

Teacher – Elizabeth (Beyeler) Jacobs

Teacher – Florence Shafer

Teacher – Don DeHass

357/

Teacher – Dale Kreischer

347/

Teacher – Elson Sommers

376/

Teacher – Catherine Snyder

348/

Teacher – Judy Mann

❧ Troyer's Hollow —————
of the Doughty

A mile to the west of Charm lies a narrow, deeply cut gorge through which flows the area's most prominent stream, the "Doughty Creek." Because of the hollow's once highly important business activities for the area, which undoubtedly influenced the original establishing of Charm along a country crossroad, a glimpse of the hollow's history is included with the Charm history. The brief history of the hollow is given in a pictorial presentation.

The narrow gorge is located in the northeast corner of Mechanic Township between the "Doughty's" Charm Creek tributary and Beck's Mills. Its business activities had been chiefly located along the midst of its length, being contained in Section 10.

Various names have been associated with the widely known and picturesque hollow of Holmes County. Originally the Doughty Valley, of which the hollow is a part, and the Doughty Creek were supposedly named in honor of an area Indian, Chief Doughty, or Colonel John Doughty, who was in charge of the early Zanesville land office. Colonel Doughty had jurisdiction in selling certain government lands in Ohio which included the local area.

Early historians refer to the ravine as "Doughty Glens." In the 1830s Isaac Aultman erected the first house and with his businesses, which were soon to follow, the glens became known as "Aultman's Hollow." The Beck family, who were area residents and involved in business activities in the hollow, attached another title, "La Booperty Hollow." Later, family speculation would point to a French

19/
p.152
22/
p.6-p.19
226/
p.22

phrase, "le beau parterre" or "the beautiful flower garden," as the only reasonable basis for that name. From 1873 to 1915 Simon D. Troyer operated a thriving woolen mill business, and accordingly the name changed to "Troyer's Hollow" during that period. With Troyer's residence in the confines of the steep grade of the ravine, the location was also known as "Sim's Loch," meaning "Simon's Hole." "The Doughty" and "Troyer's Hollow" are the most commonly used names today.

223/
230/

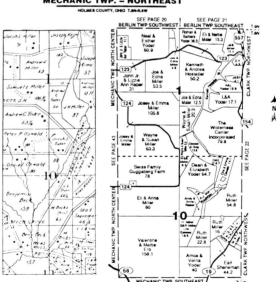

Map layouts of Troyer's Hollow. 1875 – 1992.

❧

223/
p.112

11/11-
14-1966
50/2-
14-1924
Isaac Aultman of Strasburg, Tuscarawas County, Ohio has been credited as being the original proprietor of mechanical activities in the Doughty Glens. Historians and family accounts relate that in the 1830s Aultman built the first dwelling house, along with a stable, sawmill, grist mill, and mill dam on the present Troyer's Hollow camping grounds, situated in the northeast corner of the northeast quarter of Section 10 in Mechanic Township.

309/
1834
309/
1837
V13-
389-1837
309/
1839
However, county records indicate another business ownership in the hollow at this early time. The 1834 tax records show Aultman as paying taxes for a mill right. In 1837 Isaac is taxed for a gristmill, whereas Christian Hochstetler (HS1124) is taxed for a sawmill. Also in that same year, Christian sold 15$1/2$ acres of land in the hollow to Isaac. Two years later, in 1839, Hochstetler and Aultman were both taxed for the sawmill, which indicates a partnership in the business.

Apparently the Hochstetler business involvement in the hollow was shortlived. Nevertheless, under Isaac's proprietorship the hollow became a bustle of activity.

This early photograph of Aultman's Hollow is viewed upstream and shows the original Aultman buildings. The house (enclosed by a picket fence) on the right was the Isaac Aultman residence. A son, Elijah, lived in the house on the left, while the building in the background originally housed a gristmill and later a woolen mill. A portion of the dam wall is seen in the right background of the mill.

By the early 1840s Aultman was improving a second water right a short distance downstream from the earlier location. An 1839 deed from David C. Troyer (TY32 – "Canada Dave") to Isaac Aultman gives reference to a land, stone and water right, stating ". . . so much of said quarter section as will be [s]ufficient to erect and make a [m]ill race thereon on the [w]est [s]ide of Douty's [Doughty's] Fork Creek; also privilege of conveying and using the water that runs in [s]aid Douty's Fork Creek in [s]aid [m]ill race; Also privilege of taking [s]tone out of the hill so much as will be [s]ufficient to make [s]aid [m]ill race." In 1841 Aultman acquired the northwest quarter of the southeast quarter of Section 10 from Henry Miller (ML233), a pioneer and son of early Amish bishop Jacob Miller of Sugar Creek, Ohio. Here a water-powered woolen mill and two additional houses were erected. By the late 1840s, Isaac, his four sons (George, John, Joshua and Elijah), and two sons-in-law were operating a sawmill, gristmill, woolen mill, blacksmith shop and store. At this time Aultman's Hollow was known as the best water power and largest business place in the county.

V13-
390-
1839
V13-
392-
1841
50/2-
14-1924

❧

Downstream from the original location, the Aultmans built a woolen mill and two dwellings in the 1840s. In 1862 the mill was sold to son George, who had, ten years earlier, acquired the Conrad Mill property four miles downstream, through his wife's inheritance. In 1864 the woolen mill equipment was moved to a newly constructed building on the Conrad farm and the woolen mill building in the hollow was torn down. (This new building replaced a former grist mill that was destroyed by fire.) At this time the land was sold to Kasers and was later occupied by Frederick Hedrich Ledrich.

Ledrich operated a small store along with a repair shop and did saddling, blacksmithing, tin-smithing and gunsmithing. (Fred is noted as having purchased a ri-

11/11-
14-1966
50/2-
14-1924
251/4-
16-1896
87/
204/
p.52
113/

fling machine at the estate sale of Reuben Yutzy, the renowned Amish muzzle loader builder of the 1800s.)

The Ledrich family of five (Fred, Mary, Katie, Amos and Joe) had previously lived in a log cabin two miles northeast of Walnut Creek. After the cabin was destroyed by fire, they moved to Trail, followed by the move to the Doughty in the latter 1800s.

Later, a son, Amos, lived at the home until fire destroyed the house in the early 1900s; then he moved into the Isaac Aultman home a short distance upstream. Amos continued in the retinning and repair work while living in the hollow.

The Fred and Amos Ledrich home is seen in the background of the photo.

178/

11/11-
14-1966

Isaac and Elijah Aultman sold the grist mill and saw-mill to Eash and Yoder in 1862, who, in turn, sold it to Benjamin Beck in 1864. The Becks had originally come to the Doughty Valley in 1823 from Westmoreland County, Pennsylvania. The father, Michael, as a pioneer, had chosen the lands of present Beck's Mills. He soon had constructed a dam and sawmill at the lower end of the glens and also became the founder of Beck's Mills. After the grist mill purchase in the hollow in 1864, Benjamin Beck moved the milling equipment to their four-story gristmill at the small town site. Realizing the vital loss of the manufacturing of woolen goods in the hollow when the Aultmans moved the equipment down-stream, Beck refurnished the former gristmill building with wool manufacturing machinery. In 1868 the woolen mill was purchased by Franklin Fisher, who also owned a mill at Shanesville. Fisher was joined in partnership the following year by Simon D. Troyer. Troyer became sole owner in 1873, when he bought the remaining half interest for $3,400.00.

228/
p.37
V-38-
60-1873

This change in business activities and ownerships in Aultman's Hollow reflects the progressive industrialization that was taking place during the time period. By this time, more mills were being operated along the Doughty. Customers could now have their milling needs done elsewhere and did not have to haul the heavy wagons into and out of the steep-banked hollow. A mile

downstream was the Beck sawmill and gristmill. Up-stream, within two miles, were two sawmills, a woolen mill and a gristmill. It was a commonly related expression that there was a mill for every mile for the entire length of the Doughty Creek. Albert Aultman, a grand-son of Isaac Aultman, remembered 25 water-powered mills along the stream from Berlin to Clark.

50/2-
14-1924

Another reason for the change taking place in Aultman's Hollow was the coming of steam power. Steam engines appeared in the county in the 1850s, and with this reliable power source, mills could now be established where water power was not available.

Thus the only mill to survive in the hollow was the woolen mill. Simon Troyer operated this thriving busi-ness until the early part of the twentieth century. Dur-ing the Troyer proprietorship, a Scheidler steam engine was set up at the factory's engine room to furnish the power when the water supply was low. The engine's exhaust chimney can be seen on the left of the factory. This was, supposedly, the first steam engine used for threshing in Holmes County. The mill race extending from the upstream dam is seen entering the mill between it and the house. An overshot water wheel was located on the far side of the building; it was later replaced by a Samson turbine wheel. This smaller, horizontal wheel proved more efficient and used less water to run the factory.

11/11-
14-1966

97/
p.236

121/

← Photo at left:

Beck's Mills, named after its founder Michael Beck, who was influential in early business activities. On the right is the four-story gristmill; center, store built in 1872 with larger two-story store built ca 1900. The former mill race is seen crossing the road in the center background and leading behind the store buildings, into the mill. The tail race back to the creek was underground and made of cut sandstone.

Michael's son Benjamin moved the gristmill equipment from Aultman's Hollow to their newer mill at Beck's Mills in the 1860s.

11/11-14-1966

338/

The house on the left, built by Elijah Aultman, was occupied by the Henry Aling family in the early 1900s, and by the Floyd Kasers in the 1930s. Henry's wife was a daughter of Simon Troyer. Their son, Ralph Aling, helped the grandfather in the factory readying the wool, and eventually took to weaving while yet a teenager. At fifteen he was making six blankets per day and recalls making black ladies' shawls for the locality. Young Aling's loom was located inside the double windows on the left side of the factory. Grandfather Troyer worked at his loom on the right side, while the center loom was

57/
113/
228/
p.37

operated around 1910 by Samuel Samuelson. Simon had made his special piano keyboard loom, which was used in making coverlets. The attractively woven covers were made only by Troyer, as he did not want anyone else working at his homemade loom. Another old weaver, Anthony Thiel (1841 – 1919), also worked alongside Troyer and his grandson. Thiel was born in Austria. The business at one time employed 28 persons, though it averaged only about a dozen during the 43 years of the Troyer ownership.

225/
1880

❧

90/
189/

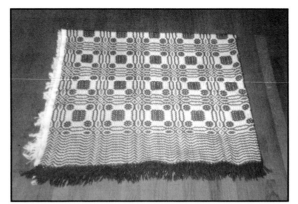

228/
p.29
113/

⟵ Coverlet made by Simon Troyer ca 1904. This blue, white and pink coverlet is made in a Whig Rose pattern. A Troyer daughter, Lucy, would hook the fringe on the borders of the coverlets.

338/

A southeast view of the house built by Isaac Aultman in the 1830s, later occupied by Simon D. Troyer and Amos Ledrich. The Ammon Kaser home is in the background. The creek bed used to be much farther east. A road (the lane today) between the homes angled behind the Troyer house to ascend the steep slope eastward.

11/11-
14-1966

Prior to Simon's association with the woolen mill, he had operated a watch repair shop at Aultman's Hol-

100/6-
30-1915

low. In 1875, soon after becoming sole owner of the mill, he married Mary, daughter of Joseph Keim. Their entire married life was lived here, across the creek from their place of business. At 66 years of age, on June 25, 1915, Simon Troyer died in the hollow that would carry his name to the present day. He was laid to rest in a local cemetery (CD-0-4-40), a mile northeast of their home in Troyer's Hollow.

❧

113/

←— An early wooden bridge spanning the Doughty Creek in Troyer's Hollow. Roads were built leading into the Hollow because of its bustle of activities. Ascending the steep grade to the east, a road led directly to Charm, closely following the 5 and 6 Section line. Going up the opposite slope from the woolen mill, a road went westward, while another angled northwest, following the steep terrain of the glens high above the creek bed. A short distance downstream at the Ledrich home, the road to the west led to the small town of Beck's Mills. On the east bank, a roadway followed the rim of the Hollow, then exited at today's County Road 19, a quarter mile east of Beck's Mills. From this road, another went eastward to the outlying farms, coal banks and the early Port Washington Road.

113/

←— A footbridge spanned the creek between the two groupings of early homes in the hollow. The bridge was located along the lower end of today's campground area, close to the large sycamore tree. This upstream view shows the Ammon Kaser home in the background.

During the 1970s, Orie Oswald had constructed a swinging bridge across the creek where the recreational dam wall was formerly located. However, because of high water, this well-made footbridge was later destroyed.

113/

—→ (photo at right) A short distance upstream from the woolen mill, a dam spanned the Doughty Creek for a reservoir and needed water supply. The main dam wall was built of wooden beams, bracing and planks across the narrow stream bed. This would raise the water to a height of twelve feet. In use from the 1830s into the early twentieth century, the dam was washed out during the flood of 1911. Apparently the dam was rebuilt, as in 1913 it was again washed out and never replaced. In the remaining two years of the woolen mill's existence, until Troyer's death in 1915, it was run by steam power. During the fateful flood of 1913, all dams in use along the Doughty at that time were destroyed.

V₃₈-60-1873
19/p.153
22/p.31-p.68
50/9-21-1911

The following is a list of water-powered mills known to have existed along the Doughty Creek between Berlin and Clark, a distance of ten miles. They are listed downstream and are followed by present day farm ownerships.

Maxwell Sawmill (Sturgis Miller farm)
Wise Sawmill (Mose T. Yoder farm)
Wise Woolen Mill (Mose T. Yoder farm)
Wise Grist Mill (David D. Miller farm)
Wise Sawmill (Jonas D. J. Miller farm)
Troyer Woolen Mill (Doughty Glens)
Aultman Sawmill (Doughty Glens)
Aultman Woolen Mill (Doughty Glens)
Beck Sawmill (Lower end of Glens)
　　This was the first mill along the Doughty to have a circular saw.
Beck Grist Mill (Beck's Mills)
Beck Oil Mill (Beck's Mills)
Asire Sawmill (Alvin H. Yoder farm)
Conkle Sawmill (David D. Schlabach farm)
Craig Sawmill (Eli A. Yoder farm)
Conrad Sawmill (Atlee J. Yoder farm)
Conrad Sawmill (John Miller farm)

113/

Conrad Grist Mill (John Miller farm)
Aultman Woolen Mill (John Miller farm)
McLaughlin Sawmill (Mattie Yoder farm)
Grist Mill (Former Charley Craig farm)
Conkle Sawmill (north of Clark)
Conkle Cider Press (north of Clark)
Keiser Grist Mill (village of Clark)

The last of these mills to be removed was the Aultman Woolen Mill on the Miller farm. Though not in use since the early 1900s, the building and some of the equipment remained until the early spring of 1993.

Thus can be seen the vital importance of Doughty Creek in early water-powered industries. With most of these mechanical businesses actually situated within one township, it was only logical for it to be named Mechanic Township.

The abutments from the bridge seen in the picture are still visible on the grounds today. Besides everyday traffic, the cumbersome steam engine and threshing machine lumbered across the bridge as they challenged the steep grades of the ravine. During the 1913 flood, all of the bridges along the Doughty were damaged except the one at the Conrad farm, 1¹/₂ miles below Beck's Mills.

113/
71/

❧

Group at the Troyer's Hollow mill dam, ca 1915, left to right: Irene Jaberg, Verna Hummel, Katie Harris, Priscilla Miller, Amanda Bontrager, Nara Blosser, Katie Mast, W. R. Mast, Clara Gardener, Carrie Troyer, Katie Mullet, Anna Miller, Ammon Gardner, Elva Immel, Sarah Hershberger, Abe Stutzman, Grace Sommers, Ura Mast, Alma Walters, Joe Blosser, Dessie Blosser, — Miller, Sarah Beachy, Gilbert Jaberg, Lizzie Jaberg.

The stream bed where the dam was located was of solid rock. To form a dam wall (background of picture), three rows of square holes were cut into the narrow width of the stream and beams with double braces set into the mortised holes. Planks were then placed on the upstream side of the structure, which formed a sturdy support to raise the water level to the needed depth.

189 /

→ (photo at right) The 10-inch x 10-inch holes, set 30 inches apart, can still be seen in the creek bed at the upper end of the campground. These were used to place the posts and braces for construction of the mill dam.

113/

← A northeast view of the Simon D. Troyer home. The cut from the road bank is seen in the background.

Soon after Troyer's death, the mill and equipment were sold at public auction, on August 21, 1915. With the equipment being purchased by junk dealers, the machinery was disgracefully smashed to manageable pieces and hauled from the premises as junk. With Troyer's death and sale, mill activity came to an end in the glens.

57/

113/

Shortly after milling ceased at Troyer's Hollow, the acreage and buildings were purchased by the Medina Oil and Gas Company. The grounds were converted to a recreational area for the company's employees; however, this was an unsuccessful venture because of the travel distance. After the real estate transferred, the mill was razed during the summer of 1916 and some of its lumber was used to build numerous cottages, as seen on the left center of the picture.

19/
p.155
167/

❧

333/

113/

Neighbor Tom Sheneman built the dam wall for the Medina Oil and Gas Company around 1917. The double drop retaining wall was constructed of cut sandstones from the foundation of the former woolen mill building.

Clayton Metzler, living southwest of Beck's Mills, cleared out the dam area with a team and slip scraper. However, because of flooding, the dam was soon filled up with soil washed downstream by erosion.

105/

Relaxing on the dam wall, from left: Harold Mast, Gottlieb Viegel, Sanford Oswald, Archie Oswald.

56/

An excellent and often used swimming hole was created at the spillway along the dam wall.

365/

Floyd and Thelma Kaser on the ice of the recreational dam in Troyer's Hollow.

365/

113/

← The Floyd Kaser home, greatly damaged from the flood of 1935. This was the former Elijah Aultman and Henry Aling home on the west side of the creek. Floyd remodeled the house at the time of their marriage (1931) and lived here until the home was destroyed in 1935.

(picture below) The grounds as they appeared during the oil company's and successive ownerships. The Simon Troyer house is at the left, with the Ammon Kaser home in the background. Remaining anchor poles of the swinging footbridge are visible on the right.

19/
p.154-
155
113/
171/

Myron Budge Pomerene acquired the grounds from the Medina-based company and eventually sold them to local residents.

The last of the residents to live in the hollow were Amos Ledrich (Simon Troyer home), Ammon Kasers and Jacob I. Hershberger (background of photo), and Floyd Kaser (immediately to the right, on the west bank of the creek). In the flood of 1935, the homes sustained considerable damage, and the residents of the hollow moved out. (See Unusual Weather and Occurrences.)

Later, however, the Jacob I. Hershberger family lived in the Kaser home until shortly after his wife's death in 1942. Thereafter, the once prosperous grounds grew up as an abandoned ghost town until the 1950s, when Orie T. Oswald restored the grounds as a camping and recreational area.

Orie Oswald, a grandson of Simon Troyer, renovated the hollow in memory of his grandparents. Once again the grounds were greatly altered. The creek bed was relocated along the steep west bank of the hollow and the older buildings were removed. A small pond was dug behind the Kaser home and eventually two shelters were constructed, one on each side of the creek, for reunions, picnics, and services.

The secluded atmosphere of the steep-banked glens has made this an ideal and well cherished spot for its residents and visitors. Its former inhabitants have described the hollow as "where the sun only shines a couple hours each day."

Presently the recreational grounds are owned by Orie's children, LaRue Oswald and Larry (Eleanor Oswald) Gray.

56/

"Sim's Loch"

Troyers Hollow

After business activities ceased and the last residents moved out, the once prosperous glens became a neglected and desolate hollow. From left: Arthur Lorenz, Lloyd and Marilyn Swaldo.

An upstream view of the three once prominent homes of the Doughty Glens. Left, Henry Aling; center, Simon Troyer; right, Ammon Kaser.

The Doughty stream winding through the glens is a majestic beauty. Huge sandstone boulders are evident along its banks. Downstream from the campground area, one of these huge boulders forms a cave. This well known cave in Troyer's Hollow is also locally known as "Gvoonah Loch" (Hole of Wonder). Its sides and front are covered with names of persons who have visited the cave. Hemlock trees, unusual for the outlying area, grow within the hollow. They are adaptable to the location because of the "Canadian climate" formed by the cold air flowing through the steep sided ravine. Wild flowers in their utmost array of colors and sunshine filtering through the heavily wooded confines display splendor amid the stream water's ripple.

Troyer's Hollow residents – ca 1915. From left: Mr. and Mrs. James (Alma Kaser) Miller, Mr. and Mrs. Elmer Miller, Mr. and Mrs. Ammon (Katie Ledrich) Kaser with children Floyd? and Ada?, Mr. and Mrs. Amos (Laura Kaser) Ledrich with daughter Jennie?.

365/

Dale and Alice, children of Floyd Kaser, at the front porch of grandparents Ammon Kasers' home in the hollow.

121/

An example of early barn building in the Doughty Valley. Built 1815, one fourth mile south of the glens. Seated: Civil War veteran Noah Schweitzer.

Tramps of the Eastern Holmes County Area

To many people, the mention of tramps brings special meaning. Older generations still vividly recall the sight of these wanderers along the road or on their way to a home in hopes of finding a measure of kindness. Recalling some of the warm acquaintances with this class of people, older people are still touched in the heart.

The tramp, shuffling along the road, dressed in either decent clothes or dirty tatters, is a scene from a bygone era. In their day to day search for food and lodging, they went from place to place asking for a handout. During the 1800s and into the 1950s, tramps were widely known in the area.

The term "tramp" was often used to designate this unusual class of persons during that time, along with "transient worker," "vagabond," or "vagrant." In the 1910 U.S. census, a descriptive title, "traveling boarder," was also used to designate them. "Hobo," "outlaw," and "loafer" were heard, and these words were, undoubtedly, apt descriptions for some tramps; others, however, were friendly, helpful, and good natured persons. Some were willing to work and offered their help in splitting firewood or doing odd jobs in return for food and an overnight rest.

71/
Occasionally, tramps used a well known trick to avoid working. In return for a handout, some would be asked to fill a barrel of firewood. When a tramp was alone by the woodpile, he would sometimes turn the barrel upside down. A small amount of wood piled on the bottom would give the appearance of a filled barrel of firewood.

Their presence was met with different attitudes. In some homes, they were taken in as guests, finding meals and a bed, while other homes would not tolerate their presence. Often, children were sent scurrying at the sight of these lone strangers coming down the road or lane.

To the county and state governments, they were considered a nuisance: "Unemployed persons roaming the countryside engaged in all kinds of evil doings."

50/2-
7-1895
In February of 1895, an article appeared in *The Holmes County Farmer* concerning a solution to the tramp problem. Its heading read: "Everything in Readiness For Feeding the Tramps – Bean Soup and Warm Fires for Those Who are Willing to Work."

The writing cited a June 12, 1879 state law concerning tramps. Section 6995 of the Ohio Revised Statues provided that "whoever, except a female or blind person, not being in the county in which he usually lives or has his home, is found going about begging and asking subsistance by charity, shall be taken and deemed to be a tramp; any tramp who enters a dwelling-house . . . against the will or without the permission of the owner or occupant thereof, or does not, when requested, immediately leave such place, or is found carrying a fire-arm, or other dangerous weapon, or does or threatens to do any injury to the person or real or personal property of another, shall be imprisoned in the penitentiary not more than three years nor less than one year; and any person may, upon view of any such offense, apprehend such offender, and take him before a justice of the peace, or other examining officer for examination."

The article further stated that arrangements had finally been made for feeding and working the "hobo," and the first ones were brought in to crush stone for their meals and lodging. Marshal Jordan was to have complete charge of the operation, which included a contract for providing food; and if for any reason they do not show up for work, it is his duty to raid their dens and layouts and bring them in to work or compel them to leave and clear out altogether.

The meals were not to be delicacies, but rather "plain wholesome food, something calculated to warm up their 'internals' and to a degree offset the wintry blasts."

The plan was to relieve the citizens of further annoyance and to provide work and food for the beggars in a "merciful way." Another aspect of the plan was to work the tramps at the homes instead of sending them to a workhouse.

The crushed stone was to be used for building and repairing streets, which would offset expenses.

To make the plan effective, all households were to refuse food or meals if any of these men came to the back door, and anyone could bring the men in for work. Should this not keep them from begging, the suggested sentence was "ten days at the stone-pile." In conclusion, the article stated, "Oh, we're gloriously fixed for the hobo if the scheme is only manipulated properly."

The government project did not put an end to the traveling boarders, as they were still found in Holmes County up to the middle of the twentieth century. The presence of the Amish and other religious groups throughout the area may, perhaps, partly explain why the county could not "stamp out" the problem. Their sympathetic, willing handouts were widely known to the transients and allowed them more freedom than crushing stone for meals and a bed.

A bed, to these men, was a place of rest, and could consist of a special "tramp bed" in the house or shop, or a sofa in the living room. In the barn, a hay or straw pile, or simply blankets, often served for the overnight rest. Out of doors, it could be a bed of leaves in the open air, under an overhanging rock or one of a number of makeshift shelters.

Meals could be anything to fill an empty stomach and might mean sitting at the table and partaking of the meal along with the family or being brought a platter of food. Others were handed a sandwich or given victuals to cook at the hangout over an open fire. Of course, some tramps appeared only at mealtime and would take advantage of their benefactors. An incident at Dan J. Schlabachs, a mile northeast of Charm, is an ex- *95/*

ample of this. A tramp, on one of his visits to the farm, was offered a piece of freshly baked cake. Contrarily, he stuck his dirty fingers in the remaining cake, saying, "Do you still want this?" His trick turned out as planned, for he was given the whole cake for his unappreciative manners, though much to the resentment of the family members.

Well known songs have been written about this unusual class of persons, including the song, "May I Sleep in Your Barn?"

> "May I sleep in your barn tonight, mister?
> For it's cold lying out on the ground,
> And the cold north wind comes a-whistling
> And I have no place to lie down." (v.1)

Or the biblical theme of "Only a Tramp:"
> "Only a tramp was Lazarus' sad fate
> He who laid down by the rich man's gate,
> He begged for the crumbs from the rich man to eat
> But was only a tramp found dead on the street." (v.1)

And "Big Rock Candy Mountain:"
> ". . . As he strolled along he hummed a song
> Of a land of milk and honey,
> Where a bum can stay for many a day
> And he won't need any money." (v.1)

Where did these people come from or what was their goal in life? For many it will never be known, as they kept their identity hidden. Some were known to be educated people who had accumulated a fair amount of money that could have changed their way of life from a listless wanderer to respectable citizens. Others, no doubt, had seen hard times and struggles in life that had left them poor, and their only desire was a sufficient handout and a place of rest.

Coming from all parts of the country and even from abroad, the traveling boarders made their visits throughout the locality. It is said that the men had a code of communication among themselves, informing each other of the occupants' hospitality. A stone on the fence post, at the lane entrance, gave others a signal that the place was occupied. Simple signs on a gatepost explained the farm's residents further (see indicators below).

143/
Jan.
1968
p.15

Indicators supposedly used by tramps in Holmes County, from top left: "Inhabitants hostile;" "No use;" "Eats here;" "You may sleep here;" "Mad dog;" "Money to be had;" "Woman and servant alone;" "Charitable women;" "Play sick;" "Talk religion."

Perhaps a mad dog symbol was used in Charm at one time, as in 1896 "Major," the night watch dog, was considered a tramp's terror and the children's friend, as reported in *The Holmes County Farmer*. The tall, well built dog was owned by the storeowner and Civil War veteran Isaac J. Miller.

50/2-
20-1896
109/

From the lone travelers, some unusual happenings and accounts have been remembered and kept alive throughout the years. One of the better known tramps was Andy Reiss, who in the early 1900s was spending the night in Rudy J. Yoder's barn, a mile east of Charm. Curled up on the hay beside the feed alley, he was constantly pestered by Rudy's goat which was shut in the barn. Getting enough nonsense from his tormentor, Andy took off after it, chasing it through the dark feed alley. A wheelbarrow was standing in the middle of the alley and, of course, the goat lightly jumped over it. As Andy did not realize that the wheelbarrow was there, he hit it full force with his shins, which sent him sprawling. After hobbling to the house, he got Rudy out of bed and dressed his painful, bleeding legs. Arriving at neighbor Dan J. Schlabachs the next day, Andy was still complaining about Rudy's goat. He is remembered as a big, strong fellow who spoke German.

75/

One day, around the year 1912, Andy Reiss stopped at the Emanuel P. Hershberger farm, two miles east of Charm, looking for a meal. Since he was willing to work in exchange for food, he became known in the area as "orbite sucher" or "rumm herr schaffer." That day, he was helping set fence posts. The men were working on the warm day and needed a drink of water, so the father called his boys, Jacob and Eli, who were playing in the sandbox, to bring them some water. With a "yep," the boys kept on playing. Again, Emanuel called, and the boys' reply was, "Yep," but still they made no effort to fetch the drinking water. At this point, Reiss made his feelings known, and with a shout to the boys, said, "Wir wollen wasser haben, nicht yep!" ("We want water, not yep!") The boys at once fetched water for the thirsty men.

6/
43/
183/

In the fall of 1938 Andy Reiss had, again, been at Rudy Yoders overnight. Before leaving, he complained of not feeling well, and afterward they received word that two days later his dead body was found east of Trail, Ohio in the barn of Owen Maust, where he had been spending the night. Andrew (Park) Reiss died of a heart attack at age seventy.

175/
183/

It was not until after his death that his real and hidden identity was revealed. Only when notice of his death appeared in local newspapers was it learned that he had relatives in Dover and Canton. Further investigations brought two daughters from Canton to Millersburg, and they identified

50/10-
6-1938

the dead body as that of their father. Reiss died Saturday, October 1, 1938, and services were to be held at Hunter Bros. Funeral Home on Monday the third. The burial had been arranged at the Holmes County Infirmary. However, when the relatives claimed the body, it was brought to Dover for burial.

Andy Reiss had been missing from Tuscarawas County for 25 years. Working and roaming from farm to farm in neighboring Holmes County, he was never recognized, nor did he associate with relatives. Seven years earlier, in 1931, the family made an unsuccessful attempt to find him during an estate settlement. Unable to locate his whereabouts, the court of his native county had declared him legally dead.

A freak accident claimed the life of a tramp between Mt. Hope and Winesburg, Ohio. The story is related that one day a stranger came to the Daniel Swartzentruber (1842 – 1918) residence and offered to help with some work in exchange for a few days' stay.

202/
p.29-30

The farmer had a large stone in the south field, across the road (County Road 160) from the lane, so he said the tramp could bury it. This tract of farmland lies a short distance southeast of the West Fairview Parochial School.

In those days, the way to get rid of boulders was to dig a large hole beside it, then roll the stone into the hole, usually a foot or two below the plow depth.

The tramp took up the offer, and with shovel and pick he set to work. Although warned by Mr. Swartzentruber beforehand of the danger involved in this kind of work, he steadily kept on with the tiresome work.

After digging for a few days, he failed to appear for supper one evening. Concerned about a mishap, or thinking that because of the hard work involved the stranger might have walked off, the farmer set out to investigate. Coming to the site, he found what he had feared. The undermined stone had rolled into the hole and crushed the poor tramp to death.

This was a drastic shock to the farmer, as he was of a nature not to wrong anyone. With sad and troubled feelings, he went to the nearest neighbor for help and advice. Since the stone was unmanageably large and no equipment was available to move it, it was finally decided to seek the advice of a lawyer.

The next morning, Daniel and the neighbor drove the twelve miles to Millersburg with horse and buggy to see a lawyer. Because they did not know of any relatives or emigration records, after much deliberation, the lawyer advised them to go home, cover up the incident, consider it buried, and leave it at that.

Another accident at Millersburg resulted in the death of one of the numerous roaming tramps. Early on Saturday morning, August 29, 1903, the body of a man was found lying along the railroad tracks. The man appeared to be about fifty years of age. He was later identified as having been in the area a short time, selling wire coat hangers. Another tramp who had been in contact with him said that he had given the name of Will Rogers and that before tramping around the country, he had been a bricklayer.

50/9-
3-1903

Apparently he had attempted to jump on a freight train during the night and had fallen under the train's wheels. The badly mutilated remains of the unfortunate traveler were taken to undertaker Cary's establishment, where Coroner Cole held an inquest. On the same evening, the body was buried in the infirmary cemetery. Nothing was found on it by which the deceased could be accurately identified.

"Trilby – William Ray Bodine 1869 – 1923" reads the tombstone reminder of a man who came to Holmes County to spend the latter part of his life. After his first house, close to Dublin, was destroyed by fire, he stayed in a small shanty in Trail.

19/
p.161
203/
p.9

In the community he was known as "Trilby" and recognized as a tramp, but he was highly respected

19/
p.162

"Trilby," William Ray Bodine

for his character and manners. Despite his paralyzed left arm, he would still seek work at a coal mine during the winter and paint mailboxes for his friends.

Only to a few trusted friends did "Trilby" reveal bits of his past life, and he did so only because of his fear of sudden death. He was born in Louisville, Kentucky as William Ray Bodine, was educated, and had been a newspaper reporter for the *New York American*.

On the day of his death, June 8, 1923, he was staying at the Dan C. Yoders, east of Limpytown (CR 70 and TR 137 intersection, Clark Township). He had been running after a horse, then while sitting on a chair during a visit to the members of the family, he died suddenly—possibly from overexertion.

The largely attended funeral was held at the German Swiss Reformed Church near Trail, Ohio. His body was laid to rest in the church cemetery with no relatives in attendance, only his later life's companions, his friends.

Friedrich Johannes Landolt is remembered in the area as "Kasefresser" (cheese eater), and was a well known tramp in the early 1900s. Landolt was found seriously ill along the road to Millersburg in November of 1933 and was taken to the Holmes County Home. It had been his custom to procure food and clothing, then sell part of them to other tramps. When he took sick, he had on his body $566.62. His illness resulted mainly from undernourishment; after a few weeks at the Home, he regained his health.

26/
p.111

While staying at the Home, Landolt asked Reverend Simon W. Sommers to contact relatives in Switzerland; they had lost all trace of him and assumed that he had died. In telling of his background, Landolt said that he had left his home country against the wishes of his parents when he was quite young and had been involved in a love affair. For the rest of his life, he described himself as "a plain and regular bum."

With Landolt wishing to return to Switzerland, a trip was arranged to go with Reverend Sommers. Sommers had been planning to make the trip across the ocean for his own interest, anyway. The tramp's money was used to cover traveling expenses, and the men left on July 19, 1934. Because of Landolt's troublesome ways, the journey was not always pleasant, but they reached his home country safely. The "Millionaire Hobo," as he was also called, was in his middle eighties when he made the trip across the ocean.

On October 18, 1940, a shuffle was heard on the outside of Eli P. Hershberger's house, $^3/_4$ mile west of Farmerstown, Ohio, and as the door opened, a heavyset stranger entered, hobbling along on

7/8-
9-1989
50/10-
24-1940

crutches. One leg had been amputated above the knee. His dirty clothes were evidence enough to identify him as one of the Holmes County tramps in search of food and lodging. The stranger sat wearily on a chair offered to him, and it seemed the cold damp weather had taken its toll on his ailing body. During the conversation with the Hershberger family, the elderly visitor said his name was Frank Plumb. After supper, Frank was given bedding to sleep on the living room davenport. The next morning, Saturday, after accompanying Hershberger to the barn, the stranger asked politely if he could stay one more night, "as I am a sick man." Frank described how he had slept in a barn, but with only one leg, he was unable to climb up to the haymow. Instead, he had rested in the hay alley, and the cold draft had left him with a bad cold. Eli readily agreed to another night's stay, to which the tramp said, "I shall never make you any more trouble hereafter, if I can stay one more night."

The following afternoon, the family was busy doing their regular work. Frank was sitting in the rocking chair after having read the newspaper. At 3:40, the rocking stopped and the mother, who was busy at the sewing machine, noticed that something was wrong with Mr. Plumb. She urgently called her husband, who was in the woodshed splitting firewood with the hired hand. When the men came into the house, the motionless man was slumped in the rocking chair and ceased to answer when his name was called. Frank Plumb was dead. Sheriff Harry Weiss, the coroner and a few neighbors soon arrived. The death was ruled as caused by "agnia pectoris." He was laid to rest at the Holmes County Infirmary Cemetery.

On Plumb's body was found $23.00 in bills, $9.92 in coins, and his identification card. Franklin Plumb was born March 17, 1876 at Grove City, Ohio, to George and Rachel (Clemmons) Plumb. He was widowed and had been a railroad worker.

Surviving were one daughter, who was living at Butte, Montana, and one brother, George D. Plumb, of Lucasville, Ohio.

8/
204/
p.309
258/

Johnny Wise, nicknamed "Osterhaas" (Easter Rabbit), is listed on the 1910 Holmes County census records as a white male, 63 years old, born in Germany and coming to America in 1869. As he walked along, he usually had his hands clasped behind his back and, at times, could be heard singing. He was a small person, wrinkly and bowlegged. Because of his habit of pipe smoking, Wise was blamed for an accidental barn fire close to Walnut Creek. As the unoccupied barn went up in flames, "Osterhaas" was seen leaving the area. It was supposed that he had been smoking in the hayhole. The barn was later replaced, and is lo-

204/
p.309

John Wise, born in 1847 in Germany.

cated today on the farm of Delbert H. Shetler.

142/
143/
Jan.1993
p.13

Pete Donald, or "Pete Donny" pretended to be nearly blind, but somehow saw the dime on the sidewalk that had been purposefully laid there for him by Gideon Troyer. (Troyer lived two miles north of Charm.) He was also seen reading a newspaper. At one place, Pete wanted to warm his outstretched hands over the "stove," which turned out to be a girl sitting on a chair picking nutmeats. Donald was also known as "Peter Pete," and is said to have formerly resided at Alliance, Ohio.

46/
143/
Jan.1993
p.11

Joe Kraus was also known as "Katie Kraus." He had people wondering whether he was male or female. Kraus was a clean and neatly dressed tramp and would help with bologna and sausage making at butchering time. But he preferred housework, which he did wearing a handkerchief on his head. Joe had good penmanship and would write family records in Bibles with artistic calligraphy.

43/

John Smith was a short fellow with a high temper. At one home, he was handed a meal, but his temper flared, as he wanted to eat at the table. Jumping up and down, swinging his arms and swearing, he took his food to the barn. He was also given blankets for the night, and the next morning they were found strewn around, with no tramp in sight.

44/
143/
Jan.1993
p.14

184/
203/
p.34

Henry Shafer, of small build, was fond of playing with children. He willingly helped with odd jobs, including carrying firewood.

340/

One day in the early 1940s, the red-bearded, friendly old man came to Henry Kauffmans, east of Berlin, and was not feeling well. As Shafer was resting in the barn, Grandpa Kauffman came to see about the sick man and asked what he could bring him to eat. His request for toast broth was granted, and on receiving it, he was greatly moved that someone would actually give him, an old tramp, what he asked for. Though sick, Shafer did not want to stay at the Kauffmans'; he wanted to go "hinna zum da Peta Joe" (back to Joe P. Miller). The Miller family lived two miles west of Winesburg, so he was taken there. Later, from there, a son, Levi, took sick Henry, with horse and buggy, to Noah Weavers at Mt. Eaton.

The next morning, Noah Weaver took Shafer to see Dr. Mayor of Apple Creek. From there he was taken either to a hospital or "poorhouse," where he died a short time later. Henry had not wanted to go to the hospital, remarking, "No gevva sie meah von de greena bottla un sell is gift" (Because they will give me of the green bottles and that is poison).

Henry Shafer died in December of 1942, being 93 years old, and was supposedly buried at the Mt. Eaton cemetery.

Henry said he emigrated from Germany, where he was born and brought up in an Amish family. He remarked that his parents were among the last Amish in Europe to be plainly dressed.

Billy Smathers was a regular visitor throughout the area during the 1940s and early 1950s. Smathers used a walking cane to help him along

20/
43/
47/
339/

128/

Billy Smathers, born in 1870 in Pennsylvania, died in 1951 at Mt. Hope, Ohio.

Example of Joe Kraus' calligraphy. (The Dan J. Schlabachs lived 1¹/₂ miles northeast of Charm.)

and as he walked, he would pitch up the cane, catch it in the middle, allow his hand to slide to the top, take a step using the cane, then pitch it again on the next step. He could be recognized at a distance by the unusual pitch of his cane. By some he was known as "Lome Bill" (Lame Bill).

50/10-
4-1951
143/
Jan.1968
p.14
186/

Billy had also been known as "Spring Chicken," a name he received when someone told him to work instead of walking from place to place. To this he replied, "I'm no spring chicken anymore."

Apr.1989
p.22
250/

Smathers was very fond of corn mush with milk and of vegetable soup, of which he could easily consume a quart.

Billy was of slender build and medium height. He was fairly clean and would greet you with a ready smile. Smathers was born May 4, 1870 in Pennsylvania. He did some tree trimming while making Holmes and Wayne Counties his home.

In the fall of 1951, at 81 years of age, he came to the Sam L. Masts on Friday, September 28. The Masts lived 2¹/₂ miles northeast of Mt. Hope. On Saturday, Billy complained of not felling well and asked to stay another night. After eating supper, he said he felt better, and Sam accompanied him to the barn where he always slept. On Sunday morning, he did not appear as usual, so before leaving for church, Sam and his father Levi checked on him. They found him dead.

On the following Wednesday, graveside services were held, conducted by a Methodist minister of Millersburg. Smathers, having no known close relatives, was laid to rest at the Holmes County Infirmary, to be buried in the land of his friends.

8/
9/
43/
Henry Stingecomb was considered a clean tramp who willingly worked for his room and board. He was well known in the Charm area. It was a common sight to see the tall, red-haired gentleman sitting on the store porch at Charm enjoying a visit.

43/
Bob King was one of the latest tramps in this area, making his appearance in the 1940s and '50s. He is believed to have originated from the southern states.

A circulating story had it that Bob would, at times, throw away food given to him. On one such occasion he came wandering to the Levi C. Miller farm at the northeast edge of Charm. For supper he was given a sausage sandwich and a cup of coffee, which he took to the shop. Later he was given blankets and had gone to the barn for the night. Afterward the Miller boys discovered that he had dropped the sandwich and coffee down a hole in the shop floor. Upon hearing this, Levi told his wife that if he came to the house for breakfast, they could tell him to get his sandwich in the shop.

The next morning as the farmer came to the barn, he heard a voice, and on closer examination found the tramp in a nicely worded, lengthy prayer, thanking the Lord for his good place of rest. With a change of heart, Miller told the women to give him breakfast if he came in.

On his return to the house that morning, Bob received a ham sandwich, and he was seen eating part of it as he headed toward Charm; he then threw the rest over the fence.

17/
143/
Jan.1993
p.14
"Swade" originated from Sweden, and to some people he was known as "Speck Menly" (Little Bacon Man). He was especially fond of bacon, and after receiving some, he would head to his retreat and, in true tramp style, fry the strips on the bottom of a tin can set over an open fire. Swade was a jolly, well built bachelor wearing a long beard. He would sing Swedish songs and was especially well liked among school children. A prayer before eating showed his respect for religion in his life.

43/
100/1-
26-1922
143/
Jan. 1993
p.11
ଏ
Max Rosenburg was a Hungarian eyeglass peddler from the first quarter of the present century. Rosenburg was a big, strong man who carried two heavy suitcases. He wore a size fourteen shoe and, instead of wearing boots, he nailed strips of automobile tires to the bottoms of his shoe soles.

202   Max is listed on the 1920 census as Solomon

56/

Henry Stingecomb sitting on the egg crates at the Charm store porch.

225/
1920
Rosenburg, a boarder in Walnut Creek Township, single and 57 years old. He is shown as coming to America in 1880.

Though Rosenburg was more like a peddler, because of his appearance he was regarded as a tramp—much to his resentment. He would sell eyeglasses at $1.50 to $2.00 a pair. On one visit to Bishop Gideon Troyer, north of Charm, Gid set the biggest suitcase on a scale and found that it weighed ninety pounds.

6/
8/
75/
100/3-
23-1893
Among other traveling boarders known to have been in the area were "Washtfresser" (Sausage Eater) and "Fresstramply" (Glutton Tramp). "Fresstramply" was a man of small stature who would, at times, get breakfast at different homes on the same morning. Such an account is reported to have happened at Sugarcreek in 1893, when a tramp received breakfast at five different placed in a single morning. An unhappy resident, Mose I. Hostetler, took after the tramp and ordered him to leave the town.

186/
Apr.1989
p.22
128/
142/
"False Tramp" would not work, as he claimed to have a headache and backache, and expressed fear of ending up with a muscle disease if he did any work. "Cider Pat," "Lutheran Preacher," and Gus Gurling are also remembered as making their appearances. Carl Hemten was a heavyset fellow who did some work for his food. Bill Mosser of

Apple Creek was fond of painting buggies. Joe Haze and "Long Eater" (a big, tall fellow) also made occasional appearances as tramps. Jim Shipman used to stay over winter in a small, 10' x 12' building at Adam Millers, between Charm and Farmerstown. During the summer months, he would be out tramping again. "Coffee Siffler" was very fond of coffee. "Knoche Fritz" (or Peter Bones) collected bones along the road. "Gla Rote Menly" (Little Red Man) and Patty O'Brian were also tramps in their time. O'Brian was a very quiet and clean person. John Osman came from the state of Massachusetts. John Carlington, a tall gentleman and nearly blind, supposedly originated from England. Some time later, the relatives in his home county erroneously received word that John had passed away. Despite the false information, Carlington did not want them to realize that he was still alive.

184/
185/
6/
204/
p.310
143/
Jan.1993
p.15

Louie Schmidt was a popular figure and was more respected among children than were some of the other strangers who appeared as tramps. He would help with chores, barn cleaning or the harvesting in the fall. As was the custom in earlier school days, the children would stay home from school when there was work to do on the farm, but when Louie Schmidt came along to help out for his room and board, the children could attend school. Schmidt was an older gentleman when he passed away.

The Peter Weavers lived two miles north of Bunker Hill along CR 77 and were accustomed to having tramps arrive for a meal or a night's rest in their special "tramp bed." On one occasion, Robert F. Mescheck came to the Weavers and took advantage of their generosity by staying too many nights in succession. To remedy the situation, Mr. Weaver had his daughter Dena tell Robert that he had "worn out his welcome." Hearing this, the gentleman became quite angry, exclaiming, "I go by Geib, I go by Zook, but never will I come back till Peter Weaver shall not live!" Storming out, he headed for the road. But within a few days, Mescheck was again seen plodding in Weaver's long lane.

205/
Family
#110
[A]

In a local newspaper of 1900 is found the following account under a "Charm" heading:

"An exciting incident happened on Saturday evening last, at about 6 o'clock, while members of the family of Jacob Mast, one-half mile west of here, were in the haymow looking for eggs. They saw what appeared to them as a peculiar bunch of hay and upon investigation they found a man of the 'Hobo tribe' imbedded beneath, laying motionless and apparently dead, which frightened the family very much. They at once gave the alarm, and Mr. Mast being at the village of Charm they

50/8-
9-1900

notified him, who with the village 'police' returned to investigate. When they arrived they found 'Weary Willy' determined to make that his resting place for the night but Mr. Mast thought otherwise and soon sent him on his way 'rejoicing' when the family again became reconciled after their fright."

An unusual situation concerning a tramp turned up in Berlin Township in the winter of 1888. On the Crist Miller farm near Berlin, a tramp had been staying for several months before being detected. Shortly after harvest, he had burrowed in the haymow in the barn, where he hid during the day, then prowled around during nighttime to find something to eat.

50/1-
19-1988

Around the middle of November his hideout was discovered and Mr. Miller sent him on his way, supposedly out of the neighborhood.

But six weeks later he was discovered in a barn belonging to a widow Boyd. Here, also, he had burrowed several feet into the hay, then cut a round hole a short distance to a window for light and ventilation, while at the same time being able to see what was happening on the outside.

The farm was close to the Boyd schoolhouse where he would go at night and cook something to eat. He would boil wheat for his meals, and when discovered there, he was also cooking some bones he had found somewhere in the vicinity.

After his arrest, he was taken to Berlin before Mr. Giauque for a hearing. Since there were no sufficient grounds for jailing him, he was again set free, much to the resentment of the community.

The fellow had displayed great intelligence when questioned. He appeared about 35 years old, with long hair and beard, along with badly soiled clothes.

Strangely, he was never seen in the area during daytime.

An account was related of how John McConnel came to the Ura J. Millers, who lived two miles northeast of Charm, one cold winter evening. Invited into the house, he was warming himself at the stove in the outside part of their cellar. Earlier that evening, Billy Smathers, a regular tramp who visited the Millers every few weeks, had arrived at the Miller home. Smathers had been welcomed to the "tramp bed" set up in the back cellar room, but hearing of McConnel's presence, he came back up the stairs and told Ura that he would leave if John stayed. Since the Millers did not want to lose Billy's visits, the father went to the outside cellar door and told John about the precidament, asking him to leave. McConnel, though very unhappy about it, agreed to leave, but said, "I'll go, but if I find Billy on the road, I'll slaughter him!"

20/

Teasing strangers could spell severe trouble. On March 10, 1921, a tramp came to the Michael E. Yoder home, a mile northwest of Mt. Hope, asking for a place to sleep. Since thirteen of their fourteen children were at home that night, the father said that there was no room in the house, but he would get blankets to fix a bed in the barn for him to sleep on. This greatly displeased the stranger, and he left and kindled a fire in the woods close by, where he stayed overnight.

200/
p.25
50/3-
17-1921

The next morning, March 11, when the father, along with his sons Eli and Obed, went to the barn to begin the chores, the tramp was still in the woods, swearing and carrying on. Michael had warned the boys to keep quiet, but on returning to the house, they heard him still growling, and Eli yelled, "Whee."

Hearing this, the tramp grabbed his suitcase and headed for the house. Michael was at the chicken house as he came by, demanding to know where "that boy" was. Michael told him not to go into the house, but he entered, anyway. Once inside, the stranger pointed a pistol at eighteen-year-old Eli. The young boy grabbed the gun and threw the stranger to the floor as one shot hit the lad in the leg. Another shot ricocheted off the table and hit the cellar steps where some of the other children were standing. The father had, by now, entered the house and was helping Eli hold the tramp to the floor. Once he was held down, Katie, twenty, tore the gun out of his hand.

The tramp was pleading to be let go, and in his earnest desire bit the boy on the hand. With the assistance of the other family members, the tramp's hands and feet were tied with a rope.

Son Obed went to neighbor Eugene Wheeler to call the sheriff, and thirteen-year-old Solomon went to Mt. Hope for more help. Later, Sheriff Henderson arrived from Millersburg and took the tied-up tramp with him; he gave his name as Gottard Brobeil. He was given a hearing and placed in jail to await the action of the jury.

Dr. Graf of Mt. Hope gave medical attention to Eli's leg, then the son and his father went to Beach City with the buggy and traveled by streetcar to the Canton hospital for further treatment.

Meanwhile, at the farm, it was discovered that chicken bones were scattered around the burned down campfire, and it was assumed that the tramp had roasted one of the Yoders' chickens that night in the woods.

The theft of chickens had been a considerable problem throughout the area. One such incident, still related today in Holmes County, is of a tramp brought before the judge because of stealing chickens. With insufficient evidence to convict the accused, the judge replied, "There is not enough

142/

❧

evidence, but if I were a chicken, I'd roost up high."

In January of 1916, three tramps were staying at the David Alleshouse residence, near Farmerstown. One evening when Alleshouse went to town, they disappeared, taking with them a lot of clothing, as well as a watch. After the Holmes County sheriff was summoned, he took them into custody the following day, near Coshocton. All of the stolen articles were found in their possession at the time of the arrest.

100/1-
19-1916

As noted, teasing the strangers could mean trouble, yet the urge apparently was not always resisted. The late Sarah M. Weaver gives this account of how her uncle Eli (1883 – 1943), son of Peter Weaver, as a young boy would sing, "Tramp, tramp, tramp, the boys are marching," when a tramp was in their reserved room. The mother greatly disliked the son's behavior and felt he possibly received a just punishment later. One day the Weavers had company staying overnight and Eli had to sleep in the "tramp bed," which resulted in his getting a bad case of lice.

205/
Family
#154
[A]

During the period of "tramping," incidents and happenings arose where tramps were connected to lawlessness. This only intensified the pressure between them and government officials to eliminate the problem of tramps and their existence. Among these accounts was the robbing and burning of the store at Charm on November 24, 1894. Five tramps were taken into custody at Coshocton, when the items they were selling aroused the suspicion that the tramps were connected to the robbery and disastrous fire. The five, known as Joseph Quinn, Mike Grant, Elmer Good, Joseph Williams and Edward Carr, were arrested by U.S. authorities as they were sitting around a huge bonfire. After a jury trial held at Cleveland, Ohio, Joseph Quinn and Mike Grant were found guilty of the store destruction and each was sentenced to three years in the penitentiary at hard labor.

50/11-
29-1894
50/1-
6-1894

50/3-
7-1895

The men had conducted their own defense and did it with ability. Although a professional hobo, Quinn, at times, spoke with eloquence. He and Grant were called before Judge Hicks, who said, "In conducting your case you have shown that you are men of intelligence. You have used good language, have ability, and your addresses have been more clear and concise than many arguments made by professional lawyers. It is plain that you are educated men and should have been in better business than tramping and robbing and burning post offices." (See a more detailed account of the robbery included with the Charm store history.)

Another account, circulated in a local paper, was headed, "Tramps Capture Train." According to the 1903 article, a dozen tramps stormed a Reading Railroad freight train which made numerous

50/9-
3-1903

stops, picking up produce from market gardeners for the Trenton and Philadelphia markets. Armed with clubs, the tramps overpowered the train crew and made a 35-mile run to Trenton Junction. During the ordeal, the crew members attempted to recapture the train, but every effort seemed futile. "Watermelons burst over the heads of the attacking parties; potatoes and hard apples struck them in their eyes and on their noses." When the train finally came to a halt at a station, officers rushed aboard and a fifteen-minute hand-to-hand fight ensued, leaving three policemen knocked unconscious. In the end, three of the tramps were arrested, while nine made their escape.

An earlier article in January of 1885 had already vividly urged a combined effort to rid the state of armed tramps. The article explained that it was no longer safe to travel alone upon country roads, and upon the railroads the train crews are powerless. Gangs of armed men under the disguise of persons seeking work were roaming the state and that should no longer be tolerated. 50/1-17-1885

"Honest men" sincerely seeking work do not go armed, and special effort should be made to search and arrest all "strangers." If people were found with concealed weapons, that would be evidence not only of lawlessness, but also of evil intent. Some special police going through every freight train and arresting every tramp would soon stop the "tramp evil."

One of the most distinguished of all local tramp accounts is a list of 38 names compiled by the late Crist C. Yoder (OAG 2749), who had lived 1½ miles north of Charm. The Yoders' hospitality can be inferred from the number of names found on the list. Their home was only a short distance from the "Big Rock Spring" tramp resting spot, so visits would have been quite frequent. The Yoders had a ready tramp bed in the shop for those seeking lodging, and the farm was apparently a widely known stopping place. 20/
45/

The list not only gives their name or identifying nickname, but it also indicates some nationalities. (It should be pointed out that Yoder's reference to "Dutch" does not necessarily mean that the individuals came from Dutch-speaking countries. They could have come from Germany, or he might have been referring to the Pennsylvania Dutch language.)

Additional information concerning these men is included in square brackets. 201/
p.41

John Carson – Irish
Pete Donald – Irish [See earlier account.]
August Horn – Dutch
"Little Gust"
"Old Strowe"
"Old Deign" – Denmark [Deign, pronounced "Dane," was of big stature and white-haired; it was said that he could speak seven languages.] 17/
Leohair Hohair
Joe Kraus [See earlier account.]
Legglo – grapevine trimmer
Opfer – Dutch [John Henry Opfer was a willing worker who always wore blue.] 204/
p.309
Houseu – Dutch
Yacob Roarer – Dutch
"Crooked Nose Smith"
John Smith – Dutch [See earlier account.]
"Cheeseeater Smith" – Switzerland
Jacob Snechenberger – Switzerland
John Mayers – Switzerland
"Irish Pat" [His real name was Patty Smith; he was a short, stocky and clean tramp who had formerly been a boiler maker.] 204/
p.309
Henry Shafer – Dutch [See earlier account.]
Carl Beaustruir – Sweden
"Bundle Henry" – Dutch
"Pox Marks In His Face" – English
"Big-Eyed Irish"
Bill Smathers [See earlier account.]
Henry Stingecomb [See earlier account.]
August Stevens – Dutch
"Little English" – always carried a basket
Bob King [See earlier account.]
Conrad Blender – Dutch basket maker [A basket maker is supposedly buried in the William E. Beachy cemetery (CD-L-23) with an unmarked fieldstone as a marker. Of the three basket makers known in the area, it would seem that this could be Conrad's grave.] 12/
John Weaver – Dutch basket maker [See following account.]
"Old Lutz" – bought old boxes and rags
Andy Reiss [See earlier account.]
"A Swede" – always wore a red handkerchief around his neck [See earlier account of "Swade."]
"Mitten Knitter" – knitted gloves
Fritz Becker – Dutch
Max Rosenburg – Hungarian [eye]glass peddler [See earlier account.]
"An Argue Tramp" – later returned to Switzerland
Matthew – English

Various locations throughout the Charm vicinity were used as gathering places by the wandering tramps. Frequently visited, the simple places of rest were sheltered by boulders, makeshift abodes or logs rolled into place around an open fire.

The "Tramps Stump," at the head of a small trickle stream known as Big Rock Spring, ¾ mile north of Charm, along TR 369, offered ideal weather protection for the transient and was widely known in that respect. The large, overhanging sandstone creating the cave, 100' wide, 30' deep and 25' high, is a natural beauty in itself. This was a favorite gathering place for those needing a rest 201/
p.41

❧

9/ or seeking the company of their kind. Huddled around an open fire as handed out coffee was brewed, the men would plan what direction each would take to obtain more handouts or to find a place to sleep.

43/ Around 1920, some tramps set up their own little abode 1¹/₂ miles northwest of Charm, along the west side of the Doughty Creek. In a gully in the woods, they gathered and laid up old split fence rails a few feet high. Once the little 8' x 10' sides were up, other rails were laid on top and the complete structure covered with leaves to keep out the rain. Piled on the inside was another heavy mattress of leaves to sleep on; it had room for about six men.

At times, as many as twelve would gather there, and if disputes arose and they couldn't get along, some would leave.

Accounts are related of how a few tramps were staying at a residence and another had come along looking for lodging. Opening the door and looking over his fellowmen, he would leave if one was present whom he didn't like.

143/
Jan.1968
p.14 Another hangout in the Charm area was in the "sheep hollow," one-fourth mile east of Guggisberg Cheese, where the lone travelers frequently congregated. The spot was situated in woods among big rocks and wild grapevines.

140/ A mile to the southeast of Charm, tramps were frequently seen sitting at a litter strewn encampment along SR 557. Their gathering spot was on today's Ammon Barkman property, a short distance west of the buildings in a shallow ravine.

175/ Halfway between Charm and Farmerstown, an old sand mine afforded the travelers protection on the former Emanuel P. Hershberger farm, which is occupied today by Jonas L. Yoder.

258/ On the Henry Shetler farm between Charm and Walnut Creek, a number of tramps wintered in the woods south of the home. Shetler had granted them permission to do so, with the understanding that they would not bother the neighbors in search of handouts. Throughout the winter, they kept the fire going for warmth, amid the huge boulders that afforded them some protection against the wintry cold.

Places highly regarded by tramps were the heated kilns at brickyards. Many spent cold winter nights by the warmth of the big brick dryers in operation at the local towns of Sugar Creek and Baltic. Supposedly, the last of the area's tramps to be seen were at these brick kilns.

Despite the serious effort to halt tramping, sympathy was expressed for the roaming characters. As the problem of tramps appeared especially evident in Holmes County, articles from outside the county were printed in local papers. In *The*

50/4-
11-1889 *Holmes County Farmer* of April 11, 1889, there appears an article about a debate in the House on a bill making it a crime for a man to become a tramp. During the session, an account was given of a poor, unfortunate person known as "Blue Jean Tramp."

The story begins with the John Hicks family, consisting of the parents and their two children, Jennie and Dwight. The young children had grown up with every possible advantage, as Hicks was a well-to-do farmer and did not spare money for his children's wants and needs. However, despite his generosity towards the children, one sorrow saddened the father. The daughter, Jennie, was of a very envious nature, "getting all you can and keeping all you can get." The brother, however, was quite the opposite and "freeheartedly" got along with his sister, who showed no charity or generosity when claiming any of his belongings as her own. In due time, she developed hatred and bitterness against her brother, who was of an indifferent yet happy nature. After Jennie's marriage, the parents died and left an estate to be equally divided between their two children.

Soon after the parents' death, Dwight met a girl who accepted his proposal of marriage. His sister, by now, had taken a great dislike to the girl. With apparent friendship, she whispered cruel words into her future sister-in-law's ears. They bore fruit. Suspicious, the slanders grew to certainty and she renounced, almost at the wedding date, the man whom she had wanted to marry. Dwight, confounded and insane, left the home. Drinking appeared as the only relief for his great sorrow. The sister now continued her method of gaining his wealth. Living under the influence of alcohol, he returned one day to the sister's house, where he lived, but was driven off to himself with not a dollar in the world.

What little of Dwight's reason that had remained was shattered, and he left, a homeless man without money or goals in life. For years he tramped, going over his regular route, always wearing a blue jean jumper, from which he got the name "The Blue Jean Tramp." No one feared him and everyone pitied him, welcoming him to their fireside warmth, where he found the food and rest that he needed.

A few basket makers are identified as having been located in the area. Though, at the time, they were categorized with the tramps, their livelihood appeared closer to that of a peddler. Also being different from the tramp, they had set up housekeeping and were more self reliant.

Conrad Blender is included on the earlier mentioned Crist C. Yoder list of tramps. He is identified as a Dutch basket maker. Nothing more of his basket making or whereabouts is known.

John Weaver was an older resident of Walnut Creek Township. He was better known as "Kaupmacher" (basket maker) and was frequently seen throughout the area, selling his supply of handmade baskets.

95/
279/

John was a German emigrant who appeared here in the early 1900s. Inquiring at the Dan S. Hershbergers, he received permission to stay in a vacant house on the 57-acre Mast plot earlier added to their farm. This, today, is a part of the Andy Y. Miller farm in the southwest corner of Walnut Creek Township.

Weaver is remembered as getting great enjoyment caring for an apple tree growing alongside the house, and with tending a small garden during the summer. Among the vegetables he grew was an unusual blue skinned potato.

The neighbors, among whom were the Hershbergers and the Levi (Leff) and Dan J. Schlabachs, supplied the old bachelor with a weekly loaf of bread, milk and eggs. In the spring, Johnny would come walking to Dans for his yearly haircut, wanting "all hair off." He would then, at times, wear a stocking cap made of old, cut off underwear legs to cover his nearly naked head.

"Kaupmacher" was a professional in basket weaving. He would cut most of his needed willow branches along the upper Doughty, close to the former Wise woolen mill on the Jake Eusey farm along SR 557 (Mose T. Yoder farm). When enough were cut and tied in bundles, Schlabach or Hershberger would haul them back home for him, where he would peel off the bark and weave them into baskets. He made many sizes of baskets; small, round, oval, sewing baskets, market and egg baskets with handles, and large clothes

95/
272/
308/
249/

Willow twig baskets identified as made by basket maker John Weaver. (This type of basket resembles the baskets known as the "Sonnenberg Basket" that appear to have been made in the Sonnenberg community of the Kidron area, ca 1880 – 1920.)

378/
p.155-159

95/
249/

Quality basket made by John Weaver.

baskets. On some, a finishing touch of design painting of various colors was done, usually in dark red, blue or green. Once a variety was made, he would strap them on his back and peddle them throughout the community for a meager income. At times, he was seen loaded with so many baskets that only his head, arms and legs protruded from the quantity of wares.

When he was sick, the neighbors would check on him and help as needed. One account is told that once, when Weaver had taken sick, the Schlabachs brought him a bottle of Hoosier medicine sold by area resident Mose L. Yoder. To their surprise, the next day he had emptied the bottle. Informed that the proper dosage was one tablespoonful, John replied, "What is it going to help if left in the bottle?"

279/

He received a German newspaper and during World War I closely watched the movements of his native country.

In his later years, ca 1920, when "Kaupmacher" was no longer able to care for himself, the Walnut Creek Township trustees were summoned, and they admitted him to the Holmes County Home. When he died, he was supposedly buried at the infirmary burial grounds.

John G. Martin was another basket maker from the area whose high quality baskets were in demand. He also found the former Wise farm along the Doughty Creek an ideal place to gather twigs. Martin cut his supply here when he lived two miles northeast of the Wise farm. After the twigs were cut, he loaded them on a two-wheeled cart, then pulled it home with a crude self made harness. Except during the springtime, the twigs needed to be boiled before the thin bark could be peeled off. The pliable branches were now ready to be woven into clothes baskets, sewing kits, hampers, pie holders and varieties of baskets so useful in a household. As a rule, Martin was busy and did basket making by order only. At Millersburg, a few stores were selling his wares, although most

48/
203/
342/
343/

were apparently sold to individuals.

Another basket credited to him was made from twisted strands of rye straw tightly sewn together. The small, delicate sewing basket was lace edged with a braided strand around the top. The zigzagged design of the lid set it off as an attractive piece of artwork.

John was a good natured, German speaking bachelor who was born in Bavaria. At one time, he had lived in the upper Trail valley, then moved to the Emanuel M. Beachy farm, a mile southeast of Berlin, in 1930 or '31. Here he stayed in their vacant house for approximately five years. (It is said that while staying here, the house was so badly infested with rats and mice that he set his bed on crocks so that the rodents couldn't crawl onto the bed.)

From the Beachys, Martin moved to the Dan E. Hershberger farm, $1^1/_2$ miles northeast of Bunker Hill. His dwelling was located at the far end of their farm along a small stream winding down to Trail. The small house he stayed in was rudely furnished with a bed made of wooden store boxes. A single bench was all he needed to sit on. He cooked in tin cans. The closest neighbor lived a half mile away. Because he was busy and also had a cat for company, the older basket maker did not consider his life lonely.

In the area, the bachelor was known as "Kaupmanlie" (Little Basket Man). When he became old, he was placed in the Holmes County Home, where he died on February 28, 1953 at the age of 88.

A common sentiment among the generous families who showed hospitality to the traveling boarder tramps was that "it was a worthwhile family experience, teaching us the virtues of caring and sharing."

Jacob Yoder (1822 – 1894), who lived $1^1/_2$ miles

northeast of Charm, had migrated with his father Michael from Hessen, Germany in 1825. Among his tramp friends he was known as "Hessen Pop" because of his former place of residence. The Yoders lived on the present Abe A. Yoder farm along TR 369 and had been caring for a sick tramp. After the boarder regained fair health and was ready to leave, Jacob's wife was moved to tears as she saw their stranger–friend, also with a heavy heart, take leave. The tramp himself was no less touched, and as he came to the end of the lane, he sat under a cherry tree weeping loudly, before heading up the road.

143/
Jan.1968
p.14

What caused the tramp era to finally fade away? Perhaps their disappearance will remain, in part, a mystery, as were some of the motives and circumstances that led these men to become tramps in the first place. With the problem of tramping already existing in Holmes County in the late 1800s, the county's concern to end their existence relaxed on their behalf during the next half century.

In 1935, the United States Congress passed the Social Security Act, creating public assistance programs to help the blind, the aged and families with young children. This federal program had a great impact on the "traveling boarder." The unemployed could now also receive benefits from the government, and retired persons were eligible for pensions under this program. The coming of Social Security would greatly affect the lifestyle of American people, including those persons who had lived as tramps. Some would still roam the countryside during the next decade or two, but eventually their visits would be a thing of the past. Their appearance and presence were once a prominent part of America, of Ohio, of Holmes County, and yes, of Charm, also.

Included among Holmes County expressions is a Pennsylvania German one, "Mol saene voos draably fallt." The term used today would be used to mean, "We'll see," or "Well, it depends." The origin of this saying is given in the following account.

245/

A tramp had arrived at a farm house and was welcomed into the warm kitchen by the mistress of the house. She had been attending her meal, which was cooking in a kettle on the stove, and great beads of perspiration covered her forehead from the heat. While stirring the contents, she asked if he would stay to eat. The tramp, watching the perspiration about to drip from the tip of the lady's nose into the kettle she was stirring, replied, "Mol saena voos draably fallt." [Let's see where the droplet falls.] His decision to stay would be determined by which side of the kettle the per-

249/
342/

Rye straw sewing basket made by basket maker John Martin.

Tapered basket and lidded basket found in the area. Both have red and blue decorative paint.

189/

spiration fell; inside or outside the kettle. Thus, today's usage of the expression would have been fitting in this instance also: "Well, it depends."

Moreover, the haphazard wanderings of the tramps were greatly dependent on the attitude, "Well, it depends," or "We'll have to see." With the uncertainty of their tomorrows, their nights, or even the next meal, the thought, "Well, it depends" was fitting to their style of life. "Mol saena voos draably fallt." ❧

❧ *Charm Interests* ────────────

Biographical Sketches

Andrew I. Miller

Andrew I. Miller was born September 6, 1855, a mile west of Charm on the farm now owned by Paul S. Erb.

50/2-
20-1896
206/
p.91

Very little is known of Andy's early life. The first connection we find of Andy at Charm is in 1896, when he operated the wagon shop. He was also engaged with carpentry, going with the Mose Keim crew. His touch of expertise as a woodworker was highly evident with the miniature tools and lathe turnings he was making during his later years. Operating his foot powered lathe skillfully, Andy made small chairs and stands, and repaired broken furniture.

The older gentleman, who was a bachelor, became an expert whittler. Pocket knives of hickory and walnut were made to snap open and closed, just like the real knives. He could make pliers, nippers and tongs that would open and close and had a resemblance of real tools. Andy was also noted for making a wooden wheel pie crust cutter. Another specialty of his was rolling pins. Often, these items were given, as a kind gesture, to children or to people bringing him something to eat.

V66-
431-
1903

At Charm, the bachelor lived at the south edge of town on the Atlee D. Schlabach property of today. In 1903, he bought the three-quarter-acre property from his brother Hiram. On the acreage stood an old two-story log house that Andy used for his home, living there by himself.

Andy was known throughout the area as "Isaac Andy," and even today, among older residents, the mention of him creates special sentiments. He was an unusual person, in that his witty sense of humor could quickly turn to violent anger. Early incidents of this are still related by his surviving relatives and friends.

❧

9/

Best remembered is the time he was "turning" a rolling pin on the lathe. When the pin was nearly finished, the chisel caught on the spinning piece of wood and gouged into the smoothed surface. Giving way to anger, he tore the pin from its rest and threw it on the floor. Still not satisfied, he jumped on it with both feet. To his surprise, the rolling pin rolled out from under him and sent the disgruntled woodworker flat on his back. Heading a short distance to the store with his clay pipe rigged with an elderberry stem, he had a smoke of "Growler," then came back and finished the "rolling" pin.

279/

Another incident took place when the house (presently occupied by Mrs. Melvin A. Raber, two miles north of Charm) was being built. The Keim carpenters of Charm, along with "Isaac Andy," were putting plaster strips on the wall and ceiling. To reach the ceiling, Andy had laid a wooden shingle across the open end of an empty nail keg. He was unconcernedly at work when the old shingle suddenly broke, leaving Andy standing with both feet inside the nail keg. His feet were thus crammed in the keg with his toes pointing upward. He couldn't free himself and was hopping around the room in anger. The other carpenters nearly exploding with laughter, knew that this

9/
249/

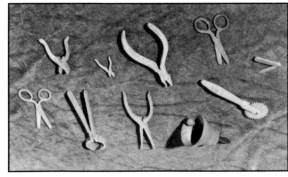

Wooden items made by "Isaac Andy."

would only make matters worse. The ordeal ended when they smashed the keg in order to free the trapped carpenter.

Not all of Andy's misfortunes turned out so badly. One day he was doing roof work on the house where the Mose L. Troyer family now resides, a mile south of Charm. Losing his footing, he began sliding down the roof, yelling, *"Ha, helf miah!"* (Lord, help me!) Sliding into a nail that was extending from the roof, he tore a hole in his new overalls, but managed to avoid falling to the ground. With this, the frenzied carpenter replied, *"Nau brauchst doch nimme"* (Now you don't need to anymore), forgetting the source of the help he had asked for and received.

At Charm, "Isaac Andy" was often a victim of teasing. The pranksters, knowing to what degree he could "boil," schemed some uncalled for plots merely for the sake of seeing him get angry. Once, his walking plank, extending over the ditch leading from the road to his house was almost sawed through. Turning the saw cut side down, the plank, of course, broke when Andy attempted to cross, and sent him falling into the ditch. Another time, the two posts were torn from the small porch roof, which crashed down over his doorway. Racing to the nearby Andy J. Miller cemetery, the boisterous ones hid to hear what would happen as the bachelor crawled out from under the toppled roof. Yet another time, the porch steps were moved away. Hearing a commotion on the outside, Andy came rushing from the house, only to be sent flying as he missed the porch steps. Getting his wits together, he grabbed a knife and took off after the boys, who had gone to a nearby woods. Jumping upon a fallen log, he yelled, "If I could find you I'd let you have it." Unknown to him, one of the boys was lying behind the same log Andy was standing on, hiding in the darkness.

Andy greatly disliked being called his given name of Andrew, and this was often a subject of teasing. One evening during the 1920s, young Howard, a son of Brisban Kaser, called him "Andrew." Immediately, Andy took off after the young boy, desperate to lay hands on him for a due punishment. The two raced down the street from the store, past the Keim Lumber building. As Howard spied the open basement door at the Mose Keim home, he darted inside to elude his captor. The fleet footed bachelor followed in close pursuit, and once inside, raced around the table which was in the room.

Mrs. Keim, who was working in the basement, was quite startled. After numerous circles around the table, Andy told the bewildered lady to hand him the wooden washing stick. The kindhearted woman solemnly rebuked him, saying, "No, you

67/

344/

107/

don't want to do that."

But Andy, determined to get the stick, made a quick dive for it. Seeing his chance, the lad rushed for the doorway and headed up the street again. He made a safe retreat into his home, which was in the upstairs of his father's butcher shop (today's restaurant building).

During the remainder of the evening, nothing more was seen of young Howard Kaser.

Around 1924, Andy became ill and was unable to take care of himself anymore. Crist Hummel, who was blacksmith at the time, was married to Andy's sister Amanda, and they were living at the north corner lot in town (today's Keim Lumber driveway entrance). Hummel accordingly built a two-story extension to the east side of their house, and Andy was moved into the second story.

Regaining his health, Andy used part of the addition for his whittling and shop area. (The top portion of this building is still intact, on the Tobe M. Yoder property at the north edge of Charm.)

While Andy lived at his sister's home, he made numerous wooden items for the Hummel children which included a doll bed, a chest of drawers, a doll stand and a small wooden scooter. The scooter lasted young Paul Hummel for two summers of "hard usage."

In 1927, the Christ Hummel family moved to Berlin, taking Andy along with them. Here, also, a small dwelling and shop was erected for him, where he could work as health permitted.

"Isaac Andy" Miller died at Berlin from a heart ailment, on April 1, 1937.

Earlier, during his old age, when an acquaintance passed away, Andy was asked if he would attend the funeral. He replied, "Hum, no, he won't come to mine, either."

He is buried at the Walnut Creek Mennonite Church Cemetery alongside his brother, Alexander, who also had never married. He had died the previous year.

206/ p.91

16/

9/

Christena Graefe

The egg market at the Charm store brought people to town, bringing eggs and butter to sell or barter for necessities. On certain days during the early 1900s, it was a common sight to see two aged women walking to town carrying their baskets of produce. The prize baskets of eggs were handled lightly to insure their safety, while the shaped butter was neatly wrapped in large rhubarb leaves to retain the coolness from the spring cellar.

The ladies had walked the two miles east to town from their homes. One, Tena Graefe, an unmarried lady, walked to the Valentine Erb farm, where she was joined by Mrs. Erb (Amanda). The

274/

route was often traveled in each other's company, as they both enjoyed the walk and the neighborly chats along the way.

225/
1880
252/

Christena Graefe was born November 29, 1859 in Germany to Frederick Graefe, who appeared in Holmes County the following year applying for naturalization.

Tena is listed on the 1880 census with her father and possibly an uncle, Lewis. Her mother was apparently no longer alive at this time. The Graefes farmed the acreage lying between CR 19 and Troyer's Hollow of the Doughty in Mechanic Township. The farm is owned today by Ruth Miller.

Tena later lived alone. She had only one brother, Theodore, who quit-claimed the real estate to her in 1889. Both had previously assumed ownership in accordance with their father's will.

As Miss Graefe became older, she was no longer able to work the seventy-acre farm, so the fields became unproductive. She died on April 9, 1929

273/

and was buried at the St. John Lutheran Church cemetery at New Bedford.

In the estate settlement, only seven nieces and nephews are noted as heirs to her possessions;

272/

❧ Christena Graefe, right, and her blind aunt Anna Raif.

none of the heirs were living in Ohio at that time. A Charm businessman, William Perry Miller, had been appointed executor. Also mentioned on the settlement papers was Christena Barbara S[cherer], who was to be paid for her labors. Apparently, Barb, a neighbor lady, was working for Tena when she was no longer able to care for herself.

Though Christena's character and morals were never known by the present generation, a glimpse of her attitude may perhaps be attained from her collection of poems, one of which is the following:

272/

Be Careful What You Say

In speaking of a person's faults,
Pray don't forget your own;
    Remember those in homes of glass,
    Should never throw a stone.
If you have nothing else to do
But talk of those in sin,
    'Tis better to commence at home
    And from that point begin.

We have no right to judge a man
Until he's fairly tried;
    Should we not like his company,
    We know the world is wide.
Some may have faults—and who has not?
The old as well as young:
    We may perhaps for aught we know,
    Have forty to their one.

I'll tell you of a better plan
And find it works full well;
    To try my own defects to cure
    Before I of others tell;
And though I sometimes hope to be
No worse than some I know,
    My own shortcomings bid me let
    The faults of others go.

Then let us all, when we commence
To slander friend or foe,
    Think of the harm one word may do
    To those we little know;
Remember curses sometimes, like
Our chickens, "roost at home;"
    Don't speak of others' faults until
    We have none of our own.

Today, at the old Graefe homeplace, there still lingers a remembrance of the lady who knew this as home for the most part of her life. The house, which had been going to shambles, was extensively restored and has been opened as a summer retreat under the direction of Miriam Weaver. The retreat is known as "Tena's House."

Sarah Beiler

The Daniel M. Yoder (OAG 1720) family lived on the farm at the north edge of Charm. Daniel was married to Fanny, daughter of Daniel D. Miller. Fanny's sister Catherine was married to Daniel E. Mast, who grew up a mile northwest of Charm. In 1886, during the time when the Mast family was thinking of moving to Kansas, Mrs. Mast died (CD-K-27), nineteen days after the birth of a baby girl. Nevertheless, a few months later, the widowed father, along with eight of the children, did make the move to Hutchinson, Kansas. The youngest daughter, Sarah (DBH 12844), only a few months old, was then cared for at the home of her aunt, Mrs. Daniel M. Yoder, at Charm. Raised as one of the Yoders' own children, she attended Charm School in her youth and remained with the Yoders until she married, on February 11, 1909. She was married at Charm by bishop Moses E. Mast to Samuel D. Beiler (DJH 6411) of Kansas. They resided in Kansas for a number of years, then later lived at Virginia Beach, Virginia.

89/ 242/ p.5

The father, Daniel E. Mast, was ordained deacon in 1891 and minister in 1914. Preacher Mast was an influential writer. His writings were later published under the title *Anweisung zur Seligkeit*.

Dr. Wesley Theodore Swarts

Older residents of the Charm area talk of Dr. Swarts as the veterinarian of Charm who made visits to farms in a high wheeled horse drawn cart or a Ford roadster. They will relate that he was married to one of the Eusey girls, who lived two miles northwest of Charm. Dr. and Mrs. Muriel Swarts are remembered as having lived across the street from the store and later in a stone house on the Eusey farm. Thereafter, nobody from the Charm area could recall what became of the Swarts family.

Wesley Theodore Swarts was born in 1871 to Cyrus and Elizabeth (Flory) Swarts. In 1906 he married Muriel Ruth Eusey, a daughter of Jacob and Jessie (Varns) Eusey, who lived on the Wise farm (Mose T. Yoder farm) two miles northwest of Charm. In 1917, Swarts bought the property across the street from the store where he had his office along the east end of the house. In the spring of 1918, they moved onto the property after it was vacated by Henry W. Aling. From his home in Charm, Dr. Swarts would race across the countryside in his high wheeled cart, attending to his veterinary practice. His well gaited horse could bring the animal doctor to the farms in a hurry.

Though the couple had no children of their own, Swarts was fond of the town's youngsters and is

172/

084-341-1917

100/4-15-1918
9/
107/

Dr. Swarts in his office (supposedly at Charm).

172/

remembered running down the street while helping a young lad fly a kite, or taking young Roman Keim to the circus rides at the school and buying a bag of popcorn for him. However, despite his kindness, the slender built vet also took in the rambunctious side of life in town.

The couple had apparently lived in town prior to the property purchase, as he was there in 1916 when he purchased a new Ford car.

100/5-3-1916

In 1923, the doctor and Muriel sold the property and lived for some time in the stone house on the Eusey farm. From there the couple moved to a small farm on Congress Road near Wooster, where he still did some veterinary practicing.

092-200-1923
142/
172/

During 1936, two children, Arthur Jr. and Alice Flory, came to live with Dr. and Mrs. Swarts. The children's father had been a brother to Wesley's mother, but by this time both parents had passed away, so the children were taken into the Swarts home and raised as their own. To the children the foster father was known as "Uncle Dora." As of 1994, both children still reside in their hometown of Wooster.

Dr. Swarts died on December 19, 1939 in an automobile accident. He was alone in the car and traveling west on US 30, apparently going home, when the car swerved and squarely hit a cement bridge. He was killed instantly. Dr. Swarts is buried in Lot 27 in the Wooster Cemetery along with his wife, who died in 1972.

Joel Beiler

8 /
16 /
107 /
146 /

Joel Beiler made his appearance at Charm on one of his traveling excursions throughout the country during the early 1900s. Meeting Mose J. Keim, he struck it off well with him. The sympathetic Charm businessman was engaged in carpentry, sawmilling, and a planing mill, and gave Beiler, a bachelor, employment. Mose overlooked Beiler's somewhat handicapped speech, poor hearing and lack of education, and thus developed a strong friendship with the Pennsylvania native.

Joel was born in 1859 at Lancaster, Pennsylvania to Johannes (1816 – 1892) and Lydia Hertzler (1820 – 1874) Beiler. To some, Joel was considered a deaf mute, and later he confided to his friends at Charm that at home he was considered *naet ganz schmaet* (not quite smart). Therefore, he was denied an education. When he arrived in Holmes County in his fifties, he was unable to read or write.

Intending to help him, Mose Keim wrote to his family, suggesting that it would be wiser to use his money to build a home for him rather than have him continue traveling and ending up broke. He asked the family to send $20,000 so that he could help Joel get established. The Pennsylvania relatives were, at first, greatly displeased by the enormous amount of money to be sent to Ohio, but they readily accepted when they learned that Mose had mistakenly added a zero and that the intended amount was actually $2,000.

V84-
107-
1915

In 1915, .85 acre was purchased from Emanuel D. Oswald along the east side of town, where a house was placed for Joel. The home today is owned by Joe D. Erb and is immediately east of the Harness Shop.

Though limited in education, Joel became able to understand the function of a carpenter's square. With the help of his employer, he got along well with the carpenter crew. In due time, Joel needed a barn on the small property, and did the layout and framing himself. Rumors were heard that Beiler was not able to fit the frame properly, but once the building was erected, everything fell into place except the side roof rafters, which he had shortened from the original length. Much to the surprise of everyone, Joel Beiler was able to build a barn for himself.

8 /

Probably the most often recalled incident concerning the bachelor was his rice cooking episode. Since he had great taste for the cooked grain, he came into the store one day saying, "I could eat rice three times a day, how much do I need?" The store owner, Bill Mast's son Harold, was at the counter that day and amusedly told the gentleman, "Oh, about three pounds. It's three pounds for a quarter." Joel, in his hunger for rice, readily bought the three pounds and went on his way home.

That evening, Mrs. Sara Ann Mast, who lived across the street from Beiler, went up to his pump to get water for supper. Hearing a commotion on the inside, she overheard Joel repeating, "*Un fa chantich, rice, rice, rice!*" (Oh, my goodness, rice, rice, rice!) Upon entering the smoke filled kitchen, she found that he had put the three pounds in one large dipper. Once the cooking rice had puffed up and the pot was overflowing, Joel began hurriedly filling containers of all descriptions with the enormous amount of rice. Joel, later relating the incident, would repeat in his broken language, "*Baumlich rice.*"

130 /

Because of Beiler's hearing problem, his fellow workers on the carpenter crew would sometimes take advantage of him for their own amusement. When working on a job, the crew would often stay for a whole week because of the length of time it took to travel with horse and carriage. After the week's work was done and it was Beiler's turn to use his horse and rig to work, the men climbed aboard for the return trip home. With Joel sitting up front driving, the men on the back would urge the horse to amazing speed. It was Beiler's thought that the frisky horse was just anxious to get home. However, while he would be hanging on the reins and talking to his horse, a soft whistle and giddap from the men on the back, that was not heard by Beiler, would get the horse into another burst of speed. As Joel tired from tugging on the lines, he would let them loose and say, "Okay, now run if you don't have any sense," and the returning carpenter gang was in for a wild ride.

Once, at Charm, his weak hearing almost caused him serious or fatal injury. He was at the Keim Brothers' sawmill in town and, unknown to him, a log began rolling down the slope toward him. Some others, seeing the oncoming log, shouted a warning, but Joel never heard their well meant cry. Seconds before the impact, he noticed the danger he was in. He jumped straight up in the air and the loose log rolled under him, as he narrowly escaped from its path.

107 /

During Joel's stay at Charm, he attempted to make a perpetual motion device. The setup was made with wheels and balls that acted as weights, but despite his efforts, the machine never kept in motion. He named it *Die Ewig Unruhe* (The Eternal Unrest). His employer, Mose J. Keim, once told him that the name was not proper. Joel seriously disagreed.

Joel was often involved in some kind of amusement around town, and was a well accepted character. His employer, Mose, had one son, Roman, and Joel could not pronounce the young boy's name because of his speech problem. He would relate to Roman's name as *baumlich wieschta nameh* (very ugly name).

One day in town the store attendant, young Harold Mast, snapped a picture of Joel. Joel took after Harold and chased him through the store aisles yelling, *"Du nat in da himmel kommst!"* (You are not going to get to heaven.) Later, Harold showed Joel the picture and told him that when he was no longer here, we would know what he looked like.

8 /

With Beiler's interest in carpentry, he was making sparrow traps and bird houses. The unique bird house which stood in the center of the intersection in Charm was made by him (see p. 28). Joel placed one of his traps along the northeast street corner at the center of town. He mounted the trap on a tube and designed it so that the birds would fall down through the opening. A small glass window at the bottom of the tube allowed him to see if he had caught anything.

As the Pennsylvania native reached his sixties, he began having heart problems and accordingly moved to the Mose L. Yoders, a mile northeast of Charm. Though not related, the Yoders were friends, and divided their living room and cared for him during his sickness. On December 16, 1921, the 62-year-old single gentleman, who had later in life become attached to Charm, died of heart failure. A funeral service was held at the Yoder farm, then the body was transported to Bird-in-Hand, Pennsylvania. At Lancaster county, a second service was held, with a Mr. Glick and ministers D. J. A. Miller, John B. Miller, and Robert Troyer of Holmes County in attendance. Joel is buried in the Beiler Cemetery, near Ronks, along with other members of the family.

16 /
50 / 12-29-1921
100 / 1-12-1922

After his death, the property was sold to Amos Helmuth, a fur buyer and taxi driver. It is owned today by Joe D. Erb.

U 91-356-1922

Bernice Unger

Who was Bernice Unger?
This question came up numerous times during the past number of years. To various older people, Bernice is remembered as a schoolmate at Charm School, but very little of her family or later life was known.

According to school records, Bernice attended the two story school from 1914 to 1921. During these years, she was living with her grandparents, Peter and Mary Anna (Miller) Hershberger, who lived halfway between Charm and Beck's Mills.

30 /

Bernice was born March 5, 1907 at Grand Rapids, Minnesota to Edward and Katie (Hershberger) Unger. Twenty days after her birth, the mother

206 /
p. 97

died. As evident by the school records, when Bernice started school, she was cared for at her grandparents' home. Further identification of her family reveals the grandmother to be a sister of Andy I. Miller, the well known bachelor of Charm known as "Isaac Andy."

At eighteen years of age, she married Enos Roy Hochstetler. At age 23, she died on September 19, 1930 at Ragersville, survived by her husband and three children.

Edgar Ott

Edgar Ott, better known as "Red Eddie" because of his complexion, appeared in Charm in 1928. He was under the care and guardianship of Waldo Getz, who came to Charm as storekeeper in 1928. Eddie was a son of Anna Getz, a sister to Waldo, who had married William Ott.

9 /
30 /
119 /
121 /
345 /

56 /

Eddie Ott with dog, and Dick, son of Perry Miller.

Edgar's mother died during his childhood, and since Waldos had no children of their own, they took the young boy into their home. He attended Charm School from 1928 to '31, from sixth to eighth grade.

The lad's character often displayed a hint of mischievousness, accented by his red hair and freckles. For example, Eddie would get a thrill seeing how close to the electric wires he could toss the town cats by placing a foot under the kitty's belly and giving it a shove skyward.

When Eddie grew to adulthood, he enlisted in the U.S. Army. On his return from the army, he was drinking heavily. He married Esther Faquay, whom he later divorced. Living at Coshocton, he worked on the railroad; or, as an acquaintance later recalled, "He was working on the railroad during the daytime and drinking at night, which eventually caused his death." His former wife moved to Texas and there remarried, having no children from the first marriage.

Jonas E. Troyer

DJH-
6370
42/
112/
346/

Jonas (DJH 6370), a son of Emanuel and Catherine Troyer, grew up on a typical Amish farm on the south edge of Charm. At age 26, he accompanied Jacob J. Yoder (OAG 2788) to North Dakota to Yoder's cousins to help with the wheat harvest during the summer of 1902. That fall, Jonas decided to stay in the western state. Jacob, with dismay, came back to Holmes County wishing he could have brought his friend along home. During his stay in North Dakota, Jonas married Bertha RaDue of Donnybrook, North Dakota in 1902.

In early married life, the Troyers moved to Charm, where they resided in the house on the south edge of town, where the cheese factory was later built. Bertha began work as a seamstress for the community. However, she was not content living at Charm, so they returned to North Dakota.

Eventually, marital problems arose, and their marriage finally ended in divorce. Bertha got custody of their only child, a son, Verna. For many years, Jonas was at Duluth, Minnesota, until he returned to his native town in Holmes County. On this occasion he moved into the lean-to formerly built on the east side of the Christ Hummel house for "Isaac Andy" when Andy was not able to care for himself. The structure had a ground level garage with the living quarters above, in an uninsulated, bare stud and siding outside wall. Here Jonas made his home while engaging in a taxi service with a Plymouth car, which he parked in the lower part of his dwelling.

On November 1, 1942, at 66 years of age, Jonas died in his single room dwelling. Prior to his death, he had said that he would like to have an Amish

112/

Jonas E. Troyer ("Jay Linn")

funeral. At the time of his passing away, Sol Schlabach, an Amish bishop of the Martin's Creek area, was contacted. Schlabach, along with Rev. Simon Sommers, speaking in English, conducted the funeral service in the house where Troyer had grown up as a boy. Burial was made on the home farm cemetery (CD-0-6), presently owned by his nephew, Levi A. Miller.

Otto Scherer

14/
76/
293/

Otto Scherer was a well known individual around Charm up to his death in the 1980s. Ott was the only living child of Michael and Barbara Scherer and was born in Mechanic Township of Holmes County, two miles south of Charm, on the present Levi V. Raber farm. Since his parents' death (Barbara on November 1, 1950 and Mike previously) and Otto moving closer to Charm, very little remains of the old home place. The house is completely gone, while the old barn still stands, but is not in good repair.

When Ott left the home place in the 1960s, he moved into a 12' x 14' building on skids a mile southeast of Charm. This was on the Andy L. Miller property at the "handle shop." Some years later, the shanty, which had originally been built as a chicken house by local carpenter John Lahm, was moved to the west side of the Raber Lumber Co. driveway.

In his compact little dwelling, a single bed stood in one corner with sleeping bag and covers piled on for warmth. A wood burning stove, close to the bottom of the bed, kept the small quarters within livable temperatures during the cold months. Overloaded shelves and a kitchen cabinet filled the small room. Overhead hung fishing equipment and racks of drying ginseng and golden seal, which he took great pleasure in digging. A manual grinder was fastened to the cabinet top and was used to grind the dried roots that he prepared for the market.

At his bed or in the vehicle usually lay his loaded handgun, in which he put great trust. Once, after a warning from an officer for having a loaded gun in the car, Ott replied, "What do you want me to do? If they take my money, tell 'em to wait till I have the gun loaded?!"

Cleanliness and tidiness was unheard of in the unkept dwelling, and Ott was frequently aided with neighborhood cleaning and washings.

He held jobs at Pallet All, Yoder Clutch Corp., the handle factory at Andy's Craft Shop, and Raber Lumber Company.

Ott was a dedicated fisherman of the Doughty and Killbuck Creeks, and many hours of stories were related to a neighbor, friend, or passerby as they stopped for a chat with the old bachelor. During the 1960s, he drove a camper pickup. With this he could go hunting or fishing as he pleased and could cook and repose while abroad. He was especially fond of turtle meat, and many snappers were given to him by friends of the community.

Mike Scherer and Barbara (Schweitzer) Scherer

121/

Otto Scherer at the door of his pickup camper with his prized garfish caught along the Doughty Creek in the 1960s.

It is reported that during his younger years, Otto was once caught in trouble, but straightened things out in a mannerly way. Albert and Joe Keim had taken over the limestone crushing operation after the death of their brothers, Abe and Dan, who died of the flu in 1920. The steam powered operation was located $1^1/_2$ miles west of Charm on today's Joe M. Miller farm. One Monday morning as they came to work, it was discovered that the tool shanty was missing most of its picks and bars, along with two cases of dynamite. Nephew Atlee Keim, a young lad, heard of the incident and recalled that his brother Billy had come upon a stranger while on a walk in the woods, who had given him a dynamite cap. Hearing this, Al and nephew Sanford Keim went to see Billy at the Charm School and came to the conclusion that the theft had been committed by Ott Scherer. After Billy was excused from school, he was taken with a group of neighbors to the Scherer residence. Once at the home, Sanford and the schoolboy started for the house while the others stayed hidden behind a stone fence. The two greeted Ott as he was splitting wood. They began talking about hunting, and asked if he owned a dog and a gun, to which he replied, "Oh, yes." In the meantime, young Billy nodded to Sanford that this was the man. After Scherer showed his gun, they began target practice, and as Sanford had the gun in his hand for a round of shooting, he signaled to the men at the stone wall to come. With the gun out of Otto's hands, all involved felt safer. With the rest of the group now present, Ott was asked about the missing tools. He readily admitted to carrying them off and said he had intended to use them, then bring them back again. With the rough terrain and the $1^1/_2$ miles to carry the tools, he had put forth quite a bit of work and effort. The men decided to give him until 9:00 P.M. that evening to return the merchandise or the authorities would

8/

🌿

be notified. He carried out the plan as intended, bringing back the tools late in the evening. After staying for a short visit, he started on his way back home.

During his last years spent at Charm, he was often seen walking to town for visits or groceries, which often included his favorite – a quart of half and half milk.

156/

In his later years, he was admitted to the County Home, where he resided until his death in June of 1985. He is buried there.

Ezra Miller

DBH
7842
15/
92/

From the early to the mid 1900s, Ezra Miller was a well known figure in Charm and vicinity. He lived along the former Port Washington Road, one mile northwest of Beck's Mills on lands now owned by Eli D. Miller.

Ezra was born January 25, 1883 at Needy, Oregon and married Esther Mishler at LaGrange, Indiana in 1910. Four children were born to them, of whom the two younger girls, Laona Fannie and Annie Mae, are remembered by the neighborhood. A son, Louis Moses, died in 1923 at eight years of age, and the oldest child, Leroy Freman, settled in Oregon.

The mother died at a young age around the 1930s, after a long illness. Thereafter, Ezra and the two daughters lived on the small acreage northwest of Beck's Mills until the girls married. He then stayed alone until the 1960s, when he moved in with a daughter who lived close to Sugarcreek, the Andy Schlabachs.

Ezra was, perhaps, better known throughout the area as "Gaysa Ezra" because of the goat herd

389/

which he cared for. He raised them for meat and profit.

In the neighborhood, he would work for people, cutting brush or mowing pasture with a scythe. The widower attended the Martins Creek Mennonite Church and, at times, would use neighbor Ben G. Yoder's horse and buggy to attend services. At Charm, he was a well known figure. He would walk the few miles to catch the bus going through town to Millersburg. A wait on the store porch could bring a visit with townspeople, which they enjoyed, along with his familiar, distinctive laughter.

Ezra moved to Sugarcreek in the early 1960s, and soon thereafter the house of a former neighbor Roy J. Miller, burned down. Shortly after the fire, he came to the Millers and offered the unfortunate family any useful items they could salvage from his now deserted house at Beck's Mills.

Thomas McPherson

22/
p.33
21/
91/

Around the 1920s, the store at Beck's Mills was operated by a Thomas McPherson. Aside from storekeeping, he had a meat route throughout the area, along which he sold varieties of meat. During this time, he converted a touring car to a pickup type vehicle to better facilitate his needs.

To the southeast of Beck's Mills, approximately two miles away, lived Walter Kaser, who was always using new ideas to come up with his own inventions. One of these was a free wheeling automobile transmission, which would allow the drive shaft to run freely when its speed was higher than that of the engine. After Kaser completed the transmission, McPherson decided to install it in his meat truck to test drive it.

According to reports, the new transmission was used in the converted car for two years, then Kaser went to a Cleveland car company in hopes of selling his new idea to them. They did not appear interested in purchasing the new invention, but they agreed to see a demonstration of the transmission's performance. The automobile company's skilled mechanics, present at the exhibition, got a good idea of the mechanical workings of the new device, but they were still not interested in purchasing the right to manufacture it. Nevertheless, the year after the transmission was demonstrated in Cleveland by the Holmes Countian, they manufactured, and put their new cars on the market with, a free wheeling transmission.

Since Wal Kaser had not patented the device, the company simply stole the new idea away from him, leaving him empty handed.

The free wheeling transmission faded from the

•

market within a few years, but it was a forerunner of the automatic transmission.

Benjamin Plank

A peddler making occasional visits through the area was Benjamin Plank, the fish peddler. Using an enclosed, horse drawn buggy hack, he sold numerous varieties of fish to his customers. Plank was originally from Lancaster County, Pennsylvania. He married a Holmes County girl, Lizzie Schlabach, a daughter of Abe Schlabach. Benjamin was a practical joker, and it is said that at their wedding, he brought another girl to his Pennsylvania friends and introduced her as his wife-to-be.

171/
183/

Benjamin and Lizzie lived two miles east of Charm on the Homer Brown place in the 1930s, then they moved ³/₄ mile south of the Holmes Lumber and Building Center, west of Berlin.

Benjamin's wife died January 7, 1948. After her death he returned to Pennsylvania, where he died on April 21, 1956, and was brought to Holmes County for burial. The Planks are buried two miles northeast of Berlin (CD-K-12).

Plank's fish wagon was later used by the Andy Burkholder family to take their children to school.

John N. Yoder

It is fitting to add a short sketch of an area transient, the late John N. Yoder, who was widely known among the Amish, of which he was a member. John was born in Kansas, on August 15, 1905, to Noah and Elida Yoder. He remained single throughout his life. Because of financial hardships early in life, he turned to a lackluster lifestyle, which earned him the name "Slow Johnny."

100/10-
17-1990
171/
288/

In the Holmes County area, he had cousins and friends with whom he stayed, helping with work and chores. At Charm, he was a well known figure, traveling through or coming to town to catch the bus, often accompanied by his brown paper shopping bags.

Having lived the greater part of his life in Holmes County, he chose to stay there during his later years, also. Doing no manual labor as he grew older, he had one day humorously written in his diary, "Don't know what I did. Guess I worked." Many kind gestures were rendered toward the gentleman; he was given room and board during his visits and stays.

During the mid 1980s, a badly infected toe required amputation. In 1984, soon after the operation, John took residence at the Holmes County Home. He died at the Home on October 11, 1990 at 85 years of age. After funeral services at the Melvin A. Raber residence, John was laid to rest at the Yoder cemetery, southeast of Farmerstown.

From his family, one brother, Benjamin, survived him. He was a resident of the nursing home at Walnut Creek and passed away ten days after the death of John.

100/10-
24-1990

Lydia P. Hershberger

Lydia P. Hershberger came to live at Charm during her feeble age when she needed nursing care. In 1967, she moved in with Mattie Miller and daughter Amanda, who lived at the south edge of town. At that time, an adjoining room was attached to the Miller home for Lydia's dwelling. While living here, the elderly woman made carpets as a pastime whenever her health permitted. The rugs were made of tightly braided carpet rags that were stitched into round or oval throw rugs. The various colored handiwork made a long lasting carpet.

42/
171/
100/5-
10-1978

Lydia Hershberger was born May 2, 1896 at Charm to Peter and Mary (Yoder) Hershberger (DJH 5654). For many years, she did housework for the Dan Crilow family of Martin's Creek, until moving to the Charm area. In 1965, she moved

169/

Violet Kaser, left, and Fannie Hummel, right, at Charm School.

onto the "Ben Kurtz" property half a mile south of Charm, then by 1967 she moved in with the Millers. While living there she suffered a broken hip, and was later admitted to the nursing home at Walnut Creek. She died May 7, 1978 and was buried at the Hershberger family cemetery a mile east of Charm.

56/

Sylvia Oswald, David Erb and Ab Schlabach

172/

Dr. Wesley Theodore and Muriel Ruth (Eusey) Swarts

374/

27/

❧

Storekeeper Isaac J. Miller family in front of their home at Charm, ca 1895. Front left: Charles, Mary (Lint) Miller, Nettie, and Isaac. Back left: Fanny, Franklin, Cora, Edward, Anna and Ida. The photograph is probably that of Herbert, who is missing from the picture. Another son, William, died at eight months of age.

Arletus and Priscilla Miller

Paul and Esther Miller with son Bob

56/

First Telephone Line

In early 1896, the anticipated telephone line to Charm was becoming a reality. In March, arrangements were made by the Millersburg Telephone Company to connect the towns of Charm, Farmerstown, New Bedford and Baltic with the Millersburg exchange. The required money for the construction of the line had been quickly raised and the needed poles were contracted for.

50/2-20-1896

50/3-5-1896

This branch was to connect with the main line on the Millersburg and Berlin road at the Charm road intersection (US 62 – SR 557). In the middle of March, the poles were distributed along the route for service to be made available soon thereafter.

50/3-12-1896

In the spring of 1902, Noah Hershberger, the implement dealer at Charm, placed a telephone line from his residence west to Troyer's Hollow, a distance of 1¹/₂ miles.

100/4-8-1902

Buster, Bambi and Doe Doe

Buster and Bambi were introduced to Charm in the early 1970s and have been favorite attractions to residents as well as to out-of-town visitors. The graceful deer provide year-round amusement in their chain link enclosure along the east edge of town. A second doe, known as Doe Doe, has since been added to the small herd.

129/

❧

189/

Deer pen at Charm

Their owner, Joe D. Erb, built a pen on his property around 1971 and accordingly has had deer on the lot ever since. Interestingly, the game animals have reproduced while in captivity, as each spring is highlighted with the birth of a few white spotted fawns. Also, yearly, the buck deer sheds its antlers, which are displayed by Erb at his sporting goods store in town.

Whitetail deer are native to the area, and have dramatically increased in numbers during the past two decades. The earlier encroachment of humans into wildlife habitat had forced the deer to almost completely vanish from the area. A quarter of a century ago, it was quite unusual to find a deer track through the immediate area. But because of sound wildlife management, the deer population has risen sharply, and they have adapted well to the smaller wooded lands found in this part of Holmes County.

229/
367/
383/
p.18

The first controlled deer hunting season for Holmes County was 1952, and the first year that the county reported a separate deer kill was 1957, with a total of 33. In the late 1960s, only three deer were taken during the gun season, whereas during the 1993–'94 bow and gun seasons, a total of 2,168 deer were harvested in Holmes County.

Charm Merchant Days

265/

Since 1983, Charm Merchant Days have been an annual event. Each year they are held on Friday and Saturday of the second week of October. During the yearly two-day bargain shopping, participating merchants offer discount prices and specials to help celebrate the occasion. Since the second year of Charm Days, a great attraction is the drawing for a Grand Prize of $1,000.00. Sponsored by the merchants, its registration to win also includes chances for prizes from each place of business. Other activities during the years have included: a two-day benefit bake sale; a flea market at the school yard; yard sales throughout town; a school benefit including old fashioned chili and fry pies; and Raber's barbecued chicken. On Friday evenings, an old time fiddling program is held, with former local fiddler Jeff Geohring serving as

56/

Busy street scene, Charm Days – 1987

The Grant helicopter landing during the 1994 Charm Merchant Days.

"master of ceremonies" and includes his own "Red Mule String Band." Various other performers have been: well known fiddler and violin maker Clifford Hardesty of West Lafayette; master fiddler Kenny Sidle of Newark, who has won national recognition for his performances; and veteran state champion fiddler Michelle Blizzard of Frazeysburg. An added interest during the Friday evening events has been guest speakers Ralph Aling and Delbert Harmon, both former Charm residents and historians.

For a number of years, "The Countrysiders" and the "Holmes County M&Ms" performed country music Saturday noon prior to the afternoon auction at the bank parking lot. In 1994, music was provided by the "Heartland Express" and "The Cherry Ridge Boys."

Also, on Saturday afternoon of 1993 and '94, a Grant Life Flight helicopter from Coshocton came to Charm to display the aircraft and explain the availability of life flight services.

A Wooly Worm Derby has been getting exciting attention during the past few years. On Friday afternoon, the lower grade children of Charm School have been competing with their favorite caterpillar crawling up a string.

To complete the Charm Days, on Saturday afternoon at two o'clock an auction is held behind the bank. Items sold are donated by the Charm residents and businesses. Since 1991, a pie contest has been held on Saturday, and throughout the auction the pies are also sold. At the latter part of the sale, the winning entries are auctioned off. Bids have been raised to $450.00 for a pie. The last items to be sold are the Charm Historical plates. Each year, the first five of the 155 plates made are sold,

189/

which are usually the only remaining plates available for that year. The highest price for a plate has been $375.00. All the money raised at the yearly auction is placed in the Charm Community Share-N-Care Fund, which is a local charity helping people in need.

The final attraction of the day is the prize drawing of all the participating merchants and the announcement of the lucky winner claiming the $1,000.00.

$1,000.00 Winners

295/

1984	Amos Swantz, Millersburg, Ohio
1985	Enos M. Miller, Sugarcreek, Ohio
1986	Robert E. Stansburg, Newark, Ohio
1987	Marilyn E. Troyer, Sugarcreek, Ohio
1988	Derrick Sampsell, Sandusky, Ohio
1989	Carl and Amy Pecoraro, Cleveland, Ohio
1990	Charles Andrews, Killbuck, Ohio
1991	Ivan L. Raber, Millersburg, Ohio
1992	Vernon M. Stutzman, Millersburg, Ohio
1993	John O'Palka, Georgetown, Pennsylvania
1994	Susan Ellen Yoder, Millersburg, Ohio

Charm Plate Prices

265/

1990	Charm School House #3
#1	$155.00
#2	$160.00
#3	$175.00
#4	$160.00
#5	$160.00
1991	Charm Flour Mills
#1	$120.00
#2	$55.00
#3	$30.00
#4	$40.00
#5	$35.00
1992	Charm Store
#1	$350.00
#2	$45.00
#3	$35.00
#4	$20.00
#5	$25.00
1993	Keim Bros.
#1	$350.00
#2	$375.00
#3	$220.00
#4	$220.00
#5	$260.00
1994	Charm Cheese Co.
#1	$275.00
#2	$175.00
#3	$50.00
#4	$50.00
#5	$35.00

Pie Contest Winners

1991

1st – Creme Cheese Nut – Sara Ann Mast 171/
2nd – Swedish Apple – Mrs. Ervin L. Raber 265/
3rd – Ground Cherry – Mrs. John O. Miller, Jr.
Heritage – Mince – Mattie Mast
Holmes Co. – Ground Cherry – Mrs. John O. Miller
Best Decorated – Cherry Nut Topping – Mrs. Abe A. Mast

1992
1st – Creme Vanilla Crumb – Mrs. Abe Mast
2nd – Pecan – Katie O. Keim
3rd – Sour Cream Apple – Sara Ann Mast
Heritage – Grape – Mrs. David J. Troyer
Holmes County – Pineapple Cream Cheese –
   Mrs. Emanuel Miller
1993
1st – Sour Cream Raisin – Mrs. John O. Miller
2nd – Cherry – Maudie Raber
3rd – Pineapple Cheese – Mrs. Ivan J. Miller
Heritage – Vanilla Crumb – Mrs. Emanuel Miller
Holmes County – Custard – Betty Raber
1994
1st – Sour Cream Pecan – Mrs. Ivan J. Miller
2nd – Pear – Mrs. John O. Miller
3rd – Peach Pineapple – Mrs. John O. Miller, Jr.
Heritage – Caramel Raisin – Mrs. Emanuel Miller
Holmes County – Grape – Mrs. David J. Troyer

Wooly Worm Derby Winners
1992 – Leroy R. Miller
1993 – David Allen Troyer
1994 – Laura A. Raber

Charm Historical Mural

The Charm Historical Mural originated from the owner of Brookline Antiques, Brooks Harris, who was inspired to present to the town a glimpse of past history and thereby aid the Charm Community Share and Care Fund. The idea was to portray a mural of the town in an early setting and to help the fund with one-dollar donations collected from the public. His goal was to provide an educational and historical project as well as financial support for the community's needy.

With this goal in mind, Brooks, a retired West Holmes high school teacher, contacted one of his former pupils, the widely known artist, Claude Ruston Baker. They drew up a contract with the agreement that the project be completed by March 1, 1990. In the meantime, Mr. Harris also contacted Vernon and Ivan Miller for help in supplying historical material. After numerous discussions and meetings between them and the charm residents, the mural was begun.

The 5' x 30' painting was done in Brooks' garage, with "Rusty" commencing in the middle of December, 1989. The main painting was completed in the second week of January, 1990.

The central part of the panel was painted from an old photograph taken soon after the store and post office burned in 1894. A shoe shop and barn known to have been in the town center during the mural's 1875 – 1920 time period have been included in the scene. To the left of the town's center, a gas well drilling rig was added. No actual picture of the rig was available, so what could be

accumulated from that time period by the artist was used. In the upper left corner was depicted a barn raising, a common event throughout the period. The artist has also added signs to buildings and shops to identify them more clearly in the setting.

On February 2, 1990, the mural was brought to the town and mounted in the former Oren Keim barn that was converted to Brookline Antiques and E and E Woodcrafts. The artist completed the finishing touches and dated and signed the painting on February 23, 1990.

Presently, the painting is displayed in a unique setting, amid the antiques in the framed barn. Above and below the picture, Brooks has displayed various tools used in the mural's time period, while a small museum in the barn's granary offers memorabilia relating to the businesses and history in the earl town. The mural, antiques and related items on display have offered the community and visitor a chance to step into a museum of Charm that has never previously been available nor exhibited.

189/

Charm historical mural – ca 1875 – 1920

Charm Merchant Days historical plates displayed among early Charm advertising at Brookline Antiques.

Charm Historical Plates

Prior to the 1990 Charm Merchant Days, the merchants decided to have a commemorative plate made. The proceeds from the plates would be put into the Charm Share-N-Care Fund. The plate's first scene chosen was the two story school building that was replaced in 1938. Its appearance on the initial plate was fitting, as there was, perhaps, no place in all of Charm history more cherished by so many people as the "old two story."

Each year, 155 plates are made, with a new scene every year. Later plates have featured the Charm Flour Mills, the Charm Store, Keim Lumber Co., and the Charm Cheese Factory.

On the plate's front is a neat sketching of the featured building, with minor background details. Its reverse side gives a brief commemorative account of its business history. The 8"-diameter gold-rimmed plates were designed and made by Larry Fox of Carrollton, Ohio. The plates are individually numbered and #1 to #5 sold at auction on the Saturday afternoon of Charm Days. Number 6 is displayed at the Commercial and Savings Bank in town. The balance are then divided among the

265/
284/

participating merchants and sold for $13.00 each.

Aside from being collector's items, the plates serve their intended purpose well as a fund raiser. At auction they have ranged in price from $20.00 to $375.00. (A price layout is given in the *Charm Merchant Days* article.)

Unusual Weather and Occurrences

1816 – This was the year of no summer. Snow fell in every month of the year. A severe snow-storm occurred on July 4. Settlers wore winter clothes when they harvested grain.

June 1, 1817 – So hard was the frost that leaves looked as they had been scorched.

June, 1819 – A tornado passed through Mechanic Township. It touched down north of Clark, following the west and northeast branches of Military Creek for some distance, then stayed aloft until it reached present day Shanesville.

May 18, 1825 – A tornado known as the "Burlington Storm" passed through Mechanic and German (Clark) Townships, leaving a path up to a mile wide. It started near Urbana and traveled northeast to Columbiana County.

108/
p.141

108/
p.141
22/
p.76

108/
p.141

❧

108 /
p.142
216 /p.7
217 /
p.160

November 13, 1833 – From approximately 11:00 P.M. to 1:00 A.M., the stars (meteorites) fell from the sky as a heavy snow. They did not shoot across the sky, but appeared as if coming straight down to earth. They lit up the sky in a strange manner.

108 /
p.142

1838 – A severe drought hit the area, causing typhoid fever to spread throughout the country.

108 /
p.142

May 2, 1841 – A violent snowstorm passed through Holmes County.

108 /
p.143
253 /

June 5, 1859 – The most destructive frost ever recorded in Holmes County was so severe that the wheat froze.

253 /

January 7–8–9, 1874 – An ice storm that broke down a large amount of timber hit the area.

108 /
p.143

December, 1877 – Temperatures were in the eighties and nineties during December. On Christmas Day, it rose to the upper nineties, it was remembered as "Summer Christmas."

50 / 4-
25-1901

April, 1881 – Up to two feet of snow fell the first week of April.

253 /

September 6, 9–10–11, 1885 – The corn froze from frost.

22 /p.77
50 / 4-
25-1901

April 16–17–18, 1901 – "The Great Snow" hit the area. The first half of April had been mild spring weather and farmers were busy with field work; oats were being sown at this time.

On Tuesday afternoon of April 16, it began raining, and the rain turned to snow during the night. A heavy snowstorm continued on Wednesday and Thursday, accompanied by occasional rain and high winds. Despite the fact that temperatures never dropped below freezing, the gale piled drifts from eight to fifteen feet deep. Roads were impassable and people were snowbound at home or wherever they happened to be. On level ground, the snow was estimated to be not less than three feet deep.

Local mail routes did not come through until the middle of the following week. East of Charm, children walking to school could touch the telephone wires while walking on drifts. The wet snow clung to the dials of the courthouse clock at Millersburg and clogged its hands so that it didn't run until the following Monday. Some of the grain drills left in the fields from sowing oats were so snow covered that only the handles could be seen. Snow in coves and drifts could still be seen on the tenth of May.

At the time, the older people said it was the worst snowstorm they had ever seen. The storm swept from Canada to Tennessee, causing great damage to railroads, streetcars, and communication systems.

22 /p.78

August 6, 1902 – A hailstorm, approximately 100 yards wide, passed north of Beck's Mills toward Charm on the afternoon of the sixth. All crops within the path of the storm were destroyed. The

hail piled so heavily on the ground that many hailstones could still be seen at noon the next day.

50 / 9-
21-1911

September 14–15, 1911 – On Thursday and Friday morning, a heavy rainstorm occurred that left heavy losses to Holmes and surrounding counties. The greatest damages were in the northeastern part of Holmes County and along the Doughty Creek. Practically all of the bridges along the Doughty were either washed out or taken downstream. At Charm, two bridges were out. Since water power was still being used along the Doughty, four mill dams were washed out. Those were the Wise dam, 1 1/4 miles west of Charm; the Keim dam, a mile west of Charm; the Troyer dam, in Troyer's Hollow; and the Fraelich dam, at Beck's Mills. Some damage was done to the Simon Troyer woolen factory and the Fraelich flour mill. The Keim sawmill, formerly known as the Dannie Miller sawmill, was washed downstream. Roads, fences and farm lands were heavily damaged.

22 /p.78
97 /
p.239

March 23, 1913 – The flood of 1913 resulted from heavy rainfall from Sunday until Tuesday. This flood ended the history of water powered mills along the Doughty Creek, as all the dams were washed out.

50 / 3-
20-1921

March 20, 1921 – On this date it was 81°, and three days in March there was 80° weather.

43 /
71 /
22 /p.78
50 / 8-
9-1935

August 6, 1935 – The flood of 1935 occurred when on Saturday, August 3, a cloudburst swelled the creeks with water and they had not receded to normal when the storm hit three days later. The stage was thus set for heavy flooding.

Around 6:00 P.M., Tuesday, August 6, one of the most severe thunderstorms in the history of Holmes County hit the area. From Tuesday evening until six o'clock Wednesday morning, close to seven inches of rain were recorded. Reportedly, throughout the night fifteen storms swept the area with torrential rain. Constant lightning kept the night illuminated.

At 7:00 P.M., lightning struck the barn of Fred Schnell at the SR 557 – US 62 junction. As news of the fire reached Charm, people headed that way to view the burning structure. Dey Troyer took a load with his car and made the return trip safely, crossing the rising Doughty Creek without difficulty. Among other locals there was farmer Abe J. Mast, who had taken the horse and top hack and picked up some neighbors along the way out. Deciding to return home from the fire, they found the Doughty Creek too high to cross at the Wise's school bridge. Unable to go any farther, the group spent the stormy night at a nearby farm. The next morning, the water was still dangerously high, but the farmers were becoming anxious to get home for milking. Finally, bishop David Miller started across the bridge, holding onto the fence and leading the Mast horse and rig. With a long pole, he searched in front of them for washouts, and in that way was able to cross the turbulent stream. The farmers arrived home around mid morning.

At the bishop's farm, immediately south of Guggisberg Cheese, the cows were stranded in the pasture field on the opposite side of the creek, close to the cheese factory. Not knowing what would be best, he called them, and one by one they jumped into the swollen stream. Rapidly going with the swift current, they passed under a bridge and, surprisingly, all of them climbed out of the water and came in for the overdue milking.

Along the Doughty, from the Wise's bridge to Clark, every bridge was washed out except the one on the Conrad farm. Eleven of fifteen bridges along the creek's entire length were out.

A mile northwest of Charm, the Joe Keims were awakened during the night when a foot tub that was floating in the water in the basement bumped against the cellar ceiling.

In Troyer's Hollow, its residents were met with disaster. Waters roaring through the narrow ravine rose rapidly and violently. The Floyd Kaser family, who lived in the remodeled Elijah Aultman house on the west side of the creek, escaped through the back door and took refuge with neighbor Peter J. Troyer. Amos Ledrich wasn't convinced as easily and wouldn't leave the house. Flood water filled their basement and was over the first floor. This flood caused the residents of Troyer's Hollow to eventually move out.

At Charm, people recalling the '35 flood said you could read a newspaper throughout the whole night because of the constant lightning. Some said if the end of the world would be coming with water, they would have thought it was coming then. The downpour was described as more like a heavy splash than rain.

1951 – '52 Winter – The Wooster Experiment Station reported 66 inches of snow during this winter. *11/2-21-1994*

July 4, 1969 – A heavy thunderstorm hit the Wayne–Holmes–Tuscarawas County area. Locally, 9¹/₂ inches of rain were reported that night, and totaled twelve inches during the next week. The storms would seemingly pass over, then come back again from the east with more intensity. Many bridges were washed out, and some roads became impassable. From the Wayne–Holmes County area, 21 persons drowned during the flooding. *218/255/11/7-22-1969*

In Troyer's Hollow, two parties were camping when the flood waters rose. Wallace and Mary Ann Schlabach and friends narrowly escaped from their camping trailer before it was washed downstream, ending up a mile below Beck's Mills. Jack Stauffer, Bruce Miller and Errol Miller of Sugar Creek had

pitched a tent on the grounds and were awakened when the high water reached their tent. Wading through knee deep water to safety, they took refuge in a trailer (later used as a post office at Charm) during the storm. The constant lightning allowed them to see the top of their submerged car above the water. As the creek rose, they beheld the Schlabachs' trailer bobbing downstream with its battery lights still on, and did not know if anyone was inside or not.

Flood cleanup efforts remain unforgettable throughout the stricken areas of the county. Killbuck was hit hardest of the Holmes County towns, with 95 percent of the village under water.

January 28, 1977 – On Friday forenoon, a heavy snowstorm arrived, with blizzard conditions. Roads were opened with locally owned wheel loaders. More snow later made opening roads worse, as the banks were piled so high that there was almost no room to dump more snow. Throughout the month, the area had around thirty inches of snow. It was below zero for sixteen days, and did not go above freezing at any time. On January 13 it was 19° below zero, and January 17 it was 22° below, with a chill factor of -51°. *218/*

January 26, 1978 – At 3:00 A.M. it was raining and 42°, then the temperature dropped to 10°. A heavy snow fell and there were forty to sixty miles per hour winds by 6:00 A.M. It turned cold so fast that the rain water froze on the road as it was running off. During the day, the temperature dropped to 0°, with a -40° to -80° chill factor. This was the biggest snowstorm in the history of Ohio, with almost everything shut down. Holmes and Wayne Counties were hit the hardest in the state. At Wooster, Ohio the barometric pressure dropped to a record low of 28.38 inches. *218/11/2-21-1994*

September 14, 1979 – The area had approximately six inches of rain overnight, which caused flash floods. There was over two feet of water in the basement of Charm Plumbing. *218/285/*

December 30, 1979 – With the temperature around freezing, a heavy fog set in and froze on the landscape in a crystal brilliance which lasted for a few days. *218/*

June 7, 1980 – A tornado passed north of Mt. Hope and left extensive damage. *218/*

July 11, 1980 – The fourth hailstorm of the summer in the Charm area left heavy crop damage. Some hailstones were the size of walnuts. *218/*

July 27, 1980 – A light earthquake at 2:50 P.M. was felt in Holmes County and throughout Ohio. *218/*

June 9, 1981 – Heavy rain caused flash floods in Holmes County, and a tornado passed through the Lake Buckhorn area and headed east toward Charm. Some trees were uprooted at Charm, which was at the tail end of the storm. *218/*

❧

218/   **January 21, 1984** – The temperature was -24° and people were putting up ice that was 14" thick.

218/   **January 20, 1985** – The temperature was -24°. With the low temperature and the wind, the chill factor was reported as -55°.

218/   **February 14, 1985** – A heavy snow fell, and roads were opened with wheel loaders.

218/   **1985 – '86** – During the fall of 1985 and again in the spring of 1986, Halley's Comet was visible. The comet, on a 75-year orbit, was last seen in 1910. The display was not as brilliant as was expected by astronomers. On November 16, 1985, it was sighted as a faint speck of light. On March 22, 1986, the comet could be seen with the naked eye. It had a tail 2° in length. During the following month, it gradually faded.

218/   **January 28, 1986** – At 11:50 A.M., an earthquake showing five on the Richter scale was felt through Ohio. Effects were noticed in eight surrounding states.

218/   **April 4, 1987** – The area was snowed in with 30° weather, a heavy snow, and a strong north wind. Many roads were closed, with sixteen inches of snow reported. The following day, the snow was rapidly melting, with drizzles and 60° weather.

218/ *293/*   **1988** – Drought conditions were evident over a large part of the United States. Charm had .4 inch of rain on June 16 and 1.1 inch on July 18. Throughout the period it was very warm, with a low humidity, allowing temperatures to rise even higher. It was 104° on June 25 and July 8. Three days in July registered 108°. Some mornings were so dry, people could have put up hay. Crops looked poor and the water supply was low.

After rains came again in late July, in August farmers put up good yields of second and third cutting hay.

Despite the record summer temperatures, August was the only month in 1988 with no frost. At Charm, there was frost July 1 and September 7.

218/   **1989** – The extreme rainfall during May and June was quite opposite of last year. It was so wet, it was hard to get crops planted or the first cutting hay made. It rained twenty days in May. In later summer, it was, again, nearly as dry as last year.

218/   **1990** – This year was one of the wettest years on record, with the rainfall of the area around 50"; the average is 38". Because of the mild weather in the fall and again in December, some apple trees had blossoms, and on New Year's Day dandelions were blooming.

218/   **1991 – '92** – It was dry and drought conditions existed from the summer of 1991 until August of 1992, when the Weather Service announced that

the water table was back to normal. During July of '92, more than 10" of rain were recorded in the Charm area, including 2.6" in thirty minutes on the 24th. Timely rains throughout the '92 summer kept vegetation growing, and no brown or dry lawns were noticeable. Harvesting grain during the fall was a problem, as some clover seeded fields had grown almost as high as the grain shocks.

218/   **March 18, 1992** – Rain developed, along with a cold east wind, which made for very icy conditions. In the Charm area, the glittering scene, especially on the windswept ridges, lasted from Wednesday the eighteenth until Saturday.

11/3-15-1993   **March 13, 1993** – 'The Blizzard of '93' was a winter storm that extended from Canada south to Cuba. With winds over forty miles per hour, the northern part of the country received heavy snows, while hurricane winds, rainfall and unusually cold weather was experienced along the southeastern coast; Florida also had tornados. Over 200 storm-related deaths were reported. The Charm area had around five inches of snow. All roads in the county were closed by the Sheriff's Department at 7:35 P.M.

218/   **1993 – '94 Winter** – Snow accumulation began December 20 and drifts were still evident by the second week of March. This was an old-fashioned winter, with lots of snow. On January 19, temperatures were reported from 24 to 40 below 0°. On January 21, Charm had -30°. On February 8 and 9, a major ice (2" to 4") and snow storm hit the country from the southwest through the mid states to the Atlantic seaboard. The vast area was paralyzed and suffered heavy damages.

310/3-24-1994   The East Holmes School District cancelled ten days of school because of bad weather, and five had to be made up in the spring.

368/ *11/5-11-1994*   **May 10, 1994** – The annular eclipse of the sun was a rare occasion for Ohio viewers. Northern Ohio was the center path of the eclipse, with the true epicenter occurring a mere 150 miles northwest of Charm. From Charm, the moon obscured all of the sun except a narrow ring, 3/4 of the way around its perimeter.

The eclipse began at 11:33 A.M., peaked at 1:16 P.M., and ended at 3:03 P.M. During its peak, the temperature dropped 7°. Also, at the peak, the sun was darkened enough that the planet Venus could be seen, 28° east of the eclipsing bodies.

11/8-10-1994   **July 16 – 22, 1994** – On July 16, the first fragments of the comet Shoemaker–Levy 9 hit the planet Jupiter. During the next week, over twenty pieces hit the planet, which caused immense explosions that astronomers could view from earth.

The Abe Mast house, built by Fred Nickles in 1891. From left: Fred Grossen, Fred Frank Nickles, Fred John Nickles, Anna Viola Nickles, Emma Margaret Nickles, Rosa Merie Nickles, Ida Mae Nickles, Eliza Marie Nickles, Elizabeth Schott Nickles. Other owners and residents living here included: Fred Grossen, Christ Hummel, Henry N. Miller, Samuel J. Miller, Lewis Kaser, Perry S. Miller, Otto Stockli, Abe P. Troyer and Ben J. Troyer.

Former residents who lived here include: William A. Mast, Abner Schlabach, Melvin B. Miller and Oren D. Keim. The house was razed in 1987 when the Charm Center Building was built.

Families residing here have included: George Price, Gideon B. Helmuth, Dr. A. M. Guittard, Jacob L. Miller, Isaac Bontrager, Harvey Oswald, William Kaser and Joe D. Erb.

62/

This house was built by Joni J. Yoder, ca 1890; later it was owned by Arletus Miller – 1916; John Oren Miller – 1956.

8/

The "Mose L." house, on the northeast street corner, being raised to add a basement.

56/

"Mose L." house shortly before being razed in 1989. Owners and residents: Isaac S. Miller, George Price, Lewis Geib, Gideon B. Helmuth, Eli Sommers, William H. Hochstetler, John J. Keim. Abe J. Keim, Joni J. Yoder, Joseph J. Miller, Abner Schlabach, Christ Hummel, Mose L. Yoder, Susan Miller, Ada Glick, John Barkman, Andy L. Miller, Anna and Malinda Mast, Ivan E. Mast, Monroe C. Yoder and Eli J. Hershberger.

295/

Harry Kauffman home, Charm Bologna factory and Miller's IGA – 1969.

295/

The "boarding house" was used as an office for Keim Lumber during the 1960s and '70s, then was later razed.

109/

This house was known as the "boarding house." Occupants and owners have included: John Burkey, Peter Remington, Isaac J. Miller, Christian E. Troyer, William McHendry, Henry A. Hochstetler, Mose J. Keim (his second ownership), Waldo Getz, Dennis Getz, Roman Keim, Susan Miller, Mary Yoder, Gerald Mast, Dey Troyer, Jonas Kauffman, Ralph Miller and Robert Kauffman.

62/

Barn on today's restaurant property; later it was moved to the John Oren Miller acreage.

Reflection Collection

The Old Charm Schoolhouse

100/5-
16-1990

In a beautiful valley is a very small town
Surrounded by hills, it is called Charm.
There was a schoolhouse; it was made of wood,
And right in the front, an old coal house stood.

The schoolhouse was immense; two stories high,
With a fire escape that reached to the sky.
I remember those days in the yard we did play,
Laughing and shouting, day after day.

Nice teachers we had; I remember them all.
They were very thoughtful of our every beck and
    call.
In the backyard was a seesaw and swing,
On the high roof, the big bell would ring.

With a pail for water to the cheesehouse we'd go
To avoid the spills, we had to go slow.
We all used the same dipper to drink, I recall,
Around the old schoolhouse we really had a ball.

Oh! Precious memories, worth more than gold,
Of the old Charm School, of the days of old.

Mrs. Dan (Martha) Wengerd

———— ≥⦁ ————

The Road of Learning

Like a road that has no end
Is the course of learning's way.
Here a hill and there a bend
Vistas changing every day.

When we meet to celebrate
The closing of this year's career.
'Tis but the shutting of the gate
That marks our journey of a year.

But still the road leads on before.
The gate which closed upon the past
Gives us entrance yet for more
Vistas for next year than last.

Travel there both young and old,
Whether days be foul or fair—
Horizons new their views unfold,
Truths revealing everywhere.

The journey of a short school year
Is but a little episode,
A pleasant jaunt, with mem'ries dear,
On learning's never-ending road.

The texts are guide books of the route.
The teacher one who points the way
Preparing pupils to find out
The course to take some future day.

Charm School souvenir [date?]

———— ≥⦁ ————

Charm School Reunion
[July 18, 1992]

Many old school friends
Came to celebrate this year,
At the Charm school house
[O]f memories we hold so dear.

≥⦁

232

Many hadn't seen each other
[F]or 60 years or more.
Many hellos were heard
"Nice to see you" o'er and o'er.

100/11-18-1992

Tables with food
Were piled "sky" high,
If [we] ate it all
[W]e'd groan with a sigh.

Five kinds of dressing
[A]nd chicken, too.
Cake, pudding, pies
[T]oo good to be true.

But, oh, how sad the message
[O]f two men who were there,
Yes, God called them home
His blessings to share.

We don't know who's next
[T]o leave this world of sin,
But how wonderful it'll be
When we, too, will enter in.

Someday soon He'll take us
[T]o that heavenly home above,
There'll be no more sorrow
Heaven's filled with joy and love.

Mrs. Dan (Martha) Wengerd

This reunion was held July 18, 1992 for former teachers and pupils (and partners) who had attended the old two-story schoolhouse (pre 1938). Those in attendance were:

Minnie (Stingel) Smith – Walnut Creek (Teacher)   *129/*
Lora B. Yoder – Millersburg
Sam M. Miller – Millersburg
Peter L. Miller – Sugarcreek
Aden M. Troyer – Apple Creek
Roman H. Miller – Millersburg
Noah T. Yoder – Baltic
Eli M. Yoder – Baltic
John E. Mast – Mt. Hope
Mose J. J. Yoder – Millersburg
Emma M. Hochstetler – Holmesville
Albert M. Miller – New Bedford
Atlee D. Schlabach – Charm
Jonas R. Yoder – Charm
Susan J. Yoder – Millersburg
Abe M. Yoder – Millersburg
Abe A. Miller – Conneaut Lake, Pa.
Henry A. Miller – Fredericksburg
Albert D. Erb – Millersburg
Henry A. Mast – Fresno

Peter M. Troyer – Apple Creek
Albert A. Keim – Charm
Jacob A. Miller – Charm
Edward R. Miller – Millersburg
Perry M. Miller – Sugarcreek
Abe L. Miller – Baltic
Roman Keim – Charm
Atlee Keim – Mt. Hope
Olive (Mast) Beechy – Wooster (Teacher)
Levi Oswald – Apple Creek
Verna Schlabach – Millersburg
Levi D. Schlabach – Millersburg
Anna M. Mast – Charm
Sarah T. Yoder – Charm
Fannie Mast – Millersburg
Fannie Yoder – Baltic
Noah M. S. Yoder – Baltic
Joe D. Erb – Charm
Amanda A. Yoder – Millersburg
Mose M. Miller – Millersburg
Fannie T. Hershberger – Baltic
Tobe M. Yoder – Charm
Amanda A. Miller – Charm
Amanda B. Yoder – Baltic
Fannie B. Miller – Millersburg
Katie Ann Raber – Millersburg
Susan B. Hershberger – Millersburg
Ada A. Yoder – Millersburg
Mattie E. Mast – Charm
Martha J. Wengard – Mt. Eaton
Lizzie M. Yoder – Baltic
Abbie A. Miller – Beck's Mills
Anna A. Miller – West Union
Jacob E. Mast – Millersburg
Dan M. Yoder – Millersburg
Mary M. Yoder – Millersburg
Katie Y. Miller – Millersburg
Susie E. Mast – Charm
Mose T. Yoder – Millersburg
Jonas A. Keim – Apple Creek
Sarah Hershberger – Sugarcreek
Lizzie Raber – Millersburg
Anna S. Troyer – Millersburg
Anna Swartz – Bern, Ind.
Calvin Otto Stockli – Newark
Ben M. Miller – Millersburg
Edna Schrock – Fredericksburg
Katie Ann Miller – Fresno
Fannie E. Mast – Millersburg
Eli D. Yoder – Millersburg
Katie Ann Hershberger – Sugarcreek
Celesta Schlabach – Charm
Ervin Keim – Charm
Robert L. Miller – Baltic

"The capitalists of this town contemplate erecting three new houses this year on account of there being too many people and not sufficient houses. This will make quite an improvement in our town. Many other changes are taking place and not a great many years shall pass [until] Charm will be to the front."

The Holmes County Farmer – March 2, 1899

———————— ❧ ————————

"The wife of George Aling, who lives near Troyer's factory [Troyer's Hollow], in the eastern part of Mechanic Township was deprived of her life on Friday evening, July 25, in a manner fearful to contemplate. We understand that Mrs. Aling was subject to fits and that while in the act of preparing supper on that evening, the family being temporarily absent, fell on the stove which set fire to her clothing and in her helpless condition was burned to death. A member of the family arrived soon after but the unfortunate woman was unconscious and soon died."

She is buried half a mile west of Troyer's Hollow (CD-N-3-3).

The Holmes County Farmer – August 7, 1890

———————— ❧ ————————

244/ In 1817–'18 and '25, Henry Yoder (YR 261) of Somerset, Pennsylvania purchased three quarter sections of Holmes County land a mile east and north of Charm in Sec. 4 T. 8 R. 5. Oral tradition says that Yoder offered this frontier land to whoever married his two remaining daughters. Within the first decade after acquiring the land, two Schlabach brothers did marry the Yoder sisters and accordingly moved to the new Ohio settlement.

The Schlabach boys had come to America from Hesse, Germany in 1820, along with their aged parents and most of the family. After a six-year stay at Somerset, the whole Schlabach immigrant family moved to Holmes County because of the brothers' marriages to the Yoder sisters.

Jacob married Barbara and resided on the present Jonas R. Yoder farm, which at that time included the David J. Troyer and Willis D. Yoder acreages as well. These three farms are still owned by descendants of pioneer Schlabach. The brother Daniel received the land of today's Eli J. Mast, Henry M. Raber and part of the Willis D. Yoder farms.

Henry L. Erb

The early egg market at the Charm store had brought a gentleman into town carrying a basket of eggs. After checking the egg price, he decided to walk the four miles to Farmerstown in hopes of getting a better price. Arriving at the distant town, he found them a cent per dozen lower than at Charm. Unknown to him, the storekeepers had connected by telephone and the lower price was purposefully offered to him. Returning the four miles to Charm, he happened to be intently watching the school children at play when he stepped into a hole in the road and upset the prize basket of eggs, only a short distance from his destination.

Levi D. Schlabach

———————— ❧ ————————

William and Elizabeth Hershberger lived immediately southwest of Charm on the farm presently owned by Jonas N. Yoder. William died January 19, 1894; the funeral was held on the twenty-second. His wife died two years later and was buried on exactly the same day of the month.

The Holmes County Farmer – January 23, 1896

———————— ❧ ————————

Charm storeowner Isaac J. Miller was a Civil War veteran. The following is a letter he wrote while at the hospital with typhoid fever.

109/

August the 26 /62
Dear brother Abraham J. Miller[,]
I will [n]ow [w]rite [a] few lines to you to let you know that I am in Philadelphia in the hospital[.] I was very sick with the typhoi[d] fe[v]er but I am over [th]at [n]ow[.] I can go out in the [c]ity now and walk [a]round any place. Now I [will] let you know that I received [a] let[t]er from Tobias. [H]e and Stephen are both well yet. I g[uess] I must quit [w]riting this time. [The] [time] go[es] very fast yet[.] [E]xcuse me for my ba[d] [w]riting.
[S]o [much] [from] your friend[,]
Isaac J. Miller

[W]rite soon an[d] often[.]
[D]irection
[U]nited States [H]ospital . . .
Philadelphia[,] P.

The two brothers, Tobias and Stephen were both killed in action eleven months later on July 18, 1863 at Ft. Wagner, South Carolina.

Evelyn Culp

———————— ❧ ————————

Ammon N. Miller was raised a mile east of Charm. Later in life he operated a blacksmith shop there.

During World War I, when Ammon (OAG 2445) was transferred from an army camp to a farm at Hartville, Ohio, he met Lizzie Schlabach, whom he married in 1919. Lizzie was a daughter of David D. and Sarah Schlabach, who, by chance were living at Hartville at this time. Both David and Sarah were born in Holmes County and, while single, migrated to Kansas in 1880. After marrying in 1887 in Reno, they moved in 1897 to Noble County, Minnesota, where Lizzie was born. From there the Schlabachs moved in 1902 to Oscoda County, Michigan; in 1909 to McMinnville, Oregon; in 1912 to Kokomo, Indiana; and to Hartville, Ohio in 1918. Ten years later, in 1928, the Schlabachs moved to McGrawsville, Indiana, where David died. Sarah moved to Kalona, Iowa in 1941, where she died.

After their marriage in 1919, Ammon and Lizzie made occasional trips from Charm to Hartville with horse and buggy.

Relating to the fact that the Schlabach family had made numerous moves, a thought in their family history includes: "A critic might rightfully say, 'A rolling stone gathers no moss,' but there also may be some truth in the reply of the opponent, 'A settin[g] hen never gets fat.'"

Roy J. Miller

92/
381/

———— ❧ ————

In the immediate area, no farm has been occupied by as many different people as the farm owned today by Crist U. Miller, along the northeast edge of Charm. The acreage had earlier been a part of the Vernon Kline farm and owned by Benjamin Helmuth. After Benjamin's death in 1895, a 72-acre parcel was transferred, in 1902, from the heirs to a son-in-law, Christian J. Yoder (OAG 1918) and his wife Mary (Helmuth). After Mose, the Yoders' oldest son, married in 1905, the farm buildings were placed, and the farm was transferred to him in 1909. In 1920, the Mose Yoder family moved to a farm one mile south of Berlin and the farm at Charm was bargained to be sold to Jacob D. Raber, whose wife was a sister of Mose. However, before the Raber family could move from Walnut Creek to Charm, they were stricken with the flu epidemic. Both Jacob and his wife passed away during the night of February 15, 1920. Their only child, Katie, was six months old at this time. The same year, the 72 acres were transferred to her; she was the only heir to the estate. The baby was taken to the home of her uncle, Christian C. Yoder, by

20/
341/

𝒱67-
376-
1902
𝒱73-
413-
1909

𝒱89-
302-
1920

whom she was raised to adulthood. The Yoders lived two miles north of Charm.

The farm was now rented out, with the following tenants among those taking up residence there: Ben Oswald, Andy Y. Mast, Benjamin E. Yoder, Alvin B. Beachy (lived here in 1931), Neal C. Yoder and Andy Y. Miller. After Katie married Ura J. Miller in 1939, they moved onto their farm until returning to her home place (Christian C. Yoder farm) in 1946 to continue farming there. Thereafter, the renters were: Neal E. Miller, Andy D. Schlabach, Eli E. Mast, Henry C. Yoder, Jonas D. J. Miller, Ervin J. Schlabach, Eli A. Raber, Eli J. Stutzman and Crist U. Miller.

In 1968, the farm was deeded to son Crist Miller, who is its present owner and also a great-grandson of the original 72-acre grantee.

Crist U. Miller

𝒱166-
565-
1968

———— ❧ ————

"The sawmill dam of D. J. Miller (better known as 'John Danny') let loose yesterday and the big carp took a trip to Simon Troyer's dam."

The Budget – July 30, 1896

———— ❧ ————

Jacob E. and Susanna (Schlabach) Mast (OAG 1549) lived on the family farm a mile west of Charm. Jacob was a grandson of the original settler and pioneer, Daniel C. Miller. Susanna was Jacob's second wife. In 1927 or 1928, she suffered a stroke, which left her greatly paralyzed. In her helpless condition, her speech also failed. With her eyes she was able to signal yes or no, according to her wishes. For 77 days prior to her death she had no bowel movement, until the last day or two before she passed away. She died January 2, 1930 at 73 years of age.

Eli A. Mast

352/
p.2

———— ❧ ————

Around 1900, William D. Fisher boarded at Emanuel Troyers while teaching at Charm School. He later married Ida, daughter of Isaac J. Miller, and resided at Baltic.

Amanda A. Miller

42/

———— ❧ ————

❧

16/ In 1909, the schoolboard at Charm consisted of: J. J. Yoder (Director), L. D. Yoder, W. H. Brown, J. W. Shafer, William Stingel and Moses Raber.

1910 school souvenir

——— 🖎 ———

The Daniel D. Erb family lived a mile southwest of Stevenson (Charm) on the farm they had bought in 1863 from Benjamin D. Miller. The farm is now the Menno A. Yoder farm in the southwest quarter of Section 6.

DJH
p.336
CD-
O-41
207/
p.101
209/
p.165

On January 25, 1868, on a Saturday evening with a heavy blanket of snow on the ground, the family bundled up to pay Daniel's aunt a visit. The young family of five (Daniel, 31; Carolyn, 25; Levi, 5; Menno, 3; and Daniel Jr., 1) did not realize what was to befall them later that evening as they drove the six wintry miles to the Jonathan Masts (DJH 2842).

The Masts were living at Troyer Valley, two and a half miles northeast of Farmerstown, on land owned today by John A. Troyer.

The Mast family was at home. It, too, was a family of five: Jonathan, 31; Elizabeth, 43; Mary, 3; Joseph, age unknown; and an adopted girl, Susan, 1, whose natural father was John Helmuth.

That evening at the Mast home, around 8:00 the oil lamp showed empty. As the father refilled the lamp, young Joseph was holding a lighted candle and got too close to the explosive kerosene oil. Instantly the can exploded, and the fiery oil blew across the room. The clothing of the ten people present caught fire, as did the heavy winter wraps and clothing stored in one portion of the room. The elders who were able to battled the blaze. Children were rolled in the snow on the outside. Daniel Erb heroically extinguished the flames which were consuming the store of clothing, then got everyone outside before going for help. The call of "Fire!" was heard by neighbors a half mile to the north. With snow eight inches deep, the trudge across the valley and up the steep hill was tiresome.

The situation the two families were in was horrible. Their hands and faces were so badly burned that some features were unrecognizable. Mrs. Erb was severely burned on the hands, neck and face, resulting from her effort to extinguish the flames on her boys. As Mrs. Mast raised her arms to see the extent of her burns, strands of flesh hung from her hands. One of the first three neighbors who arrived went for the Shanesville doctor, while the others helped the injured back into the house and into bed. Mr. Erb, in the meantime, was heading northwest, apparently in hopes of summoning Dr.

Abraham Mast of Walnut Creek. He left a trail of blood in the snow and burned flesh from his hands froze to the rail fences that he crossed. Arriving at the home of John Stuver (presently known as the Knerr farm and owned by Roman E. Miller), he was unable to go any father or return to the scene of tragedy because of exhaustion and from his injuries.

At the grim scene of disaster at the Mast home, it is said that they were singing a German hymn as help arrived. Its equivalent in English would be:

59/
p.299

> The clock does strike and means to say,
> That time has elapsed for me,
> I've made another step this day,
> Ever near'r my grave to be.
> My Jesus thus reminds me so,
> Because the hour I do not know,
> When my time is at hand.
>
> Even though if this be the last,
> Of my life's earthly hour,
> So keep me in my faith steadfast,
> Through your great suffering pow'r.
> Another chance Thou givest me,
> So let me like a Christian be,
> Hon'r you and in death be blest.

Jonathan Mast died around midnight. His son Joseph, who had been dutifully shining a light for his father, died the following day, Sunday. On Tuesday a funeral was held for the two. Elizabeth Mast died February 8, in accordance with her cherished wish. In the meantime, baby Susan Helmuth and Menno Erb were laid to rest.

The remaining five of the two families recovered from the accident, although they carried scars for the rest of their lives. Daniel Erb was cared for at the Stuver home for six weeks. Eventually, as the four surviving members of the Erb family recovered, they were brought home in an enclosed bobsled. It was eighteen months before Carolyn was able to do any work. Her hands remained disfigured for the remainder of her life, with none of her fingers in perfect shape. Young Daniel Jr. was so badly burned on the scalp that no hair grew back; part of an ear was also missing.

Twenty-one years later, in 1889, the Daniel Erb family moved to Hubbard, Oregon, where they lived the remainder of their lives. Daniel died in 1915 at the age of 78 and Carolyn died in 1919 at age 76.

Mary, the only surviving member of the Mast family, married Benedick B. Mullet and they lived in Yoder, Kansas. She died in 1892.

——— 🖎 ———

"Isaac Andy" Miller, 1855 – 1937, added a bit of humor as he burned his bedbug-ridden bedding: *Wann des naet guwt fa wannsah is, dan weys ich naet was bessah is* (If this isn't good for bedbugs, I have no idea what is).

372/

Eli E. Miller

———— ❧ ————

"My grandfather, Emanuel Troyer, living at the south edge of Charm, remembered when all of the houses in Charm were log homes."

257/

Emanuel J. Yoder

———— ❧ ————

Levi D. Schlabach wanted to be remembered as the first person to make a deposit at the Charm bank. While excavating was being done in 1987, he tossed a penny onto the proposed bank building site.

Leroy D. Shetler

———— ❧ ————

Daniel D. and Lydia B. (Troyer) Miller purchased the farm southwest of Charm from her parents in 1872 (presently owned by Jonas N. Yoder).

212/
p.29

When the two oldest children (Eli, born in 1868, and Edward, born in 1869) were still young, they were placed on a blanket in a wheat field where the parents were cradling the grain. The mother had also set some bread and milk on the blanket to keep the boys content while they were at work.

Some time later, Mrs. Miller returned to the boys to see what their laughter was all about, and was quite surprised to find a snake drinking the milk. Young Eli had a small pocket knife and was trying to cut the snake's tongue off while telling it to *es sum brucka* (eat some bread crumbs). The snake was soon killed by the protective mother when she came upon the scene.

Daniel D. and Lydia B. (Troyer) Miller Family History – 1974

———— ❧ ————

A New Electric Railroad

In this electric age and while [capitalism] is looking for investments in electric roads which would pay, we would call attention to a feasible project of an electric line connecting Millersburg and New Philadelphia. The line to start from near the depot [Millersburg] or the foot of Main Street, run up Main Street and out what has been known as the Port Washington road through Saltillo and crossing Doughty Creek at the head of what we call Doughty Glens, thence on through Charm and across into the south branch of Walnut Creek along the road leading to Farmerstown to the summit of the ridge between Walnut Creek and Troyer valley . . . and across the Tuscarawas River, striking New Philadelphia on West High Street . . . .

The line would without doubt be a feasible one and comparatively easy and inexpensive to build, as there would be no extra heavy grades, but few bridges and no trestles, about 27 miles long and run almost due east and west, with but few curves. The line would connect the two county seats, and run through a thickly settled and prosperous community and through several growing towns . . .

There are also several special features which would be of great value to the line. Such as the run along the summit of the ridge from the Farmerstown road to Shanesville along which a most enchanting view of the surrounding country can be had and at several points three or four towns can be plainly seen. But the most important special feature would be the "Doughty Glens." This is a narrow, deep valley somewhat in the shape of a letter "s" about $1^1/2$ miles long and at the widest place $1/2$ mile wide and from 100 to 200 feet below the surrounding country, its sides lined with rocky ledges and covered with spruce trees, laurel and with wild roses and other wild flowers and several rocky precipices with waterfalls and also caves and a number of springs of clear, cold water and several springs of sulphur and other mineral waters, forming as it were a natural pleasure and health resort, to which as it is at present without any special privileges or conveniences . . . would become a famous pleasure and outing resort and would be patronized by the people of the towns and cities of eastern Ohio . . . .

The Holmes County Farmer – August 9, 1900

———— ❧ ————

❧

"Another soldier boy, Henry Kleinknecht, has returned home at Charm, Holmes County, after being at Fort McHenry and Fortress Monroe for the past five months. While at the latter place he lost one of his fingers and had his hand otherwise badly hurt."

The Holmes County Farmer – December 29, 1898

———— 🙠 ————

140/ Around 1920, farmer Emanuel Oswald, living at the east edge of town, would hitch his trusty sorrel horse to a wooden sled for hauling milk. With the milk loaded, the horse was sent on its way the short distance to the cheesehouse. Arriving at the factory, the cheesemaker unloaded the milk, refilled the cans with whey, then sent the horse on its way homeward again.

Roman H. Miller

———— 🙠 ————

State Route 557

145/3-
2-1993
Ohio State Route Five Fifty-Seven
Was once just a narrow gravel road;
Rough and dusty in the summertime,
And a mess when it rained or snowed.

It still turns south off Sixty-Two,
And meanders o'er the bridges into Charm.
Then across the hills through Farmerstown,
To Six Forty-Three at the old Shutt farm.

Sometimes after a severe snow storm
The road would be closed for days.
That's when men and boys with shovels
Formed an army of means and ways.

With summer came the threshing rigs;
Pulled by a steamer or perhaps an oil-pull.
An occasional car, and buggies would go to trade
Everything from butter and eggs to raw wool.

Yes, Old 557 is blacktopped today,
And is trimmed in yellow and white.
There are still some landmarks along the way;
They bring memories that as yet haven't died.

There is the site of Wise's first school,
And across Doughty Creek, the Eusey place.
The Pomerene farm and bits of a dam
That ran the Wise's mill in the olden days.

In Charm there's the old flour mill;
The cheesehouse and the little watch shop.
In Farmerstown there's the Township Hall;
Once the school, no longer has the bell on top.

The U.[nited] B.[rethren] Church house stands without its steeple.
The Luke and Koontz homes are also there.
And beyond the town at the road's last bend
Is the farm that once belonged to Eli Fair.

Today the old road still serves those who travel;
Be it home folks, stranger, friend or foe.
The hills, the valleys, and the creeks are still there
Where they were in those days, long ago.

Delbert Harmon

———— 🙠 ————

382/ Harold Patterson recalled visiting his uncle Lewis Kaser who lived at Charm and operated the cider press. On one Sunday while at the Kasers, the neighbor's pigs were running, squealing and grunting. The pigs had come across the creek and eaten of Kaser's discarded apple pulp that had aged, and they became intoxicated.

Harold Patterson

———— 🙠 ————

107/ "I don't think anyone has more pair of socks than I do. When I'd go buy a pair I always thought I might as well get two pair yet actually ended up buying six or eight. But I can tell you one thing, I always paid for them myself."

Roman Keim

———— 🙠 ————

"Fences are very poor in this locality, especially around the supposed oil well. Cattle were ordered to be kept off from the road, but when cattle break in other pastures from lack of building a few rods of fence, [it] shows little principal [principle].

"A man ought to make enough cider to buy coal, instead of tearing down what fences there are for starting fire."

The Budget – September 13, 1906

———— 🙠 ————

243/ Peter C. Troyer (DBH 10401) married one of David Schlabach's daughters who lived a mile northeast of Charm in 1889. The Schlabach farm lay along the dividing range and it was decided to divide the large acreage and place buildings for the Troyers on the south half (the David J. Troyer farm today). A new house and barn were built and the smaller buildings were moved across the field from the Schlabach home to the new farm setting. The Troyers were renting the farm. One morning in 1895, Peter did not appear for breakfast at his usual time. Coming in late, the wife, Catherine, inquired about his delay, and he told her he had just returned from buying the farm.

Since the farmland and countryside were hilly, Peter was later thinking about moving to the level plains of Stark County, or Plain City to where some of his siblings had moved. The Troyers had also thought of building onto their house, as the family had grown to eleven and the addition was necessary. Catherine was not in favor of moving out of her home community, much less of adding to the house before they left, for someone else. During one of Peter's scouting trips to his distant siblings, the mother told the children, "When Father returns home we will not inquire anything about his trip or ask questions." The following morning, after Troyer came home, he announced that they were going to the woods that day and fell trees. As the others wondered why, he said, "To put an addition to the house and stay here." Apparently, coming home to family and home far exceeded in importance the move to a strange but level countryside. Their decision to stay is reflected today in the large number of their descendants living in the area.

John P. Troyer

──────── ❧ ────────

Mei mutter war ein rechtshaffichs weibsmensch (My mother was an upright woman). 107/

Roman Keim

──────── ❧ ────────

"Menno Troyer, a young man residing near Charm, met with a horrible accident Monday evening, which may result fatally. He was engaged at work in the barn, unloading wheat, and had left a fork standing at the entrance to the mow. Forgetting about the fork he slid down out of the mow, alighting on the fork, which penetrated his body a considerable depth. He was extricated from his perilous position and medical aid summoned as quickly as possible. He was placed under the influence of opiates, and after an examination it was deemed best, owing to the extent of his injuries to take him to a Cleveland hospital. He was brought to this place Tuesday morning and accompanied by Dr. J. M. Hyde and Jonas Bitschy was taken to Cleveland, where an operation will be performed."

The Holmes County Farmer – August 1, 1907

From relatives, it is reported that Menno was single at the time of the accident. At first it did not appear that he had suffered much harm, but toward evening he was experiencing great pains, so he was taken for medical attention on a spring wagon carriage, lying on a pile of blankets. 112/

After marriage later in life, Menno was among the early settlers at the Stark County Amish settlement.

Levi A. Miller

──────── ❧ ────────

In 1948, the telephone number of Miller's Grocery and Market was 25 F3. 120/

──────── ❧ ────────

"I feel and act like an old man." 107/

Roman Keim (79 years old)

──────── ❧ ────────

During the 1930s, Ben G. Yoder was working for Crist J. Raber in the Harness Shop. Ben was mending a collar that he had clamped in a harness jack, using a long needle and pliers. The tough leather caused the stitching to pull hard. As he was straining with the pliers, the long needle unexpectedly slipped through the leather and penetrated his breast. Luckily, Ben escaped serious injury, as the needle narrowly missed his heart. 161/

Emanuel E. Hershberger

──────── ❧ ────────

"I work, not because I have to, but because I enjoy it." 19/p.39

Mose J. Keim (93 years old)

──────── ❧ ────────

Daniel D. Miller (ML 22329), born in 1847, was big and strong for his age. As a teenager, he worked for his brother-in-law, Daniel J. Yoder. One day while pulling straw from the strawstack, a ram hit him from behind and knocked him head over heels. Feeling a bit shaken up and angry, Dan took off after the ram and gave it a good kick, which caused it to fall over, and it died. It so happened that the day before, Dan Yoder had sold the ram to a neighbor, Mr. Shetler, for $7.00. The question arose of who should sustain the loss. It was de- 212/p.20

❧

cided to select a committee to resolve the issue. Yoder and Shetler would each appoint a man and the two appointees would name a third person. The three-man committee consisted of Levi D. Yoder and Jacob E. Mast of Charm, along with Daniel Miller. The committee decided that Yoder and Shetler should each lose $3.50.

———— ❧ ————

257/ A hired girl returning to the farmhouse on the farm (owned today by Mose L. Troyer), one mile south of Charm, saw a bear close by. After being alerted, the neighbors went after it and shot the bruin in a nearby woods. This is reported to be the last bear sighted in the Charm area.

Emanuel J. Yoder

———— ❧ ————

"Well, Stark Co[unty], we will surrender to your jottings in regard to drilling for 'apple jack' instead of oil, for the Oil Co[mpany] that arrived here from Pittsburg[h], Thursday, failed to find in their inspection what they hoped would be oil. They are putting another well down on Andy Troyer's farm, 1 mile south from here, and we all hope they will succeed in finding oil there."

The Budget – September 13, 1906

———— ❧ ————

244/ In February of 1994, a large poplar tree was cut down on the Roy L. Miller farm, a mile east of Charm. According to family lore, the farm's earlier resident, Joas Schlabach, had a heart condition and often needed a walking cane. Returning home one day, he stuck a poplar walking stick in the dirt of the spring house floor. After his death in 1914, at 42 years of age, the poplar twig, which had sprouted in the moist and cool cellar, was replanted along the road and grew into a large tree.

Henry L. Erb

———— ❧ ————

81/ John V. Erb (1893 – 1981) used a stump puller to help in barn raisings when straw sheds were being built. The puller was staked to the ground in back of the barn, then a rope passed over the barn roof and attached to the heavy frame lying on the floor. The young boys were kept busy turning the long handle on the wheel, which slowly wound

the rope on the drum and pulled the wooden framework into place. John sold the puller, mounted on a Champion box wagon, to Emanuel A. Miller, who continued using it for some time thereafter.

Valentine J. Erb

———— ❧ ————

The town boys were always looking for some type of amusement back in the teens and twenties.

107/ One evening, Mose E. Mast came to the store after dark carrying an oil lantern, which he set on the porch before going inside. The unattended lantern seemed quite appealing to the boys, who took it and hung it at the top of a pine tree across the street. The lantern was kept lit, up in the tree, for weeks, with the lads climbing the tree with a bottle of kerosene and refilling it. By them it was known as and called the "North Star."

Roman Keim

———— ❧ ————

191/ Jacob Yoder ("Davy Jake"), a farmer who lived one mile south of town in the early 1900s, planted a field of corn northeast of the farm buildings. When he was finished, he ended up having only two rows in the whole field. He used a two row planter and circled the field until coming to the center.

Mose N. Raber

———— ❧ ————

"We saw Will Nirote of Charm, O[hio] in our neighborhood last Sunday and we think we know where the attraction lies."

The Budget – June 12, 1890

———— ❧ ————

227/ The Henry O. Lahm family lived a mile east of Beck's Mills. In this family ". . . many of the men learned carpentering and the girls, in order to earn money, often walked to the mill in Troyer's Hollow, where they were given a supply of knitted stockings. These had no completed heels or toes and these girls would shape and knit them by hand, return them to the mill and collect their earnings . . . ."

Frances (Patterson) House

———— ❧ ————

On January 14, 1985, Ivan J. Miller slid from his wheelchair and broke his leg. Paralyzed from a previous accident, he did not feel any pain or notice what had happened. After a few games of ping-pong, he returned upstairs, and when getting into bed, he realized that he had broken his leg.

218/

———— ❧ ————

Cinda D. Troyer attended Charm School for grades 3 and 4 in 1972 – '73 and 1973 – '74. Throughout her eight grades of elementary schooling in the East Holmes Local District, she had a perfect attendance.

368/

Daniel A. Hershberger

———— ❧ ————

"We believe every person will try to tell how or where they spent the glorious Fourth, so we will attempt to do the same as we feel proud to say that that day was so well celebrated at this place this year. Just scores of fun was had from morning till night. Quite a nice crowd of people was present in the afternoon and all stayed for the fireworks in the evening. On account of the rain at noon, the parade was not until later in the afternoon. Music by the Charm band."

The Holmes County Farmer – July (?), 1896

———— ❧ ————

"The store of Edward Hochstetler at Charm, a small hamlet in Holmes County about five miles north of this place [New Bedford] was burglarized Tuesday night. An entrance was effected through a basement window and about fifty dollars in cash was taken from the drawers. Nothing else was disturbed. The work is supposed to be that of local talent and investigations are now on foot to bring the culprits to justice."

54/

Coshocton Daily Age – February 24, 1905

———— ❧ ————

During the 1930s and '40s, boxing matches offered a sort of entertainment to the younger generation and boxing was often a sport to be called upon.

75/

A young lad of Millersburg heard of the events and came to Charm one evening, feeling he could whip anyone around. Buck Barthlemeh, who ran

the egg route for the Getz Bros. store, was in town at the time and accepted the gloves. The feat was held inside the store. Buck was considered a fair boxer and soon sent the out-of-town boy sprawling against the end of a long row of filled, stacked egg cases. The cartons, when hit, acted like dominos and ended up in a messy heap. The next day, Mose L. Yoder, a store attendant, got to clean up the mess.

Levi Schlabach

———— ❧ ————

Mary J. Yoder, daughter of "Davy Jakes," who lived in Andy Miller's house beside the cheese factory, was blind in one eye because a hen pecked it when she was gathering eggs.

90/

John B. Kurtz

———— ❧ ————

"Several boys came through here Sunday, having their dress changed who were trying to fool people, but they must understand we know who they are, and I think it is a shame and disgrace to this community to have our young Amish boys degrade themselves in such a way. One of the boys lives near the Weaver school house and the other near the tile factory, north of Berlin. They had bonnets on and ladies' dresses. (Read D[eu]t. 22:5) To parents: 'Train up a child in the way he should go, and when he is old he will not depart from it.'"

The Budget – October 7, 1907

"A statement appeared in last week's *Budget* concerning two boys who went through Charm having their dress changed. I do not intend to succor the boys or take their part, as it was a poor policy for them to go to public in such a way, but I think it is a poor policy for an older person to publish a false statement in such an extensively circulated paper. The boys only had ladies' bonnets on and no dresses."

The Budget – October 14, 1907

———— ❧ ————

The Charm school closed last Tuesday with H. W. Ledrich, of Walnut Creek, as teacher. In the evening Mr. Ledrich made his farewell speech and said ["][T]here is a certain class of people that don't study the high branches, and when they come to town they don't know what the sidewalks are for, and walk in the middle of the streets, when the mud is knee deep.["] I was in many towns already where there were sidewalks and never saw the class of people that he had spoken of do that, but one person that did not belong to that class, walked on Main St. in Millersburg, through the mud, and that was a stoop-shouldered fellow that looked like that teacher that made that farewell speech and I think it was him; and I think he spoke about himself that time. He also said this class of people work and work until they become stoop-shouldered, and never have any pleasure in their life. Again he said the greatest pleasure that people will ever have is in this world. Does it take a true [c]hristian that says that? The greatest pleasure that a [c]hristian will ever have is in that world which is to come; "An house not made with hands, eternal in heaven." He said in his speech that any man can go to the public and say what he pleases about him, so I thought I would tell you what I think about his speech. If a man has anything against another man, he should not take the whole class of people together to insult them.

The Budget – April 5, 1900

—————— 🙠 ——————

30/ Moses T. Yoder could not take school examinations due to a broken jaw.

1934 – '35 Charm School enrollment records

—————— 🙠 ——————

"I never knew my husband before he was gray-haired. As a teenager he had a bad case of measles which turned his hair white while yet a young boy."

Mrs. Simon (Mattie) Troyer, 90 years old

—————— 🙠 ——————

171/ Arletus Miller died from an apparent heart attack while eating breakfast at his home in Charm, October 9, 1954.

John O. Miller

—————— 🙠 ——————

18/
168/
194/

Around the turn of the century, Louie Kaser ("Amish Louie") lived 2½ miles southeast of Charm. This was on the former Ammon D. Miller farm or today's Vernon M. Miller acreage. Their dwelling, no longer present, stood south of the Miller farm buildings.

At one time, the family was very sick and one of the Kaser children came to Ammon Millers asking them to summon a doctor. Hearing of their need of help, the Miller farmer accompanied the child back to his home. When the neighbor entered the house, he found the family in serious condition. Everyone was sick. He found seven members of the family lying in one bed. Louie was not around the house, which aroused suspicion as to the cause of the sickness. Finally, one of the family said they had eaten *schwem* (a poisonous mushroom). Louie was later discovered by the straw stack; he, too, was very sick.

After the doctor arrived, he administered another poison to counteract the food poisoning, and they all recovered.

The "Amish Louie" poisoning incident was a frequently related account at Charm.

Nothing is known of what later became of the family except that they had also lived two miles south of Charm and a short distance east of the CR 600 – TR 188 intersection. No buildings remain at either of these homes. An eighteen-month-old daughter, Elizabeth, is buried on the Henry M. Miller farm, two miles south of Charm (CD-O-14).

Noah A. Raber

—————— 🙠 ——————

90/ Threshing and a good thresher with a steam engine was a highly regarded work in the early community. Among these were Perry S. Miller with Levi Keim, and Peter Erb. During the first quarter of the century, Erb bought a Rummley Oil Pull tractor to take on the threshing jobs. Miller was working on his steam engine at the school yard, while Erb was at the blacksmith shop. As the town boys gathered from one engine to the other and had the owners saying how much their engines would pull, they soon had a pulling contest set up. The ends of a pipe were flattened and drilled for the hitch bar. Their first try was on the school yard, and as the power was turned loose, the Oil Pull dug down in the dirt, while the heavy steamer would not move, either. The next try was pulled on the road. This time the steam engine run by Miller and Keim, with all the traction it needed, outpulled the lighter Rummley, which bounced fiercely as it was being dragged up the road, digging ruts into the hardened roadway surface.

John Kurtz

——————— ❧ ———————

"Our mail carrier tumbled backwards off the cart the other day, but nobody hurt."

The Budget – February 8, 1892

——————— ❧ ———————

On June 19, 1948, Charm schoolteacher Ethel Miller married Dale Stutzman at Wissembourg, France, where he was doing relief work for the Mennonite Central Committee. She returned to the states in November and continued teaching at Charm. Her sister Ruth taught classes for her as a substitute while she was gone.

5/

Before marriage, Ethel lived with her parents. D. D. and Maggie Miller, in the present Helping Hands Quilt Shop at Berlin. After her last year of teaching at Charm in 1950, she moved with her husband to Goshen, Indiana. After that, the Stutzmans lived at Holmesville, Ohio, again at Goshen, and are presently living at Bristol, Indiana.

After teaching for a total of 28 years, she relates to them as "good, fulfilling years, being able to touch many lives, and gaining a very satisfying experience."

Ethel (Miller) Stutzman

——————— ❧ ———————

In the 1930s, Grover Boker, Lee Miller and Jonas E. Troyer ("Jay Linn") did taxi service in the area. We used to say, "They're hauling the Amish over to the Pennsylvania hills to the quack doctors."

51/

Paul R. Miller

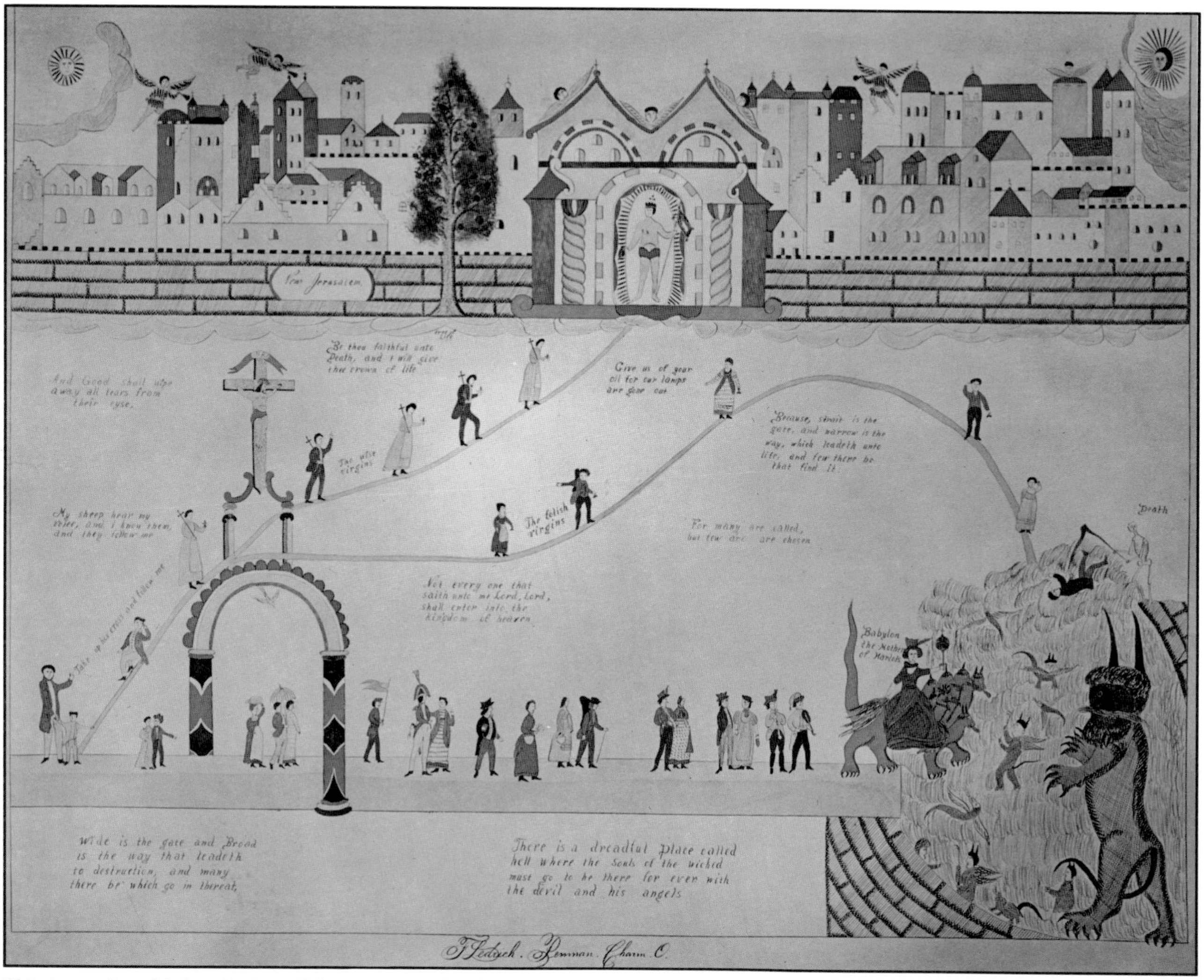

189/
361/

100/1-14-1892

❧

This is a colored ink painting of the two ways leading to heaven or hell signed by "F. Ledrich, Penman, Charm, O." Frederick Hedrich Ledrich was a tinsmith, gunsmith and blacksmith at Troyer's Hollow at the turn of the present century. During January of 1892, Ledrich was trying to start a class for ornamental penmanship at the Charm School.

Dar McKinley is elect un em Benj Helmuth si hawna henkt der kub (McKinley is elected and Benjamin Helmuth's rooster hangs its head).

The Budget – November 12, 1891

———— ❧ ————

"A burglar tried to get into J. J. Yoder's house Monday night, but was discovered before he gained entrance. J. J. Y. got up and awakened Henry _____; he took the shotgun and went out after the burglar. Finally he thought he saw him going along the picket fence, and Henry gave him the load. The next day he found that he had shot an old sow in the back."

The Budget – June 22, 1899

———— ❧ ————

5/ "The fall of 1946 I was so hoarse and was diagnosed as having 'singer nodes' (small growth on my larynx). Instead of surgery, the specialist at Cleveland suggested I whisper for 6 weeks to remove the strain. I did—and taught school [at Charm] every day. It was amazing how well the children cooperated."

Teacher Ethel (Miller) Stutzman

———— ❧ ————

75/ The front porch of the Charm butcher shop was a usual gathering place for the local residents. Sylvia Oswald, its owner from 1929 to 1934, lived in the dwelling part of the building and had a taste for practical amusement. After fashioning a bare copper wire through the wall, he connected it to an unused crank type telephone that was still mounted to an inside wall. The wire on the outside was left to dangle freely from the ceiling. Within a short time after the setup was made, the porch bench and railings were again occupied with townspeople. One of the boys was absentmindedly playing with the old wire and neatly wrapped the soft copper wire around his thumb. In the meantime, Sylvia was watching from the doorway and quickly slipped inside and started cranking on the old telephone. As he whirred away on the handle, the unsuspecting victim on the outside was shocked to a frenzy by the electrical current, while the rest of the group shook with laughter.

Levi Schlabach

"Joel Keim and [William] Helmuth must of got on the wrong track last week. They wanted to go to Massillon but happened to get to the State Fair at Columbus."

The Budget – September 22, 1892

———— ❧ ————

42/ John W. Hershberger (1851 – 1913) occupied the farm immediately west of Charm and approached his neighbor, Emanuel Troyer, telling him the east line fence was set too far on his land. Agreeing to have a surveyor check it out, Hershberger was very much astonished to find that the fence was too far on the Troyer farm. Clearly ashamed, John asked to buy the land along Troyer's west line fence. Hershberger, at the time, was selling new clocks in his jewelry business, and Emanuel agreed to have a new clock as a settlement to the land.

At present, the 42-inch high wall clock is still at Charm and ticks away at the home of Amanda A. Miller, who is a granddaughter of Emanuel Troyer.

Amanda A. Miller

———— ❧ ————

379/ Star was a small, dark bay gelding and "tough as leather." He was owned by the Henry J. Shetler family in the 1940s. Despite the fact that he could be a plain outlaw, he also showed great intelligence. At times when the boys rode him to Charm and had another ride home, they would tie up the reins and send Star on his way home by himself. As the horse went the $2^1/_2$ miles, occasionally a neighbor would stop him, ride him someplace, then send the horse on his way home again.

Mervin Shetler

———— ❧ ————

"Joel Keim thinks he has a good engine [steam] and the best whistle in the county."

The Budget – October 1, 1891

———— ❧ ————

"Henry Hostetler our enterprising lumber man started to go New Bedford last week but lost the road and drove in the woods to turn around so that no one would find out, but he happened to stall and at the end had to get a man to help him out."

The Budget – June 11, 1896

—————— ❧ ——————

"[Isaac Miller and Noah Hershberger, store owners,] bought a safety bicycle the other week, but we suppose Hershberger did not think it was a safety [bicycle] when it [ran] into a wagon and landed him on the wheel. Noah tried it again and this time tried to run over the jewelry man's dog. Lots of fun in our town this week, but Noah can ride better now although he is sitting a little crooked on the seat."

The Budget – October 1, 1891

—————— ❧ ——————

During the 1940s, the Charm boys staged a pest hunt which included mice, rats, sparrows and starlings. The one group went to the Millersburg courthouse clock tower and caught 2,400 starlings in one night. Seven burlap bags of carcasses were carried out.

279/

Atlee Schlabach

—————— ❧ ——————

"We will always be grateful for the good family relationship we had with the neighboring people while we lived at Charm."

96/

Mrs. Ray Mast Jr.

—————— ❧ ——————

In the early 1900s, the boys on the Henry N. Miller farm got amusement from their dogs. The one was fond of ice cream, and they would feed it to him until his tongue was cold. After getting the dog to chase the horses, they shared a good laugh, as its tongue was still cold and stiff and he couldn't make a loud bark.

67/
341/

The other, a terrier, was extremely bad tempered; because of being teased a lot. At times, he was set on an engine spark plug. Biting and clawing anything within reach, the bewildered doggy could be fed pickles and red beet, and one fall ended up eating thirty-six locusts.

Ammon H. Miller

—————— ❧ ——————

"J. J. Farmwald has a new Charm make buggy and likes it well."

The Budget – July 23, 1891

During the 1940s, Malva H. Shetler was baching in his newly constructed chicken house type building on the Mose J. Keim property in Charm. One evening the stove suddenly began smoking badly. Hearing light footsteps on the roof, he assumed someone had covered the chimney. A dipper of sour milk was setting close by, which Malva took outside and flung up on the roof, then returned inside without saying a word. Later that evening, Atlee D. Schlabach stopped in at the shanty for a visit and, unknown to him, still had some milk in his hat.

379/

Mervin H. Shetler

—————— ❧ ——————

The sons of Dan J. Mast, the grist mill owner (living in Charm from 1913 to 1920) were pros on the stilts and had made some tall ones. They would climb on them from the front porch at a height of twelve feet. At times, when walking on the road, they would straddle cars.

99/

Mrs. Aden (Franny Mast) Keim

—————— ❧ ——————

At the Mast farm, one mile northwest of Charm, the hams were hung in the granary until needed, which was a usual custom during the early 1900s. At one time, it was noticed that some of the meat was being carried off.

71/

Stealing cured meats from a farmer's storehouse was an often related happening in the early days. The Mast boys, on learning of the occurrence, decided to set a trap for the intruder. The door leading into the granary was opened by sticking a finger through a hole and unlatching it on the inside. Here they placed a cutter used for cutting straw for the straw tick. The knife was set to a trigger that was released when a finger was stuck through the hole. On making a trial run, the keen, heavy knife sliced off a corn cob that was put through the hole. When all was ready, the trap was set for its intended purpose. One morning when the trap was checked, it was discovered that the blade was tripped. Further investigation showed nothing serious—no blood or finger lying around.

The suspect was never apprehended, but at this time a local horse trader had a shortened and bandaged finger.

Eli A. Mast

❧

—————— ❧ ——————

57/ The residents of Troyer's Hollow received their mail at the Beck's Mills post office until its closing in the early 1900s. After this, they got their mail at Charm. Ralph Aling, who lived at Troyer's Hollow, would walk the mile to Charm every two days to get the mail for his grandfather, Simon Troyer. To run the errand, he was given ten cents per trip. With this money he was able to buy his first M. Hohner harmonica. Ralph's first tune that he could play was an old favorite, "Red Wing."

Ralph Aling

———— „ ————

90/ A worship service planned to be held at the Charm School was aborted when the intended minister didn't show up.

Bishop David A. Troyer (1827 – 1906), upon coming to the barn one morning, was surprised to find that a stranger had slept in the hay alley. This was not too uncommon at the time, as tramps needing a place of rest were frequent guests in the area. Upon further consultation, the stranger turned out to be his long-gone brother, with whom he had had no contact for quite some time. (Apparently, this was brother Jonathan (TYc1d), who was living in Prairie Creek Township, Nebraska in 1880.)

The newcomer refused to come to the house for breakfast and claimed to be a Dunkard minister. The bishop, longing to hear his brother preach, offered to arrange a special weekday service at the Charm School for the visiting preacher, to which he agreed. When the appointed evening came, the benches at the schoolhouse were filled, but the intended preacher never showed up.

John B. Kurtz

———— „ ————

293/ Dan D. Keim used to relate how one fall, some boys put a corn shock on the road, hoping a car would run into it. Incidentally, no car hit it that night, so the group decided to scatter it by running their own car into the shock. To their surprise, the car stalled on top of the corn pile, and with the hot muffler resting on the fodder, it was ignited, burning the car along with the corn shock.

Floyd E. Troyer

———— „ ————

90/ A big chestnut tree standing along the road between the John P. Troyer and Rudy J. Yoder farms, east of Charm, was to be removed. Area resident Jacob I. Hershberger buried sixty pieces of dynamite under the big tree to fell it. When the explosive was set off, the giant load force blasted the tree up so fast that all of the limbs were broken off. The trunk came down to rest again, in an upright position, in the same spot where it had stood.

John B. Kurtz

———— „ ————

On June 28, 1960, Dan and Lovina Schlabach were driving along CR 207, east of Benton, with a horse and buggy. Coming to the Joe Weaver residence, they were suddenly apprehended by a pony stallion which had broken from his stall in the Weaver barn. Galloping onto the road, it annoyed the Schlabachs' mare they had hitched. Lovina left the buggy to calm their own horse and to drive off the offender with a whip when the stallion turned and kicked the 77-year-old woman in the face. She suffered nose and cheekbone fractures and was hospitalized a short time at Millersburg.

On July 7, she had a relapse and was returned to the hospital. By the tenth, she died of a heart attack which medical authorities related to her earlier injuries.

The Schlabachs resided a mile and a half northeast of Charm on the present Willis D. Yoder farm.

The Budget – July 14, 1960

———— „ ————

The following is a complete list of deaths of Charm residents during the past forty years.

Name	Date of death	Age at death
Arletus Miller	10-09-1954	68
Peter J. Yoder	06-22-1955	66
Mose L. Yoder	03-07-1957	84
Levi J. Raber	12-16-1959	68
Alvin J. Schlabach	12-15-1960	62
John Lahm	08-18-1966	73
Crist B. Miller	05-16-1967	77
Mrs. John (Katie) Erb	06-16-1968	71
Mrs. Mose (Lizzie) Keim	01-07-1969	86
Mrs. Levi (Katie Ann) Raber	03-18-1969	78
Mrs. John (Sarah) Miller	08-09-1969	79
Mrs. Alvin (Mattie) Schlabach	07-19-1971	76

171/

Name	Date of death	Age at death
Mrs. John (Ella) Lahm	04-16-1972	76
Dan D. Keim	01-18-1972	52
Mrs. Ben (Sarah) Troyer	06-03-1972	67
Mrs. Lee (Priscilla) Miller	06-11-1972	83
Al Keim	01-15-1973	82
Mrs. Crist (Lizzie) Miller	11-11-1973	85
Mose J. Keim	04-15-1974	93
Harry Kauffman	04-26-1974	83
Oren D. Keim	05-08-1975	59
Mrs. Tobe (Amanda) Yoder	11-04-1975	77
Ben J. Troyer	05-04-1976	81
Mrs. Andy (Mattie) Miller	03-27-1978	92
Lydia P. Hershberger	05-11-1978	81
Melvin Domer	09-13-1978	81
Aden E. Miller	10-26-1978	43
Mrs. Roman (Mary) Keim	01-26-1979	67
Raymond L. Raber	07-18-1979	65
Mrs. Al (Lovina) Keim	07-06-1980	91
John V. Erb	03-21-1981	87
Mrs. Harry (Mary) Kauffman	12-08-1981	90
Forrest G. Miller	12-20-1981	65
Shana Danell Yoder	02-16-1982	7 months
Levi D. Troyer	07-13-1982	67
Mrs. Levi (Lizzie) Troyer	04-01-1991	76
Atlee D. Schlabach	03-25-1993	82
Anna D. Keim	04-12-1993	75
Mrs. Atlee (Ada) Schlabach	05-13-1994	80
Mrs. Jonas (Sarah) Yoder	02-09-1995	78

Mrs. John O. Miller

(Mose J. Keim became the oldest person to have lived in Charm when he died at age 93. Today, 1995, his age is shared by Tobe M. Yoder, who resides at the northwest edge of town. Mrs. Andy (Mattie) Miller was the oldest person who had lived her entire life in Charm, when she departed this life at 92 years of age.)

——— ❧ ———

On the afternoon of July 4, 1993, distant thunder was heard from an approaching storm in the south and west. On the warm and humid Sunday afternoon, Daniel R. Yoder, 19, had ridden to Charm on a bicycle. On his way home, around 2:00 P.M., he stopped at his sister's trailer at the Charm Engine property. Leaving the trailer around 4:00, he checked the lowering storm clouds and noticed neighbor Ben D. Miller relaxing on a double swing which sat under a maple shade tree. Daniel, of a talkative and friendly nature, joined Miller in the appealing shade at the edge of the lawn; he was only a few feet from him. The short visit of the deacon and young lad was abruptly ended when a bolt of lightning struck the tree. Daniel, who had been leaning on a wooden fence, was thrown back

235/

a few feet and killed instantly. Miller, aside from being stunned momentarily, was not injured.

The incident seemed even more unusual because this was the only streak of lightning seen in the area; it appeared well ahead of the storm, while the area was still partly sunny. Aside from a few drops of rain, the storm passed by without a shower that afternoon. It was believed that the same lightning streak also killed some cattle in the Sugarcreek area.

Ben D. Miller

——— ❧ ———

On February 7, 1934, a stillborn son was born to the Eli P. Troyers and was buried at the southeast edge of town, at Miller Cemetery (CD-0-6). The Troyers lived at Charm at this time and operated the harness shop.

152/

Eli Troyer Jr.

——— ❧ ———

In the mid-1940s, a campaign was initiated to destroy and eliminate the barberry plants from local woods and fencerows. The three-pronged, native thornbush was considered responsible for the rust found on the stalks of wheat. The campaign was supervised by George Holmes of Columbus, who, with local help, zigzagged across the countryside to weed out the troublesome bush. A bag of salt was carried along and some applied to the base of the plant wherever it was found. Among those helping from the area were: sons of Mose E. Hershberger; Perry S. Miller's boys; John O. Miller; Emanuel D. Miller; and Donny Kaser. Later, Tom Sheneman of Beck's Mills combed the countryside in search of the plant. At the time, destroying it was important for wheat-growing areas of the country. It had earlier been proven that the rust found on the plant and that on the wheat were separate stages in the life cycle of one fungus. Today the barberry plant can still be found, and though it is a host to the rust on wheat, a proper fungicide can be applied to the seed wheat and thus be successfully controlled.

171/
78/

——— ❧ ———

Schlak sell deeale nat so hat zu (Don't close the door so hard).

Mel Domer, former Charm resident

——— ❧ ———

Soll ich di oahrah losseh? (Shall I leave your ears?)

Oren Keim, former Charm resident

———— * ————

120/   In 1948, the telephone number of the Charm General Store was 25 F21.

———— * ————

"Charming Charmer of Charm."
     Menno D. Miller used this pen name during the period he was a scribe of the Charm area for *The Budget* (1930s to 1950s)

———— * ————

Remember that it is always wise,
to buy your feed and farm supplies,
     at Charm Feed Mill
                    Advertising pen – 1960s

———— * ————

298/   Around the late 1960s, Alvin B. and Edna Yoder were heading home from Charm to Walnut Creek with the horse and buggy while leading a brood mare behind the buggy. Nearing the crest of the long hill a half mile east of town, they were alarmed to see a team of mules come galloping down the road hitched to a loaded wagon of hay with no driver. Fearing for their own safety as well as for that of the team heading for the steep grade, Yoder left his wife with the buggy and ran toward the frantic team. To his amazement, the mules did slow down as he approached, and they stopped for him just before continuing down the hill. With no farmer in sight, he turned the rig around and headed it in the opposite direction. A short distance up the road, he found the owner attending to a mishap that had occurred with the team running off.

     What had happened in the first place was that farmer David J. Troyer had been helping neighbor Jonas R. Yoder put up hay. Finished, Troyer was taking home a load for himself and had placed a bale elevator on top of the load which extended out above the team. As he started toward home, the rattle from the overhead elevator put the mules on the run, with no intention of slowing down. The road, at that time, had teed into CR 70 at the very crest of the ridge. Coming to the intersection, they met a Hershberger buggy whose horse got scared and jumped down the steep embankment on the south side of the road, overturning the buggy. At this point, Troyer jumped off to help the women occupants and decided, "whatever" with the runaway mules.

*
248

No serious injuries occurred with the women in the buggy, and Yoder's timely interception of the team before they started down the hill with the loaded wagon delivered them from a potentially disastrous situation.
                              Alvin B. Yoder

———— * ————

43/   When the Christian B. Miller family acquired the farm at the east edge of Charm in 1938, it was said that the old farmhouse had been moved fifty years ago. It had stood across the stream to the east, along TR 369. This is owned today by Vernon Kline.
                              Levi C. Miller

———— * ————

171/   As a young boy, Ivan J. Miller had taken an interest in collecting watch fobs. At the time, collecting the ornamental fob was a fast-growing and attractive hobby among collectors and businesses alike.

     On July 4, 1973, when Ivan was twelve years old, he traded Keim Feed Mill fobs with Edward Raber, who lived southwest of the schoolhouse. Returning from the Rabers, he came down the hill toward SR 557 on a bike with no brakes. Coming to the Charm Creek, he went off the left side of the bridge and his face hit the opposite embank-

380/

From the 1972 – '73 to the 1993 – '94 school years, Elson Sommers taught lower grades at the Charm School. His 22 consecutive years of teaching have not been surpassed by any other known teacher in the school's history. When he retired, an open house was held for him on June 3, 1994. This "schoolhouse" cake was made for Mr. Sommers and was displayed at the reception at the schoolhouse.

ment. The impact broke his back and badly bruised his face.

Ivan was transported to Millersburg, then to Timken Mercy Hospital at Canton, where he underwent back surgery to remove the fractured vertebra and plastic surgery to repair his badly lacerated face.

After a five-week stay at the hospital, he came home on August 10, then was admitted to Akron Children's Hospital a week later. Here he was placed in a halo hoop brace to straighten and immobilize his back. The brace had a halo around his head with pins firmly imbedded in the skull and a larger halo around the waist with its pins protruding through the hip bones and out the lower back. Surgery was performed on September 14 to fuse the broken back. He returned home on the 29th.

Since the accident, Ivan has remained paralyzed from the waist down and must use a wheelchair. Though handicapped, he stays active, with employment at Keim Lumber Co. On June 3, 1993 he married Sara Ann Mast, a Charm resident.

John O. Miller

——— ❧ ———

56/

Henry H. Miller was handling his loaded shotgun in his harness shop one day and accidentally shot a hole through the front door.

Dey Troyer

——— ❧ ———

189/

"Do you pay people to dress up that way?"
A 1989 Charm tourist asking Brooks Harris about the Amish people

——— ❧ ———

5/

"[In the 1940s, the] [s]tudents and I covered [the] [northwest] corner of the room with plastic and carried in soil to build a farm to go along with our studies. We had houses, other buildings, fences and fields where we planted crops, etc."
Teacher Ethel (Miller) Stutzman

——— ❧ ———

244/

Bevzy and Coony	Canary Bird
Sweet Anna	Molly
Betzy	J. H. L.
Reporter	Correspondence
Dandy Sammy	Guess Who

X Y Z	An Old Reporter
Charmer	Yockob Patch
Democrat	Dic – Tom
Papa Lint	Judge
Harry	Charm Pappy
E. I. Z.	Sam Patch

Charm newsletter pen names in *The Budget*, 1892 – 1895

——— ❧ ———

8/

During the early 1900s, Henry N. Miller was challenged to ride a bucking pony for $15.00. He succeeded by tying himself onto the bronco so that he couldn't fall off.

Atlee Keim

——— ❧ ———

341/

"We could argue about this; which side do you want?"

Harry Kauffman – former Charm resident

——— ❧ ———

9/

Oscar Miller lost his new set of dentures when swimming at the often used Troyer's Hollow swimming hole. He had to buy a new set.

Paul Hummel

——— ❧ ———

Ein gute platz fa kaufe (A good place to buy).
Keim Feed Mill pen – 1960s

——— ❧ ———

11/6-
1-1974

"Some days are dark but the next day is usually brighter. You need some dark days to keep you on your toes."

Raymond L. Raber

——— ❧ ———

326/

During the sub-zero January 1994 weather, a frozen box turtle was found by Abe H. Yoder, 1/4 mile east of Charm. The initials of the boy's great-grandfather, Christian B. Miller, were found carved on the shell: CBM-1941.

Henry B. Yoder

——— *Reflection* ——— ❧

57/ "I have seen two centuries, and if I live until I'm 104, I will see the third."

Former Charm resident Ralph Aling
at the 1989 Charm Days

———— 🕊 ————

"I was born about four thousand years ago,
And there's nothing in this world I do not know;
I saw Peter, James and Moses playing ring-around-
a-roses,
And I'll whip the guy that says it isn't so."

Oren Keim, singing to the town children

———— 🕊 ————

131/ "It's a match – Abe and Fannie"

Mast wedding book match cover

———— 🕊 ————

44/ "Often when teacher Perry Miller would start telling a story to the children, he would begin with, 'When I was a pretty little boy . . .'"

Lovina Kaufman

———— 🕊 ————

Dees ist das Jahr das dah Jupayter raygiahat im land dee planawten (This is the year that Jupiter reigns in the land of the planets).

Mose J. Keim, former Charm resident

———— 🕊 ————

"This is not 'Putschtown,' it is the charming city of Charm."

Menno D. Miller, former area resident

———— 🕊 ————

'S nemt gift fa gift fadriva (It takes poison to expel poison).

Mose L. Yoder, former Charm resident

———— 🕊 ————

"Call the lumber number."

Keim Lumber Company

🕊
———— 🕊 ————

248/ Longtime Charm resident Atlee D. Schlabach needed a new horse to replace old Charlie in 1988. Finding a safe horse suitable for older people could, at times, be a problem. But the 77-year-old grandfather found a bay horse to his liking at Emanuel A. Millers. Taking him for a trial drive from his home, he was pleased with the horse, except he seemed a bit sluggish when turning. Returning home and stopping at a neighbor's place, he was quite surprised to find that he had not placed the bit in the horse's mouth.

Roy E. Miller

———— 🕊 ————

Oren D. Keim and Fannie Coblentz were married on January 12, 1935. On February 4, 1940, their first child was born, and the mother passed away—two hours after the son's birth. The baby died an hour later. Both mother and baby were laid in the same casket. They are buried in the Keim family burial plot, a mile northwest of Charm (CD-0-4).

The Budget – February 8, 1940

———— 🕊 ————

The last three living children of Dan J. "Younie Dan" and Amanda J. (Miller) Troyer, who lived south of Charm, were Mose, Mary and Noah. Mose suffered a stroke some years ago. He recovered well enough that he was able to stay active until he had another stroke in the spring of 1990. During Mose's stay at the hospital, his granddaughter's wedding was held at his home, and he was unable to attend. His brother, Noah, who had regained better health from his bout with cancer, and sister Mary did attend the wedding.

A few weeks after the wedding, on Saturday, May 26, 1990, Noah died. Mary attended the funeral on the following Tuesday, then died unexpectedly the next day.

Mary and a group of widows had gone visiting and, during a stop at Mt. Hope Fabrics, she had a stroke and passed away. Her funeral was held on Saturday, June 2. On the day of Mary's funeral, her brother Mose died. He had been seriously ill from his stroke.

Within one week's time, the three Troyer children died, each from an individual cause of death. Mose was 80, Mary 77 and Noah 71 years old when they died.

———— 🕊 ————

Sometime from 1932 to 1936, when the Henry A. Hershbergers lived a half mile southwest of Charm, Henry carved his initials on a box turtle found on the farm. Twenty years later, the same turtle was found by John Kurtz, who now lived there.

240/

Henry A. Hershberger

———— ❧ ————

"Putchtown" de Davy gmey" ("Putchtown" the Davy church district).

Referring to the church district of Bishop David Troyer

———— ❧ ————

Ebbes ksenneh vom "Hen" sei katz dah bawm drovveh? (Have you seen "Hen's" cat up in the tree? – Henry N. Miller's cat was treed by a coon hunting party.)

Mose Keim, former Charm resident

———— ❧ ————

Ride the Amish Bus

Come take a different ride with us
We'll hop aboard the Amish bus
And ride the roads both up and down
Across the hills to Limpytown.
Back ways are always best to ride
To view the Amish countryside;
The hilltop woods, each field and farm
Who knows, we may wind up in Charm.

323/

The Amish bus may make a stop
In Whiskerville, as like as not
Then drive on up to Farmerstown
Where one can really look around
The rural, scenic, Alpine view;
They have a livestock auction too
Where sale is held once every week
Much like the barn in Sugarcreek.

Charm lies a hill or two away
A village out of yesterday,
But in each valley in between
The fields are nestled snug and green,
With many a picture postcard view
Of creeks and buildings, horses, too
As Lizzie Ann would often say
I'm glad we rode the bus today.

Unknown

———— ❧ ————

Wee kann des sei, do kommt ein buggy onney gaul (How can this be, here comes a buggy without a horse).

57/

Lena Beam, seeing her first auto-buggy in Charm, 1904

———— ❧ ————

"There wasn't one birdie nest along this part of the Charm Creek that we children didn't know about."

99/

Franey (Mast) Keim

———— ❧ ————

"If I want a good time I attend church and listen to a good sermon."

Mose J. Keim, former Charm resident

———— ❧ ————

"The only thing that people freely give is advice."

114/

Mrs. Ervin (Hulda) Kaser, 98 years old

———— ❧ ————

"Eat ginseng every day and you will get older than your neighbor" —Indian Greyhound

57/

Ralph Aling's speech at Charm Days, 1989

———— ❧ ————

Selly dummey buvarrah (Those uneducated farmers).

164/

John Mueller

———— ❧ ————

"Hatpin Hatty"

Brood mare boarded at Levi A. Miller farm

———— ❧ ————

"A great excitement was caused at this place [Charm] last Saturday by the first street car ever [to pass] through town. Samuel Lint was the owner."

The Budget – April 8, 1897

"C. W. Brightman, of the Brightman Mfg. Co. [they lived at the Victorian House in Millersburg], purchased in Cleveland recently an automobile

which arrived here yesterday. This is a two passenger machine run by steam with gasoline as fuel.
It is the first machine of this kind in the town or
county, and will prove quite a novelty as well as
convenience to its owner."

The Holmes County Farmer – April 25, 1901

———— ● ————

169/   Cousins Irene and Esther Mayer were teachers
at Charm during the 1920s. They came to school
from Berlin in their early Ford car.

Irene (Keim) Raber

———— ● ————

293/   Saloma, daughter of Simon P. Troyer, died of
pneumonia during the 1941 – '42 school term.

Floyd E. Troyer

———— ● ————

67/   The Joel Keim family lived a mile northwest of
Charm on the present John S. Miller farm. Around
the 1920s, the young boys took a barrel on one of
the hills and wanted someone to crawl in and roll
down the slope. Joel's daughter Dena volunteered
and climbed inside. The lid was nailed shut, and
off she went, rolling and bouncing, until she came
to a stop in the fence at the foot of the hill. The lid
was taken off and Dena climbed out, with no serious bruises.

Ammon H. Miller

———— ● ————

    "Wm. H. Hostetler of Charm [sent] us word on
Monday that we should not mention anything
about that little daughter that came to his home
on Sat. No, Will, we will not tell anybody, we will
only publish this so you may know that word
reached us safely. Other people don't need to read
this."

The Budget – July 20, 1899

———— ● ————

67/   A son of Henry N. Miller pounded on a loaded
cartridge, which exploded, and the shell lodged
itself in one of his nostrils. A brother, Ammon,
extracted the hot metal with pliers.

Ammon H. Miller

●

———— ● ————

60/   Sisters Lydia Ann and Emma Erb were employed at Miller's IGA Market at Charm during
the early 1960s.

    One day they went to a funeral at Plain City and
stopped at a restaurant along the way. Both girls
decided to order a footlong hot dog. Lydia Ann
was thinking about the price, 25¢, when the waitress unexpectedly tapped her on the shoulder, asking, "What is for you?" She quickly answered, "I'll
have a 25" hot dog." To her astonishment, the
waitress said, "Sorry, but we have only footlongs."

    Sharing a good laugh with their driver, Mrs.
Floyd Miller, their trip was completed. However,
later the driver's husband, who made frequent
stops at the Miller's Market at Charm, presented
Lydia Ann with a package containing a specially
made 25" hot dog. "And I had a few good meals
from it, too," she later recalled.

Lydia Ann Swartz

———— ● ————

218/   Construction was begun on a new 70' x 200 pole
building at Keim Lumber in early 1977. The building was to provide more storage area for the constantly growing building material company. The
80' trusses arrived in town in the evening of February 15 on a specially built trailer. The trusses
were hauled upside down, and the 80' span extended well fore and beyond the trailer, making a
very top heavy load. Everything appeared well
until the truck made the left turn at the Keim Lumber driveway. As the rig rounded the turn, the back
wheels of the trailer rode over a pile of snow, which
shifted the high load's balance and flopped the
complete rig on its side. The back end of the load
lay across the road at the hitching rail area, and
traffic was stopped for a few hours until local
heavy equipment was brought in to set it up. Despite the accident, no injuries occurred.

———— ● ————

371/   Four Charm area residents have had open heart
surgery.

    Erma Miller was diagnosed as having Idiopathic
Hypertrophic Subaortic Stenosis, a hereditary
heart disease, in 1970. This is a rare disease where
heart muscles are enlarged. Blood will come into
the heart faster than the restricted channel will
return it to the body.

    Erma was operated upon February 3, 1971 at

the National Institute of Health at Bethesda, Maryland, during the early stages of open heart surgeries. She was released from the hospital on February 20. Her surgery was successful.

Eli E. Miller suffered a heart attack on April 20, 1983. On June 23, he underwent triple bypass surgery at the Cleveland Clinic. Seven years later, on September 14, 1990, his wife Mattie also underwent heart surgery at the clinic. She had an aortic valve replaced with a microvalve and repaired an aneurysm.

372/

Mrs. Crist U. (Ada) Miller had heart surgery on October 24, 1988 after she had suffered two earlier heart attacks. She had surgery for a triple bypass at the Aultman Hospital at Canton. Ada Miller died February 27, 1995

341/

———— ❧ ————

Ich bin ayns fon dee drub vo see dee alta leut haysa und von meah ebba hen fa abheiha kenna miah feel sacha fazayla (I'm one of the group that they call the old people and if we have someone to listen, we have many stories to tell).

8/

Atlee Keim

———— ❧ ————

During a natural health meeting held at the Charm schoolhouse on the evening of March 2, 1978 and conducted by Nancy Travis, she offered an iridology examination to interested persons. When she was checking the eye of 71-year-old Abe J. S. Yoder, she stared at him in disbelief and claimed that according to his eye, he should be a dead man already.

218/

He purposefully had her look into his artificial glass eye.

———— ❧ ————

"I don't care if you can't recite the Constitution forward and backward. But if I can teach you where to find the information and how to look for it I will have accomplished my job."

40/

Howard Kaser

———— ❧ ————

A. B. Huperich, a teacher at Charm School from 1914 to 1918, was later in life killed in a tractor accident.

8/

Atlee Keim

———— ❧ ————

On September 30, 1991, LeAnn, a daughter of Dan and Ann DeHass, was heading east of Charm. She was driving along CR 70, in the midst of picturesque farming country. Upon reaching the crest of the hill, she noticed a team of horses hitched to a mower, standing idle and seemingly unattended. Upon further investigation, she saw someone lying at the back of the mower, with a straw hat close by. Immediately alarmed and fearing a mishap or that the farmer, David J. Troyer, might have had a heart attack, she raced back to town and summoned the Berlin Emergency Squad. Returning to the scene, LeAnn was totally astonished to see the team and driver busy at work again. Making another hasty drive to Charm, she called off the squad, which was already on its way.

141/

As it turned out, the team and the farmer's son needed a well-deserved rest break.

LeAnn Miller

———— ❧ ————

On June 3, 1994, Charm businessman Bill Keim and his recently wedded wife, Eva, were unsuspecting victims of a post-wedding belling.

A few days earlier, the members of the Walnut Creek Mennonite Church had asked the Keim couple to go along on an evening hayride, to which they consented. Because of the amount of people going along for the evening of fun, it was decided to take a semi with a flatbed trailer.

The weather turned out beautiful for the Friday evening event. After the "hayriders" were all picked up, the enjoyable evening was begun, traveling through the picturesque countryside. Eventually the load came to Charm and stopped at the schoolhouse. Here they were met by another group which included some of the Keim Lumber employees who had brought along a large-sized lawn cart.

At this time, the purpose of the planned event was made known. The group demanded that Eva sit in the lawn cart and Bill cart her to the far side of town. The procession was now met with probably the most deafening sound and commotion ever produced in the village. Truck and car horns were blaring and an alarm siren was wailing. Sledges and hammers were pounded on steel plates. Small engines were roaring and pot and pans were banged together.

The belling-walk ended at Miller's Dry Goods, where the "honored couple" climbed back onto the semi trailer. As the rig made the return trip through town, another round of serious belling was given for the newlyweds.

The semi left Charm heavily decked with balloons and streamers.

75/ In 1929 Dan and Lovina Schlabach's eight-year-old son Levi was sick with appendicitis.

The family lived 1¹/₂ miles northeast of Charm.

On the way to the hospital with an ambulance they came to the east edge of Charm where a road crew was replacing a culvert; the ditch across the road was being dug by hand. After the driver informed the crew of the emergency situation, foreman Waldo Getz called on the men to refill the ditch (by hand) so the vehicle could pass over.

After the sick boy was again on his way, the road crew reopened the culvert ditch. (It was found Levi had a ruptured appendix.)

Levi D. Schlabach

———— ❧ ————

It's Not [P]utchtown Anymore

145/
/May
3-9,
1994

Charm has left the past behind,
Where crafts are a treat in store.
There's a place where you can eat and sleep,
It isn't [P]utchtown anymore.

The town is still big in lumber,
But there was no bank before.
Neither was there any tourist traffic.
It's not the same Charm anymore.

Hey, they're selling furniture,
And, unbelievable, a museum, too.
All these new things and much more,
There even is a zoo.

There used to be two feed mills,
And a little watch shop was there.
It was the home of Charm Bologna,
And a blacksmith and repair.

There always was a post office,
As well as a general store.
And, of course, a harness shop
Was a business there before.

There also was a cane press,
And a slaughterhouse, too.
There was a cheese factory,
To mention just a few.

Gone, but far from forgotten,
Are the old gentlemen we'd see,
As they made their daily rounds,
With whatever the news might be.

Today, Charm is a tourist town,
With "Welcome" on its front door.
It's all dressed up for company.
It sure isn't [P]utchtown anymore.

Delbert Harmon

———— ❧ ————

244/

PUBLIC SALE!

The undersigned will offer at Public Sale at his residence in German Tp., Holmes county, Ohio, on the road leading from Becks Mills to Charm,

ON THURSDAY, MARCH 28th, 1889,

Commencing at 10 o'clock A. M., the following property:

4 HEAD OF HORSES!

ONE A YOUNG MARE WITH FOAL.

1 YEARLING COLT,

4 HEAD OF COWS!

2 OF THEM FRESH.

5 Head of Young Cattle,

1 Large Buck, 9 Head of Shoats,

1 Sow with 8 pigs, 1 Sow with pig, two 2-horse Wagons and a 4-horse wagon, 3 spring wagons, open buggy, top buggy, Reaper, Mower, one horse-power Threshing Machine, Plows, Harrows, Corn Cultivator, 3 Sleds, a lot of Harness, a lot of Dry Lumber, lot of Oak Shingles, Oats and Corn by the bushel, Hay by the ton, Cornfodder, a lot of Chickens, also 1 STALLION 5 years old.

Household Furniture,

Such as Bureaus, Bedsteads, Cupboards, Tables and Chairs, Cooking and Coal Stoves, Apples, Potatoes, 3 Barrels of Cider, and many other articles.

ALSO ON THE SAME DAY

Five acres of Land with Good House, Stable and Fruit, will be offered. If not sold will be for rent.

TERMS MADE KNOWN ON DAY OF SALE.

DANIEL ERB.

TROYER & BONER, Auctioneers.

315/

PUBLIC SALE

The undersigned will offer for sale at public Auction at the late residence of JACOB MILLER deceased, 1 mile west of CHARM, HOLMES COUNTY, O.,

ON WEDNESDAY OCT. 22, 1902.

Commencing at 9 O'clock A. M. The following property to wit:

Five Head Of Horses,

2 Yearling & 2 Spring Colts, 5 Cows, 9 Head of young Cattle, 8 Sheep, 11 Hogs, 2 Sows with pigs, 1 Four-Horse wagon, 1 Two-Horse wagon, Spring wagon, Buggy, Hay Ladder, Grain Drill, Binder, Mower, Hay Rake, 1 Spring & 1 pick tooth Harrow, 2 Plows, Cultivators, Sleigh, Corn Sheller, 500 bu Oats, 40 bu Corn, Hay by the Ton, Corn by the shock, 2 set draft harness, buggy harness, 2 cook & 1 heating stove, sink, chairs, desk, sewing machine, counter scale tables, chests, cupboard, bureau, lawn mower, cream separator, copper kettle, rifle and a variety of other articles.

Terms. All sums under $3.00 must be paid in cash, above that amount a credit of 9 months will be given by giving their note with two approved sureties.

F. W. ANDREWS, Auc.

Jacob E. Miller.

Administrator.

PUBLIC SALE!

94/

The undersigned will have public sale at her residence 1 mile east of Charm, Ohio, and 3½ miles southwest of Walnutcreek, Ohio, on the Charm-Walnutcreek road, on

FRIDAY, FEB. 18

3 — Head of Horses — 3
Consisting of One Bay Mare, 17 years old, weight 1350; Two Bay Horses, 9 years old, weight 1400.

5 — Head of Cows — 5
Consisting of Four Holsteins, one fresh Feb. 27th, the rest will be fresh in March. One Grade Cow.

1 Sow and 15 Shoats
Sow due to farrow April 1st and 15 Shoats, weight about 60 lbs.

Black Hawk Manure Spreader; McCormick Binder; McCormick Mower; Osborne Side Delivery Rake; Dump Rake; Osborne Tedder; Hoosier Grain Drill, Fertilizer Attachment; Krause Corn Cultivator; One-Horse Cultivator; Oliver Riding Plow; Syracuse Walking Plow; Springtooth Harrow; Spike Tooth Harrow; Land Roller; Two-horse Wagon; Ladder Wagon; Sled; Spring Wagon; Single Buggy; Sleigh; Portable Saw Rick, 10-horse power; 1½ H. P. Domestic Gas Engine; Letz Grinder No. 8; Fodder Shredder; Ensilage Cutter; Corn Sheller; Bone Cutter; Grind Stone; Stewart Horse Clipper; 30-ft. Extension Ladder; 2 Sets Work Harness; Single Buggy Harness; Horse Collars; Bridles; A lot of Carpenter Tools; Feed Cooker; Copper Kettle; 2 Cook Stoves; 600-lb. Platform Scale; Apple Butter by the gallon. Some Household Goods, also Fanning Mill and many other articles too numerous to mention.

TERMS MADE KNOWN ON DAY OF SALE

Sale to Commence at 1:00 O'clock

L. C. YAKLEY, AUCTIONEER

Mrs. Joas D. Schlabach

PUBLIC SALE

94/

The undersigned will sell at public sale on the premises of Joas Schlabach the property of Catharine Schlabach dec., 1 mile east of CHARM, O.,

ON FRIDAY JANUARY, 18, 1907

Commencing at 1 O'clock P. M. the following property to wit:

1 Family MARE 18 years old, 1 Buggy, 1 Sleigh, Buggy Harness, Cook Stove, Sink, Heating Stove, Cupboard, Bureau, Chairs, Ward-Robe, Table, Stand, Desk, Domestic Sewing Machine, 3 Bedsteads, Grindstone, 1 800 lb. Scale, Sausage Stuffer, a lot of Carpenter Tools, Work Bench, Lard Press, Meat Barrel, 1 Copper & 1 Iron Kettle, and many other articles.

L. C. Yakely, Auctioneer.   J. J. Yoder, Clerk.

L. D. SCHLABACH.

PUBLIC SALE

244/

The undersigned will offer for sale at Public Auction at his residence, 2 miles southwest of Charm, in German Township, Holmes County, on

THURSDAY, FEB. 28, '07

Commencing at 12 O'clock M. the following Property. Consisting of

Six Head of Horses
1 black mare 18 years old. 1 roan mare 9 years old. 1 bay mare 7 years old. 1 gray horse 5 years old. 1 black horse 3 years old. 1 bay colt 2 years old.

Seven Head of Cattle
Consisting of 2 cows coming fresh in April. 1 heifer coming two years old. 2 steers coming two years old. 1 steer coming year old. 1 bull coming 1 year old.

Twenty Head of Hogs
Consisting of 4 brood sows due to pig in April. One full-blooded Berkshire boar 18 months old. 15 Shoats.

Some Chickens, one 15-horse power Russell traction engine with extra heavy gearing, has been running only three seasons to hull clover only, two Birdsell clover hullers, has been run four seasons with self feeder and wind stacker. one has been run stout eleven seasons with self-feeder and web stacker. one Russel grain thresher. This machinery is in good running order. One buzz saw, one Piano mower, two 4-horse wagons, one 2-horse wagon, one spring wagon, one bob-sled. one field roller. one spring tooth harrow, two spike-tooth harrows, three plows, one 2-horse corn planter, two feed grinders one corn sheller, one fanning mill, one blacksmith forge, one anvil, one vice, one grindstone, one feed cooker, one copper kettle, one fruit dryer, one heating stove, three sets of harness, one set singly buggy harness, two grain cradles. Hay by the ton and a lot of corn and oats by the bushel. Lots of other articles not mentioned.

TERMS MADE KNOWN ON DAY OF SALE
FRED ANDREWS
Auctioneer

MICHAEL ERB

PUBLIC SALE!

71/

The undersigned will offer for sale at public auction at his residence, ¼ mile west of

CHARM, OHIO,

=ON= *1911*

SAT., MAY 27th, '11

THE FOLLOWING PROPERTY, VIZ.:

ONE EIGHT-DAY GRANDFATHER CLOCK,

1 weight mantel clock, 1 cupboard, sink, water bench, wash stands, bureaus, desk and bookcase, stand, chest, 2 wood chests, 3 tables, 3 bedsteds and bedding, cradle, a lot of chairs, 2 rockers, 1 Martyrs' Mirror and a lot of other books, a lot of crocks and jars, and a variety of other articles.

Sale to Begin at 1:00, P. M.

Terms and conditions made known on day of sale.

L. C. YAKLEY, Auct.
J. J. YODER, Clerk

JACOB E. MAST,
Agent for the Heirs of Eli and Rebecca Mast, Deceased

106/

PUBLIC SALE

The undersigned will offer for sale at public auction on the David Erb 1½ miles east of Charm on

Fri. MAR. 31 '16

2 Head of Horses,

1 coming 8 years and one 7

1 Jersey Cow,

2 Shoats

60 Barred Plymouth Rocks, 2-horse wagon, broad tire wagon with hay ladders, buggy, 2-horse cultivator, one horse cultivator, Imperial plow, spring and spike tooth harrow, sled step ladder, 2 sets double work-harness, single buggy harness, grind stone, some carpenter tools, heating and cook stove, cupboard, sink, water bench, table, dough-tray, bedsteads and bedding, two rocking chairs and other chairs, two clocks, Standard sewing machine, hay by the ton corn fodder by the bundle, corn, oats, potatoes and apples by the bushel and a lot of other articles to numerous to mention.

SALE TO BEGIN AT 1:00, P. M., Sharp

L. C. YAKLEY, Auct.

Terms made known on day of sale.

DAVID ERB

76/

PUBLIC SALE!

I, the undersigned, will offer for sale at public auction on my farm located ½ mile South of Charm, Ohio, on the Charm-New Bedford road, on

WED., SEPT. 24th 1941.

BEGINNING AT 12:30 O'CLOCK

FIVE HORSES

1 Gray Horse 10 yrs. old; 1 Gray Mare 15 yrs. old; 1 Road Horse 5 yrs. old, sound and family broke; 1 Bay Mare 9 yrs. old, sound and good broke; 1 Roan Mare 15 yrs. old, good work mare.

FOUR DAIRY COWS

One to be fresh in February, the others in March

2 SOWS WITH 10 PIGS EACH   150 LEGHORN PULLETS   100 2-YEAR-OLD HENS

FARM IMPLEMENTS: Binder, Mower, Hay Loader, Side Delivery Rake, Dump Rake, Land Roller, 10-hoe Drill, good as new; Hay Tedder, Corn Planter, Two-Horse Cultivator, Fanning Mill, John Deere Riding Plow, Burch Plow, 3-section Spring Tooth Harrow, Spike Tooth Harrow, New Idea Manure Spreader, 1-Horse Grain Drill, Double Set Work Harness, Extension Ladder, Brooder House, DeLaval Cream Separator, good as new, No. 12; Home Comfort Cook Stove, good; 2 Heating Stoves; Power Washer in good condition, 50-gal. Beet Cooker, Wheel Barrow, Platform Scales, 2 Iron Kettles, Copper Kettle, Single Trees, Double Trees, Shovels, Forks, and many other articles not mentioned.

1 Bu. Big Clover Seed; 1 Bu. Small Clover Seed; Alfalfa and Clover Hay by the ton; 5 Gal. Lard; 250 Shocks Corn; 100 Bu. Oats

JONAS KEIM, Auct.   J. A. RABER, Clerk

TERMS: Six Months Time with Two Approved Sureties.

DANIEL J. TROYER

94/

PUBLIC SALE!

I, the undersigned, will sell the following items at the residence in Charm, Ohio, on

SAT., SEPT. 13

at 12:30 P. M. (E.S.T.)

CARPENTER TOOLS — Power Saw and Table; Planer & Jointer; Band Saw; Craftsman Jig Saw; 2 to 3 h. p. Gas Engine; Wood Lathe; Belt Sander; Delta Drill and Mortise Machine; Briggs & Stratton Gas Engine; Tenon Machine; Lathe Tools; ¼-inch Power Drill; Line Shaft; Automobile Engine Power Plant; Two Skill Saws; Two Stoves; Generator and Engine; New Pulleys; Hand Sander; 20-ft. Sandpaper Belts; Drills; Bits; Chisels; Hammers; Saws; Planes; Nuts; Bolts; Nails; Levels; Screwdrivers; Wrenches; Files; Pliers; Saw Set; Clamps; Punches; Hydraulic Jack; New 1½-inch Bearing; Stapler; Cabinet Hardware; Cabinet Lumber, including Plywood and Quarter Sawed Lumber; .22 Cal. Rifle with Telescope Sight, like new; Hardy Sprayer; Duster; Walking Plow; Wagon; Road Cart; Milk Hack; and Many Other Items.

Good, Safe Driving Horse

JOHN F. ANDREWS, Auct.   TERMS — CASH
Beach City, Ohio

Mrs. Abe P. Troyer, Owner

50/4-
15-1897

The undersigned will offer for sale at public auction, at his residence in Charm, Holmes county, O., on Tuesday, April 27, 1897, commencing at 1 o'clock p. m., the following property to-wit: 1 good driving mare, coming 4 years old; sire by American Boy, dam a Hiatoga mare; 1 Grade Jersey cow, 5 years old and just fresh; 1 yearling Jersey heifer, household and kitchen furniture of all kinds, including a new bed room set; 1 stand of Italian bees, number of hives and fixtures, 20 head thoroughbred Langshan chickens, several hundred bushels of seed potatoes, and various other articles too tedious to mention. Terms made known on day of sale.   A. M. GUITTARD.

Lewis Conkle, Auctioneer.

&a

August 11, 1915

PUBLIC SALE.

The undersigned will offer for sale. at public auction, at the late residence of Simon D. Troyer, deceased, in Mechanic township, Holmes Co., Ohio, on Saturday, Aug. 21st, the personal property of said Simon D. Troyer, deceased consisting in part: bay mare, 2 buggies, spring wagon, 2 sets single buggy harness, lot of double and single bed blankets, batting, several hundred yards of flannel, cassimere, cassinette, chain and overcoat goods, stocking yarn, men's socks, ladies' hose, ladies' woolen shawls and lot of other goods, 8-day clock, chests, 2 iron safes, a number of knitting machines, patterns, heating stoves, a number of cans lubricating oil, drum full of gasoline, gasoline engine, drill machine, platform scales, small scales, tools, pipe wrenches, pipe die, cupboard full of dyes, saws, printing press, telephone, roll of asbestos, emery wheel, many tools and other items too numerous to mention. Sale to commence at 10 o'clock a. m. Lunch will be served at reasonable prices. Terms: Purchases amounting to $3.00 or less to be paid in cash; above that sum, notes on 6 months time, with two or more sureties, will be taken. E. D. Oswald, B. C. Fisher, Adms.

362/

COW SALE

The undersigned will sell at public sale, at CHARM, OHIO, on
MONDAY, APRIL 16
Commencing at One o'clock p. m.

25 HEAD OF
CHOICE COWS, FRESH and CLOSE UP

10 HEAD OF HOLSTEIN COWS
8 DURHAM COWS
2 GUERNSEY COWS
5 Durham and Holstein Heifers
1 four-year-old SHETLAND PONY, Cart and Harness.

BOYD & DUGAN

L. C. YAKELY, Auct.
E. D. OSWALT, Clerk.

189/

PUBLIC SALE!

I, the undersigned, will offer for sale at public auction on my farm, located 1½ miles northeast of Charm, Ohio,

Wednesday, Nov. 17th
BEGINNING AT 12:00 O'CLOCK E. S. T.

9 Head of Horses

Black Mare 14 years old, Black Horse 14 years old, Black Mare 8 years old, blind; Black Mare 14 years old; Sorrel Horse 20 years old; Black Road Mare 5 years old; Bay Mare Colt 18 months old; Bay Colt 6 months old.

 ## 12 Head of Cattle

8 MILK COWS: Cow 3 years old, due Feb. 6th; Cow 3 years old due June 20; Cow 5 years old due May 20; Cow 10 years old due Mar. 28; Cow 3 years old due April 29; Cow 10 years old due Mar. 4. All Holsteins. One Jersey Cow 8 years old due June 25; Jersey Cow 7 years old due July 7th 1 Holstein heifer, pasture bred; 1 Holstein 1 year old; 1 Holstein Heifer 6 months old; Holstein Bull 6 months old.

30 HEAD HOGS: 2 Spotted Poland Sows; 3 White Sows; 1 Boar; and 24 Pigs

FARM IMPLEMENTS: Deering Binder; Deering Mower; Superior 9-hoe Grain Drill; 2 International 2-horse Cultivators; Hay Tedder; Dunham Cultipacker; Two 3-sec. Spring Tooth Harrows; 4-sec. Diamond Tooth Harrow; 2-sec. Spike Tooth Harrow; Oliver Riding Plow; 2 Oliver Walking Plows; Three 1-horse Cultivators; 1 Clover Buncher; Dump Rake; Lime Spreader; Sled; Log Sled; 4-in. Tire Wagon with Hay Rack; 2 Box Wagons; Two 1½ H. P. International Engines; International 8-in. Feed Grinder; Corn Sheller; Platform Scale; 2 Hog Self Feeders; Extension Ladder; Top Buggy; Milk Hack; Wheel Barrow; Work Harness; Collars; Myers Spray Barrel; Butcher Tools; Shop Tools; Bee Hives; Single Trees; Double Trees.

HOUSEHOLD GOODS: 2 Beds and Springs; Lounge; Baby Bed; Wood Boxes; Dough Tray; Churn; McCormick-Deering Cream Separator; Four 10-gal. Milk Cans; Crocks, Barrels, Iron Kettles, Sugar Pan and Pails; Other articles too numerous to mention.

TERMS MADE KNOWN ON DAY OF SALE

L. C. YAKLEY, Auctioneer   L. L. Schlabach and A. J. Schlabach, Clerks

DAN J. SCHLABACH ❧

71/

PUBLIC SALE

The undersigned will sell at public sale at his residence, one-half mile west of CHARM, OHIO, on

SATURDAY, OCT. 12

1911

Commencing at 9 o'clock a. m. the following property:

23 HORSES

Consisting of 7 Breed Mares as follows: One 10-year-old registered black Norman mare, in foal, one 4-year-old roan mare in foal, one 8-year-old gray mare in foal, one 4-year-old gray mare in foal, one 13-year old mare in foal, one 4-year-old bay mare, one 12-year-old black mare in foal, one black team of heavy draft horses 4 and 5 years old, one 3-year-old gray horse, one 3-year-old roan horse, one 3-year-old sorrel horse, one 4-year-old roan road horse, automobile broke; one 4-year-old bay road horse, automobile broke; one black road horse 7 years old, one sorrel draft colt 2 years old, two yearling colts, five spring colts.

13 HEAD OF CATTLE

Consisting of 3 milk cows with calf, 3 yearling heifers, 1 yearling steer, 1 2-year old Holstein bull, 1 yearling roan bull, 4 spring calves.

20 HEAD OF COARSE WOOL EWES

19 HEAD OF HOGS

Consisting of 3 breed sows, 1 Berkshire boar, 15 shoats that will average 125 pounds each, also 8 pigs that will be 3 months old on day of sale.

FARMING IMPLEMENTS: Two 4-horse wagons, 2 2-horse wagons, 1 hay loader, 1 mower, Osborne mower, Superior fertilizer grain drill, 2-horse Superior fertilizer corn planter, 2-horse Hoosier corn planter, single Superior corn planter, Osborne hay tedder, Osborne hay rake, riding corn cultivator, 2 Oliver chilled plows, 2 spring-tooth harrows, spike-tooth harrow, land roller, corn wonder, bob sled, Humphrey bone grinder, carborundum grinder, grind stone, feed grinder, set heavy draft harness, 2 sets of draft harness, set single buggy harness, 2 sets check lines, collars and bridles, Chatham fanning mill, corn sheller.

HOUSEHOLD GOODS: Six bedsteads, bed springs, 2 cupboards, clothes press, wood chest, 3 tables, water bench, lot of chairs, Round Oak heating stove good as new, wood heating stove, copper kettle, churn, cider barrels, meat hogshead, 2 20-gallon jars, 2 milk cans, 1 pair Peafowls and many other articles not mentioned.

TERMS MADE KNOWN ON DAY OF SALE

JACOB E. MAST

F. W. ANDREWS & SON, Auct.   J. J. YODER, Clerk.

There will be a LUNCH STAND on the grounds.

71/

Imported Percheron Stallion

VILLARCEAU 29829

Will make the season of 1903 at Jacob E. Mast's barn, 1 mile west of Charm, Holmes County, Ohio.

DESCRIPTION — *Villarceau* 29829 is a dark iron gray with star, light mane and tail, 16-3 hands high, weighs 1900 pounds, and when fully matured will weigh one ton. This is an extra strong and well made horse, well muscled, heavy bone, good feet neck and head, a free and prompt actor, quality and quality in abundance, in fact a model of power, strength and endurance. From his general conformation, disposition and high class breeding, any good horse man will say "he is sure to be the sire of good ones."

PEDIGREE: *Villarceau* was foaled April 7th 1899; sired by Besigne (19602) he by Brilliant III, he by Fenelon, he by Brilliant, he by Coco, &c. Dam La-Perle (34997) by Malbrouck 10810-(13200;) 2nd Dam Blene (6147) by Fleurus (14997;) 3rd Dam Pelobpe I.

TO FARMERS AND BREEDERS.

This horse was imported by the Darby Plain Importing Company direct from the Pearch district of France. He was bred and raised by one of the most extensive and up-to-date breeders in France. The Charm Stallion Company is composed of good farmers and practical stock men. This colt was bought to improve our stock, and all others who desire to breed to him. Don't fail to see this horse before you breed your good mare, for he is just the horse to breed to.

Terms: To insure a colt 10 days old, - - - - - $15.00

This horse is under the care of a competent keeper and the company will not be responsible for any accidents.

CHARM STALLION COMPANY,

JACOB E. MAST, Manager.   Owners.

252/

PUBLIC SALE!

I, the undersigned executor of the estate of Tena Graefe will offer at public sale at her late residence, one mile west of Charm, Ohio, and one mile east of Becks Mills, Ohio on the Charm-Becks Mills road, on

Sat., June 1

— THE FOLLOWING PROPERTY —

Included in this property are many antique articles, relics 50 and 100 years old; One Clock, a very rare one; Two Bureaus; Chest, brought from Germany; One Solid Walnut Chest; Good Walnut Cupboard with glass doors; Cook Stove; Heating Stove; White Sewing Machine; 4 Beds with bedding; Many German Books; Song Books; Histories and other religious books; 241 beautiful and rare dishes; 8 Beautiful Quilts; A number of pieces of dry goods ranging from 2 to 28 yds in a piece; Civil War Whiskey Bottle; 3 beautiful old-fashioned stands; 2 Tables; Sink; Several very old German Bibles; New Mirror; 14 yds. Home Made Carpet; 3 Rocking Chairs; Garden Tools; Iron Kettle; Kitchen Utensils; Knives and Forks and other articles too numerous to mention. All interested in antiques should not miss this sale.

Will also take bids for the 70-acre farm. This farm has a lot of good timber on it and thousands of bushels of limestone.

SALE TO BEGIN AT 12:00 O'CLOCK

TERMS WILL BE MADE KNOWN ON DAY OF SALE

L. C. YAKLEY, Auctioneer   ABNER SCHLABACH, Clerk

WM. PERRY MILLER

EXECUTOR

LUNCH STAND ON GROUNDS

❧ Credits and Sources ———

1/ East Holmes Local School District Administrative Office (Holmes County)

2/ Holmes County Office of Education

3/ Elizabeth Beyeler Jacobs (Charm School teacher)

4/ Amanda Kurtz Yoder (Charm School pupil)

5/ Ethel Miller Stutzman (Charm School teacher)

6/ Melvin E. Hershberger (area resident)

7/ *Gemeinde Register* [Millersburg – Ragersville, Ohio], [A bi-weekly church paper serving the Amish community of Ohio].

8/ Atlee Keim (former Charm resident)

9/ Paul and Mary Yoder Hummel (former Charm residents)

10/ Clayton Miller (son of Charm School teacher)

11/ *The Daily Record* [Wooster, Ohio], [daily newspaper].

12/ Emanuel B. Beachy (area resident)

13/ Wayne and Sarah Miller Troyer (area residents)

14/ Amanda Speicher Erb – private ledger (former area resident)

15/ Dan B. Yoder (area resident)

16/ Tobias M. Yoder (Charm resident)

17/ Roy Beachy (area resident)

18/ Henry A. Raber (area resident)

19/ Clarence Troyer, *History of Villages – People – Places in Eastern Holmes County*, Berlin, Ohio: Berlin Printing, 1975.

20/ Ura J. Miller (area resident)

21/ Alfred Kaser (area resident)

22/ Harry C. Logsdon, *The Silent Streams*, [Historical sketch of the Doughty and Military Valleys of Holmes County], N.p.: n.p., 1950.

23/ *Ohio Revised Code*, [Sections 3321.01 to 3321.08].

24/ Thomas A. Billings, *The Old Order Amish versus the Compulsory School Attendance Laws: An Analysis of the Conflict*, [Thesis], University of Oregon, 1950.

25/ Jacob J. Mast, et al., *Reasons for not Sending our Children to School Beyond the Elementary Eighth Grade*, ts, Holmes County Board of Education, [Minutes of Sept. 11, 1954].

26/ Oscar R. Miller, et al., *Sesquicentennial History of the Berlin Community*, Sugarcreek, Ohio: Middaugh Printers, 1966.

27/ Herb Miller (grandson of former Charm storekeeper)

28/ Menno A. Yoder (area resident)

29/ *The Ohio Law for State Support of Public Schools*, ts, (Charm School Records), n.d.

30/ Charm School Records

31/ Lloyd J. Miller (area resident)

32/ John L. Yoder (area resident)

33/ *The Traveler (The Holmes County Traveler)* [Millersburg, Ohio], Graphic Publications Inc. [magazine].

34/ Map of Holmes County School Districts (Holmes County Office of Education), [1990]

35/ *Revision of the 1964 School Philosophy*, ts, [By the teachers of Clark Local School District – Holmes County], 1966.

36/ Priscilla Miller Falb (Charm School teacher)

37/ Elizabeth Hershberger Keim (former Charm resident)

38/ Isaac J. Miller (Civil War record)

39/ Laura Mast Kaser (former Charm resident)

40/ Sam E. Hershberger (Charm School pupil)

41/ Lorene Mast Kaser (wife of Charm School teacher)

42/ Amanda A. Miller (Charm resident)

43/ Levi C. Miller (former Charm resident)

44/ Lovina Miller Kaufman (Charm School pupil)

45/ Crist C. Yoder – private list of tramps (former area resident)

46/ John and Fannie Raber Yoder (area residents)

47/ Sam L. Mast (area resident)

48/ Emanuel M. Beachy (area resident)

49/ *Holmes County Board of Education Record of Proceedings*, [Minutes]

50/ *The Holmes County Farmer (The Holmes County Farmer Hub) (The Holmes County Hub)* [Millersburg, Ohio], [weekly newspaper].

51/ Paul R. Miller (former Charm resident)

52/ Crist J. Raber (former Charm resident)

53/ Andy Mast (area resident)

54/ *Coshocton Daily Age*, [Coshocton, Ohio], [daily newspaper].

55/ [*Business Calendar of Charm, Ohio*], 1928.

56/ Dey Troyer (former Charm resident)

57/ Ralph Aling (former Charm resident)

58/ Henry E. Mast (area resident)

❧

Credits and Sources

59/ N. a., *Eine Unparteische Lieder-Sammlung zum Gebrauch beim Oeffentlichen, Gottesdienst und der Häuslichen Erbaung*, Scottdale, Penn.: Mennonite Publishing House, 1963.

60/ Lydia Ann Erb Swartz (former Charm resident)

61/ J. H. Beers and Co., *Commemorative Biographical Record of the Counties of Wayne and Holmes, Ohio, Containing Biographical Sketches of Prominent and Representative Citizens, and of Many of the Early Settled Families*, Chicago: John Morris Company, 1889.

62/ Marlene Miller (descendant of former Charm resident)

63/ John Y. Schlabach (area resident)

64/ Minnie Stingel Smith (Charm School teacher)

65/ Paragon Geophysical Inc., Mt. Gilead, Ohio

66/ Sherman Drilling and Bakerwell Inc. personnel (oil and gas well exploration)

67/ Ammon H. Miller (former Charm resident)

68/ George F. Newton, *History of Holmes County, Ohio*, [unpublished manuscript], 1889 (Holmes County Library).

69/ Mose V. Hershberger (area resident)

70/ *Commissioners' Journal #1* (Holmes County Recorders Office).

71/ Eli A. Mast (area resident)

72/ Jonas T. Miller (former area resident)

73/ Atlee J. Miller (former area resident)

74/ Melvin Mullet (area resident)

75/ Levi D. Schlabach (former area resident)

76/ Dan L. Troyer (area resident)

77/ Holmes County Health Department

78/ Holmes County Cooperative Extension Office

79/ Mose J. Keim – private ledger (former Charm resident)

80/ Robert Clark (former area resident)

81/ Valentine J. Erb (former Charm resident)

82/ Sara Hershberger (former area resident)

83/ Rollin McCelland (former gas well operator)

84/ George D. Irving, *The Millersburg Glass Story*, ts, Millersburg, Ohio: *privately printed*, 1971.

85/ Joe L. Raber (area resident)

86/ Lester Scherer (area resident)

87/ Reuben Yutzy, Estate #1851, Holmes County Probate Court

88/ Albert M. Miller (area resident)

89/ Levi L. Yoder (former Charm resident)

90/ John B. Kurtz (former area resident)

91/ Esther Varnes Rine (former area resident)

92/ Roy J. and Abbie Miller (area residents)

93/ Andy M. Bontrager (grandson of former Charm harnessmaker)

94/ David J. Troyer (area resident)

95/ Roman and Sarah Schlabach Hershberger (area residents)

96/ Ray Jr. and Gladys Yoder Mast (former Charm storeowners)

97/ Jack Nowels, et al., *Holmes County, Ohio to 1985*, Salem, West Virginia: Walsworth Publishing, 1985.

98/ Ervin Keim (Charm resident)

99/ Franny Mast Keim (former Charm resident)

100/ *The Budget*, [Sugarcreek, Ohio], [weekly newspaper].

101/ Adrian Miller (former Charm resident)

102/ Delbert and Arletta Lahm Harmon (former Charm residents)

103/ Francis Miller Mast (former Charm resident)

104/ David D. Miller (area resident)

105/ Adrian and Irene Oswald Scheetz (area residents)

106/ Sam Erb (area resident)

107/ Roman Keim (Charm resident)

108/ W. S. Hanna, *Holmes County History*, ts,:1932 (Holmes County Library).

109/ Evelyn Culp (granddaughter of former Charm storeowner)

110/ Leroy and Anna Miller Raber (former Charm residents)

111/ Wm. McKinley, Jr. et al., *Official Roster of the Soldiers of the State of Ohio in the War of the Rebellion 1861 – 1866*, 12 vol., Akron, Ohio: The Werner Company, 1893.

112/ Levi A. Miller (Charm resident)

113/ Orie T. Oswald (area resident and former Charm storekeeper)

114/ Hulda Brand Kaser (former Charm resident)

115/ Roy L. Miller (area resident)

116/ Eleanor Oswald Gray (area resident)

117/ Jeff Schrock (collector of Civil War items)

118/ Mrs. Ben F. Miller (area resident)

119/ Adrian Ott (area resident)

120/ *The Baltic, Ohio Centennial 1848 – 1948*, N.p.: n.p., 1948.

121/ Helen Kaser Lorentz (area resident)

122/ Margaret Ely Miller (area resident)

123/ Pauline Forsh Giaugue (granddaughter of former Charm blacksmith)

124/ William McHendry, (oil and gas leases), (Holmes County Recorders Office)

125/ Edward and Lorene Raber (area residents and Charm storeowners)

126/ Sara Ann Mast Miller (Charm resident)

127/ Roy A. Miller (Charm resident)

128/ Mrs. Aaron Lehman (Wayne County resident)

129/ Joe D. Erb (Charm resident)

130/ Eli M. Yoder (area resident)

131/ Abe A. Mast (Charm resident)

132/ Noah A. Keim (Charm School pupil)

133/ Jeremiah J. Miller – private ledger 1901 – 1905 (former area resident)

134/ Eloise Shott Miller (wife of Charm School teacher)

135/ Donald and Barb Hines (former Charm business owner)

136/ National Archives and Records Service, Washington, D.C.

137/ Paul J. Yoder (grandson of former Charm jeweler)

138/ *Holmes County Republican* [Millersburg, Ohio], [newspaper].

139/ *The Columbus Dispatch Magazine* [Columbus, Ohio].

140/ Roman H. Miller (area resident)

141/ Le Ann DeHass Miller (area resident)

142/ Ben G. Troyer (area resident)

143/ *Family Life*, [Aylmer, Ontario], Pathway Publishers [magazine].

144/ Marty Van Reeth, *History of the Commercial and Savings Bank*, ts: 1993.

145/ *The Holmes County Bargain Hunter*, [Millersburg, Ohio], Graphic Publications Inc. [weekly newspaper].

146/ Abner Beiler (Lancaster County, Pa. historian)

147/ William W. Mast (grandson of former Charm storekeeper)

148/ Jonas Kauffman (former Charm resident)

149/ Amanda Erb Miller (Charm resident)

150/ Vernon J. Miller – personal notes of Charm (author)

151/ Menu of Homestead Restaurant, Charm, Ohio [1993]

152/ Eli Troyer, Jr. (area resident)

153/ Janet Korns (great-granddaughter of former Charm blacksmith)

154/ William M. Chupp (son-in-law of former Charm blacksmith)

155/ Aden P. Troyer (son of former Charm blacksmith)

156/ Jonas J. Yoder (Charm resident)

157/ Garnett Spurgeon (daughter of former Charm blacksmith)

158/ Levi Oswald (former Charm resident)

159/ Charm School souvenir – 1913 [Brooks Harris]

160/ John E. Troyer (former Charm resident)

161/ Emanuel E. Hershberger (area resident)

162/ Vera Nussbaum (granddaughter of former Charm cheesemaker)

163/ Peter C. Troyer – private ledger (former area resident)

164/ John L. Mueller (former Charm cheesemaker)

165/ Paul Hershberger (former Charm cheesemaker)

166/ Eric Guggisberg (Charm resident and cheesemaker)

167/ Stanley Kaufman – Stanley Kaufman private notes (area resident and historian)

168/ Noah A. Raber (Charm resident)

169/ Irene Keim Raber (former Charm resident)

170/ Levi S. Erb (area resident)

171/ John and Susan Troyer Miller (Charm residents)

172/ Alice Swanson (step-daughter of former Charm veterinarian)

173/ Olen Mast (Charm resident)

174/ Jacob J. Yoder (Charm resident)

175/ Jonas R. Yoder (area resident)

176/ Henry A. Schlabach (Charm resident)

177/ Jacob J. Hochstetler (area resident)

178/ Wayne Hochstetler (area resident)

179/ Calvin Stockli (former Charm resident)

180/ Violet Kaser Hochstetler (former Charm resident)

181/ Mose D. Troyer (area resident)

182/ Ruth Oswald (former Charm resident)

183/ Atlee D. Miller (area resident)

184/ Levi J. P. Miller (area resident)

185/ Sam P. Miller (area resident)

186/ *The Diary*, [Gordonville, Pennsylvania], [A Church Newsletter Serving the Old Order Society].

187/ Melvin A. Barkman (area resident)

188/ Anna D. Keim (former Charm resident)

189/ Brooks Harris (Charm business owner and historical collector)

190/ Clarence H. Scherer – receipt book (former area resident)

191/ Mose N. Raber (area resident)

192/ Jacob D. Yoder (area resident)

193/ John J. Yoder – private ledger (former area resident)

194/ Melvin A. Raber (former area resident)

195/ Andy E. Raber (Charm resident)

196/ Roman and Mattie Miller Yoder (former area residents)

197/ Joe D. Yoder (area resident)

198/ Dan M. Miller (area resident)

199/ Mose M. Miller (area resident)

200/ Eli A. Yoder, *Descendants of Michael E. Yoder*, Holmesville, Ohio: n.p., 1980.

201/ J. A. Caldwell, *Caldwell's Atlas of Holmes Co. Ohio*, Condit, Ohio: H. J. Toudy and Co., 1875.

202/ Joe D. Yoder, et al., *Swartzentruber Family History*, Baltic, Ohio: Gordonville, Pennsylvania Print Shop, 1988.

203/ Abe C. Schrock, *A Record of Deaths*, N.p.: n.p., 1957.

204/ Roscoe Miller, et al., *Sesquicentennial History of New Carlisle and Walnut Creek Township*, Strasburg, Ohio: Gorden Printing, 1977.

205/ Sarah M. Weaver, *Peter Weaver Family History*, N.p.: n.p. 1978, [N.pag.].

206/ Oscar R. Miller, *Descendants of Eli S. Miller and Marie Kauffman Volume 1 – Descendants of Isaac S. Miller and (1) Rachel Troyer (2) Fannie Erb Volume 2*, Berlin, Ohio,: n.p., 1981.

207/ Henry L. Erb, *Descendants of David Erb*, Baltic, Ohio: Gordonville, Pennsylvania Print Shop, 1990.

208/ Daniel M. Yoder – private account ledger (former Charm resident) [Ohio Amish Library]

209/ Val[entine] J. Miller, *Memorial History of Emanuel Hershberger*, Sugarcreek, Ohio: Gordonville, Pennsylvania Print Shop, 1968.

210/ Joseph P. Helmuth, *Family Records of Friedrich Helmuth of Germany*, Arthur, Illinois: Arthur Graphic – Clarion, 1933, [Reprint of the 1933 edition].

211/ Ervin Gingerich, *Ohio Amish Directory, Holmes County and Vicinity*, Millersburg, Ohio: Hiland Printing, 1988.

212/ Oscar R. Miller, *Descendants of Daniel D. Miller and Lydia B. Troyer*, Berlin, Ohio: n.p., 1974.

213/ Thomas Aquinas Burke, *Ohio Lands – A Short History*, Columbus, Ohio: n.p., 2nd ed., 1989.

214/ Paul Kaufman, *Indian Lore of the Muskingum Headwaters of Ohio*, [Millersburg, Ohio]: n.p., 2nd ed., 1987.

215/ Betty Miller, *Amish Pioneers of the Walnut Creek Valley*, Berlin, Ohio: Atkinson Printing, 1977.

216/ Albert A. Raber, et al., *Descendants of Jacob Raber*, [Baltic, Ohio]: n.p., 1977.

217/ David A. Troyer, *Hinterlassene Schriften*, [Charm, Ohio]: Wayne County Amish, Reprint of 1920 ed., n.d.

218/ Vernon J. Miller – Vernon J. Miller private diary (author)

219/ Roy R. Bontrager, *The Descendants of Isaac J. Bontrager*, Logan, Ohio: n.p., [1985].

220/ Allen W. Eckert, *The Frontiersman*, Boston, Massachusetts: Little, Brown, 1967.

221/ William R. Collins, *Ohio the Buckeye State*, Englewood Cliffs, New Jersey: Prentice Hall Inc., 5th ed., 1974.

222/ Ruth W. Gavian, et al., *United States History*, Boston, Massachusetts: D. C. Heath and Company, 1965.

223/ A. J. Stiffler, *The Standard Atlas of Holmes County, Ohio*, Cincinnati, Ohio: The Standard Atlas Publishing Company, 1907.

224/ Henry Howe, *Historical Collections of Ohio*, 2 Vol., Cincinnati, Ohio: C. J. Krehbiel, 1902.

225/ U.S. Census Records, [Holmes County].

226/ Evelyn Beck Ulmer, et al., *Our Beck Family History*, N.p.: n.p., 1982.

227/ Frances Patterson House (descendant of former area resident)

228/ Stanley A. Kauffman, *Germanic Folk Culture in Eastern Ohio*, Walnut Creek, Ohio: Tope Printing Inc., 1986.

Credits and Sources

229/ Andy A. Schlabach (area resident)

230/ *Holmes County 1992 Plat Directory – Ohio*, Dayton, Ohio: Great Mid-Western Publishing Company, Inc., 1992.

231/ Stephen Yoder, Estate #195, Holmes County Probate Court

232/ Aden B. Raber (area resident)

233/ Abner J. Schlabach, *Descendants of Jacob D. Schlabach and Magdalena Miller*, Souderton, Pennsylvania: Indian Valley Printing Ltd., 1980.

234/ Willard Miller (former Charm business owner)

235/ Ben D. Miller (area resident)

236/ Shirley Yoder, *What's a Hershberger*, N.p.: n.p., [1979?].

237/ Roy O. Keim (former Charm resident)

238/ Paul D. Shetler (area resident)

239/ Samuel D. Yoder (area resident)

240/ Henry A. Hershberger (former area resident)

241/ Bob Gerber (area resident)

242/ Daniel E. Mast, *Anweisungen zur Seligkeit*, Baltic, Ohio: J. A. Raber, n.d.

243/ John P. Troyer (area resident)

244/ Henry L. Erb (area resident)

245/ Ella Miller Keim (area resident)

246/ *Our Ohio*, [Columbus, Ohio], [A Digest of Ohio History].

247/ James A. Rhodes, *A Short History of Ohio Land Grants*, [Columbus, Ohio]: n.p., n.d.

248/ Roy E. Miller (area resident)

249/ Ed Hershberger (photographer)

250/ Holmes County Health Department (Death Records)

251/ *The Millersburg Sentinel*, [Millersburg, Ohio], (newspaper).

252/ Christena Graefe, Estate #3319, Holmes County Probate Court

253/ Joni J. Yoder – Private Death Record Ledger (former Charm resident) (Ohio Amish Library)

254/ Fred J. Herr, *Ohio Archeological and Historical Publications*, Vol. 36, Columbus, Ohio: n.p., 1927.

255/ Jack Stauffer (area resident)

256/ Les Howell (historical collector)

257/ Emanuel J. Yoder (former area resident)

258/ Delbert H. Shetler (area resident)

259/ Silva Beachy (former Charm business owner)

260/ Johann E. Schlabach (area resident)

261/ Ivan A. Yoder (area resident)

262/ William Isaac Hummel (former Charm resident)

263/ Lula Schlabach Beachy (former Charm resident)

264/ Mary Erb Miller (former Charm resident)

265/ Vernon J. Miller – personal notes of Charm Days (author)

266/ John B. Yoder (area resident)

267/ Ada Glick (former Charm resident)

268/ Pauline Mauer (area resident)

269/ Melvin H. Raber (former Charm business owner)

270/ Larry Andrews (Charm business owner)

271/ Aretta Keim (former Charm resident)

272/ Eli M. Kuhns (area resident)

273/ St. John Lutheran Church Cemetery – New Bedford, Ohio

274/ Amos and Amanda Troyer Yoder (area residents)

275/ Ervin L. Raber (Charm business owner)

276/ Bertha Miller Yoder (former Charm resident)

277/ Emanuel M. Miller (Charm resident)

278/ Tom Kalinowski (former Charm business owner)

279/ Atlee D. Schlabach (former Charm resident)

280/ *Cleveland Plain Dealer*, [Cleveland, Ohio], (daily newspaper).

281/ Ken J. Hetter (historian)

282/ Vernon J. Miller – private notes of The Commercial and and Savings Bank – Charm Branch

283/ Paul Mueller (former Charm resident)

284/ Ivan J. Miller (Charm resident)

285/ Andy N. Miller (former Charm business owner)

286/ Holmes County Soil and Water Services – Oil and Gas Division

287/ Ohio State Auditor's Office

288/ Jacob A. Miller (former Charm resident)

289/ Melvin J. Miller (area resident)

290/ Ervin A. Schlabach (former Charm resident)

291/ Zip Code Publishing Company, Inc., *National Zip Code Directory*, N.p.: W. T. Rogers Co., 1972.

292/ Amos Hoover (historian – Pennsylvania).

293/ Floyd E. Troyer (area resident)

294/ Ben J. Raber (area resident)

295/ Bill Keim – Keim Lumber Company (Charm business owner)

296/ Robert R. Troyer (area resident)

297/ Jim Neff (area resident)

298/ Alvin B. Yoder (area resident)

299/ Perry Sampsel (area resident)

300/ C. Henry Smith, *The Story of the Mennonites*, 4th Ed., Newton Kansas: Mennonite Publication Office, 1957.

301/ *N.a., Die Ernsthafte Christenpflicht*, [Revised Edition], Scottdale, Pennysylvania: [Mennonite Publishing House], 1978.

302/ E. L. D. Seymour, et al., *The New Garden Encyclopedia*, New York, New York: Wm. H. Wise and Co., 1943.

303/ George W. White, *Geology of Holmes County*, 4th Series, Bulletin 47, Columbus, Ohio: F. J. Heer Printing Co., 1949.

304/ Levi D. Yoder – private ledger (former Charm resident)

305/ Roman Hershberger, *Descendants of Jeremiah Miller and Lydia Troyer*, Middlefield, Ohio: n.p., 1984.

306/ Gary Ray Bolen, *The Nickles Family*, 2nd ed., N.p.: n.p., 1986.

307/ Jacob J. Mast, *History of Preachers, Deacons and Bishops*, Gordonville, Pennsylvania: Gordonville Pennsylvania Print Shop, 1970.

308/ Leroy Beachy (area resident and historian)

309/ Holmes County, Ohio Tax Records

310/ *The Times–Reporter*, [Dover, Ohio], (daily newspaper).

311/ Dan and Mattie Troyer Schlabach (area residents)

312/ Noah J. B. Miller (area resident)

313/ Holmes County Recorders Office

314/ Holmes County Tax Map Office

315/ Eli J. M. Miller (area resident)

316/ Melvin A. Stutzman (area resident)

317/ *The Meadow Mart*, [Wooster, Ohio], (newspaper).

318/ Roscoe Miller, et al., *A Century and a Half with the Mennonites at Walnut Creek*, Strasburg, Ohio: Gordon Printing, 1978.

319/ [*The New American*] *Calendar*, [Baltic, Ohio], [Raber's Almanac].

320/ Emanuel J. Miller, *Family History of Joni Miller and His Descendants*, Wilmot, Ohio: n.p., 1942.

321/ Emanuel J. Miller, *Family History of the Descendants of Jeremiah Miller and Lydia Troyer*, Wilmot, Ohio: n.p., 1943.

322/ *The Feed Bag*, [Wooster, Ohio], (newspaper).

323/ Susie E. Mast (Charm resident)

324/ Carl Weidman (Wayne County resident)

325/ Richard Kaser (son of former Charm blacksmith)

326/ Henry B. Yoder (Charm resident)

327/ *Holmes County, Ohio Official Farm Plat Book and Directory*, La Porte, Indiana: County Plat and Directory Co., Inc., [1965].

328/ *Holmes County, Ohio Official Farm Plat Book and Directory*, La Porte, Indiana: County Plat and Directory Co. Inc., [1964].

329/ Levi N. Yoder (area resident)

330/ Emanuel Schlabach (photographer)

331/ Emma Weaver Hershberger (area resident)

332/ Rhoda Raber (Charm resident)

333/ Myrl and Joyce Frontz (descendants of former Charm residents)

334/ Larry and Sally Hockenberry (Charm business owners)

335/ Vernon A. Kline (Charm resident)

336/ Noah Hershberger, *A Struggle to be Separate*, Orrville, Ohio: n.p., 1985.

337/ Lora Miller Yoder (area resident)

338/ Claude F. Lahm (area resident)

339/ Daniel J. Schlabach family Bible (former area resident)

340/ Mrs. Noah Weaver (former area resident)

341/ Crist U. Miller (area resident)

342/ Roy A. Yoder (area resident)

343/ Warner Farver (local historian)

344/ Jonas V. Hershberger (area resident)

345/ Robert Miller (former Charm resident)

346/ Mose J. Yoder (area resident)

347/ Elson Sommers (Charm School teacher)

348/ Judy Mann (Charm School teacher)

349/ Bob and Arvada Everhart (Charm business owners)

350/ George W. Varns, *The Varnes Family of Doughty Valley Holmes County, Ohio*, Sugarcreek, Ohio: Middaugh Printers, 1970.

351/ Yoder Lumber Co. Inc. (area business)

352/ D[aniel] E. Mast, *Ein Vermahnungsschreiben*, [pamphlet], N.p.: n.p., n.d.

353/ Sunshine DeHass (Charm business owner)

354/ Bonnie Oswald Sadd (granddaughter of former Charm resident)

355/ Atlee A. Miller (area resident)

356/ Anna Miller (area resident)

357/ Dale Kreisher (Charm School teacher)

358/ Robert and Delia Patterson Ramseyer (area resident)

359/ Mary Pauli Schmidt (area resident)

360/ Andy L. Miller (former Charm resident)

361/ Sarah Scheuffler (area resident)

362/ Henry R. Miller (area resident)

363/ Ivan Kline (Charm business owner)

364/ *Berlin Quadrangle – Ohio*, [Topographic Map], Washington, D.C.: U.S. Geological Survey, 1961.

365/ Alice Kaser Miller (area resident)

366/ David Farver (area resident)

367/ Ohio Department of Natural Resources – District #3 Office, Akron, Ohio

368/ Daniel A. Hershberger (area resident)

369/ Monroe C. Yoder (area resident)

370/ Holmes County Clerk of Courts

371/ Erma Miller (Charm resident)

372/ Eli and Mattie Raber Miller (Charm residents)

373/ Venus Zuercher (Charm School teacher)

374/ David E. Miller (Charm resident)

375/ Clark Township Local School Board Minutes (East Holmes Local School District Administrative Office – Holmes County)

376/ Catherine Snyder (Charm School teacher)

377/ *New Bedford Quadrangle – Ohio*, [Topographic Map], Washington, D.C.: U.S. Geological Survey, 1961.

378/ Paul G. Locher, et al., *Decorative Arts of Ohio's Sonnenberg Mennonites*, Kidron, Ohio: Tope Printing, Inc., 1994.

379/ Mervin H. Shetler (former area resident)

380/ John A. Miller (Charm resident)

381/ Adam A. Miller, et al., *A Brief History of the Married Life of our Parents David D. and Sarah (Miller) Schlabach, and the Family*, [pamphlet], N.p.: n.p., 1964.

382/ Harold Patterson (area resident)

383/ Richard B. Pierce, *Ohio 1994–95 Hunting and Trapping Regulations*, Columbus, Ohio: n.p., 1994.

384/ Deborah D. Morgan, *The Kaser Family*, Goshen, Indiana: Instant Copy of Goshen, 1994.

385/ Archie Carpenter (former Charm resident)

386/ Ivan R. and Katie Miller Barkman (Charm residents)

387/ Henry J. C. Yoder (area resident)

388/ Peter P. Hershberger, Estate #506, Holmes County Probate Court

389/ Warren Miller, *Martin's Creek Mennonite Church Centennial Book 1865–1965*, N.p.: n.p., 1965.

390/ *Road Notice Petition*, ts: 1881 (Ben D. Raber)

School Enrollment Index

❧ *Index* ——————————————

A

❧

❧ Index